REFIGURING
the ARCHIVE

REFIGURING
the ARCHIVE

Edited by
Carolyn Hamilton, Verne Harris, Jane Taylor,
Michele Pickover, Graeme Reid & Razia Saleh

Kluwer Academic Publishers
DORDRECHT / BOSTON / LONDON

A C.I.P. Catalogue record for this book is
available from the Library of Congress

First published 2002

in Africa by David Philip Publishers, an imprint of New Africa Books (Pty) Ltd,
99 Garfield Road, Claremont, Cape Town, South Africa

and in the rest of the world by Kluwer Academic Publishers,
P.O. Box 17, 3300 AA Dordrecht, The Netherlands

Sold and distributed in North, Central and South America
by Kluwer Academic Publishers,
101 Philip Drive, Norwell, MA 02061, U.S.A.

In all other countries except Africa, sold and distributed
by Kluwer Academic Publishers,
P.O. Box 322, 3300 AH Dordrecht, The Netherlands

ISBN 1-4020-0743-4 (Kluwer)
ISBN 0-86486-507-4 (David Philip)

Printed by Clyson Printers, Cape Town

Inventory

*(1)   A finding aid listing and describing in varying degrees of
detail the contents of one or more record/archive groups, fonds,
classes or series, usually including a brief history of the organisation and functions of the originating agency/ies, institutions
or organisations and, if appropriate, indexes. In US usage, the
normal unit of entry is the series. According to the degree of
descriptive detail, an inventory (1) may be referred to as an
analytical inventory (calendar), descriptive inventory or list,
preliminary inventory, repertory or summary inventory.*
*(2)   A document containing a list of things, e.g. furniture
and fittings, often, as in the case of the property of deceased
persons, with an indication of value.*

Peter Walne, ed., *Dictionary of Archival Terminology*, ICA
Handbooks Series vol. 7 (Munich, New York, London, Paris:
K. G. Saur, 1988).

*Prefaces along with forewords, introductions, preludes, prelim-
inaries, preambles, prologues, and prolegomena, have always
been written, it seems, in view of their own self-effacement.
Upon reaching the end of the pre- (which presents and precedes, or rather forestalls, the presentative production, and, in
order to put before the reader's eyes what is not yet visible, is
obliged to speak, predict, and predicate), the route which has
been covered must cancel itself out. But this subtraction leaves
a mark of erasure, a remainder which is added to the subsequent text and which cannot be completely summed up within
it. Such an operation thus appears contradictory, and the same
is true of the interest one takes in it.*

Extract from Jacques Derrida, *Dissemination* (Chicago: University
of Chicago Press, 1961), p. 9.

Carolyn Hamilton, Verne Harris & Graeme Reid

(RE)FIGURE

We begin our ending – for this is our editorial summation – with a
lexical interlude. The word 'figure' enfolds multiple meanings – as a
verb: to appear, be mentioned, represent, be a symbol of, imagine, pattern, calculate, understand, determine, consider – all remultiplied by
the word's hospitality to prefixes. Almost as complex – to assert what
this book attempts to demonstrate – is the word 'archive' (the noun),
which plays (is played) as idea, as institution, accumulation of physical or virtual objects, profession, process, service. Conjoining these
words 'figure' and 'archive' is to open up a cornucopia of meaning.

THE PROJECT

The archive – all archive – every archive – is figured. Acceptance of
this in South Africa has shaped fundamentally the argument – and the
processes built upon it – that the country's archives require transformation, or refiguring. The figuring by our apartheid and longer pasts
must be challenged, and spaces must be opened up in the archives by
a transforming society. Undoubtedly *Refiguring the Archive*, the book,
can be positioned within this imperative. However, it is our hope that
it will invite – and deserve – other positionings. For the archive is also
always already being refigured: the technologies of creation, preservation and use, for instance, are changing all the time; physically the
archive is being added to and subtracted from, and is in dynamic relation with its physical environment; organisational dynamics are ever
shifting; and the archive is porous to societal processes and discourses
– although at certain junctures, like the one South Africa finds itself
in now, formal conduits need to be put in place. So that beyond any
call for refiguring, or intention to refigure, *Refiguring the Archive*
acknowledges and seeks to engage the (re)figuring that is happening,
in South Africa particularly, and wherever there is archive.

The book was conceptualised as an extension of a project with the
same title hosted in 1998 by the University of the Witwatersrand's
Graduate School for the Humanities and Social Sciences in conjunction

with four archival institutions: the National Archives, the University's Historical Papers, the Gay and Lesbian Archives and the South African History Archive. Its centrepiece was a series of thirteen seminars, which attracted twenty-two speakers, nine of them from outside South Africa (four from the United States, three from other African countries and two from Europe). The speakers and seminar discussants were drawn from a wide range of academic disciplines and professions.

A medley of interrelated events were constellated around the seminar series. The project launch was celebrated with the simultaneous opening of *Holdings: Refiguring the Archive*, an exhibition, curated by Jane Taylor, of work by contemporary South African artists who explore the activities of documentation as processes of interpretation. Each of the participating institutions offered a workshop linking the intellectual explorations of the seminar series to a particular area of archival practice. Most of the workshop presenters were South African practitioners or academics, but there was representation from Botswana, Zimbabwe and the United States. The Moving into Dance Company performed *Tranceformations*, choreographed in 1991 by Sylvia Glasser and inspired by San rock art and trance dancing. Before the performance Glasser spoke about the conceptualisation of the dance, its use of archive and its constitution as archive. The Gay and Lesbian Archives offered a free stage performance of the musical *After Nines!* based on interviews about gay and lesbian township life, as well as a slide show on the Lesbian Herstory Archive (New York) presented by Maxine Wolfe. The National Archives hosted a guided tour of the National Archives Repository in Pretoria. And the films *Doodkry is Min* (director Jamie Uys) and *Die Skerpioen onder die Klip: Afrikaans van Kolonialisme tot Demokrasie* (director Zackie Achmat) were screened at the Graduate School for the Humanities and Social Sciences.[1] Uys' film is a classic propaganda piece on Afrikaner nationalism which Achmat self-consciously echoes in both style and composition and which draws radically different conclusions from his rereading of the archive of the Afrikaans language, demonstrating its heterogeneous origins. The events constituted a kaleidoscope of spaces, forms, media and voices, designed to stretch as far as possible both an interrogation and a process of (re)figuring.

The collaboration of the four participating institutions was designed to bring into a single frame of reference the concerns of archival practitioners, historical researchers who work with a particular concept of archive and who use archives, as well as public and community interests around archives. It was, further, an attempt to look

1 The literal translation of the former title is 'To die is nothing'. 'As tough as they come' is closer to the intended meaning. As an expression in Afrikaans, the title is used with reference to something/someone that cannot be killed, but also, more figuratively, to something/someone that is extremely tenacious and cannot be subdued or contained. The latter title can be translated as 'The scorpion under the stone: Afrikaans from colonialism to democracy'.

beyond the idea of archives as physical records, so as to engage the idea of the taken-for-granted, often implicit, 'archive' that is the foundation of the production of knowledge in the present , the basis for the identities of the present and for the possible imaginings of community in the future. To investigate this idea of archive is to bring to bear on 'archive' an interrogation similar to that which concepts like 'canon' or 'orientalism' have undergone. Attempts to refigure the archive chime with other postcolonial interventions such as the Subaltern Studies project, and more specifically the 1999 publication *Africana: The Encyclopedia of the African and African American Experience*, edited by Kwame Anthony Appiah and Henry Louis Gates.[2] The difference lies in the particular claims of the archive to constitute the record, to provide evidence and to act as source.[3]

An inquiry around archive(s) also demands an attempt to understand the conditions and circumstances of preservation of material as, and the exclusion of material from, the record, as well as attention to the relations of power underpinning such inclusions and exclusions. In the effort to open the discussion around the refiguring of the archive we were mindful of Michel Foucault's engagement with archive: his view that archive is not simply institution, but rather the law of what can be said, the system of statements, or rules of practice, that give shape to what can and cannot be said.[4] In our project, Foucault's influence was strongest in the proposition – articulated neatly in this book by Stoler – that archives are often both documents of exclusion and monuments to particular configurations of power.

Historians and other scholars are increasingly concerned to understand how knowledge is produced and, more specifically, how knowledge of the past is produced. Where previously historians 'mined' the archives for 'nuggets of fact' in a manner conscious of problems of bias in the record, today scholars pay greater attention to the particular processes by which the record was produced and subsequently shaped, both before its entry into the archive, and increasingly as part of the archival record. This approach draws attention to the way in which the record is altered over time, as well as to the gaps and omissions in, and excisions from, the record. In South Africa historians have been cautious about relying exclusively on public and more specifically government records, because of their colonial and later apartheid biases. That the record is biased is widely recognised by researchers, but a great deal of work remains to develop our understanding of the circumstances of the creation of the archival record in general, and of specific collections in particular.

2 Basic Books, New York.

3 The recently published *Harvard Guide to African-American History* (Cambridge: Harvard University Press, 2001), edited by L. Litwack and D. Clark Hine, is one of the few publications in this area which looks beyond alternative histories to examine the sources on which they are based.

4 See *Archaeology of Knowledge and Discourse on Language* (New York: Pantheon, 1972), pp. 79-134.

In an effort to overcome some of the biases in the official record, researchers have undertaken extensive oral interviewing amongst those whose voices find scant place in government files. Often these interviews remain in the hands of the researcher, and all too rarely are they placed in public repositories. The circumstances of the production of specific oral archives require close attention, subject as they are to many of the same processes of modification, selection and exclusion as the documentary record. (Important differences mark off oral records from written ones: some of these have been identified, even rarefied.) In other respects the full possibilities and limitations of the oral record remain the subject of investigation. The project suggested an approach to archives that is wary of the claim that one or another corrective intervention can 'fill the gaps' in an archive. The very idea of a discernible 'gap' was problematised, with the archive being stressed as sliver rather than as incomplete whole.

The oral record is not the only alternative to public documentary archives. Literature, landscape, dance, art and a host of other forms offer archival possibilities capable of releasing different kinds of information about the past, shaped by different record-keeping processes. In short, many established ideas about the nature and location of the archive are under challenge.

The project further created an opportunity for the National Archives to participate in a partnership which promised to open that institution to transformational energies and to provide a forum in which it could reach out to new constituencies. The legal mandate of the National Archives defines powerful imperatives to work co-operatively and to find ways of extending services to all South Africans. Given a still-resilient apartheid legacy, the institution faces numerous systemic barriers in seeking to fulfil this mandate. Participation in the project by the staff of the National Archives offered a way forward to that institution. The project also provided a unique opportunity to inject ideas, influences, perspectives and values into South African archival discourse which until then had found no currency. The post-apartheid transformation of South African archives failed to trouble the positivist assumptions of the apartheid era. In the series, then, for the first time, formal space was being created for a post-positivist critique of the archive in South Africa, and therefore for the emergence of a truly radical archival discourse. The organisers were keenly aware of the influence of deconstruction, in particular the writings of Jacques Derrida, on the proponents of a postcustodial approach to archives in other parts of the world. And, as has been suggested above,

CAROLYN HAMILTON, VERNE HARRIS & GRAEME REID

academic users of archives in South Africa have been exposed to some of the same influences. It was felt, then, that the time was ripe to create space, formally, for deconstructive perspectives on archive within South African critical discourse; and to link these concerns to the pressing political need in South Africa to draw on an archive outside the archival inheritance of colonialism and, later, apartheid.

The project sought to bring together the realms of theory and practice. Key areas within the archival profession in need of overhaul, such as methodology and practical procedures, were highlighted. It raised important questions around what archivists do and how they perceive themselves. It also provided a valuable forum for examining the contextual milieu, both socio-political and theoretical, within which archivists craft their policies and conduct their day-to-day business. Attention was paid to past and existing notions of access to, and the destruction of, documents in South Africa. This is a particularly pertinent discussion given the apartheid past and quest of the Truth and Reconciliation Commission (TRC) to locate documents and other evidence relating to gross human rights violations during the apartheid era. (In the Commission's attempts to reconstruct the past it became clear that many documents had been systematically and deliberately destroyed without intervention from the Archives Commission or the Director of Archives.) Paradoxically, access to the archive of the TRC itself raises important questions around restriction of access to information, the sanitising of documents and the role therein of government. The participation in the project of a wide range of archivists and academics allowed for vigorous debate on these topics.

The archive is not, of course, simply the concern of researchers and government. It is part of the everyday activity of identity formation and maintenance by ordinary people. Community archives like the South African History Archive (SAHA) and the Gay and Lesbian Archives (GALA) brought to the project the concerns of marginal archives and the possibilities of their engagement with the archival mainstream. They also raised questions about the inclusion in the archive of documents and objects not usually placed in archival custody, such as the SAHA collection of political banners, posters and lapel badges, or GALA's assemblage of personal memorabilia, significant artefacts, art works and dresses. Marginal archives often preserve materials excluded from the mainstream repositories but are themselves no less constructed than mainstream archives, and are likewise the product of processes of both preservation and exclusion. Collections compiled in opposition to a particular hegemonic discourse are equally shaped by the kind of material collected, and the way it is arranged and described, as well as by what is excluded from an alternative recording of history.

Traces of marginal lives are by no means absent from mainstream archives. For example, the records of South African police surveillance of gay 'bottle parties' in the 1960s provide valuable information about gay social networks, police surveillance strategies, and the extent and nature of moral panics in white suburbia. What is required here is a sensitive and informed rereading of existing archival material. While the records were initially compiled for a very particular police function, the material may also be read creatively, against the grain.

There is no easy remedy, no obvious redress to past exclusion from mainstream archives. What was left out cannot simply be put back in. There are many projects designed to include previously absent or muted voices within existing mainstream institutions (such as state-sponsored oral history programmes[5] or by establishing independent community archives).[6] Both types of project have limitations and flaws. Some material has simply been lost or destroyed, and will never be recovered. Other mnemonic devices, such as features in the landscape, elude the archive and can resist being captured even by oral testimony.

Aside from the constructedness of the archive, whether mainstream or alternative, the cultural and social mores of the time also shape collections in profound albeit less visible ways. For example, a gay and lesbian archive is predicated on a particular concept of individual and collective identity. Will this sense of a common identity based on sexual orientation endure indefinitely? It seems unlikely. If this is the case, how will a gay and lesbian archive be viewed and read in a hundred years from now?

There are limits to constructedness, as the geneticists have demonstrated through DNA testing. The myth of origin of Lemba people in South Africa may have been understood as precisely that – an elaboration on oral tradition that linked this community to a Jewish ancestry. Yet scientific investigation into the archive of DNA has established a veracity for this claim. The authority vested in scientific evidence suggests that some archives do in fact exist outside of human agency – some things happen and are preserved beyond the self-conscious construction of the archive.

It would be premature (and, given that we were all involved in the project, presumptuous) to assess the project's impact. But interim comments are possible. By most measures, the debates and discussions were vigorous and invigorating, and on occasion their substance was

5   The National Archives launched a National Oral History Programme in 1999, specifically to fulfil its legislated mandate to document voices excluded from formal repositories in the past.

6   In South Africa the late 1980s and 1990s saw a flowering of such archives.

CAROLYN HAMILTON, VERNE HARRIS & GRAEME REID

reported in the local press. There were many special moments. One of them was Henry Louis Gates, Achille Mbembe and Bheki Peterson sharing a platform at the project launch. Another was Jacques Derrida weaving a tapestry with archives, power, remembering, forgetting and knowing, before a huge audience spilling over into an adjacent venue. As 'an event', and according to measures common in the 'archival world', the project made a significant impact. But its 'real' test is the degree to which it is successful in weaving an awareness of (re)figuring into both archival discourse and practice, and into historical reconstruction and imagining. The signs at this stage are good. Archivists who participated are discussing ideas and making connections that have been absent from their discourse until now. Academics and students are responding to the invitation to make an archival turn. At a more tangible level, the energies generated by the project have been channelled by the University of the Witwatersrand into a new postgraduate archives course, Reading the Trace: Memory and Archives, designed to meet the needs of both archivists and historical researchers. Developers of archival and related courses at Technikon South Africa, the University of South Africa, the University of the Transkei and the University of Natal participated in the project. The 1998 issue of the South African Archives Journal was wholly dedicated to the proceedings of the project's workshop series.

The project should be seen as part of wider processes of refiguring in archival discourse internationally. The later 1990s saw numerous voices in a number of countries articulating some of the concerns, perspectives and issues brought into focus by the project. Some of these voices were given space by the project organisers. By the end of the decade fundamental theoretical debates had become common in institutional forums and publications. To quote a few examples. In 1998 and 1999 the British journal *History of the Human Sciences* devoted two issues to exploring 'the archive' from a range of disciplinary perspectives. Through the 2000/1 academic year the University of Michigan's Center for International Studies hosted a programme entitled 'Archives, Documentation and the Institutions of Social Memory', which attracted scholars from many countries and hinged around seminar and lecture series. In planning for several years before 2000/1, this programme's organisers established a dialogue with the organisers of the *Refiguring the Archive* project from 1998. Also in 2000, the Dutch-based international journal *Archival Science* was launched, dedicated to tapping and disseminating fresh energies in international archival discourse. And in 2000 the South African Society of Archivists convened a national conference with the theme 'Renaissance and Archives', with the intention of providing a forum for engaging such energies in the particular circumstances of South Africa at the turn of the century.

The Book

The decision to produce a book based on the project's seminar series is motivated primarily by three considerations (other than the pleasure of it, and the recognition that it is important for all kinds of reasons). Firstly, so many of the seminar contributors confessed (in some instances, demonstrated) that they were using the space afforded by the series for exploratory work. The book offers an opportunity for recording development, assimilation, refinement, extension and debate. (Eleven of the essays in this book are re-workings of papers from the seminar series.) Secondly, we wanted to reach a wider audience for the work. We wanted to ensure that the project was not confined to two circles, researchers and academics on the one hand and practising archivists on the other. Thirdly, we wanted to extend the scope of the project by going beyond merely presenting a compilation of thematically linked essays. It is our intention to present the essays figured by parallel, supplementary, superimposed and juxtapositional texts – writing and images, reproduced either partially or fully. This is an intellectual (re)figuring using as vehicle a technical (re)figuring. The resulting intertextuality – which both acknowledges and plays the blurred boundaries between form and content, text and context – provides a shifting space for multiple voices.

The essays in the book are collected around three themes. The contributions on the first theme (Mbembe, Peterson, Derrida, Van Zyl and V. Harris) deal with new thinking around the archive, extending its boundaries and theorising its exclusions, thereby setting the scene for the two sections which follow.

The following theme includes essays by Stoler, Hayes, V. Harris and B. Harris that offer a view of the making of the archive(s). They look at certain archives as products of state machinery and as technologies that bolstered the production of those states themselves. They draw our attention to the processes of recording and remembering, of omission and forgetting, as well as to the relations of power involved in all of these processes. The essays position us to ask what insights might be gained from attending not only to archival content, but also to the particular and sometimes peculiar form of specific archives, through what Stoler terms a reading along the archival grain.

They draw our attention to archives as one of the foundations of epistemology and suggest that archives are crucial elements in epistemological challenge and experimentation. Through these essays archives emerge not simply as sources, but as sites of contested knowledges. The essays experiment with ethnographies and histories of archives. What constitutes an archive, what form it takes, and what systems of classification signal at specific times, the essays suggest, are the very substance of the politics of the times. As Derrida puts it, there is no political power without control of the archive.

The third theme revolves around the extension of the boundaries of what might fall within the compass of 'archive'. Here essays on gay and lesbian materials (Reid), DNA (Soodyall, Morar and Jenkins), oral texts (Hamilton and Mpe), art (Taylor), literature (Nuttall and Roberts), place and materiality (Hall) and electronic records (Bearman) are offered as part of an effort to widen and shift the meaning of the term archive.

This book extends the project's explorations in a number of directions. It suggests that it may now be fruitful to consider the archives as but one facet of a range of institutions including libraries, museums, local records and special collections all designed to create a particular vision of society. The institutional (and conceptual) range, of course, is expanded dramatically by the electronic technologies that underpin an archive at once actual and global. Clearly the materiality of archives, for so long simply assumed in archival discourse, is troubled by this reality. In his essay, Hall argues that the traditional significances accorded to materiality endure. Bearman, by contrast, offers a vision in which these significances find little place. These two essays go some way towards grappling with the implications of the shift from archives as purportedly stable repositories of original material – places where the body historically has gone physically to engage with the material trace – to electronic archives, unconstrained by space and place, and eschewing the claim to be original.

This book accords considerable space to public archives, some of them located at the heart of political power, others marginal and challenging of that power, even where they are not labeled 'archives'. But certain elements in the exhibition curated by Jane Taylor, *Holdings: Refiguring the Archive* – such as the highly charged family photographs collected and exhibited by Santu Mofokeng – draw our attention to archives which, until they surface as works on exhibition, remain in private custody, sometimes in domestic or intimate settings. The works are sometimes such archives made manifest; at other times, as

Taylor puts it, they imagine the private domestic archives of subjective life. The essay by Taylor on *Holdings* also articulates a latent theme of the rest of the book, the archive as a conception of what is valuable, and of how such value should be transmitted across time.

The essays in the book look most closely at how archives are made: at which traces survive and under what circumstances, as well as what is excised or excluded. They look closely at the activities of those who generate the record, and those who subsequently shape it. They draw attention to the processes of the establishment and maintenance of the repository and its policies and protocols. The essays reflect rather less on those who use the archives: on their strategies for approaching archives; on the way in which archives are made to yield their treasures through intimate acquaintance and 'readings against the grain' which can reveal precisely what the controllers of the record sought to obscure; on the fault lines of the archives which reveal their processes of construction. The essays merely touch on how a steeping in the record can enable the researcher to discern the hidden logics of the record; on the way in which researchers themselves also construct the archives; and on how their reading, interpretation and citation of materials shape the archives. They only hint at the deep attractions of the archives and the enduring passions that researchers develop with the contents of buff folders. They begin the work of looking at archives which emanate from different intellectual fields, but they barely touch on how archives are taken up in these fields.

Alternative visions require alternative archives. The third section of the book begins to point out some such alternatives. The book embraces the dynamics of refiguring and of such alternative vision. It ventures into the undefining of archives. Nevertheless, its editors and the contributors share a profound respect for the value of archive(s). Jacques Derrida, a contributor to this book, and arguably the most radical interrogator of archive in the last decade of the twentieth century, devotes the first section of his *Archive Fever: A Freudian Impression* (1996) to an extended lexicon of the word 'archive'. His etymological analysis demonstrates that every archival deconstruction must both respect and work with the stuff of tradition. No refiguring can sever the rootedness of archival concepts in the Greek words *arkhe* and *arkheion*. Equally, no refiguring can discard the necessity of an agreement between archivists and society – an archival contract. The nature of that contract is usually assumed, and not made explicit. This book challenges that silence: what is it that archivists undertake to do in return for the enormous power invested in them by society? (What constitutes an acceptable exercise of what Derrida calls 'archontic power'? What does it mean to 'preserve' a document, lapel badge or dress?) Everything in this book, indeed the book's very rationale, assumes the contract to be indispensable.

Clearly, however, new realities are placing strain on the archival contract and are modifying the concept of preservation: archivists interrogating the epistemological foundations of their practice; the difficulty of identifying and preserving records in electronic environments; the growing imperative for media conversion even in paper-based environments; the preservation of ever smaller proportions of increasingly voluminous records accumulations; contestation around legitimate limits to freedom of information; the difficulty of documenting ever more complex organisational and record-keeping processes; and so on. At the same time, new realities offer archivists opportunities to build on the contract: for instance, by exploiting technology to document collections (including archival interventions in collecting) more fully and to make them available more widely. Obviously, seeing this opportunity and utilising it requires appropriate expertise and resources. In countries like South Africa, positioned within global peripheries, this constitutes a serious challenge in itself. However, we remain convinced that in all global positionings, across professional landscapes and genres, archivists should aim to engage new realities with a passionate commitment to fulfilling the archival contract.

Such commitment is much needed in a South Africa that seeks to imagine itself and its past in ways not constrained by the colonial and apartheid pasts. What South Africa needs and does, of course, has wider resonances. For the archive is increasingly not a national patrimony, but today circulates, as Hall notes, 'in global systems of loan, exchanges and markets'. Likewise, global initiatives concerning the archive, like Gates' project mentioned earlier, affect the local situation. For much of the nineteenth century the treasures of the archive were forcibly relocated to imperial centres. At the turn of the millennium they continue along similar paths from poorer centres to richer metropoles as wealthy institutions snap up private collections, purchase microfilms and 'facilitate' digital availability. Based in Western centres, those institutions thus aggregate to themselves the power to define and delimit the archive. This book represents a challenge to the assumptions that underpin their activities, suggesting that a refigured archive might escape the kinds of boundaries they enforce, and find expression in new sites and in new forms.

Entrance to the former Roeland Street gaol, Cape Town; now the Cape Archives Repository.

The Power of the Archive and its Limits

Achille Mbembe

The term 'archives' first refers to a building, a symbol of a public institution, which is one of the organs of a constituted state. However, by 'archives' is also understood a collection of documents – normally written documents – kept in this building. There cannot therefore be a definition of 'archives' that does not encompass both the building itself and the documents stored there.

FROM DOCUMENT TO ARCHIVE

The status and the power of the archive derive from this entanglement of building and documents. The archive has neither status nor power without an architectural dimension, which encompasses the physical space of the site of the building, its motifs and columns, the arrangement of the rooms, the organisation of the 'files', the labyrinth of corridors, and that degree of discipline, half-light and austerity that gives the place something of the nature of a temple and a cemetery: a religious space because a set of rituals is constantly taking place there, rituals that we shall see below are of a quasi-magical nature, and a cemetery in the sense that fragments of lives and pieces of time are interred there, their shadows and footprints inscribed on paper and preserved like so many relics. And so we arrive at the inescapable materiality of the archive as well as at its resulting role, as this essay will endeavour to show, as an instituting imaginary.

In terms of the rituals involved, we might look at how an archive is produced, that is, at the process which culminates in a 'secular' text, with a previously different function, ending its career in the archives – or rather, becoming an archive. We often forget that not all documents are destined to be archives. In any given cultural system, only some documents fulfil the criteria of 'archivability'. Except for private documents (church documents, documents from private institutions, families, companies . . .), the majority of documents deemed archivable are related to the general work of the state. Once they are received, they have to be coded and classified. They are then distributed according to chronological, thematic or geographical criteria. Whatever criteria are used at the time of coding, classification and distribution, these procedures are simply a matter of creating order. Documents are thus immediately placed in a system that facilitates identification and interpretation. More seriously, the documents are then placed under a seal of secrecy – for a period of time, which varies according to the nature of the documents and local legislation. The process that results in a document becoming 'archivable' reveals that there are only products which have been deliberately stripped of what would make them simply 'secular' documents; thus there are no archives as such.

Archives are the product of a process which converts a certain number of documents into items judged to be worthy of preserving and keeping in a public place, where they can be consulted according to well-established procedures and regulations. As a result, they become part of a special system, well illustrated by the withdrawal into secrecy or 'closing' that marks the first years of their life. For several years, these fragments of lives and pieces of time are concealed in the half-light, set back from the visible world. A ban of principle is imposed upon them. This ban renders the content of these documents even more mysterious. At the same time a process of despoilment and dispossession is at work: above all, the archived document is one that has to a large extent ceased to belong to its author, in order to become the property of society at large, if only because from the moment it is archived, anyone can claim to access the content. Over and above the ritual of making secret, it seems clear that the archive is primarily the product of a judgement, the result of the exercise of a specific power and authority, which involves placing certain documents in an archive at the same time as others are discarded. The archive, therefore, is fundamentally a matter of discrimination and of selection, which, in the end, results in the granting of a privileged status to certain written documents, and the refusal of that same status to others, thereby judged 'unarchivable'. The archive is, therefore, not a piece of data, but a status.

THE STATUS OF THE DEBRIS

What status are we actually talking about? First of all, it is a material status. The material nature of the archive – at least before digitalisation – means that it is inscribed in the universe of the senses: a tactile universe because the document can be touched, a visual universe because it can be seen, a cognitive universe because it can be read and decoded. Consequently, because of its being there, the archive becomes something that does away with doubt, exerting a debilitating power over such doubt. It then acquires the status of proof. It is proof that a life truly existed, that something actually happened, an account of which can be put together. The final destination of the archive is therefore always situated outside its own materiality, in the story that it makes possible.

Its status is also an imaginary one. The imaginary is characterised by two properties already mentioned above: the architectural nature and the religious nature of the archive. No archive can be the depository of the entire history of a society, of all that has happened in that society. Through archived documents, we are presented with pieces of time to be assembled, fragments of life to be placed in order, one after the other, in an attempt to formulate a story that acquires its coherence through the ability to craft links between the beginning and the end. A montage of fragments thus creates an illusion of totality and continuity. In this way, just like the architectural process, the time woven together by the archive is the product of a composition. This time has a political dimension resulting from the alchemy of the archive: it is supposed to belong to everyone. The community of time, the feeling according to which we would all be heirs to a time over which we might exercise the rights of collective ownership: this is the imaginary that the archive seeks to disseminate.

This time of co-ownership, however, rests on a fundamental event: death. Death to the extent that the archived document *par excellence* is, generally, a document whose author is dead and which, obviously, has been closed for the required period before it can be accessed. The test represented by this closure, this extension of the period of time and the resulting distance from the immediate present, adds to the archive content of the document. Other than in exceptional cases, it is only at the end of this period of closure that the archived document is as if woken from sleep and returned to life. It can, from then on, be 'consulted'. The term 'consulted' shows clearly that we are no longer talking about just any document, but of this particular document, which has the power, because of a legal designation, to enlighten those who are engaged in an 'inquiry' into time inherited in co-ownership.

On a more basic level, the archive imposes a qualitative difference between co-ownership of dead time (the past) and living time, that is, the immediate present. That part of its status falling under the order of the imaginary arises from the fact that it is rooted in death as an architectural event. A death has to occur to give rise to a time characterised by not belonging to a private individual, precisely because this time, from that moment on, founds or institutes something. The power of the archive as an 'instituting imaginary' largely originates in this trade with death. There are three dimensions to this trade. The first involves the struggle against the fragments of life being dispersed. In fact, death is one of the most radical attempts to destroy life and to abolish all debt in relation to it. The act of dying, inasmuch as it entails the dislocation of the physical body, never attacks totally, nor equally successfully, all the properties of the deceased (in either the figurative or the literal sense). There will always remain traces of the deceased, elements that testify that a life did exist, that deeds were enacted, and struggles engaged in or evaded. Archives are born from a desire to reassemble these traces rather than destroy them. The function of the archive is to thwart the dispersion of these traces and the possibility, always there, that left to themselves, they might eventually acquire a life of their own. Fundamentally, the dead should be formally prohibited from stirring up disorder in the present.

The best way to ensure that the dead do not stir up disorder is not only to bury them, but also to bury their 'remains', the 'debris'. Archives form a part of these remains and this debris, and that is why they fulfil a religious role in modern societies. But – always remembering the relationship between the document and the architectural design in which it is stored – they also constitute a type of sepulchre where these remains are laid to rest. In this act of burial, and in relation to sepulture, is found the second dimension of the trade between the archive and death. Archiving is a kind of interment, laying something in a coffin, if not to rest, then at least to consign elements of that life which could not be destroyed purely and simply. These elements, removed from time and from life, are assigned to a place and a sepulchre that is perfectly recognisable because it is consecrated: the archives. Assigning them to this place makes it possible to establish an unquestionable authority over them and to tame the violence and cruelty of which the 'remains' are capable, especially when these are abandoned to their own devices.

THE ARCHIVE AS A TALISMAN

Up to now, we have treated archives on the basis of their power as a relic, and their capacity to function as an *instituting imaginary*. We have deliberately left aside two aspects: the subjective experience of the archive by individuals, and the relationship between the archive

ACHILLE MBEMBE

and the state. As far as the first is concerned, it is enough to state that however we define archives, they have no meaning outside the subjective experience of those individuals who, at a given moment, come to use them. It is this subjective experience that places limits on the supposed power of the archives, revealing their uselessness and their residual and superfluous nature. Several factors are involved in this subjective experience of the archives: who owns them; on whose authority they depend; the political context in which they are visited; the conditions under which they are accessed; the distance between what is sought and what is found; the manner in which they are decoded and how what is found there is presented and made public.

The relationship between the archive and the state is just as complex. It rests on a paradox. On the one hand, there is no state without archives – without its archives. On the other hand, the very existence of the archive constitutes a constant threat to the state. The reason is simple. More than on its ability to recall, the power of the state rests on its ability to consume time, that is, to abolish the archive and anaesthetise the past. The act that creates the state is an act of 'chronophagy'. It is a radical act because consuming the past makes it possible to be free from all debt. The constitutive violence of the state rests, in the end, on the possibility, which can never be dismissed, of refusing to recognise (or to settle) one or another debt. This violence is defined in contrast to the very essence of the archive since the denial of the archive is equivalent to, *stricto sensu*, a denial of debt.

This is why, in certain cases, some states have thought that they could do without archives. They have therefore attempted, either to reduce them to silence, or, in an even more radical manner, to destroy them. By doing this, they thought they could defer the archive's ability to serve as proof of a suspect fragment of life or piece of time. More interested in the present and the future than in the past, they thought that they could shut down the past for once and for all so that they could write as if everything was starting anew. Because, in the end, such methods affect the materiality of the archive more than its dimension as an instituting imaginary, they have, on occasion, run into trouble.

The power of the archive for all that has not been abolished. On the contrary, it has, rather, been displaced. Material destruction has only succeeded in inscribing the memory of the archive and its contents in a double register. On the one hand, in fantasy, inasmuch as destroying or prohibiting the archive has only provided it with additional content. In this case that content is all the more unreal because it has been removed from sight and interred once and for all in the sphere of that which shall remain unknown, therefore allowing space for all manner of imaginary thoughts. On the other hand, the destroyed archive haunts the state in the form of a spectre, an object that has no objective substance, but which, because it is touched by death, is transformed into a demon, the receptacle of all utopian ideals and of all anger, the authority of a future judgement.

In contrast, other states have sought to 'civilise' the ways in which the archive might be consumed, not by attempting to destroy its material substance but through the bias of commemoration. In this framework, the ultimate objective of commemoration is less to remember than to forget. For a memory to exist, there first has to be the temptation to repeat an original act. Commemoration, in contrast, is part of the ritual of forgetting: one bids farewell to the desire or the willingness to repeat something. 'Learning' to forget is all the easier if, on the one hand, whatever is to be forgotten passes into folklore (when it is handed over to the people at large), and if, on the other hand, it becomes part of the universe of commodification. Thus we pass from its consumption by a Leviathan seeking to liberate itself of all debt (that is, to acquire the right to exercise absolute violence) to its consumption by the masses – mass consumption.

By democratising the act of chronophagy and returning to an order where the consumption of the archive becomes a communal tool of the state and of society, two possibilities arise which repression alone does not allow. On the one hand, the urge that would have meant a desire to repeat, in a different time and with other actors, the original act is attenuated. In those cases where such an act involved murder, an assassin or a massacre, it is not difficult to see the benefit a society might gain from such a severance. On the other hand, by making such a severance a part of the universe of merchandise thanks to mass consumption, the archive is removed from the sphere of 'remains' and 'debris' and transformed into a talisman. A pagan cult then results, at the heart of which can be found numerous other institutions and artefacts (for example, museums).

The transformation of the archive into a talisman, however, is also accompanied by removing any subversive factors in the memory. In giving those who carry it (in this case those who consume it) a feeling of being protected or of being co-owner of a time or co-actor in an event, even if in the past, the talisman softens the anger, shame, guilt, or resentment which the archive tends, if not to incite, then at least to maintain, because of its function of recall. Thus the desire for

ACHILLE MBEMBE

revenge is removed just as the duty of repentance, justice and reparation is withdrawn. The commodification of memory obliterates the
distinction between the victim and the executioner, and consequently enables the state to realise what it has always dreamed of: the abolition of debt and the possibility of starting afresh.

CONCLUSION

Examining archives is to be interested in that which life has left
behind, to be interested in debt. However, it is also to be preoccupied
with debris. In this sense, both the historian and the archivist inhabit a sepulchre. They maintain an intimate relationship with a world
alive only by virtue of an initial event that is represented by the act
of dying. This being the case, writing history merely involves manipulating archives. Following tracks, putting back together scraps and
debris, and reassembling remains, is to be implicated in a ritual
which results in the resuscitation of life, in bringing the dead back to
life by reintegrating them in the cycle of time, in such a way that
they find, in a text, in an artefact or in a monument, a place to inhabit, from where they may continue to express themselves.

Dealing with dying also evokes the possibility of the spectre.
The archive could not have a relationship with death without
including the other remnant of death – the spectre. To a very large
extent, the historian is engaged in a battle against this world of spec-
tres. The latter find, through written texts, a path to an existence
among mortals – but an existence that no longer unfolds according
to the same modality as in their lifetime. It may be that historiography, and the very possibility of a political community (*polis*), are
only conceivable on condition that the spectre, which has been
brought back to life in this way, should remain silent, should accept
that from now on he may only speak through another, or be represented by some sign, or some object which, not belonging to any one
in particular, now belongs to all.

This being the case, the historian is not content with bringing
death back to life. S/he restores it to life precisely in order better to
silence it by transforming it from autonomous words into a prop on
which s/he can lean in order to speak and write beyond an originary
text. It is by the bias of this act of dispossession – this leaving out of
the author – that the historian establishes his/her authority, and a
society establishes a specific domain: the domain of things which,
because shared, belong exclusively to no one (the public domain).

And this is why the historian and the archivist have long been so useful to the state, notably in contexts where the latter was set up as an appointed guardian of that domain of things that belong exclusively to no one. In fact, both the historian and the archivist occupy a strategic position in the production of an instituting imaginary. One might ask what their role from now on may be, especially in contexts where the process of democratising a chronophagic act — that is, the abolition of the archive — is at an advanced stage.

The curious thing is the long-held belief that the state rested on something other than on this desire to abolish the archive, to free itself of debris. What could be more noble? But perhaps it is a condition for the existence of all societies: the need permanently to destroy the 'debris' — the taming, by violence if necessary, of the demon that they carry.

(Translated from the French by Judith Inggs)

The Evolution of the Bantu.

(By H. I. E. Dhlomo.)

Under this title we shall discuss the evolution of the black man since he came into contact with the white man. Bantu progress may be divided into several distinct periods or stages. However, progress has been so slow in some respects and so rapid in others that the divisions we shall make and discuss below, have come almost at one and the same time, and are not easily distinguishable, one from another. To day, in Bantu society may be found men who are at the van of modern thought and progress, and others, the majority, who live as of yore. This state of affairs aggravates the problems of race as the laws that are necessary for one section of the black population are a nuisance to the other. Before we proceed to consider stages and difficulties in Bantu growth, let it be said that Europeans—especially the advocates of segregation—should pro. mote, not obstruct, Native progress till the important stage of self expression is reached. For only after reach ing this stage can Natives develop along their own lines. At present this is impossible, but when that point is reached, Natives will show their race genius in creative work —and here will begin developing along their own lines (whatever that means) for each race can express and create that only which is within, or inherent in it.

The first stage in the evolution of the Bantu is that of the early contacts of the black and the white man. Of the events and conditions at that time much remains obscure and unknown. In view of this fact we have to content ourselves with discussing the ques tion of the writing of the history of that period in particular, and of the writing of S. African history in general. Unfortunately most S. African historic al books and documents were written when history was still viewed from a dynastic rather than from a humanis tic point of view ; from a strictly racial and political than from a correlated evolutionary and inter racial point of view. Some historians were (and are) influenced by, and their research work and ideas devoted to, classicism. They bamboozle and terrify the uninitiated by means of elaborate statistics, bom- bastic scientific formulæ, and by rhe toric. Historical truths and facts are distorted by the imaginative, fanciful and logical reflections and conclusions of writers. Instead of giving us facts they shower us with evidence confirm ing their conclusions. Evidence is a very dubious thing as judges and psychologists will tell you. Prejudice, credulity and scepticism and other human frailties make evidence preca rious. Above all illusion may deceive

H. I. E. Dhlomo, 'The Evolution of the Bantu' I, II and III, *Umteteli wa Bantu*, 14, 21 and 28 November 1931.

The Archives and the Political Imaginary

Bhekizizwe Peterson

Let me start by commending the conveners of the seminar series for organising what I regard as an intriguing range of talks, themes and speakers. Quite clearly, judging from the absorbing range of presentations and the essays in this book, the processes of refiguring the archives are extremely complex, multi-layered and multi-disciplinary.

Because of South Africa's racialised and divided history, the problem of its archive, particularly with regard to how it is constituted and its accessibility, has been a long-standing one. In the early 1930s, the pioneering playwright and journalist H. I. E. Dhlomo complained about the 'difficulty of . . . [n]atives getting access into public and state libraries and into the archive Departments'.[1] The significance of the archives for Dhlomo and his contemporaries stemmed from the political and symbolic duality that seemed to be at the heart of archival projects. Underlying the archive is the aim of ordering the past as inheritance. As we know, colonial and apartheid authorities consistently denied the existence of any legacy among Africans worth preserving, an attitude borne out in their insistence that Africans had no history. Alternatively, where robust forms of local knowledge could not be ignored or denied, colonial authorities sought to reshape and appropriate such 'archives' into the service of colonialism. The denial and active suppression of a native archive meant that its import, in the larger African nationalist project of transforming inheritance into deliverance, could be partially checked. Dhlomo pointedly noted that 'time and again our position and future have been prejudiced and made insecure by reference to our past'.[2] The archives, for Dhlomo, were a crucial component of the active labour of creating the political imaginary, that is, the intellectual and cultural horizons that shape our grasp of personal and social identities and histories: where we come from and where we are destined. In a sense then, archives, like history, draw on the impulses of introspection and anticipation, as they seek to systematise the chaos of the past, organising the fragments of the old world in ways that can renew the world we inhabit. Archives cannot, therefore, escape the thick imprint of their institutional and political nature.

So, how do we refigure the archives? Bearing in mind that mainstream archival traditions in South Africa have been exclusionary, I find the topic of refiguring the archive somewhat mis-

1   H. I. E. Dhlomo, 'The Evolution of the Bantu II' in *Umteteli wa Bantu* (21 November 1931).

2   Dhlomo, 'The Evolution of the Bantu II'.

men of the highest moral intergrity and intellectual ability These, then, are the dangers of imaginative and logical historical work which, of course, is necessary in certain cases where data is either unavailable or incomplete. Briefly the danger is that a fertile, imaginative mind may weave and propound theories which are not based on available facts The common fault of scientific, philosophic and historic speculations, is that facts are made to fit into the theory instead of the theory being based on available facts.

In making a musical composition what is important is not the sounds as such, but the relations between them. Likewise in history,—the ev nts, the people, and the conditions are of secondary importance. Of primary and supreme importance is the relation, interpretation and meaning read into historical data. The motives of individuals, their ideas, laws, mental states, merits and deme, its; the judgment, explanation and results of events and institutions; the customs, laws, arts, sciences, and beliefs of the people; how, and how far these affected their ordinary daily life—these are the vital, difficult and interesting problems that face writers of historical documents. We cannot gainsay the fact that time, place and conditions produce great figures just as great figures in turn give birth to new ideas and changes. Tshaka, Khama, Napoleon and other great or even notorious men (e.g. Al Capone) are the products of the time, place, and conditions. Al Capone could never be produced in, say, S. Africa today under the conditions prevailing. A Tshaka would have failed under the conditions, time and place that produced a Khama,—and the reverse is true It is these relations and connections that ARE history, and which give rise to distorted and incomplete historical pictures. Historians should be well versed in anthropology psychology, geography and art. To write intelligently about the story of a nation, one must take into account all the factors that affect the mind, growth and composition of the people. It is significant that until recently historians paid no attention to such important factors as music which expresses the profundity of the soul and mind of nations, and displays the people's emotions and instincts. The country's history of war, its sparkling biographies of heroes and leaders, its traditions, its spectacular achievements, its prospects, aspirations and fears, all are told and recorded in song Little wonder, then, that writers of historical documents have given us false and incomplete descriptions and conclusions Geographical and climatic influences were of paramount importance in the past for man's knowledge and ability were not able successfully to fight against geographical and climatic onslaughts. So that these had a definite and important stamp on early racial evolu

chievous. In other words, should we not, initially, occupy ourselves with locating, understanding and foregrounding the various forms of oppositional experiences and knowledge systems that are currently omitted from the archives in their present figuration? I say this because I am acutely aware that at the moment we are under the siege of various metropolitan theories that proclaim that we are 'post' this or that grand narrative, not forgetting the pitfalls of African nationalism. I would still like to insist, though, that we must strongly resist the lure to underplay the imperative to discover and construct the canons of previously marginalised groups, whatever the limitations that come with canon-formation. Otherwise, we will be unable to inscribe a local and Pan-African provenance in the production of knowledge (a concern that is frequently intimated in the calls for an African Renaissance), and will continue to proceed as if the contradictions and challenges that face South Africa now, especially with regard to the politics of race, ethnicity, class, gender, identity, culture, nation and so on, are novel developments, untheorised by past generations in South Africa or on the African continent. Unless there is a nuanced awareness of the complex social factors and intellectual traditions that have shaped Africans, the desire to refigure the archive may be nothing more than another sophisticated strategy of containment: ensuring the tacit continuation of the status quo – in all its whiteness – at the very moment when other cultures and systems of knowledge are being ostensibly recognised under the rhetoric of 'change'. In short, without a subtle grasp of the forms, contents and intentions of seemingly 'informal' canons or archives, any remaking of the archives is bound to be informed by the assumptions of the official archival processes and discourses.

If one recognises the vexed issues around the procedural, political and institutional questions that determine archives, then, quite clearly, archives cannot be naively approached as spaces or custodians of documents and information. Such an approach is untenable because of the problem of access that seems to stalk the archives. Access must be comprehended in at least two senses. First, as intimated above, we have to establish what other forms of knowledge and records have been deemed inconsequential and inappropriate and consequently excluded from archival holdings. We have to be critical of the methods that have gone into the acquisition, cataloguing and interpretation of material. Except for a few cases, archives, and, in particular, public archives in South Africa, have

30

been monolingual: they have embodied and voiced only the experiences and discourses of the successive white oligarchies that have governed throughout the twentieth century. The experiences and insights of Africans, women, workers and other communities were generally either ignored or criminalised, at times even banned and destroyed.

We well remember the apartheid government's obsession with confiscating the statements, publications, T-shirts and other paraphernalia that it suspected of 'furthering' the aims of 'communism' or 'illegal' organisations. In effect, the paradox was that only the apartheid state was sanctioned to keep and store 'subversive' material publicly. Often, activists, writers and cultural practitioners were prohibited even from having copies of their own work, lest they should be negatively influenced by their own thinking!

Beyond the political terrain, we have to wonder how much has been overlooked and lost in many other spheres such as religion, culture and sport. I am sure that much material has survived, and is stored in the stubborn memories of people, in suitcases and plastic bags under beds, in wardrobes and in ceilings. We must desist, however, from consoling ourselves by imbuing such material with a subversive, underground anonymity, as when we talk about the 'experiential archive' of black people that is somehow simply 'out there' beyond the soiled fingers of officialdom. The challenge is to find, assemble, catalogue and elucidate as much as possible of this material and to bring it into play in the public or institutional orbit. Although we may concede the presence and significance of an 'experiential archive', simply to proclaim that it is 'everywhere' is perilous. If the black 'experiential archive' is 'everywhere', then it is 'nowhere'. It is definitely not to be found in our schools' curricula or the public spaces that project our historical, cultural and educational inheritances.

If I may draw on the area with which I am most familiar, the arts, I can provide several illustrations to my observations. Let us take black theatre, where, since the 1960s, an extraordinary number of plays have been produced. A resurgence of performances among workers has been witnessed since the 1970s, constantly combining and shifting between drama, music and praise poetry. Off the top of my head I believe that only just over a dozen of these plays or texts have been published. In the absence of publication, I know of no systematic attempts to archive the notes, cast-lists, programmes, songs, manuscripts, garments, posters, or videos from

portant stamp on early racial evolution. Historians should give us a clear account of all these factors and influences before they rush to condemn or commend national actions Further our ideas of right and wrong change in accordance with the growth of our idea of morality and the evolution of our minds. Many national undertakings and customs, in war and in peace, that historians obscure and condemn, and which they term barbarous, may have been the only right and proper things to do then and there. Now and here they may be wrong as conditions have altered and ideas have changed. When a historian has come to a decision, "such a decision, however, lays on him the duty of stating his own position with the utmost precision and of setting out the facts that tell against him with equal clearness. When he has done this, he will be wise to consider whether he may not be in danger of incurring the reproach that he has wasted skill and energy on a hopeless enterprise."

(To be continued.)

The Evolution of the Bantu.

(By H. I. E. DHLOMO.)
II.

Another difficulty in the writing of S. African history is the lack of that chastening, helpful power of criticism and controversy due to the fact that S. African history is written by members of one race from their own particular point of view Until we have history written by Natives from their point of view, Union history will remain incomplete and one sided. It is time our educated young people produced history books that will inspire, encourage and be a source of pride to us and posterity. We want history of facts and records, not of mere opinions and false partisan interpretations; history established by study and observation, and not by logical arguments; history which is guided by principles of humanism, rather than the dictates and niceties of scholasticism; history that takes into account human nature and geographical and other factors, rather than that which blindly adheres to rules of classicism and scholarship. Such events as The Zulu War, The Kafir Wars, Bambata's Uprise etc., need revision. Dingane, Hintsa, Ntsikana etc., all form subjects of interesting biographies The difficulty, of course, is that Natives cannot get access into public and state libraries and into the archives departments, and, therefore cannot make use of historical records that lie unknown or partially understood by writers. However, many educated Bantu young people could collect invaluable information from our own "amakehla" who often bring to light many obscure and unknown facts and occurrences. This work can be undertaken by Natives living in rural districts for urban Native writers cannot do this owing to exigencies of finance etc.

In considering questions of race relations and adjustment we are forced to look backwards and to think re prospectively. We must needs study anthropology if we are to hold our own today, and prepare for the future. Time and again our position and future have been prejudiced and made insecure by reference to our past. Mud and ashes of discouragement and contempt are often thrown at the faces of aspiring Bantu men and women by pointing out that they come from an inferior stock of Homo sapiens, that their entire culture was primitive (a word that seems to carry opprobium and a stigma owing to ill and indescriminate use of terminology amongst writers), that their customs and beliefs were barbaric. Happily, despite lack of complete and accurate figures and facts, we have enough information and sufficient anthropological evidence to make up a good case for our past, to bring to the world the truth about human evolution, and to show our real selves. It puzzles many to find Union administrators who are well versed in the history of the past, embarking on such futile policies as are characteristic of this country's administration. The trouble is that while on material, educational and industrial lines the country is advancing rapidly, applying new schemes, and thinking of the future, in the case of Race Relations little progress has been made. When administrators consider this question, they are inclined to think of the past only, and to apply the ill-conceived policies of their predecessors. In this question we are told that the "Golden Age" was in the past when the white man had no competitors, but servants and dependents. It is in this connection only that the progressive whites sigh for "the good old days." Preposterous Instead of teaching the people the inevitableness and the ethics of competition and imbuing them with the spirit of useful rivalry, politicians delude their followers into believing that the government will remove these "competitive obstacles" by policies of Segregation, "Civilized Labour," "Colour Bar" etc. However each day makes it harder for the government to keep down the facts of the real situation, and in the near future the white rank and file will

black theatre. The few theatres that may keep some information are under-resourced, and likely to focus only on productions performed on their stages. So where is this material and is it adequately kept? I have serious doubts about this, since many black artists and groups still lead tough and itinerant existences. These predicaments impinge on attempts to refigure the archives. How are we to make sense of the traditions, new directions, themes and aesthetics of black theatre without access to performances or texts? It does not matter that scholars constantly acknowledge Gibson Kente as the 'father' of black theatre when only one of his plays is currently in print and the rest are unavailable. Dukuza ka Macu, arguably one of the most important and eloquent dramatists from the 1970s, is still unpublished and untaught in literature and drama departments, and his 'absence' and that of many others are ascribed to the lack of primary manuscripts. So, if manuscripts are not in print or circulating within the easy reach of scholars, it is as though these works and their authors simply do not exist. The end-result is a self-perpetuating cycle of neglect and ignorance of many areas of cultural life in South Africa. If we do not have adequate insight into black theatre, or any sense of indigenous language literatures, to use another example, then on what basis do we talk and write about South African theatre or literature?

Let me move to my second point concerning the problem of the archives and access. Whatever the nature of acquisitions in the archives, we have to consider who can engage, consult or use the material in the holdings. Here, it is not enough to hide behind well-meaning platitudes such as 'devising open-door policies to ensure that a wide range of possible users is reached'. Such policies are not likely to overcome such crucial barriers as the geographies in which most archives are situated, the dominance of English and Afrikaans as 'archival languages', and social factors such as low literacy rates. I have been struck, for instance, by the ways in which the Truth and Reconciliation Commission (TRC), undoubtedly the major archival project undertaken in South Africa, has been battling to accommodate and effectively deal with the cultural imagination of the black people who testified before the TRC. English is the medium of expression, with its dominance complicated rather than undermined by the use of translators; and testimonies have been received in a quasi-legalistic framework. These factors have often served to undermine rather than validate the testimonies of lower-class people and those who are not proficient in English, however eloquent they may be in African languages.

There are many possible ways in which the staid nature and inaccessibility of archives – both due largely to the workings of archivists – could be freed and rendered more dynamic and interactive with a range of communities who do not ordinarily 'visit' the archives. The starting point is to consider what the relationship should be between archives and other social and educational sites such as museums, libraries, cultural centres, writers' organisations, schools and churches. Archivists need to accept the importance of these sites as archival centres in their own right. Apart from the material and documents that are stored within them, these centres are populated by people who often prove to be dazzling raconteurs if allowed to express themselves in ways over which they have command; they have lived through much of the history of our vibrant yet troubled cities. Secondly, a considerable amount can be learnt from community and cultural organisations about where the nerve-centres of marginalised communities are, what their experiences have been, and what their fears and hopes are for the future. Yet many cultural and community organisations are struggling for survival. How can we talk of refiguring the archives when less than a few kilometres from the venue of this seminar series, cultural centres that have been on the cutting edge of black creativity since the 1970s – the Federated Union of Black Artists, the Afrika Cultural Centre and now even the Workers Library – are persistently plagued by the prospect of closing down because of difficulties in securing funds? My concern is the amount of vital material and knowledge that disappears with the demise of such institutions.

Surely archivists can devise more creative encounters between archival material and different sites and communities, given their familiarity with the contents of their holdings and taking due cognisance of the fragility, scarcity and safety of the material? Important days and events on the national calendar, at community and cultural centres, schools and churches, all provide obvious opportunities for fostering a more creative and stimulating encounter between archival material and the non-traditional users of archives. On such occasions, exhibits and workshops can be arranged in ways that seek to overcome the barriers of geography, language, class and literacy. I am certain that when archivists have the courage to engage other spaces, communities and insights, not only will access be broadened but the notion of the archive itself will be enlivened by being redeployed in fresh ways in new contexts. Such experimental encounters can deliver new insights, con-

be disillusioned, but, as it so often happens, disillusionment will come too late when Nemisis has also come. Indeed the harder the lot of the black man is made, and the easier that of the white, the better it is for the evolution of the Bantu.

As I have said, the cleverest administrators and writers often think of past and of current history only, and forget the history of the future. Herein lies the stumbling block in the way of race adjustment in this country If demagogues, politicians and writers were to be forced to write the history of, say, 60 years hence and tell us precisely how their policies and theories will be working then, and what the conditions would be like, many of them would not only be at sea and find out that they are blind steersmen (be they historians, demagogues, writers or administrators) of the state ship, but would, perhaps, realise their imbecility and inability.

(*To be continued.*)

The Evolution of the Bantu.

(By H. I. E. Dhlomo.)

III.

Openmindedness, research and constant revision are essential if we would keep our historical facts up to date. Our ideas of the past, present and future do not rest on a firm unchanging impregnable rock of finality or perfection, but are dependant upon the shifting sands of conditions and doctrines and thoughts. The history of the Middle Ages was distorted and tainted by theology and religion. Eminent scholars wasted their time on religious dogma on philosophical quiddities and obscurities, weaving far-fetched theories round these unproved "unprovable" theological points It was a fashion, then, to view all knowledge in the light or darkness of theology "Theology and Art," "Theology and History," "Theology and Geology" or titles of that description were not uncommon During the Renaissance history was expended upon, and distorted by love of literature. History was sacrificed to, and became a matter of literary aesthetics. It was the age of scholars and humanists. In America today there is a movement to revive humanism, but its exponents—Keyser, Potter, Babbitt, Lippmann and Samson are at loggerheads. Rousseau and his disciples attempted to force the doctrine of "Back to Nature." Then along

nections and even material for the archives. So, what I am suggesting is that there is no need to be paralysed by the problem of the
archives and access. The dynamism that is implicit in the notion of
refiguring the archives should be projected back onto archivists,
who then have to confront the locations, gaps and silences, and
methods that have informed the making of the conventional
archive.

In conclusion, my observations on refiguring the archive can be
encapsulated in the two broad processes that I have highlighted as
indispensable to the exercise. These are: first, rethinking the nature
and institutional processes that go into the making of the archives;
and second, making sure that the act of refiguring takes due cognisance of the experiences and worldviews of Africans. Underlying
these two processes has been my other provocation: given the racist
and exclusionary nature of South African society, how do we lock
into the experiences and knowledge that have had to find sanctuary
in the rituals, ceremonies, songs, literature, performances and popular culture produced by black people? I am thinking here about
the sophisticated ways in which, for example, independent churches have received and produced religious texts, artefacts and worldviews that they then enmesh in intricate enactments of bodily and
spiritual knowledge. There are the proclamations of self that black
youth seem to find in fashion, hair styles and music. To broach such
interventions solely from the perspective of pronouncing their con-
testatory nature is to miss a lot in what is a manifold canvas. I am
always struck when, with friends, we look at photographs of plays
we staged in the past. Often, the pictures do not trigger off memories of the themes and characters of the works. Instead we seem
always to be taken up by another drama, the events that inevitably
accompanied our existence as a group. I remember a hilarious (now,
anyway) stand-off we had with members of the security police at a
deserted border post between South Africa and Zimbabwe – the
police insisting that we perform for them the play we were then
touring. These are the scenes that we now re-enact and chronicle in
addition to the standard trajectory of the history of the group.
There are so many fascinating ways in which the dis-membering of
the land under apartheid was resisted by writers and artists as they
sought to re-member it in the light of their memories of and hopes
for a different, time, place and existence. As a character notes in
Mongane Serote's *To Every Birth Its Blood*, 'You know that it is only
in our memory that this is our land.'[3] Dhlomo opined that the act

BHEKIZIZWE PETERSON

of remembering 'is to defy and transcend Time and geography, to search for the perfect democracy', since 'no dictator, censor, law or prison can prevent you entering this paradise'.[4] Rather, accepting their important role in the elaboration of the political imaginary, archival projects should enrich the various ways in which personal and social memories are made, giving space for different and differing recollections of the journeys that we have travelled and those that still lie ahead. In refiguring the archives, the 'battle against forgetting' must be a guiding principle. We have to create new expanses where one is 'able to reclaim the past, revisit the legacies of suffering and triumph, in ways that will help to transform our present reality'.[5]

affairs, and the History of Civilization, which discusses the influence upon human beings of their art, literature, philosophy, religion and ethics." The treatment of Bantu history is most unbalanced. It is not full It is one-sided. It does not cover the divisions made above. Of course there are two or three notable exceptions Writers forget that there is nothing in life—be it only unscented sea weeds or tiny burrowing creatures, let alone human beings that does not require thorough faithful study. We have many who claim to be experts in Native law, psychology, culture etc What is the cause of all this confusion? Perhaps, to quote Buny, "it is because the historians of today were trained by the Germanizing hierarchy to regard history as a 'science' that they have so much neglected what is after all the principal craft of the historian the art of narrative."

Another common, if more dangerous, practice in South Africa is to use history as propaganda. This is the kind of history about which Valery writes, "It is the most dangerous product that the chemistry of the intellect has elaborated ..... It induces dreams, it intoxicates peoples, makes them breed beguiling memories, exag- gerates their reflexes, nourishes their old wounds, torments them in repose, drives them to megalomania or persecu- tion mania and makes nations bitter, proud, insupportable and vain." The fact that some writers of historical literatu.e cannot rise above the level of political prejudice and of the pro- paganda mania, serves to indicate that they rushed to print before doing research work. Resea·ch teaches in- dependence, good judgment and the virtue of precision. When a reseron worker reads and considers the vast store of human experience, he feels not only humble and sheepish but learns the great lessons of the disasters caused by folly and irresponsibility.

3   Mongane Serote, *To Every Birth Its Blood* (Johannesburg: Ravan Press, 1981), p. 78.

4   Dhlomo, 'The Evolution of the Bantu I' in *Umteteli wa Bantu* (14 November 1931).

5   bell hooks, 'Choosing the margin as a space of radical openness' in *Framework* 36 (1989), p. 20.

Refiguring the Archive Seminar Series
Graduate School for Humanities and Social Sciences, University of the Witwatersrand, August 1998

Archive Fever

(A seminar by Jacques Derrida, University of the Witwatersrand, August 1998,
transcribed by Verne Harris)

JD: Thank you. Well I won't tell you how pleased I am and honoured
to be here with you, and to thank my guests here, and Carolyn
Hamilton, to start with. I won't tell you how pleased I am, because I
am not pleased – I am absolutely paralysed by the situation. I am happy
to see so many people, but I thought it would be a seminar with questions and improvisation and so on and so forth. And now after these
very generous and lucid accounts, and critiques,* I am in a position to
go back to the book – and I've totally forgotten the book! Almost totally. I brought it with me, and I thought that perhaps at some time I
could just consult. And I say this sincerely, because I tried yesterday
because I wanted to prepare this improvised session. I tried to read it,
and I couldn't do it. And I was thinking that the choice you have made
of this modest essay – it was a lecture in fact (I will tell you more about
the archive of this lecture in a moment) – I thought that your choice of
this lecture would have to do with precisely the questions that were
addressed by you – that is, the current situation of the archive in this
country, the challenge of memory, the reference to the past, the TRC,
and so on and so forth. So I was just preparing myself to address not
my book – to plead for my book – but just to share with you a number of concerns. So let me try and say something about the book, but I
hope that very quickly we will leave the book and just discuss burning
things here.

About the lecture, just to describe the limits of this essay, which
was a long lecture but a short book I wrote in a very peculiar situation
– in this part of the book as archive. It was a conference in London
organised by the people in charge of Freud's archive, and close to the
house of Freud in London. And preparing this lecture about memory
and psychoanalysis, the relation – and you've said this very well, I
won't go back to this – about memory and consciousness, the technology of archive in psychoanalysis, and after psychoanalysis, I, knowing that Yerushalmi, the famous historian of Judaism, would be here,
having written this book on Freud and Judaism, I orientated everything I had to say in his direction. I wanted to pay homage to him,
while of course discussing his book. And what happened was this.

* Derrida was speaking after short critiques of
Archive Fever by Sue van Zyl and Verne Harris.
Revised, expanded versions of these critiques
are reproduced alongside this transcription.

Psychoanalysis and the Archive: Derrida's *Archive Fever*

Susan van Zyl

PART I

If the concept of the archive ever was an untroubled one, it certainly is no longer so. Postmodernism and deconstruction have made sure of that. What the archive is, how it works and in which ways it may be reconfigured are all questions that the elaborate, intertextual thought of our times tackles with characteristic self-consciousness and often unashamed opacity. In this context, Derrida's extraordinary evocation of the intermingling of questions concerning the archive and psychoanalysis in *Archive Fever* is no exception.[1]

Faced by a work of this kind one is tempted to identify with Derrida, to enter into the spirit of his text by adopting his style and method. My intention, instead, is to extract from his elliptical text those ideas and examples that demonstrate the importance of psychoanalysis to an understanding of the archive, and to present and discuss them in a way that does not attempt to do justice to *Archive Fever* as Writing.

Despite this proviso it is necessary to begin with some indication of the nature and construction of *Archive Fever*, which Derrida describes as 'three plus n essays'.[2] The text is concerned not only with what a knowledge of psychoanalysis (as a body of content or discipline) can contribute to an understanding of the archive, but also with the archive of psychoanalysis itself. It evokes a particular set of writings, episodes and relations in the history of psychoanalysis, all of which reveal that if we are to understand the workings of the archive, and how and why archives might reconfigure themselves, we must turn not only to the inevitable surface vicissitudes of history, power and knowledge, but also to what as post-Freudians we know of the depths of its subject, the archivist. A science of the archive must concern itself not only with the way in which the archive becomes an institution and the laws that govern this institutionalisation, but also with those who authorise (in both senses) this process.[3] This concern with the archivist does not mean, however, that Derrida's contribution to an understanding of the archive is a conventionally psychological one. What is of interest is not the by now commonplace understanding that archives (or any other institution or organisation of knowledge for that

1   J. Derrida, *Archive Fever* (Chicago: University of Chicago Press, 1996).

2   Derrida, *Archive Fever*, p. 5.

3   Derrida, *Archive Fever*, p. 3.

First failure – something which is repeated, which is being repeated all the time around this problem – that Yerushalmi, whom I met the day before the lecture, didn't come the day of the lecture because he was sick. He stayed at his hotel, so I just had to pay homage to him, to discuss him, while he was not here. It was a very strange situation. Something like today – well, I was not exactly prepared towards what is happening. And then of course I sent him the manuscript. He read the manuscript. He wrote to me very generously, and then we met in New York, we became close friends. And last fall, people in New York wanted to organise a real debate, a public debate like this, between him and myself. There was a crowd. And it was a total failure, because that time he tried to reply in a very aggressive way. I was totally paralysed at the situation, and nothing happened once more. So, there must be a fate here.

Let me go back to some of the points which were made by Sue van Zyl and Verne Harris. Some of them, because I agree with almost everything they said, and I don't want to repeat this. Let me simply insist on a question that they haven't emphasised – about Judaism. It's not simply a question of Judaism itself, but a certain difference within Yerushalmi's book, between what he calls Judaism and Jewishness. And this has to do with the question of the future, the archive as being not simply a recording of the past, but also something which is shaped by a certain power, a selective power, and shaped by the future, by the future anterior. Yerushalmi says that at some point in this fictional debate – and of course the fiction is an important point here – in his fictional debate with the ghost of Freud, he says that of course he would easily give up everything in Judaism except what he considers to be Jewishness – the Jewishness, that is, what is the essential feature of being Jewish. Which has nothing to do – or has nothing essential to do – with religion, belief in God, tradition, etc., etc., but simply, he says, the constitutional reference to the past (which he thinks is essentially Jewish, and inscribed in Jewish texts) and another essential, and unique, relation to the future. As if Jewishness was characterised by precisely this double relationship to the law of gathering and being true to the past, and the promise, the future. And I, discussing, of course objected to this definition, to the attribution only to Jewishness of this double desire for the past and for the future. I, of course, discussed a number of, let's say, political and historical implications of this definition of Jewishness in Yerushalmi.

And this has to do, of course, with the point both of you have correctly emphasised, that is, the archive doesn't simply record the past. It

matter) are often driven by, and even at the mercy of, the conscious beliefs, attitudes and interests of individual archivists. In Derrida's hands, the productivity of the archive's encounter with psychoanalysis stems from his demonstration that the apparent unities of the archive are always threatened by those unconscious forces and their often unexpected effects that Freud has shown to threaten continually the psychological unity of the archivist.

I

Derrida's enterprise in *Archive Fever* is, I believe, rooted in two related assumptions concerning the relevance of Freud to questions of the archive. The first is that the psychoanalytic archive in particular, dominated as it is by what Derrida calls the 'signature' of Sigmund Freud, is an especially rich site in which to uncover conflicting principles of authority and theories of origin still actively at work in archives today. The second is that psychoanalysis is itself an archival science, unceasingly concerned with questions of memory and forgetting, with the necessary and accidental destinies of desire and thought and the substrates that sustain or obliterate them.

In an attempt to give some focus to the major questions and themes that provide the surface play and dispersion of *Archive Fever* with its own unity, it is probably best to begin where Derrida begins. *Archive Fever* opens with a brief archival account of the notion of the archive: an etymological analysis of the term 'archive' itself.[4] By way of this etymology Derrida generates three ingredients central to the concept of the archive. While the contemporary meaning of the word emphasises its sequential dimensions, its Greek and Latin origins in the word *archon* or magistrate signal the archive's status as a place from which authority emanated, a place where legal documents were stored and preserved. The concept of the archive is thus temporal, juridical and material, and it is to the dynamic principles at work in each of these aspects, to the classic questions of time, space and power located at the point of intersection between archive and archivist, that *Archive Fever* makes its seminal contribution.

Turning first to the question of authority, a term that threads its way throughout Derrida's text is the word 'patriarch' (or 'archpatriarch'), a word that signals a concern with the often secret and mysterious power that those who appear to found the archive or, crucially, the family have over those that follow them. In *Archive Fever* (as one might expect from a work that is both analytic in form and psychoanalytic in nature) familial, intellectual and religious authority are

4 Derrida, *Archive Fever*, pp. 2–3.

also, of course, constitutes the past, and in view of a future which retrospectively, or retroactively, gives it its so-called final truth. And in that respect I of course take into account Freud's gesture – that's what is the major contribution of Freud, and I think something to which deconstruction will be forever, let's say, indebted – Freud's contribution consists in saying that the psyche is structured in a way that there are many places in which traces are kept, which means that within the psyche there is an inside and an outside. First. So, since the archive does not consist simply in remembering, in living memory, in anamnesis; but in consigning, in inscribing a trace in some external location – there is no archive without some location, that is, some space outside. Archive is not a living memory. It's a location – that's why the political power of the *archons* is so essential in the definition of the archive. So that you need the exteriority of the place in order to get something archived. Now, because of this exteriority, what is kept in the archive, of course can be erased, can be lost, and the very gesture which consists in keeping safe – in a safe, so to speak – is always, and from the beginning, threatened by the possibility of destruction. That's one point.

The other point is that the possibility of the destruction of the archive – and we could give examples as burning as the ones you gave about the destruction of archives in this country, of actual or potential archive – the destruction of archive is not simply a risk which is run because of this exteriority – the fact that it's located in a place which by definition is threatened. The risk has to do with what Freud defines as a death drive – that is, a drive to, precisely, destroy the trace without any reminder, without any trace, without any ashes. So, on the one hand you have a device, a structure, in which what is repressed – that is, forgotten in the trivial sense – is kept safe in another location of the psychic apparatus. Okay? And, in this economy of repression, nothing is lost. Okay? What is forgotten or repressed is kept safe somewhere else, and then, in some situation, the repressed can of course come back. And of course we can, not only illustrate this, but confirm this through a number of historical and political examples. But this economy – and this is an economy according to which nothing is annihilated, or destroyed forever – this economy is, let's say, threatened or in conflict with the aneconomic death drive, that is, a drive which motivates, so to speak, the radical destruction of the archive. There is a destruction which doesn't leave anything in place, which is even more radical than repression. It's the repetition of a possibility of a, let's say, burning into ashes the very trace of the past. So that's what I call in *Archive Fever* the archiviolithic power, the power to destroy the archive. Which means

seen as intimately connected, and the nature and intricacies of this connection are exemplified in the movements of the text itself.

Three important sets of relations to authority are evoked in *Archive Fever*: those of Freud to his father Jakob, of contemporary historian Yosef Hayim Yerushalmi, author of *Freud's Moses: Judaism Terminable and Interminable*,[5] to Freud and, finally, those of Jacques Derrida himself to both Yerushalmi and Freud. Each of these pairs of relationships is examined primarily through the lens of Yerushalmi's key question about whether psychoanalysis is a 'Jewish science', a question in turn significantly understood by Yerushalmi as inseparable from that of Freud's own relation to his Jewishness.

As the text of *Archive Fever* unfolds, something that evidently strikes Derrida is the contradiction at the heart of the question of Freud's Jewishness. This contradiction reveals itself vividly in the two different forms in which archivist Yerushalmi attempts to answer the question. The first attempt is that of the conventional modern historian, revealed in the manner in which Yerushalmi seeks and treats the evidence that might help him to answer his question. A key example discussed is the family Bible that Jakob Freud recovered and reinscribed to give to his son Sigmund on his thirty-fifth birthday – a piece of evidence used by Yerushalmi to show, for example, that Freud knew more Hebrew and more of the Bible than he sometimes implied. This in turn suggested that Jewishness (although not necessarily Judaism) was important to Freud in ways that become central to the project of *Freud's Moses*.

The second attempt is something very different. It is the final section of Yerushalmi's book, entitled 'Monologue with Freud', deconstructed by Derrida with characteristic perspicacity. The monologue, Derrida points out, represents a substantial change from the classical style of the rest of the book. Up to this point in his book Yerushalmi complies with the traditional objective norms of knowledge and scholarship that dominate the historical and scientific communities. But he concludes in a new mode. In the fictive monologue he breaks the traditional historian's code and enters into conversation with Freud's ghost, addressing Freud as 'you' and questioning him directly. What is more, having asked Freud whether his daughter Anna spoke in his name when she said that if psychoanalysis were to be described as a Jewish science it would be a 'title of honour', he promises (in defiance of all that historian and archivist alike supposedly hold dear) to keep Freud's secret and not to reveal his answer to anyone.

What strikes me with increasing force when reading Yerushalmi's

5   Y. H. Yerushalmi, *Freud's Moses: Judaism Terminable and Interminable* (New Haven: Yale University Press, 1991).

the limitation of the archive – the fact that the power, and often the social and political power of the archive, which consists in selecting the traces in memory, in marginalising, censoring, destroying, such and such traces through precisely a selection, a filter, and which, of course, is made possible by, let's say, the finitude, the limitation, let's say of human power, of space, the place where to accumulate the archive and so on. And we have a number of such problems today of the economy of the accumulation. That's finitude. But this finitude does not account for another kind of destruction, which is the death drive. That is, the radical desire for the destruction of the archive is incommensurable with the finitude of, let's say, the human power to keep in a certain space a certain amount of accumulated traces. So, you have here a conflict, or a competition, between the consequences of finitude and the radical drive to destruction. And it is because this radical drive to destruction is always at work – and we have to take account of it – that the desire for archive is a burning one. If we knew that it's only because of the limitations in time and space, because of the technological limits – that we cannot keep this or this – there would not be such a fever, a passion. You said that there is no archive to be embraced without passion. There would be no passion. If there is a passion, it is because we know that not only the traces can be lost by accident or because the space is finite or the time is finite, but because we know that something in us, so to speak, something in the psychic apparatus, is driven to destroy the trace without any reminder. And that's where the archive fever comes from.

Now, a question that I was asking. I'll make two more points, and then open to discussion with the audience. Two more points. One has to do with technology. The question has been raised about the history of technology after the etymology of the word archive, and *archon*, and so on and so forth. You're right, I didn't really take into account the whole history of technology – in details what's going on today. Nevertheless, I tried to address the question not simply of the progress of technology today and the consequences it might have on the work of the archivists of all kinds – political, archaeological, scholars, and so on and so forth – I also asked the question whether psychoanalysis itself should not be transformed by the transformation of these writing, or archiving, apparatuses. Not at all as if, let's say, psychoanalysis being what it is, the mutation, the technological mutation, could have changed the record we keep of psychoanalysis, or could have changed something in the way that we archive the results of psychoanalysis, or the way we archive the history of psychoanalytical institutions and scholarship. No. My

book together with *Archive Fever* is the importance of Derrida's crucial demonstration that a deconstruction of Yerushalmi's text reveals a point that lies at the heart of the Western historical archive. Two different concepts of truth are revealed respectively by the form of the monologue and the example of the Freud Bible. The first concept is that backed by personal authority represented by the word of the patriarch, in this case that of Freud himself. The second, by contrast, is founded on the demand for objective evidence as represented in documents, separate from any particular voice or people. While in modernity the first may seem to have been superseded and almost obliterated by the second, it is only a matter of seeming. As Freud and Derrida know, the role of patriarch continues to reveal itself in the psyche of the archivist; obedience may be deferred but it is obedience nevertheless.

Derrida's treatment of deferred obedience marks for me a key characteristic of his reading of psychoanalysis: an orientation towards what is most radical in Freud. That ambivalence to authority reflected so often in the deferred obedience of those who record and make history can be explained by way of Oedipus. In Oedipal terms it is necessary only to draw attention to the fact that freedom from the desire for the father is ironically bought by way of an identification with him, an identification that brings not just imitation but also that often insidious type of obedience that necessarily goes with it. But this is not the route Derrida chooses to follow. Freud offers us another, and for many far more problematic, explanation of deferred obedience – the phylogenetic account, primarily associated with *Totem and Taboo*,[6] which sees the inherited memory of the murder of the primal father and the subsequent complicit banding together of the brothers in their guilt as the source of an archaic psychic constellation latent in all members of the species. This constellation, the importance of which the late work of Freud continually emphasises, not only accounts for the power of the patriarch and the ambivalence of the sons, but acts as the precondition for the social bond itself. The very possibility of the archive as repository of knowledge, and thus of a history of culture, is rooted in the traces of phylogenetic memory.

This commitment to the power of the phylogenetic archive is not limited in the work of Freud or to the forces that surround the patriarch in the making of history. Its dynamic psychic work is complemented by an always implicit, often explicit, epistemological correlate. It underpins a crucial distinction between what Freud called, somewhat misleadingly for our purposes, 'historical' (collective,

6   S. Freud, *Totem and Taboo* (1912) (London: Pelican Freud Library, vol. 13, 1985).

assumption was that the mutation in technology changes not simply the archiving process, but what is archivable – that is, the content of what has to be archived is changed by the technology. And this has also a number of political implications. That is, the way we experience what we want to keep in memory, or in archive – and the two things are different – is conditioned by a certain state, or a certain structure, of the possibility of archiving. So the archive, the technological power of the archive, determines the nature of what has to be archived. Then, of course, for that reason – because the content and the meaning of the archive is constantly reshaped by the archivists of all sorts (and not only the scholars – everyone in the city which takes part in this process) – the structure and the meaning of the archive is of course dependent on the future, on what is coming, on what will have come.

And here I would like to say one more word about what you correctly recalled about what I called messianicity. The problem of messianicity is of course at the centre of my discussion of Yerushalmi's thesis. What I call the messianic, of course, the messianicity, is not reducible to what one calls messianism in religious traditions. It is irreducible to a determined figure of the Messiah in a number of Jewish, Christian or Islamic traditions. What I call the messianic is simply the relationship to the future, the expectation of what comes, with no horizon of expectation. Anyone, anything, might happen or arrive, and this openness, this relation to the future, is a universal experience – it's not reserved to cultures in which the Messiah appeared as a determined name and figure. So for that reason there is a messianic, a messianicity, implied in the very experience of the archive. And that's also why it is impossible to close the archive. It is impossible to saturate a context in which we could say, 'Well, now it's done, we have gathered all the documents and monuments, we know how to interpret it, we have all the contextual elements necessary for that, and it's done.' No! It's always possible to re-interpret an archive. And this future-oriented structure of the archive is precisely what confronts us with a responsibility, an ethical and political responsibility.

Now, of course, I know that today what South Africa is experiencing is from that point of view on the one hand unique – and we'll come back to this probably – and on the other hand, very analogous to a number of situations today in the world. I could give a number of examples in Europe or out of Europe, of the same problem of the archive of what happened during, let's say, the last century – not to say more than that – in France we have our problems too, from that point of view. Now, I've been constantly even before coming here, but spe-

unconscious, phylogenetic) truth and 'material' (actual, individual, ontogenetic) truth. To refer to Derrida and Yerushalmi, Freud may have rejected the Bible's material truth but not its historical truth – its reflection of true and truly archaic psychic material.

Just such a distinction probably informs Derrida's own reading of Freud's famous analysis of Jensen's novel *Gradiva*.[7] Jensen's *Gradiva* is the story of a young archaeologist Hanold who, despite his scientific training and its resulting archaeological knowledge, sets out for Pompeii to find the woman whose unusual gait is, he believes, the inspiration for the figure on an ancient frieze with which he has become fascinated. In Pompeii he meets and talks for two hours with a woman he takes for a ghost, but whom he later recognises as his childhood sweetheart, Zoë, whose distinctive high step was evoked by that of the figure on the frieze.

Derrida's reading of Freud's reading of the book emphasises the piece of the story that resists conventional rational explanation. Faced by Hanold's symptoms, Freud marshals the entire aetiological machinery of psychoanalysis, beginning with the mechanisms of repression. In the end, however, for Derrida at least, it is the truth of insanity, of hauntedness, that returns because it too belongs to some spectral 'historical' and not just 'material' truth that Freud's archive, perhaps despite himself, cannot do without.

II

If Derrida and Freud together trouble our understanding of the archive with questions of authority and truth, Derrida is equally merciless when it comes to our ideas around time and the sequential. Lest we think of it as available to completion, Derrida repeatedly reminds us that the archive is always open to what he calls the future-to-come. There are undoubtedly many meanings to this phrase in *Archive Fever*. The first is the obvious one that reminds us of the provisional nature of all scientific work; new archives can be discovered, and may emerge from the merely private or even actively secret sphere. Another emerges from Yerushalmi's question as to whether we shall ever know whether psychoanalysis is a Jewish science because so much will depend on how these terms are defined in the future. In this he is pointing to more than a change in the meaning of words. Yerushalmi is, according to Derrida, raising a no lesser question than that of the (perhaps unimaginable) nature of future historiographic tradition in which interrelationships between language, science, nation and religion may be construed quite differently.

7   S. Freud, *Delusions and Dreams in Jensen's Gradiva* (London: Pelican Freud Library, vol. 14, 1985).

cially since I arrived here, constantly thinking of and meditating on and discussing about the Truth and Reconciliation Commission. On one hand, we could say that it is a problem of archive – that is, the Commission is trying to gather a number of testimonies, and to make them public. (And that's another feature of the archive. There is no, in the strict sense of the word, there is no private archive. An archive has to be public, even if it's hidden provisionally or appropriated by someone. It belongs to the concept of the archive that it be public, precisely because it is located. You cannot keep an archive inside yourself – this is not archive. Because of the exteriority that I mentioned at the beginning, an archive has to be public.) Now, the TRC could be considered a place of archive. A number of testimonies are gathered, and there is a recording of it – I understand it's often publicly broadcast by the media – then there will be books, reports. It's going to be a public archive. And the very publicity, the inscription in a public space, of these testimonies and these interpretations of the testimonies, will have no doubt a powerful effect on the history and the future of South Africa. Difficult to know what this effect is or will be, but no doubt the project of the archive, and of the inscription of the archive in the public space – to make it available publicly, not simply in South Africa, but all over the world – will have powerful effects. Now, as you know very well, this Commission is very controversial. For many reasons. (Perhaps we'll come back to this in a moment.) But one of the reasons that I would select here – because of the theme of this seminar – is, on the one hand, the limitations, the selection, on many sides – many people complain about these limitations – not everyone can testify (not everyone because not everyone is living, but there are a number of people who are dead who cannot testify). So there is active and passive selection. I won't enter into details here, but you can imagine how selective the process has to be. It cannot be otherwise. If only because of the limitation in time. And this Commission, by contract – and we can [. . .?] on why – had a limited space of time, period of time, to gather these testimonies. This is a serious limitation. But they had to limit themselves, if only because the work of mourning, which is at the centre of this experience – a work of mourning, Freud would say, has to be limited in time – if you want a work of mourning to be efficient, it has to come to an end at some point. And then there are other deadlines, and the report, and the elections. So a number of such limitations. For some of them some responsibility can be assigned, of course. It's a decision made by a determined number of people who decide this and this about these limitations.

Presenting the question of the future-to-come in yet other terms, Derrida revisits Freud's attempt to represent memory as internal archivisation by way of 'The Mystic Pad',[8] or 'Magic Slate', and then raises the question (significantly the only one referred to on the cover of the book) of informatic culture and the archive. Freud did not have, as possible models to represent the functioning of the psychic apparatus, those archival machines available now, machines that could hardly have been dreamt about earlier in the century. Do these new archival machines change anything? Do they, Derrida asks, affect the essentials of Freud's thought and discourse? The questions raised by Derrida's evocation of the possible consequences of information technology for the archive are of many kinds, and it is sometimes difficult when reading the text to separate them out and to establish their respective levels and forms. One class of questions concerns the structure of the psychic apparatus itself as a system of memory and forgetting, and asks whether it resists or responds to the evolution of archival technoscience or not. Is the nature and functioning of the psychic apparatus different, Derrida asks, as a result of the existence of new archival mechanisms?[9]

A second class of questions concerns those of representation or modelling and, by implication, the consequences for Freudian metapsychology of the existence of other discursive resources as a result of the coming into being of different types of objects and processes. Is the psychic apparatus better represented by mechanisms more complex than 'The Mystic Pad', by microcomputing, by computerisation and so on?

Finally, what would the effect on the psychoanalytic archive have been if, instead of all those remarkable but time-consuming letters, Freud and his colleagues had communicated by way of e-mail?

These are not questions Derrida answers in *Archive Fever*, although he confesses he would have liked to. What is clear, however, is that it is important not to confuse changes in our capacity to represent the psychic apparatus with alterations in the psychic apparatus itself. For, as Derrida writes, if we encountered changes in terms of spatial architecture or economy of speed it would no longer be a question of the representative value of the model, but rather of an entirely different logic.[10] This would indeed be an illustration of the power of the future-to-come upon the archive.

8   S. Freud, *A Note upon the 'Mystic Writing-Pad'* (London: Pelican Freud Library, vol. 11, 1991).

9   Derrida, *Archive Fever*, p. 15.

10   Derrida, *Archive Fever*, p. 15.

But, in addition to these, let's say, decided or calculable limitations, there is an uncalculable limitation. Some archive has been, forever, destroyed. Not simply as documents, but simply people have
disappeared. And the pain, or the violence, on many sides cannot be
recorded in an archive. The destruction of the archive was part of the
painful things that are in question here. The destruction of the
archive was precisely, precisely, the problem. The disappearance, the
death or the killing or the forgetting or simply the impossibility just
to testify to what happened. So, there was a radical destruction at the
centre of the experience to be recorded, to be archived, so to speak.
Then there is another problem of course. This archive is not simply
a mass of facts, of true facts, to be gathered and delivered and made
available. They are interpreted facts, interpreted by the witnesses of
course (testimony is not simply the unveiling of a truth; a testimony
is an active interpretation of what happened). So the concept of truth
in 'truth and reconciliation' in that case does not simply mean information, because there is interpretation, there will be interpretation.
And now the way the Commissioners, the people in charge, those
who have the power in fact to build the archive and to publish the
archive and to interpret the archive, have, of course, their own interpretations, their own motivations, their own pre-shaped schemes of
interpretation. For instance, if you interpret reconciliation as conditioned by confession, repentance, forgiveness, and so on and so forth,
then you introduce within the very text of the archive a number of,
let's say, values or assumptions, which are linked, let's say to, for
instance, not only religious beliefs – for example forgiveness, reconciliation, salvation, redemption and so on and so forth – but within
such or such religion you introduce an interpretation of the religious
tradition itself. That's what I tried to say modestly in lectures I gave
before coming here on forgiveness, an act of forgiveness, pure forgiveness, usually in the Christian tradition – which is dominant in
the ideology of this unique and exemplary process – an act of forgiveness should be conditioned by confession, that is the one who
asks for amnesty, asks for forgiveness as amnesty, should ask for forgiveness, that is, repent, confess, transform himself/herself and so on
and so forth. That's the traditional interpretation of forgiveness. But
I would say, that in the same tradition you may interpret forgiveness
in a very different way, and say, 'well forgiveness has nothing to do
with asking for forgiveness, with this economy of confession, repentance, and so on and so forth. Forgiveness, if it happens, should be
totally foreign to this economy of asking for forgiveness – this con-

III

Turning, perhaps too late, to the title of Derrida's text, one is struck once again by what is central to *Archive Fever*, to what one has come to expect from Derrida, the commitment and capacity to work at the limits of his material. That psychoanalysis is a science of memory, of unwanted remembering and active forgetting on the individual level, is of undoubted importance to what Freud has to contribute to an understanding of the archive. But again Derrida chooses the strongest hypothesis available and reminds us that psychoanalysis is also a science of the death instinct, of that which dies and is destroyed as much as of that which defies it.

Early in the text Derrida raises the central idea of the death drive by way of a reading of the opening of Freud's *Civilization and its Discontents*,[11] in which Derrida points to the paradox at the heart of Freud's archival gesture: his laborious investment in the archive invokes the very principle that aims to ruin the archive as an accumulation of memory in some exterior place.

With the death drive, Freud introduces, in Derrida's terms, 'an a priori forgetfulness into the heart of the monument, that which works against itself, a principle that threatens every principality, an archive fever'.[12] With Derrida and Freud then, the archive appears before us as that driven by the eternal warring between Eros and Thanatos, in a fever provoked by the principle of death but bravely defended by all that the libido can marshal against it.

PART 2

I

Any attempt to say something more general concerning the implications of psychoanalysis for archival enquiry can usefully begin with a return to Derrida's text and the particular, some would say characteristically postmodern, reading of psychoanalysis that *Archive Fever* represents. It has already been pointed out that at key points in a work that brings psychoanalytic insights to bear upon a study of psychoanalysis's own archive, Derrida chooses what I have called the most radical readings of the material, and there is, I think, much that flows from his having adopted this particular orientation.

Two ways of signalling the complex ontological and epistemological status of the archive are particularly striking. The first of these ways (briefly discussed earlier) is to see the institution of the archive itself as existing in an ambiguous and symptomatic relation to time: as an

11 S. Freud, *Civilisation and its Discontents* (London: Pelican Freud Library, vol. 12, 1985).

12 Derrida, *Archive Fever*, p. 12.

ditional economy. And to the horizon of redemption, salvation, even reconciliation.' Now, the very concept of truth – let me be quick now because I told you at the beginning that I was paralysed and I'm seeing that I can't stop speaking – the very concept of truth, which is on the one hand at the centre of the work of an archivist. (The archivist wants to, and Freud gives us striking examples in the text that I quote, wants to establish the truth – that's what it was, okay? The way it was, and beyond my interpretation, the stones speak, as Freud said. The truth is not simply historical truth in Freud, but it is the truth itself, the thing itself, which speaks the truth.) So, on the one hand the archivist looks for the truth, and on the other hand the Commission in question, for understandable political reasons, looks for the truth considering that the truth is the condition for a reconciliation, that is, making the truth public would be the condition for precisely a, let's say, political therapeutical healing away of a number of wounds from which this country, and these nations in this country, suffer. But the truth in that context is not objective truth. It's not scientific truth. It's the truth according to which St Luke for instance would say, when I confess, when I make the truth as he says, when I make the truth I don't simply inform God, or the others, because God knows. When I confess, I'm not informing the other what I've been doing. When I confess, I say I was guilty, and I, through a lack of love, called the others to love God and so on and so forth. So the truth, in that case, is not simply an objective, theoretical act of knowledge. The truth has to do, in that case, with confession, with the transformation of the subject. And I think that if the Truth and Reconciliation Commission is so interesting today – not only crucial – for this country, whatever follows from it, and to me it is unpredictable, unpredictable, it's crucial for this country not because of what is at stake – obviously at stake – but because it forces one to ask questions such as – and the lesson has to be drawn not only by South Africans but by everyone in the world who observes what is going on here – to ask questions such as 'what is an archive today, the archive of the [hero?], the archive of traumatisms and so on and so forth, and the archive of the repression of the archive, the archive of the destruction of the archive?'. We had a number of examples in this century, not only in South Africa. So, questions such as, 'what is the archive as including the destruction of the archive, including forgetting, and what is the truth in that case, what has the truth to do with politics, and with the recovering of a nation, and reconciliation, and so on and so on?'

apparently solid place of material storage and accumulation on the one hand and as an unstable and ever-changing site always open to the exigencies and recastings of the future-to-come on the other. The second way concerns the status of the archivist as always subject to unexpected unconscious forces and desires, as perpetually at risk of being driven by what is commonly described in psychoanalysis as the symptomatic field. A productive approach to archival enquiry, then, would be to take this emphasis on the symptomatic to another level and to align both archive and archivist as objects of investigation to psychoanalysis as a knowledge that has the symptom and its conditions of possibility as its primary object. If we trouble the archive, as Derrida does, by way of psychoanalysis, what can we learn, not merely from key aspects of psychoanalysis as a body of content, but from the nature of psychoanalysis as a knowledge, from what could be called its characteristic epistemological stance?

II

As an example of this approach, let us revisit the question of the future-to-come via a phenomenon at the heart of Freud's thought – that of retrospective causality – which I believe is another way of saying (paradoxical as this may sound given the term 'retrospective') that the psychic as an archiving apparatus is always open to the future and, more strongly, that events and experiences that occur later in the series may change, not just the significance, but the nature of prior events.

In other words, Freud suggests that subsequent events may be necessary even to establish the very identity of earlier ones, and that the psychic work done by events defined in retrospect can often be understood only when we admit to the power of this complex operation. The most telling example in Freud's work of this phenomenon is the famous 'Wolf Man'[13] case – the longest, most complex and demanding of his case histories. In this case Freud focuses on the importance of an understanding of an infantile neurosis to the subsequent analysis of his still floridly neurotic aristocratic Russian patient. Many remember the case for its evocation of the panoply of exotic symptoms from which the patient suffered, and for the crucial part played in the analysis by the young Wolf Man's extraordinary dream of the seven white wolves perched in the tree outside his window.

For our purposes, however, it is the primal scene with its nature and consequences that is especially interesting. What the case history makes clear is that the identity and the significant details of his parents' sexual intercourse, witnessed by the Wolf Man when he was only

13 S. Freud, *From the History of an Infantile Neurosis (The 'Wolf Man')* (London, Pelican Freud Library, vol. 9, 1979).

Now just one last point. Even in the case of let's say – by hypothesis – a successful archive – even if you really succeed in gathering
everything you need in reference to the past, and that you interpret it
in a way which is totally satisfactory (then we'll have here a full
archive, correctly interpreted and no one would disagree on the truth
and the fidelity of this archive, everything is now kept safe and everyone agrees on that; so, we'll keep this archive safe, okay?). Now,
because of that, because of this very fullness, the hypothetical fullness,
of this archive, what will have been granted is not memory, is not a
true memory. It will be forgetting. That is, the archive – the good one
– produces memory, but produces forgetting at the same time. And
when we write, when we archive, when we trace, when we leave a trace
behind us – and that's what we do each time we trace something, even
each time we speak, that is we leave a trace which becomes independent of its origin, of the movement of its utterance – the trace is at the
same time the memory, the archive, and the erasure, the repression,
the forgetting of what it is supposed to keep safe. That's why, for all
these reasons, the work of the archivist is not simply a work of memory. It's a work of mourning. And a work of mourning, as everyone
knows, is a work of memory but also the best way just to forget the
other, to keep the other in oneself, to keep it safe, in a safe – but when
you put something in a safe it's just in order to be able to forget it,
okay? When I handwrite something on a piece of paper, I put it in my
pocket or in the safe, it's just in order to forget it, to know that I can
find it again while in the meantime having forgotten it. If there is
pure forgetting, it's because the archive, in order to be safe, in a safe,
should be external to me, okay? So, suppose that one day South Africa
would have accomplished a perfect, full archive of its whole history –
not simply apartheid, but what came before apartheid, and before
before, and so on and so forth, and a full history – suppose that such a
thing might be possible – of course it is impossible – let us suppose
it's possible – everyone in this country, who is interested in this country, would be eager to put this in such a safe that everyone could just
forget it, okay? And perhaps, perhaps, this is the unconfessed desire of
the Truth and Reconciliation Commission. That as soon as possible
the future generation may have simply forgotten it, okay? Having
kept everything in the archive, meaning the libraries, in the hands of
remarkable archivists, okay, just let us forget it to go on, to survive.
That's what we are doing – just archive against memory. Well, I think
I should stop here. Thank you.

eighteen months old, came into focus and acquired their shape and significance only in the light of subsequent events. Without his subsequent observation of animals copulating, for example, the Wolf Man would not have recognised his parents' act (sex *a tergo*) as a sexual one at all and it is only in this retrospectively determined form that the event came to play so central a part in the formation of his symptoms.

In other words, the effect of Derrida's emphasis on the necessity of recognising the archive's openness to the future-to-come, as read through the psychoanalytic concept of retrospective causality, is to point not just to the cumulative role that additions to the archive play, but to their potentially transformative capacity. If Freud had not understood the fact and power of retrospective causality he would not have been able to understand the Wolf Man's attraction to women whom he saw on all fours nor, more broadly, would he have been able finally to reconstruct the sequence of significant causal events with which he ends the case history.

The details of the Wolf Man's early history, finally expressed in the ordered listing of approximately ten key events covering the period from when the Wolf Man was eighteen months old until he was six years old, make very interesting reading. More important still, the reconstruction provided by Freud's careful analysis (covering some 140 pages in total) also proves surprisingly convincing. This is even more surprising when we consider the obvious difficulties of working with pre-verbal, repressed and often very bizarre material – material, like the primal scene itself, which Freud himself admits might only have psychic rather than 'actual' reality. In addition, this intellectual operation – this satisfying historical reconstruction – occurred in a context in which an intervention, some form of impact on the symptoms (hopefully leading to change or cure), was also expected and did, at least in Freud's eyes, occur.

What is important about this example is Freud's response to what by any standards is an extremely difficult task. As objects to be explained, few things could be more initially opaque than the symptoms that make up a neurosis. Symptoms, in having unconscious origins, are separated from the reasons that caused them, are aberrant in form and anomalous in time. They seem, that is, strenuously to defy reason, and in this to resist explanation. Freud, however, despite his obvious fascination with the symptomatic field, was not content to remain blinded by this fascination. The existence of psychoanalysis, both as metapsychology and as a set of (if only roughly) specifiable clinical techniques, attests to this fact. In addition to Freud's now

QUESTION: I've been following the Truth Commission process pretty closely and really grappling with these issues around memory and forgetting, and also the ethics of the process. Coupled with the political constraints, recognising perfectly well what those constraints were, how the discourse and the laws around the Truth Commission have been shaped – in terms of instead of examining crimes committed by the apartheid state and agents of the state and investigating crimes against humanity, and prosecuting crimes against humanity, we've hedged. And we now have a discourse that seems to equate both sides of the political spectrum, examining gross human rights violations on both sides. And there's a profound relativism at work in that, implicit in the Act.

JD: Please, no, slowly and louder, because . . .

QUESTION: There's a very strong relativism at work that says that the acts perpetrated on both sides of the apartheid struggle – for apartheid and against apartheid – are equated. And there's a profound loss of memory that operates immediately in the Act. And I, over the last couple of years, have been very troubled by the way people apologise – well, not apologise – apologetic defences for apartheid, for apartheid ideology, and indeed for the crimes committed by agents of apartheid, have adopted deconstruction as their explanation for their justifications. Such that you have the National Party going to the Truth Commission and refusing to give any kind of evidence as to what they authorised, what they were in fact responsible for.

JD: That's what they call deconstruction?

QUESTION: No, no, no. But simply offered their perspective on the past, said they were there to explain, and to offer a perspective, and simply to provide their interpretation. That what has happened is not so much an affirmation of truth, and of historical objectivity, but using notions of multiplicity of interpretations, multiplicity of truths, to justify the refusal actually to even affirm a truth. And, I'm just wondering if perhaps you could speak to that tension.

JD: Thank you. Now, of course, here is one example of a problematic interpretation, because in your question or remark, you are just assuming, interpreting, deconstruction as relativism, multiplicity of interpretation, and so on and so forth. And, of course, I find this absolutely problematic. Deconstruction, if there is such a thing, is not relativistic

famous structural theory of the psychic apparatus, he put forward a considerable body of work that now constitutes the basis of psychoanalytic psychopathology, work that significantly includes some general ideas concerning the nature of symptom and its formation.

If, on the basis of Freud's conception of the dream, the symptom can be defined broadly as the disguised and partial satisfaction of a repressed Oedipal wish,[14] on the basis of Freud's work as a whole we can extend the meaning of each of these terms in such a way as to reveal more clearly that set of general ideas. The 'disguise' referred to is made possible by the overdetermination of sound to meaning within and across languages. The word 'Dick' in the 'Rat Man'[15] case is the name of the patient's English rival and the German word for fat. This double meaning allows the repressed desire to get rid of Dick (the rival) to be satisfied by way of jogging – a means of getting rid of fat. And 'Oedipus' of course provides us with a developed metanarrative called to do considerable explanatory work in psychoanalysis, one that Derrida clearly has in the forefront of his mind in *Archive Fever* when he considers the relations between Freud, Freud's father and Yerushalmi. Even repression, as active forgetting, is based upon the possibility of the separation of 'word' and 'thing' presentations in the unconscious and their subsequent alternative realignment in the preconscious in order to take a disguised route to satisfaction. The relevance of these details concerning psychoanalytic metapsychology and psychopathology to questions of the archive turns on the question of explanation. The psychic archive may be divided, subject to an alternative and at first opaque logic, but for Freud these mysteries, however difficult to explain, are explicable in principle, and there are even conceptual and practical guidelines to aid those involved in the process.

III

To reinforce this point it is useful to return to Derrida's reading of Freud's reading of Jensen's *Gradiva*. This text is rich in material that has special significance to questions of the archive. Its central character is an archaeologist, someone whose work is prototypical of the process of both establishing and interpreting the archive, someone who wishes to make the 'very stones speak'. To be an archaeologist, then, is to be committed to the production of archival evidence of the most solid, material kind from that which was most hidden, and to the most careful and rational process of interpretation. Small wonder, then, that Hanold's 'madness', his search for the living figure

14 S. Freud, *The Interpretation of Dreams* (1900) (London: Pelican Freud Library, vol. 4, 1976).

15 S. Freud, *Notes upon a Case of Obsessional Neurosis* (The 'Rat Man') (London: Pelican Freud Library, vol. 9, 1979).

and doesn't consist simply in multiplying interpretations, in taking into account a multiplicity of interpretations. Many other philosophies, or movements, have taken into account the possible multiplicity of interpretations. So, I don't recognise deconstruction in this picture. But now, it is interesting that some people – anywhere – say well as soon as someone abuses or strategically exploits such relativism, such multiplicity of possible interpretations, then that's deconstruction, or deconstructionists are responsible for that. And I would like to testify, and to complain about this injustice. But of course I cannot convince you or convince anyone briefly without asking for some more home-work. Then you would see that deconstruction is something else than simply this relativistic activity. But it's not the first time that this hap-pens. I remember – if I may recall this – I remember when I was in the United States four or five years ago giving a seminar, at the very moment when the Rodney King affair – perhaps you know what it is, okay? – this long trial, during which the attorneys of the policeman tried to analyse the archive precisely – that is the film, the record, the tape of the film which this young man, having a camera, had made at the moment when the policeman was beating this young black man in California. And some people said well you see what this attorney is doing trying to analyse every second in the film, well, at the moment when the so-called victim tried to react, even to do whatever he did to the policeman, the policeman was not beating him, okay? So there was an endless discussion about a second in the movement of the bodies as they were precisely archivised by this improvised cameraman, okay? And people say well, this attorney used deconstruction. So then I was implicitly charged with being on the side of the police. No, there is something in the interpretation . . . excuse me, you want to say some-thing?

QUESTION: I'm not accusing you of defending apartheid apologetics. I'm simply trying to . . .

JD: I hope not.

QUESTION: Really not the point. I'm trying for myself to separate out precisely what you're saying – how the kind of abuse of certain forms of discourse is used for political ends. I think I wasn't clear enough in my point. I'm really interested in how in a way those kind of apologetics exemplify the death wish. So that where the multipli-city of interpretations can be about memory rather than mourning,

represented on an ancient frieze and his dealings with a 'midday ghost', should stand in stark contrast to all that archaeology as a knowledge represents.

Derrida's reading of Freud's account, as has been suggested above, focuses on Hanold's 'madness', the always possible, often actual, intrusion into the supposed rationality of the archive of the symptomatic, of hauntedness and ghosts. Freud's purpose is very different. He aims to uncover the origins in Hanold's early sexual history of what Freud describes, even in the title itself, as Hanold's 'dreams and delusions' and to show that it is only in so far as she spontaneously acts like an analyst that his childhood sweetheart dissolves those delusions and Hanold can return to himself, at least to that self now able to be both lover and (rational) archaeologist.

IV

Finally there is the question of the death drive, the centrality of which is reflected in the title of *Archive Fever* itself. Without the death drive, Derrida argues, there would be no drive to archive, no compulsion to maintain and store in material form all that the death drive seeks to destroy without remainder, to annihilate even beyond the point of ashes. But in Freud the death drive, at least as it appears in *Beyond the Pleasure Principle*,[16] is one of the most mysterious and controversial aspects of the so-called second two-instinct theory. Reading *Beyond the Pleasure Principle* situates one at the heart of what is most daring and debated in Freud. The extended dialogue he conducts with his previous work, the range of argument and evidence and the resulting generic complexity of the text, all attest to the extremely difficult task Freud has set himself – that of demonstrating the existence of a death instinct located at the biological, phylogenetic level – an instinct beyond that of forgetting, of repression or of the more domestic destructiveness of the superego. And this, finally, is not a principle that can be fully retrieved by an (albeit alternative) rationality – even by Freud himself.

While there is, in my view, space for a reading of the contribution psychoanalysis can make to questions of the archive that is different from that of Derrida in *Archive Fever*, a reading that might trouble the archive in less mysterious ways, his emphasis on the death drive clearly sets limits to any 'modernist' reading of psychoanalysis and in this returns the archive to the mercy of all that acts without predictable form even against its most fervent productive energies.

16 S. Freud, *Beyond the Pleasure Principle* (London: Pelican Freud Library, vol. 11, 1984).

what we're seeing here is a mourning process at work which doesn't allow the work of memory.

JD: No, I was not charging you either. I was just trying to give a form to the debate. In fact, everyone can use a deconstructive style, can make it a weapon in a given debate. It is always possible. And that's why everyone has a responsibility in precisely analysing the use and the abuse, and to see at what point these people – these people in favour of apartheid – use deconstructive devices in order just to apologise, let's say, dissolve the charge. Now, nevertheless, the very premises of this Commission give, of course, offer themselves to, a very very difficult interpretation. Because, of course, if the protocol of the Commission says that they would simply put on the same level crimes in the name of apartheid and crimes, or killings, or violences, in the struggle against apartheid, this is already a very problematic interpretation. That's why many people react, and rightly so I would say. But why is it so? It's because at the centre of this axiomatic they refer to the archive of this concept called 'crime against humanity'. As you know, the concept of 'crime against humanity' is a very new concept. It is not a natural given. It has a history. It was produced by a court after the War during the Nuremberg trial, and it is in the name of precisely this concept – crime against humanity – that a number of actions and trials, have been organised. And today the concept of the rights of man is indissociable from the concept of crime against humanity. So what is a crime against humanity? I think this concept was a progress. I have nothing against the progress that is considered. Nevertheless, it remains a very problematic concept. Very problematic. And I hope that one day it will be refined, because every crime, as a crime, is a crime against humanity. What is a crime against humanity? Now, once you refer to this concept of crime against humanity as a concept which was coined and performed and institutionalised rather recently, then you level all the crimes said to be political. As far as I understand, the criminal assassination today is not part of the agenda of the Truth and Reconciliation Commission. It's only violences with political motivations. Now, once you take this axiom for granted, of course many people may say well on the one hand of course we were not guilty because we were fighting against apartheid, but on the other hand, well we were simply fighting for a political cause and we were given political orders, and so the guilt might be neutralised. So there is a whole space of interpretation opened by precisely these two sets of axioms. And in order to distinguish between legitimate

A Shaft of Darkness: Derrida in the Archive*

Verne Harris

Conclusions

This essay is not an account of Jacques Derrida's *position* on, or *delineation* of, the archive. That would be to repeat the mistake of those who attempt to define postmodernism or deconstruction or Derridean thinking. Ultimately it is impossible to say *what* these things are. They are what they are becoming. They open out of the future. We can, at best, mark their movements and engage their energies. So the essay offers a shaft of darkness in all the harsh light of positivist discourse, a shaft aimed at Derrida in the archive. In taking aim I strive to be as open as possible to Derrida aiming at me.

In a sense all Derrida's work is about the archive. He converses with it, mines it, interrogates it, plays in it, extends it, creates it, imagines it and is imagined by it. It is impossible to speak of Derrida without also speaking of the archive. It is impossible to speak – now, at the turn of the century – of the archive without also speaking of Derrida. Of course, all these assertions assume a concept associated with this word, this noun, 'archive'. This is an assumption that Derrida questions. Not only are there numerous competing concepts associated with the word, but from within the word itself – coming from behind linguistics or semantics or etymology, coming from the very processes of archiving – there is a troubling of meaning. However we understand the word 'archive', it remains true to say that all Derrida's work is, in a sense, about the archive. It is about the archive in a sense, and in sense and sensing, for his work – the sense of Derrida and the non-sense of Derrida – insistently, searingly and joyously embraces the dimensions of reason, emotion and instinct contained in the word 'sense'.

Derrida's work can be typified as an extended reading, or rewriting, of what others have written. Always the canon of Western philosophy and literature, the tradition, the archive, is his point of departure.[1] In the archive he generates archive, opening the future in the past. He reads, and reads again, the canonical texts: 'I think we have to read them again and again and I feel that, however old I am, I am on the threshold of reading Plato and Aristotle. I love them and I feel I have to start again and again and again. It is a task which is in front of me, before me.'[2]

* This essay has its origin – to the extent that anything has *an origin* – in a paper entitled 'Jacques Derrida's *Archive Fever*: a critique', presented at a seminar in the 'Refiguring the Archive' series, University of the Witwatersrand, August 1998. This essay draws heavily on that paper and a later one, entitled 'Blindness and the archive: an exergue', presented at the conference 'Listen to their Voices', University of Natal, Pietermaritzburg, June 1999. At the August 1998 seminar, intimidated by Derrida's presence and concerned for my own archivability, I offered several warning signals, including the following:

* I have read far more writings *about* Derrida than *by* him.

* I have read considerably more writings by *archivists* than writings by *philosophers*.

* It was only on my third reading of *Archive Fever* that I began to dispense with dictionaries and to discern the enchanting coherence of Derrida's argument.

Since then I have read several more of Derrida's works and have overcome my feelings of complete inadequacy, but the disclaimers remain worthy of repetition.

1   In Edmund Husserl's *Origin of Geometry* (1978), for instance, Derrida engages Husserl and Joyce. In *Glas* (1986) he engages Hegel and Genet. *The Gift of Death* (1995) is a conversation with Kierkegaard and Jan Patocka. In *Politics of Friendship* (1997) he tackles the Western canonical discourse on friendship.

2   Jacques Derrida, in John Caputo, ed., *Deconstruction in a Nutshell: A Conversation with Jacques Derrida* (Fordham University Press, 1997), p. 9.

recourse to interpretation – the one who testifies, or the one who listens to the testimony, both of them can say well I can interpret, this can be interpreted, okay? There is an interpretation possible. You can't deny the right to interpret. Then you have to interpret the interpretation, and to discern between some legitimate one, some abuse. You can say, well I was not guilty for having done this and this – I won't give examples – because I was given the order, or because the cause of apartheid was considered legitimate. So, that's the responsibility. This will be the responsibility of everyone to decide what is an abusive interpretation and what is not. And finally, the conclusion will be, rightly or wrongly, let's say, a decision between at least two interpretations. At the end we won't have the naked truth. We'll have the most convincing, that is the most powerful interpretation. Today it is this. In the given situation, post-apartheid situation, the interpretation will be this one. Suppose that there would have been a Truth and Reconciliation Commission during the apartheid. Let's dream, okay? You can imagine that everything would have been different. And the conclusions, the report, would have been different. This doesn't mean relativism. This means that there are responsibilities, there is a transformation, there are, let's say, decisions to be made, sides to be taken. And, of course, the people who are against apartheid, for a number of principles and reasons that I won't recall here, will have a reading of the result of this Commission which will be very different from the people who still believe in apartheid. And no one at the end will be able to make a final – to reach a final – consensus. There will be a conflict of interpretations. And there is no archive which could be decisive, which could reach some point beyond interpretation. And saying this is not a relativistic stand. I could try and argue this much longer, but I wouldn't think that this point is a relativistic or empiricist one.

QUESTION: Hi. My name is Windsor, from the Sociology Department at Wits University. I've got four points which are somehow questions, concerning what you've said this afternoon. The first one is – and this is what I sense from Susan and Mr Harris and you also – there is a sense in which there was no articulation of the language that constitutes the archive. I think there was a talk about the archive as something somehow rarefied at one level. At a level something which is political, social and socially constituted in terms of authority figures. But I didn't get a sense of what is the language that's involved in archival process, archival purposes, and what is that language specifically? And I think that language can be anything in terms of its con-

Out of his reading comes new text, which is old in its newness. He discloses – for himself and for all readers of text, readers of archive – that we are always and already embedded in archi-text.[3] There is nothing outside of the archive.[4]

Yet, at the same time, in what could be called an aporetics of being, or of becoming, everything is outside of the archive. In every(thing) known is the unknown, the unknowable, the unarchivable, the other. Every other is wholly other. This is not so much, though it is this, a marking of reason's limits. It is more a disclosing of structural resistance to closure. Every circle of human knowing and experience is always already breached – breached by the unnameable, by an (un)certain divine particularity, by a coming that must always be coming. In his more recent work, Derrida has opened more fully what could be called religious and autobiographical dimensions to his explorations.[5] These dimensions coalesce in an ever closer heeding to the call of the other, or, more precisely, the call of otherness. In heeding closely, he has been drawn, in one movement, to the otherness outside and the otherness inside: the otherness of the self or of the selves, an otherness marking and marked by, but never found in, the personal archive.

So the quest for Derrida in the archive is one without (delimitable) horizon. In this essay I limit myself, for editors do have horizons, to consideration of two specific works by Derrida: *Archive Fever: A Freudian Impression* (1996), his most direct engagement with the archive as concept, and *Memoirs of the Blind: The Self-Portrait and Other Ruins* (1993), in which he posits explicit connections between archiving and ways of knowing, of being and of becoming. It is a bifurcated shaft of darkness, then, and in a double sense. For with *Archive Fever* I strain to hold the shaft steadily on Derrida; with *Memoirs* I gather the shattered reflections projected back at me.

Archive Fever

Derrida's engagement with the archive in *Archive Fever* is more a lingering embrace than an engagement. His stated objective with this work is the positing of theses which define the 'impression' left by the Freudian signature. He arrives there via an extended foreplay. His moves are at once heavy and light, focused and multi-layered; they are always deliberately and self-reflectively complex. No word or term is safe from the passion of Derrida's embrace. No Derridean gesture is without a flourish of new terms. He demands of the read-

3 John Caputo describes 'archi-text' as 'various networks – social, historical, linguistic, political, sexual networks (the list goes on nowadays to include electronic networks, worldwide webs) – various horizons or presuppositions . . .' Caputo, *Deconstruction in a Nutshell*, pp. 79–80.

4 This is a reading, a re-writing, of Derrida's possibly most misunderstood, most abused, statement: 'there is nothing outside of the text'. (*Of Grammatology*, 1974).

5 See, for instance, *Memoirs of the Blind* (1993), *Circumfession* (1993), *Passions* (1993), *The Gift of Death* (1995), 'Foi et savoir: les deux sources de la "religion" aux limites de la simple raison' (1996), and *Monolingualism of the Other* (1998).

tents – it can be French, it can be Afrikaans, it can be English, it can be Zulu, whatever – but I'm more concerned about the notion of language implicit in the process of archival practice. I think that's something that I want to get clarity on, because that is linked to the whole question of the self-deconstruction of the archive, something that you seem to be alluding to this afternoon. Meaning that certain forces seem to lead to the deconstruction of the archives. You mentioned the limits of the archive from the failure to accumulate enough information, people are dead, and so forth, but at the same time the sense in which the archive is limited in terms of *thanatos*, the death instinct. And I think that for me it's important in terms of the language that is implicit in the deconstruction of the archive. So I want to link that into that point. The second question . . .

JD: Let me respond one by one. So what is the first question?

QUESTION: The question is the language which constitutes the archive. I'm trying to understand what is your notion of the language that constitutes the archive.

JD: Well, of course you're right, there is no archive without the signature of the archivists. By 'signature of the archivists', I don't mean the individual signature of the person in charge, but the signature of the apparatus, the people, and the institution, which produces the archive. This signature is a language. The archivist doesn't simply perceive the documents, doesn't simply receive the documents. It organises it, it produces it in a certain way, and in this production implies the language on the part of the archivist. Now, the language is not simply here the idiom, that is, the verbal national language. Although it plays a role, because, to go back for a moment to the TRC, as you know, as well in your parliament you have eleven, twelve, thirteen languages that have to be translated, first, and the translation must of course transform the testimony. Testimony as a singular performative act is essentially embodied in a singular idiom, so to translate the whole archive into English – I suppose that the main, the prevailing, language in the report and the available books will be English. I don't know how they will be, eleven or twelve or thirteen translations, but throughout the world it will be read in English, I can assure you. So this hegemony of English is a problem about the interpretation of the testimonies, of testimonies which originally were not performed in English. First. And then, even in the metalanguage, so to speak, of the

er a reciprocal commitment: consummation is inconceivable without a willingness to play and replay Derrida's moves. (Which makes one wonder how it must have been for the audience that first heard the text as a lecture on 5 June 1994.)

Derrida's moves in epistemological space offer nothing new to deconstructionist discourse, but his focus on the archive brings a freshness to his fundamental assertions. I want to signpost four assertions:

1.   The event, the origin, the *arkhé*, in its uniqueness, is irrecoverable, unfindable. 'The possibility of the archiving trace, this simple *possibility*, can only divide the uniqueness.'[6]

2.   The archiving trace, the archive, is not simply a recording, a reflection, an image of the event. It shapes the event. 'The archivization produces as much as it records the event.'[7]

3.   The object does not speak for itself. In interrogating and interpreting the object, the archive, scholars inscribe their own interpretation into it. The interpretation has no meta-textual authority. There is no meta-archive. There is no closing of the archive. 'It opens out of the future.'[8]

4.   Scholars are not, can never be, exterior to their objects. They are marked before they interrogate the markings, and this pre-impression shapes their interrogation.

This last assertion Derrida buttresses through analysis of Yosef Yerushalmi's book *Freud's Moses: Judaism Terminable and Interminable* (1991). Yerushalmi concludes with a fictional address to Freud – the 'Monologue with Freud'. Up to the 'Monologue', Derrida points out, Yerushalmi presents himself as a historian 'exterior to his object'.[9] He is neither Jew nor psychoanalyst as such. But in the 'Monologue' he demonstrates this exteriority to be a chimera; he is Jewish and his discourse bears a Freudian pre-impression. Ironically, one of Yerushalmi's intentions in the 'Monologue' is to posit the pre-impression of Jewishness on Freud. He asks the question 'Is psychoanalysis a Jewish science?', and seeks to demonstrate that Freud believed that it was, but secretly: he never allowed this belief to become a part of the 'public archive'.[10] Derrida uses this as a platform for probing at Freud's discomfort with the influence of his own marking on his work. In doing so, Derrida is, I think, marking the shadow of another related question: 'is *deconstruction* a Jewish science?'[11]

'Nothing is less reliable, nothing is less clear today than the word "archive". . . Nothing is thus more troubled and more troubling today than the concept archived in this word "archive."'[12] In fact, Derrida

6   Jacques Derrida, *Archive Fever: A Freudian Impression* (Chicago: University of Chicago Press, 1996), p. 100.

7   Ibid., p. 17.

8   Ibid., p. 68.

9   Ibid., p. 53.

10 Ibid., p. 47.

11 John Caputo offers an extended exploration of this question in *The Prayers and Tears of Jacques Derrida: Religion Without Religion* (Bloomington: Indiana University Press, 1997).

12 Derrida, *Archive Fever*, p. 90.

TRC, that is the language through which the people responsible for the TRC defined the task of the TRC, they used some notions which are problematic. One, you shift from one language to another. The notion of forgiveness and repentance (I know I'm incompetent, but I know that in some African languages it is difficult to translate rigorously such a notion). There is another, according to such or such a culture, African culture, there is another cultural set of meanings around what this one wants to call repentance or forgiveness. So in that case the very actions in which the TRC is shaped from the beginning is a linguistic intervention. And this is the position. It's not simply negative. There are some negative effects, but without this risk there would be no project of any archive. But we have to remember that there are such risks. So the language is the beginning of the very project of the archive, the very institution of the archive. Not to speak of many other possible linguistic interventions.

QUESTION: Given that that's where I was going to ask you about the notion of the death instinct. Given that the death instinct, or the death drive, given that language is central to the archive, at what level does the death instinct develop or emerge in the whole process? Because if we take the death instinct from Freud and link that to language itself, and in South Africa the TRC is conceptualised in terms of a struggle practice, a political practice, how does the death instinct emerge into the TRC to deconstruct the whole process of searching for the truth, searching for meaning, and so forth?

JD: I tried to interpret – that's the right word I think – interpret what I call 'archive fever' by reference to this death drive. Not only, but mainly, by reference to this death drive. And I think the death drive is at work at least in two ways. One is the drive to destroy the very memory, the very trace and the very testimony, of the violence, of the murder. The perpetrator tries not only to kill, but to erase the memory of the killing, that is, to do, to act in such a way that no archive is left. And we have experienced this in mass murders here or in Europe – and though we know that the perpetrators, sometimes in an industrial way, in a massive way, try to kill not simply their victims but the memory, the names of their victims. That's one effect of a radical death drive. Now, another part of this effect appears on the opposite side. That is, when in order to oppose the destruction, you want to keep safe, to accumulate, the archive, as such, not simply living memory – because we don't trust living memory, you trust the archive. Now, the gesture

argues, we do not have a concept for the word; all we have is a notion, an impression, associated with the word. The very process of archiving, the structure of archivisation, will not allow it to be otherwise. Derrida's positing of the notion begins with a lexicon, an archive of the word 'archive'. He demonstrates how in the 'original' Greek usage it is inseparable from the idea of consignation; the marking on a substrate (through impression on paper, through circumcision on the human body) implies both process (the power of consignation) and place (the place of consignation). Control of consignation, the exercise of a topo-nomological 'archontic power', is at the heart of political power. For South Africans it takes only a slight jiggling of memory to recall the obsessive guarding, patrolling and manipulating of consignation by apartheid's *archons*. Apartheid's memory institutions, for instance, legitimised apartheid rule by their silences and their narratives of power; the media were controlled by an oppressive censorship regime; official secrets were protected by the Protection of Information Act and numerous other pieces of interlinking legislation.

Unfortunately Derrida's lexicon is restricted to the Greeks and the Romans. He offers no analysis of developments over more than two millennia; he declines to acknowledge archives as a discipline, one with its own discourses and histories;[13] and, while he describes the impact of the computer on archivisation as an 'archival earth-quake', he does not explore how virtual electronic records have dizzied the *archons* and transformed how we conceptualise the place of consignation. What he does explore, drawing heavily and explicitly on Freud, is the 'anarchontic' 'instinct of destruction' at work within consignation. Aside from deliberate destruction, there is an instinct of forgetfulness, a death drive indissociable from memorisation: '. . . the archives take place at the place of originary and structural break-down of . . . memory.'[14] The archive, in other words, always works against itself. This is the 'archive fever' of the book's title. Moreover, Derrida points out, Freud made possible the idea of a substrate that cannot be reduced to memory (that is, memory as conscious reserve or as act of recalling). Freud gave us the tools to expose repressed or suppressed (or super-repressed) texts, attested to by symptoms, signs, figures, metaphors and metonymies. We must, Derrida concludes, reconceptualise the archive to accommodate this 'archive of the vir-tual'.[15]

This conjuring of virtual space, of spectrality, within the archive, together with the idea of the death drive in archiving, establishes what Derrida calls a Freudian theory of the archive. It is a theory that we

13 Was this move, I wonder, archontic or anarchontic?

14 Derrida, *Archive Fever*, p. 11.

15 Ibid., p. 66.

which consists in accumulating the archive, in the monument of the document, is another way, as I said earlier, of producing forgetting. That is, there is a perverse, a perverse, desire for forgetting in the archive itself. The death drive is not simply at work in killing, in producing death, but in trying to save, in a certain way, the memory. And you can't escape forgetting, and forgetting in that case is not simply repression in psychoanalytical terms. There is repression in the psychoanalytical sense, but there is more than repression, there is an erasure that doesn't keep the repressed thing in some other place, but which produces forgetting by remembering, so to speak. And you have in many interesting texts, such as Blanchot for instance and others, the suggestion that remembering is forgetting – the accumulation, the capitalisation, of the archive is in fact a destruction of the memory and thus another symptom, let's say, of the death drive.

QUESTION: Just very briefly, it relates quite closely to the last question in any case, so you might be able to answer it quite briefly. It goes back to the issue of technology and the changing role and proliferation of technology in archival processes and in the process of recording of cultural memory. Now, it's interesting that, you know, the conclusion of your initial response to Sue and Verne, it seemed to me what was most important about your conclusion is that the truth of the archive is the truth of the other, or that's an aspiration for the truth of the archive. And it seems that technologies, particularly digital technologies and recording technologies and those kind of forms, seem to force us into a position which dramatises quite strongly the play in technology between, or the ambivalence in technology, between the death drive – you know, the death drive through the prosthetic effect of technology – and its kind of extension, its instrumentality. You know, a nice acute case in point is Bill Clinton's testimony, where you know, in anticipation – I mean there are others, the O. J. Simpson trial is also a good kind of high-profile case – but, in anticipation of the kind of scientific proof, objective valid proof of their criminality and infidelity respectively, they confess. You know, Clinton has just done this. And this seems to me – and he's doing this, it's a kind of technological mediation of the truth of the other that is happening there – so I mean, basically, does that change the nature of, rather than simply the content, of archival process?

JD: Certainly I can only agree with you on this. I'm constantly during the two weeks I spent here, I was constantly dreaming of the number

must take account of, and account for. Not that psychoanalysis offers us a concept of the archive, or even a means of resolving the contradiction, the unreliability and the lack of clarity inherent in the concept. Indeed, Derrida argues, in analysing the *trouble de l'archive*, psychoanalysis succeeds only in heightening it, for 'it repeats the very thing it resists or which it makes its object'.[16] In the theses, the culmination of *Archive Fever*'s foreplay, Derrida unfolds the internal division in Freud's discourse on the archive.

Interpreting Freud on the archive is but one thread in the tapestry of *Archive Fever*. The central thrust of Derrida's argument is that the archive, as concept, is cleft, contradictory and always dislocating itself, because it is never one with itself; but that, far from being reason for despair, this is the very strength, the future, of the archive. One need not share Derrida's particular presuppositions and perspectives to recognise the accuracy of the diagnosis. Intrinsically unstable (rather, dynamic), the archive is being turned inside out by postmodernist epistemologies and technological revolution. Here in South Africa it awaits, it urgently needs, a turning inside out by epistemologies that we might label 'African' or 'indigenous'. But there is convincing evidence, none more so than in the work of Terry Cook and other heralds of a postcustodial era, that the archive is keeping its head above the troubled waters. Derrida's own exposition of the *trouble de l'archive*, in my view, demands serious consideration. Let me rephrase that. One does not respond to a playful seduction, nor a feverish coming on, by considering it seriously. It demands a hot, or a heated, response. Of course, braving the *trouble du Derrida* is no easy ride, and consummation is not guaranteed.

Pleasures are guaranteed. For me, as an archivist, three stand out. First, there is the compelling demonstration that we are in need of archives. To quote John Caputo on *Archive Fever*: 'The living past cannot rise up from the dead and speak to us like dead stones . . . We must pick our way among the remains, wrestle with and conjure the ghosts of the past, ply them with patient importunity in order to reconstruct the best story we can.'[17]

Secondly, there is the equally compelling demonstration that this need for archives should be embraced with passion. 'Archive fever' should not render us cynical and arid. On the contrary, it is invitation to enchantment, to the play of ecstasy and pain, as we exercise that immemorial passion for the impossible. It is a passion that plays out in a waiting for a coming, more precisely in the inciting of a coming to come, a passion that is both response to and unfolding of the archive's

16 Ibid., p. 91.

17 Caputo, *Prayers and Tears*, p. 274.

of places and countries in which a TRC should be instituted. In the United States, would that be possible? Not simply on the example that you . . . Also, as far as I could see, there is a scene of reconciliation in the family Clinton story. No, but if you . . . Just two points. If today you ask yourself where and why the institution of such a Commission could be impossible – possible or impossible – this could provide you a very interesting, let's say, reading thread, interpreting thread, for the analysis of what's going on in the world today. Where the TRC can be used as a laboratory, example laboratory, where it couldn't take place, and for what reasons, in the history of the state, in the history of the nation, and so on and so forth. That's just a suggestion. Now, the other point has to do with the definition of the technology, the *techné*. Where does it start? In my first, old, essay on Freud and the scene of writing, I tried to show that for Freud, despite his interest in the externality of the psychic apparatus, he was reluctant to consider the illustration of what they call the 'mystic pad' as something more than an illustration, because he wanted to go back to the psychic life itself without any essential intrusion of any technological instrument or prosthesis. The question of the prosthesis. Now the prosthesis is not simply something external, and something we could simply dissociate from the living body and the living memory. Which means that the *techné* is not something, let's say, foreign to the body, the body proper. The *techné* starts as soon as there is a living life – there is some prosthesis at work. So, by saying this, by saying that the prosthetic structure is not simply what we call technology – it starts from the beginning – saying this, I don't want to of course homogenise or erase all the technological mutations and the breaks in the history of the technology. Of course what we are experiencing today in the technology of recording is absolutely heterogeneous to a number of earlier possibilities. But these differences, however formidable they may be, are made possible by, let's say, the strength of the body itself, in which the prosthetic is always already here. And the language is prosthetic – not simply instrumental – but prosthesis. Prosthesis is constantly here. So what we have to rethink, I think, here is not simply such serious themes as reconciliation, truth, politics and so on – is the relation between truth and technology, the relation between forgiveness and technology, the relation between interpretation and technology, from the very beginning, from the very origin of it. And that's, and I think that, in that purpose Freud's contribution was at the same time a major one, because the way he described the unconscious, the systemic partition of the psyche and so on, was introducing some prosthetic structure within the living psy-

messianic dimension. Thirdly, there is the devastating rebuttal of the notion long cherished by archivists that in contextualising text they are revealing meaning, resolving mystery and closing the archive. Derrida demonstrates that, at best, archival contextualisation reveals the multiple layers of construction in text, and in doing so adds yet another layer. Properly conceived, archival contextualisation, indeed archival endeavour as a whole, should be about the releasing of meanings, the tending of mystery and the disclosing of the archive's openness.

Memoirs of the Blind

In 1990 Derrida inaugurated a new series of exhibitions at the Louvre Museum in Paris with his *Memoirs of the Blind*, a selection of drawings from the Louvre's collections with an accompanying text. The exhibition became a book, first published in English in 1993,[18] with a fuller text and a wider selection of drawings. It is a book about vision and of vision, if ever there was one, which explores a congeries of ideas around ways of seeing and knowing: perception as originating always in recollection; the gaze of psychic interiority (eyes turned inward); the blindness of so much seeing; the profound seeing in blindness; the blind as the archivists of vision; the blindness of tears; eyes given for weeping as much as for seeing. I first read *Memoirs of the Blind* in 1998 during a stay in Budapest for an International Council on Archives meeting. The book's energies threw into grubby relief the passionless proceedings of the meeting. It also connected powerfully with South Africa's just-released Truth and Reconciliation Commission Final Report, with that image of Archbishop Desmond Tutu in tears, the myriad stories of weeping and the sense of the Report's writers with tear-stained cheeks, providing at the same time a way of understanding Hungary's very different approach to dealing with its past. It resonated as well with a great lesson of my youth, the memory of which shafted in with Derrida like ancient darkness.

As always with Derrida, he conjures with the general in the particular and the particular in the general. So, while at a certain level he is moving in epistemological space, and at another level probing the blindness cohering in the very structure of archivisation, at the most obvious level – insistently at the reader's eye-level – he is simply deconstructing the process of drawing, demonstrating that in or by drawing, the drafts(wo)man does not see. For in observing the subject (the object) of the drawing, the drafts(wo)man 'sees' out of memory, out of the pre-impression of archi-text. S(he) is pre-shaped to see cer-

18 Jacques Derrida, *Memoirs of the Blind: The Self-Portrait and Other Ruins* (Chicago: University of Chicago Press, 1993).

che, on the one hand. But on the other hand, this contribution was limited by Freud himself when he wanted constantly to go back to living memory, to the pure present of the trace. I tried in *Archive Fever* to take two examples of this, the *Gradiva*, namely, in which what he wants to finally discover, uncover, using the analogy of archaeology – which was one of his favourite analogies – what he wanted to discover is not simply the monument of the document. It is the thing itself, the past itself, being made present. That is, finally, to cross the work, the archaeological and the archivistic work, in order to reach as a classical philosopher would do, the thing itself as it appeared itself at a certain moment. So there are these conflicting drives in Freud himself. On the one hand acknowledging that the *techné*, the prosthesis, the archive, that is the upomnesis, as Plato would say, not anamnesis but upomnesis, was really irreducible – I think this is a major contribution, and I think that deconstruction is absolutely indebted to this contribution – and on the other hand there is a metaphysical resistance to what he was then discovering, dreaming still of, let's say, being an archaeologist or an archivist who finally discovers the truth of the thing itself, pure and simple. And we have many examples of this. And we cannot of course give up this metaphysical dream, okay? And it is self-irreducible, but it is part of the death drive. That is, when you once reach this absolute presence of absolute life without any prosthetic, any *techné*, any archive, then you have pure life and pure death. Pure life and pure presence is exactly pure death. So, even in the pure desire for absolute truth of life and being in themselves, there is this perversion, this possible perverse repetition of the death drive.

QUESTION: All right, I was just wondering if you could comment on the notion of justice – if there can be any true reconciliation without justice. Perhaps just to mention Emmanuel Levinas and perhaps if you can comment on that, on him and when he writes in one of his essays on, Talmudic essays, on repentance, that in the face of infinite obligation to the other, one requires at least some sort of material compensation.

QUESTION: You ended your first presentation with two very strong and somewhat troubling statements, and I would be happy if you could come back to them. The first was the impossibility to close the archives. And the second was the possibility, and even the desirability, to forget. So, my first question is how can one forget, if the archive is, so to say, unclosable, never closed, or to put it differently, if it cannot be closed?

tain things and not to see others. Moreover, there is always a delay – even if only for a second – between observation and the inscription of image on a substrate. In that pause memory plays. The drafts(wo)man is always confronted by the blankness and the blindness of the substrate, which 'reflects' his/her own blindness.

Here is the resonance in my own memory, a resonance humming with the convergence between drawing and photography. Throughout my youth, my father was an avid photographer. He specialised in shots of people, captured at what he called 'the significant moment', usually unaware of his camera, they and their surroundings transposed into the gorgeous hues of black and white. I remember him explaining to me his technique, closely modelled on that of his idol, the French photographer Henri Cartier-Bresson. 'You have to absorb the atmosphere of a place and the people in it,' he said. Feel its rhythms, its energy, allow yourself in turn to become absorbed by it, until you and your camera are invisible. Only then will you be able to sense a significant moment developing, and position yourself to capture it in an absolute unity of observer, observed, and instrument of observation.

It was a lesson in vision and in a way of seeing, but, more fundamentally, a lesson in blindness and in seeing with and through blindness. To even begin to close with the significant moment, the photographer must learn to become invisible. People are blind to his or her presence. The closing and the moving into position are in response to far more than visual perception, since the crucial energies happen beyond vision, in the realm of feelings and instincts. What the photographer 'sees', most people do not see, precisely because they are seeing only with their eyes. In the moment of capture, of course, the photographer is literally blinded. The release button is pressed by a finger wired to a complex of energies, the shutter closes, and for an instant – the critical moment, the critical five-hundredth of a second perhaps – the photographer is in darkness. He or she only 'sees' the image when it emerges later in the darkroom. The moment and its image have been anticipated, and the image is not the product of sight, but of prescience, prevision, that vision that 'sees' into the future. It is a seeing in blindness, the soul's gaze. The photographer is figured, or prefigured, by Tiresias, the blind seer. And the photograph is the archive of the invisible.

If my father were still alive, this extrapolating from his simple lesson would give him a good laugh. 'Intellectual bullshit,' he'd say, 'you can't explain inspiration. You can't even describe it. It kills me how

JD: How can we forget?

QUESTION: Yes. As long as the archive is still open. The second question, which is in fact not a consequence, but it ensues from the first one, is about the possibility to forgive. I wonder if you can expound a little bit on the relationship between forgetting and forgiving. Is it that to forgive one has to forget first, and since the archive is never closed does it mean that in fact we can never forgive? If that is the case, what about vengeance, the status of vengeance?

JD: Thank you. Difficult questions. Usually I try to distinguish between justice and law, or right, or *recht* in German. There is a history of law, there are processes, trials, and legal devices and legal texts and so on – that's the law, and the law as a history can be improved, can be criticised and so on and so forth – can be deconstructed. But justice is beyond the law. It is not reducible to the legal process, or to the legal experience. Now, reconciliation, it depends on the way you interpret reconciliation. If by reconciliation you imply, let's say, that we just forget that we were enemies, or just we heal away, as you say, the wounds and become one – not one, but form a possible community again – I don't see a necessary link between reconciliation and justice. You can – and that's why a legal process, and I think that that's why the TRC is at the same time legal and non-legal (it's not a judiciary experience, but there is something judiciary in it, processes of amnesty and so on and so forth), so as a legal, or quasi- or para-legal process, it can lead – and that's one of its aims, objectives – to some reconciliation. But this has nothing to do – nothing to do, no – it's not reducible to pure justice. Okay? Of course, when I distinguish between pure justice and the law, and when I say these two things are heterogeneous, I don't mean they are dissociable – they are indissociable, because the law refers to justice, the justice to be embodied and determined must take the form of the law. Okay? So, there is a link between them. But, in their structures they are irreducible to one another. So, justice is heterogeneous to the law. And reconciliation, if it's just a reconstitution of a community, of a friendship, the reconstitution of a healthy body, of experience, has nothing to do with justice. You can't be reconciled, that is to make arrangements, compromises, negotiations and peace treaties, or armistice, or cease-fire – there are a number of types of reconciliation – you can experience a number of reconciliations without any justice being involved. Okay? Justice, pure and simple. Now, of course, if you want to distinguish an authentic reconciliation – I suppose that's what

it's always people who patently haven't got it who can't stop talking about it.' But his seeing in blindness, his archiving of the invisible, speaks directly to the 'intellectual bullshit' of epistemological debates. In Western thinking, still in thrall to the 'Age of Reason' despite the inroads made by romanticism, existentialism and postmodernism, knowledge is linked to sight and ignorance to blindness in a binary opposition. As Derrida argues in *Memoirs of the Blind*: '. . . the whole history, the whole semantics of the European idea, in its Greek genealogy, as we know – as we see – relates seeing to knowing.'[19] Light is opposed to darkness, reason to passion. These oppositions spawn a plethora of others, one of which is that of remembering and forgetting. What we remember we keep in the light; what we forget is consigned to darkness. To remember is to archive. To archive is to preserve memory. In this conceptual framework the archive is a beacon of light, a place – or idea, or psychic space, or societal space – of and for sight. Its hallways ring with the cries of the initiated: 'once I was blind, but now I see'.

This notion of the archive, as Derrida has shown in *Archive Fever* – but using now my father's semantic bluntness – is bullshit. There is no remembering without forgetting. There is no remembering that cannot become forgetting. Forgetting can become a deferred remembering. Forgetting can be a way of remembering. They open out of each other, light becoming darkness, darkness becoming light. Between consciousness and the unconscious there are no stable boundaries. Dancing between remembering and forgetting, at once spanning them and within each, is imagining. No trace in memory, not even the image transposed onto film by a camera lens, is a simple reflection of event. In the moment of its recording, the event – in its completeness, its uniqueness – is lost. The dance of imagination, moving effortlessly through both conscious and unconscious spaces, shapes what is remembered and what is forgotten, and how the trace is configured. Each time the trace is revisited, this dance is busy with its work of shaping and reshaping. The archive, then, is a trilectic, an open-ended process of remembering, forgetting and imagining. Here, whether 'here' be understood as the archival record, as individual memory, as collective memory, or as the assemblage of society's discourses; here the cry of the initiated should be in the words of that great twentieth-century poet Leonard Cohen: 'I am blind, but you can see, please don't pass me by.'[20] Or, as another Canadian poet, Anne Michaels, expressed it in reflection rather than invocation: 'I did

19 Ibid., p.12.

20 From the song 'Please Don't Pass Me By (A Disgrace)', on the album *Live Songs* (1972).

you have in mind – an authentic reconciliation, from, let's say, a practical compromise, then of course this authentic reconciliation would be closer to justice than the compromise. In the same way, if you want to distinguish between – that's a classical distinction – between peace and amnesty or armistice or cease-fire, then peace as a pure promise of non-violence, is closer to justice than cease-fire, for example. Then you have to distinguish between two ways of becoming peaceful – the peace, properly, or the cease-fire. And the amnesty is not simply an act of justice. It's something else. Now, as you know, when you make peace – and it is difficult to dissociate peace from authentic reconciliation – when you make peace, you imply the promise of eternal peace. And you can't make this point too strongly – in the very concept of peace you imply that the war will never start again. So, what you call the eternal peace is not simply a peace to which you add the predicate eternal. No, the eternity is included in the concept of peace, because if you make peace without promising that you will never resume war, it's not a peace, it's a cease-fire. It's an act of war. It's just a suspension of aggressivity. So, the same would be true for reconciliation. If you reconcile just in order to go on doing business and surviving and so on, it has nothing to do with justice. If you reconcile forever, if it is possible, with the promise of perpetual peace, then this could require something closer to justice. So, it depends on the way you interpret reconciliation. And as you know, in the common language some people when they say reconciliation they mean something very practical, easy, empirical, provisional, and others think precisely of the promise of indefinite friendship and peace. And justice would be on that side. Now again, once you have distinguished these two poles of concept, these two concepts, you have also to articulate them. They are absolutely heterogeneous to one another, and nevertheless our responsibility is to articulate them to one another, to make the law more just and to make justice more effective. That's the ethical and political responsibility.

Now, the second set of questions is as difficult. Logically you made a point in saying if it is impossible to close the archive. I think it is impossible. To get back again to the example of the TRC, the archive will be closed in a certain way, it is closed already, okay, and it will be closed when the public record will be published and available, but as we know, this will not mean being closed – everyone will be able to add something, to criticise, to reinterpret. It will be open infinitely to readings, interpretation, contestation and so on, so this closure is not a final closure. So your question is very pertinent. If the archive is never closed, how can we forget, given the fact that I said the archive is also an act of

not witness the most important events of my life. My deepest story must be told by a blind man.'[21]

In positing a blindness in the archive, and in delineating a seeing in blindness, Derrida neither dismisses reason nor abandons realities outside human subjectivity. This blindness has no essential quarrel with reason. It insists only that the knowing of reason, the seeing of the eye – in light, by light, knower and known separated – be always joined to the knowing of passion, the seeing in blindness – in darkness, in the immediacy of feeling and touching. This I would call a knowing of soul.

At this point I imagine the frantic squawking of the *archons* of light: Go on then, play your ridiculous games of blind-man's buff! Follow the throbbings of your heart. Obey the voices which speak to you in the night. See where that takes you. Maybe into a mystical space all of your own, disengaged from the world around you. Or worse, into the spells of the myth-makers, and of their foot-soldiers – the creators of apartheid hit-squads, builders of the holocaust ovens.

Derrida's response to such squawking is to talk of tears, and the blindness of tears: 'Deep down, deep down inside, the eye would be destined not to see but to weep.'[22] It is ordinary that when we weep, it is our eyes that fill with tears. Is this not an extraordinary thought – that we weep not from any other organ, but only from the organ of sight, and that we do so in a way that blinds us? It is precisely this blindness and its seeing, the seeing of tears, which captivates Derrida. He ends *Memoirs of the Blind* with a poem by Andrew Marvell that includes these lines:

> Thus let your streams o'erflow your springs,
> Till eyes and tears be the same things:
> And each the other's difference bears;
> These weeping eyes, those seeing tears.[23]

If seeing in blindness provides an image of knowing in passion, then the seeing of tears is an image of knowing in compassion. I care for what I know; I weep at its suffering. I weep for those parts of myself struggling with alienation. I weep at the suffering of those I love, my neighbourhood, my community. I care also for what I do not know, the other. I weep at its suffering. For I know that in loving and tending my child I sacrifice the thousands of children around the world who have no love, no tending. I know that in buying a new pair of running shoes I sacrifice the workers in a sweatshop in some godforsaken part of the world.[24] I weep for the world, for the soul of the

21 Anne Michaels, *Fugitive Pieces* (Toronto: M and S, 1996), p. 17.

22 Derrida, *Memoirs of the Blind*, p. 126.

23 Quoted in Ibid., p. 128.

24 In sacrifice there is a double blindness, the blindness that enables sacrifice (see pp. 98–100 of *Memoirs of the Blind*) and the blindness (of tears) that accompanies comprehension of sacrifice. For an exhaustive account of sacrifice, see Derrida's *The Gift of Death* (Chicago: University of Chicago Press, 1995).

forgetting? It is impossible to be sure that an act of forgetting has been successful. Of course, we may forget as soon as we record and keep safe the archive in the safe, but what we think we have forgotten may come back through a number of ways, unpredictable ways, okay? It may come back, it may not come back, it may come back, it may not come back. So because it always may come back, the impossibility of closing the archive is not in contradiction with the possibility to forget. Because of that. Now, that's why we can forget, but we are never sure that we have forgotten, okay? There is no final criterion to decide that something has been forgotten. It may have been forgotten for someone at some moment, then, as you know, repression may be defeated, or through a number of generations something which has been forgotten for generations can come back. That's what we experience all the time in modern times. The coming back of the forgotten, in many ways. And because the context remains open, there is a future for the archive. Now, the last question posed, about forgetting and forgiving, is even more difficult for me, because I have been constantly during the last year, I would say, and the last weeks, speaking about this distinction between forgetting and forgiving. So I have a number of examples and arguments, and I don't know how to choose between them. Let me say this very briefly. Of course, according to the most traditional concept of forgiving that we inherit from a number of traditions, in order to forgive you should not forget. Okay? Everyone says that. I can forgive only if I remember and if I keep the memory of what I forgive, of the one I forgive and for what I forgive this one. If I forgive simply because I just forgot, it's not forgiveness. It's just something else. So there is a sharp and irreducible distinction between forgetting and forgiving. So that in order to forgive, you have not only to remember the violence, or the offence and the harm done, the misdeed, but you have to keep it so vivid, so, let's say, active, that you can forgive only in a situation in which forgetting being so much excluded that you have a quasi-hallucination of the violence that you are forgiving. You have to remember vividly, otherwise if you forgive only to the extent that the wound has disappeared and it's less painful – because there are so many ways of forgetting; you can simply forget the representation of the violence; or you can forget the intensity of the pain; you can simply take a distance. Okay? That is a number of ways of forgetting. To the extent that you forget the crime, you cannot forgive it. What you are doing is, let's say, excusing, acquitting, giving amnesty. There are a number of ways of doing something else than pure forgiving. So the pure forgiving implies pure memory. That's why a process of reconciliation as a process of healing away, of healing,

world. All my weeping originates in this, takes me to this. I plead for suffering to end, for justice to come, for God to appear. As another great twentieth-century poet, Allen Ginsberg, has wept:

> I'm crying all the time now.
> I cried all over the street when I left the Seattle Wobbly Hall.
> I cried listening to Bach.
> I cried looking at the happy flowers in my backyard, I cried at the sadness of the middle-aged trees.
>
> Happiness exists I feel it.
> I cried for my soul, I cried for the world's soul.
> The world has a beautiful soul.
> God appearing to be seen and cried over . . . [25]

As a student I took up photography, modelling my approach on that of my father and of Cartier-Bresson. For nearly a decade I searched for 'significant moments' with my camera. Later, career obligations and other pursuits squeezed photography out of my life, but my experience with it had marked me in fundamental ways. Crucially, it had sensitised me to and exercised me in ways of seeing and knowing beyond the boundaries of sight, ways that appear subversive, and can be subversive. I carried with me into archival work – as a metaphor, as a pre-impression – the irony of the camera's eye being positioned by the seeing of blindness, of it 'seeing' in the moment of literal blindness. I was, then, predisposed to question notions of the archive as a reflection of reality and as necessarily an instrument of power. Without my realising it at first, the archive's seductiveness for me lay in its dance of remembering, forgetting and imagining, a dance that ultimately can only be danced in blindness, and the dancing of which unravels the archontic strappings designed to bind archives and archivists into the work of subjugation.

BEGINNINGS

Derrida in the archive is as Derrida is wherever he chooses to be – relentlessly, radically, subversive. Nothing, except the right to question, is sacrosanct. No rhythm is left undisturbed by his determination to always, in one movement, get behind and in front of the pace, so as to disclose, and hold, the tension, the *aporia*, the unknowable, which is always already there. Bob Dylan expressed it well in his 'Ballad of a Thin Man':

25 Allen Ginsberg, *Collected Poems 1947-1980* (New York: Harper and Row, 1984), p. 151.

of curing, and so on, is incompatible with forgiving as such. With pure forgiving. Because the healing, the work of mourning, the therapeutic work, implies that you do whatever you can in order to forget. Not simply to forget that the violence has taken place, but simply to forget the effects, the suffering, the pain, and so on and so forth, the violence itself, the intensity, the quality of the violence. So, if the reconciliation, and all these processes, is conditioned by such a healing, it is perhaps very necessary – and I have nothing against that under certain conditions – but it has nothing to do with forgiveness. So the distinction between forgiveness and forgetfulness is absolute in the purity of the concept of forgiveness. Now, it is difficult, it is difficult. That's why it's so difficult to forgive, to be sure that you forgive without forgetting. The contamination between the two is always a risk, and it's difficult to cancel, to destroy the risk. But the risk of a contamination between forgiveness and what is not forgiveness . . .

QUESTION: What about vengeance?

JD: Ah, that's . . . in principle, punishment, legal punishment, legal penalty, should be foreign to vengeance. That's the principle of the law, of our laws, of the law which prevails in our culture, no vengeance. The justice and the law are established in order to avoid vengeance. Okay? Now, it's all the more the case with forgiving, with forgiveness. Forgiveness, nothing can be more foreign to vengeance than forgiveness. But there are, let's say, thinkers of forgiveness who say – like Hannah Arendt or [. . .?] – that you can forgive only something that you could punish. Okay? Not take revenge, that's something else. Revenge and vengeance, it's another order. But punish, legally punish. That you can forgive only something that you could, in principle, punish. And so there would be a symmetry between punishment and forgiveness. And I would disagree with this. I think that of course we may produce some amnesty or an acquittal, or remit someone for his guilt, on the same level of punishment by simply not punishing him or her, but that's totally foreign to forgiveness. Forgiveness is transcendent to the order of the law, to the legal order, so transcendent to punishment. You can punish someone and forgive him, okay, that's some [guess?]. You can, if someone is guilty, you can just apply the law if you think you have to. And the other forgiveness is singular, secret, foreign to the law, to the legality of the law. So I would disagree with Hannah Arendt or [. . .?] when they say that there is a symmetry between punishment and forgiveness. That's a huge problem. Thank you.

You're very well read, it's well known;

But something is happening here and you don't know what it is,

Do you, Mr Jones? [26]

Derrida's deconstructing, contrary to the superficial reckoning of his many critics, is not designed to lay waste. He is not the herald of an arid relativism. On the contrary, with pounding heart, feverishly, he invites us always to re-spect, look again. The archive is not simply a resource to be plundered. It can never be closed, neither by the exercise of reason, nor by any work, even of the most impeccable scholarship. Always there is an unknowable 'something is happening here', which Derrida will not allow us to ignore. Nor does he allow himself to escape its reach; he acknowledges that he is, as we all are, another Mr Jones.

Many of those who attended Derrida's seminar at the University of the Witwatersrand in August 1998 were surprised to discover not the dry, arrogant, cynical, almost incomprehensible deconstructionist that popular caricature had led them to anticipate. Instead they discovered a person combining profound humility with the passion of an Old Testament prophet, speaking a language at once simple and poetic. (Although he claims difficulty with English, his use of it is masterly.) His principal concern was to disturb positivist notions of the archive, particularly in relation to South Africa's Truth and Reconciliation Commission. The archive, he argued, draws us forward in taking us back. Every beginning gathers energies from and carries pre-impressions from antecedent endings. All perception begins in recollection. But all recollecting, all remembering, is also forgetting. (So that forgetting in the Commission's work is to be found not only in its exclusions – forgetting works within its inclusions.) All forgetting of the past is also a forgetting of the future. Always, always, the energy of·the archive draws us forward, not to an end but to a coming that must always be deferred, to a beginning that will always be about to begin. 'Something is happening here and you don't know what it is.' The challenge is not to detain the 'something happening', to find out what it is, but rather to affirm the unknowable (embrace, with a 'yes!', otherness) as the very core of our humanity. In this psychic space 'beginning' and 'ending' lose meaning, and initiates cry with infinite meaning: 'I am blind, but I can see!'

26 From the album *Highway 61 Revisited* (1965).

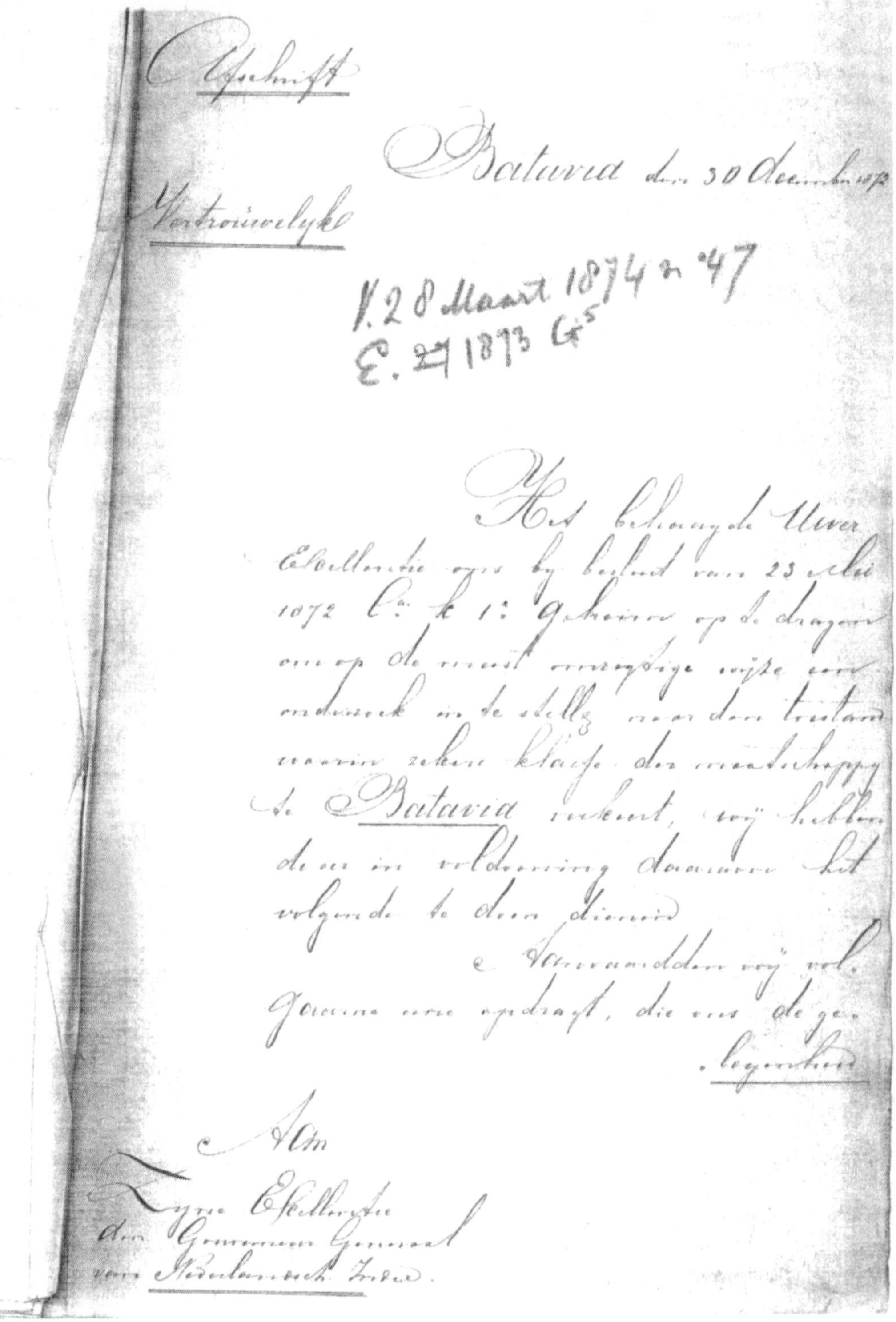

Afschrift

Batavia den 30 December 1873

Vertrouwelyk

V. 28 Maart 1874 n° 47
E. 27 1873 G5

Het behaagde Uwer Excellentie ons by besluit van 23 Mei 1872 La k 1: Geheim op te dragen om op de meest omzigtige wijze een onderzoek in te stellen naar den toestand waarin zekere klasse der maatschappij te Batavia verkeert, wij hebben de eer in voldoening daaraan het volgende te doen dienen

Aanvankelijk waren wij vol. gaarne uw opdragt, die ons de ge. legenheid

Aan Zyne Excellentie den Gouverneur Generaal van Nederlandsch Indie.

'Secret Document', 1874.

Colonial Archives and the Arts of Governance: On the Content in the Form*

Ann Laura Stoler

Genealogy is gray, meticulous and patiently documentary. It operates on a field of entangled and confused parchments, on documents that have been scratched over and recopied many times. (Foucault)[1]

This essay is about the colonial order of things as seen through its archival productions. It asks what insights about the colonial might be gained from attending not only to colonialism's archival content, but also to its particular and sometimes peculiar form. Its focus is on archiving as a process rather than to archives as things. It looks to archives as epistemological experiments rather than as sources, to colonial archives as cross-sections of contested knowledge. Most important, it looks to colonial archives as technologies of rule in themselves. Its concerns are two: to situate new approaches to colonial archives within the broader 'historic turn' of the last two decades, and to suggest what critical histories of the colonial have to gain by turning further toward a politics of knowledge that reckons with archival genres, cultures of documentation, fictions of access and archival conventions.

ARCHIVES, EPISTEMOLOGICAL SCEPTICISM AND THE HISTORIC TURN

Some four decades after British social anthropologist Evans-Pritchard's unheeded warning that anthropology would have to choose between being history or being nothing and Lévi-Strauss' counter claim that accorded history neither 'special value' nor privileged analytic space, students of culture have taken up a transformative venture, celebrating with unprecedented relish what has come to be called 'the historic turn'.[2] Some might argue that anthropology's engagement with history over the last two decades, unlike that recent turn in other disciplines, has not been a 'turn' at all, but rather a return to its founding principles, enquiry into cumulative processes of cultural production but without the typological aspirations and evolutionary assumptions once embraced. Others might counter that the feverish turn to history represents a significant departure from an earlier venture, a more explicit rupture with anthropology's longstanding complicity in colonial politics.[3] As such, one could argue that the historic turn sig-

* This essay represents a condensed version of Chapter I from my book in progress, *Along the Archival Grain* (Princeton: Princeton University Press). Parts of it are based on the 1996 Lewis Henry Morgan Lectures I delivered at the University of Rochester entitled 'Ethnography in the archives: movements on the historic turn'.

Batavia, 30th December 1872

Confidential

Your Excellency has honoured us by entrusting us in undertaking a secret mission which involved a confidential investigation into the living conditions of a specific section of the Batavia community.

We now, after the completion thereof, have the honour in presenting the following to you after having accepted the commission which gave us this opportunity.

To His Excellency

The Governor General of the Dutch East Indies

Translation of 'Secret Document' by Ena Jansen

1 Michel Foucault, *The Archaeology of Knowledge and the Discourse on Language* (New York: Harper, 1972), p. 76.

2 E. E. Evans-Pritchard. 'Social anthropology: past and present, the Marett lecture, 1950', in *Social Anthropology and Other Essays* (New York: Free Press, 1951), p.152; Claude Lévi-Strauss, *The Savage Mind* (Chicago: Chicago University Press, 1966), p. 256.

nals not a turn to history *per se* but a different reflection on the politics of knowledge – a further rejection of the categories and cultural distinctions on which imperial rule was once invested and on which post-colonial state practices have continued to be based.

Engagement with the uses and abuses of the past pervades the disciplines but nowhere more than in this burgeoning area of colonial ethnography. Over the last decade students of the colonial have challenged the categories, conceptual frame and practices of colonial authorities and their taxonomic states.[4] Questioning the making of colonial knowledge and the privileged social categories it produced has revamped what students of the colonial take to be sources of knowledge and what to expect of them. Attention to the intimate domains in which colonial states intervened has prompted reconsideration of what we hold to be the foundations of European authority and its key technologies.[5] In treating colonialism as a history of the present rather than as a metaphor of it, a new generation of scholars is taking up Michel de Certeau's invitation to 'prowl' new terrain as they reimagine what sorts of situated knowledge have produced both colonial sources and their own respective locations in the 'historiographic operation'.[6] Some students of colonialism are rereading those archives against popular memory;[7] others are attending to how colonial documents have been requisitioned and recycled to confirm old entitlements or to make new political demands. As part of a wider impulse, we are no longer studying things but the making of them. Students of colonialisms in and outside of anthropology are spending as much time rethinking what constitutes the colonial archive as they are reconsidering how written documents collide and converge with colonial memories in the postcolonial field.

But if Evans-Pritchard's warning some thirty-five years ago that 'anthropologists have tended to be uncritical in their use of documentary sources' had little resonance at the time, it has more today. For however deep and full the archival turn has been in postcolonial scholarship of the 1990s, what is more surprising is how thin and tentative it can still remain.[8] Anthropologists may no longer look at archives as the stuff of another discipline. Nor are these archives treated as inert sites of storage and conservation.[9] But archival labour tends to remain more an extractive enterprise than an ethnographic one. Documents are still invoked piecemeal and selectively to confirm the colonial invention of traditional practices or underscore cultural claims.

Anthropology has never committed itself to 'exhaust' the sources, as Bernard Cohn once chided the historical profession for doing with

3   For some sense of the range of different agendas of the current 'historic turn' see *Culture, Power, History*, eds. Nicholas Dirks, Geoff Eley and Sherry Ortner (Princeton: Princeton University Press, 1994); *The Historic Turn in the Human Sciences*, ed. Terrence J. MacDonald (Ann Arbor: University of Michigan Press, 1996); specifically on history in the anthropological imagination see Gerald Sider and Gavin Smith eds., *Between History and Histories: The Making of Silences and Commemorations* (Toronto: Toronto University Press, 1997). Also see Richard Fox's 'For a nearly new culture history' in Richard G. Fox ed., *Recapturing Anthropology: Working in the Present*, (Santa Fe: School of American Research Press, 1991), pp. 93–114, and James Faubion, 'History in anthropology', *Annual Review of Anthropology* 22 (1993), pp. 35-54.

4   See, for example, the introductions to and essays in Nicholas Dirks ed., *Colonialism and Culture* (Ann Arbor: University of Michigan Press, 1992) and in Frederick Cooper and Ann Laura Stoler eds., *Tensions of Empire: Colonial Cultures in a Bourgeois World* (Berkeley: University of California Press, 1997).

5   See my 'Genealogies of the intimate' in *Carnal Knowledge and Imperial Power: Race and the Intimate in Colonial Rule* (Berkeley: University of California Press, forthcoming).

6   See Michel de Certeau, 'The Historiographic Operation' (1974), in *The Writing of History* (New York, Columbia University Press, 1985).

7   See Ann Laura Stoler and Karen Strassler, 'Castings for the colonial: memory work in New Order Java', *Comparative Studies in Society and History* 42, 1 (2000), pp. 4–48 and the references therein.

8   E. E. Evans-Pritchard, *Anthropology and History* (Manchester: Manchester University Press, 1961), p. 5.

9   See Carlo Ginzburg, *Clues, Myths, and the Historical Method* (Baltimore: Johns Hopkins University Press, 1989).

ANN LAURA STOLER

such moral fervour. But the extractive metaphor remains relevant to both.[10] Students of the colonial 'mine' the content of government commissions and reports but rarely attend to their peculiar form. We look at exemplary documents rather than at the genealogies of their redundance. We warily quote examples of colonial excesses – if uneasy with the pathos and voyeurism that such citings entail. We may readily mock fetishisms of the historian's craft, but there remains the shared conviction that access to what is 'classified' and 'confidential' procures the coveted findings of sound and shrewd intellectual labours.[11] The ability to procure them measures scholarly worth. Not least is the shared conviction that such guarded treasures are the sites where the secrets of the colonial state are really stored.

There are a number of ways to frame the sort of challenge I have in mind, but at least one seems obvious: steeped as students of culture have been in treating ethnographies as texts, we are only now critically reflecting on the making of documents and how we choose to use them, on archives not as sites of knowledge retrieval but knowledge production, as monuments of states, as well as sites of state ethnography. This is not a rejection of colonial archives as sources of the past. Rather, it signals a more sustained engagement with those archives as cultural artefacts of fact production, of taxonomies in the making, and of disparate notions of what made up colonial authority.

As both Ranajit Guha and Greg Dening long have warned, 'sources' are not 'springs of real meaning', 'fonts' of colonial truths in themselves.[12] Whether documents are trustworthy, authentic and reliable remain pressing questions, but a turn to the social and political conditions that produced those documents, what Carlo Ginzburg has called their 'evidentiary paradigms', has altered the sense of what trust and reliability might signal and politically entail. The task is less to distinguish fiction from fact than to track the production and consumption of those facticities themselves. With this move, colonial studies are steering in a different direction, toward inquiry into the grids of intelligibility that produced those 'evidential paradigms' at a particular time, for a particular contingent and in a particular way.[13] Students of the colonial have come to see appropriations of colonial history as infused with political agendas, making some stories eligible for historical rehearsal and others not.[14] Troubling questions about how personal memories are shaped and effaced by states, too, have placed analytic emphasis on how past practices are winnowed for future uses and future projects.[15] Such queries invite a turn back to documentation itself, to the 'teaching' task that the Latin root 'docere'

10 Bernard Cohn, 'History and Anthropology: the state of play', *Comparative Studies in Society and History* (CSSH) 22, 2 (1980), pp. 198–221.

11 On the trips to archives as 'feats of [male] prowess' in nineteenth-century middle-class culture see Bonnie G. Smith. 'Gender and the practices of scientific history: the seminar and archival research in the nineteenth century', *American Historical Review* 100, 4–5 (1995), pp. 1150-76.

12 Ranajit Guha, 'The process of counter-insurgency' [1983] in *Culture, Power, History: A Reader in Contemporary Social Theory*, eds. Nicholas Dirks, Geoff Eley and Sherry Ortner, (Princeton: Princeton University Press, 1994), pp. 336–371; Greg Dening, *The Death of William Gooch: A History's Anthropology* (Honolulu: Hawaii University Press,1995), p. 54.

13 Carlo Ginzburg, 'Clues: roots of an evidential paradigm' in *Clues, Myths and the Historical Method* (Baltimore: Johns Hopkins University Press, 1989) pp. 96–125.

14 David William Cohen, *Burying SM: The Politics of Knowledge and the Sociology of Power in Africa* (Portsmouth NH: Heinemann, 1994).

15 Joanne Rappaport, *Cumbe Reborn: An Andean Ethnography of History* (Chicago: University of Chicago Press, 1994). Also see the contributions to Sarah Nuttall and Carli Coetzee, eds., *Negotiating the Past: The Making of Memory in South Africa* (Cape Town: Oxford University Press, 1998).

16 See Andrew Ashforth, *The Politics of Official Discourse in Twentieth-Century South Africa* (Oxford: Clarendon Press, 1990), p. 5.

17 Michel de Certeau, *The Writing of History* (New York: Columbia University Press, 1988), p. 75.

18 A phrase used by Jane Sherron de Hart to underscore the 'problematics of evidence' in contemporary historical reconstruction ('Oral sources and contemporary history: dispelling old assumptions', *Journal of American History* (JAH) (1993), p. 582).

19 Jacques Derrida, *Archive Fever: A Freudian Impression* (Chicago: Chicago University Press, 1995).

20 Natalie Davis, *Fiction in the Archives: Pardon Tales and Their Tellers in Sixteenth Century France* (Stanford: Stanford University Press, 1987); Richard Thomas, *The Imperial Archive: Knowledge and the Fantasy of Empire* (London: Verso, 1993); Roberto Gonzalez Echevarria; *Myth and Archive: A Theory of Latin American Narrative* (Cambridge: Cambridge University Press 1990); Sonia Combe, *Archives Interdites: Les Peurs Françaises face a l'Histoire Contemporaine* (Paris: Albin Michel, 1994). See Dominick LaCapra, 'History, language, and reading', *American Historical Review* (AHR) (June 1995), p. 807, where he also notes that the 'problem of reading in the archives has increasingly become a concern of those doing archival research'.

21 See, for example, Dening's *The Death of William Gooch: A History's Anthropology* (Honolulu: University of Hawaii Press, 1995).

22 Michel-Rolph Trouillot, *Silencing the Past: Power and the Production of History* (Boston: Beacon, 1995); David William Cohen, *The Combing of History* (Chicago: Chicago University Press, 1994).

23 Bonnie G. Smith, 'Gender and the practices of scientific history' *American Historical Review* 100, 4–5 (1995), pp. 1150–1176.

24 On the history of archives and how archivists have thought about it see Ernst Posner's classic essay 'Some aspects of archival development since the French revolution' [1940] in *A Modern Archives Reader*, eds. Maygene Daniels and Timothy Walch (Washington, D.C.: National Archives and Record Service), pp. 3–21 and Michel

implies, to what and who was being educated in the bureaucratic shuffle of rote formulas, generic plots and prescriptive asides that make up the bulk of a colonial archive. The issue of 'bias' gives way to a different challenge: to identifying the conditions of possibility which shaped what could be written, what warranted repetition, what competencies were rewarded in archival writing, what stories could not be told and what could not be said. Andrew Ashforth may have overstated the case in his study of South Africa's Native Affairs Commission, when he noted that 'the real seat of power' in modern states is 'the bureau, the locus of writing', but it may not be far off the mark.[16] That every document comes layered with the received account of earlier events and the cultural semantics of a political moment makes one point clear. What constitutes the archive, what form it takes and what systems of classification signal at specific times, is the very substance of colonial politics.

FROM EXTRACTION TO ETHNOGRAPHY IN THE COLONIAL ARCHIVES

The transformation of archival activity is the point of departure and the condition of a new history. (De Certeau)[17]

If one could say that archives were once treated as a means to an end by students of history, this is no longer the case today. The pleasures of 'a well-stocked manuscript room with its ease of access and aura of quiet detachment' are a thing of the past.[18] Over the last decade, epistemological scepticism has taken cultural and historical studies by storm. A focus on history as narrative and history-writing as a charged political act has made the thinking about archives no longer the pedestrian preoccupation of 'spadework' historians, of flat-footed archivists, nor the entry requirements of fledgling initiates compelled to show mastery of the tools of their trade. The 'archive' has been elevated to new theoretical status, with enough cachet to warrant distinct billing, worthy of scrutiny on its own. Jacques Derrida's *Archive Fever* compellingly captured that impulse by giving it a name and by providing an explicit and evocative vocabulary for its legitimisation in critical theory.[19] But Davis' *Fiction in the Archives*, Roberto Echevarria's *Myth and Archive*, Richard Thomas' *Imperial Archive*, and Sonia Coombe's *Archives Interdites*, to name but a few, suggest that Derrida's splash came only after the archival turn had already been made.[20]

This move from archive-as-source to archive-as-subject gains its contemporary currency from a range of different analytic shifts, practical concerns and political projects. For some, as in the nuanced archival forays of Greg Dening, it represents a turn back to the meticulous 'poetics of detail'.[21] To others, like Michel-Rolph Trouillot, in his treatment of the archival silences of the Haitian Revolution, and David William Cohen in his 'combings of history', it signals a new grappling with the production of history, what accounts get authorised, what procedures were required, and what about the past it is possible to know.[22] For Bonnie Smith, archival research, like 'the seminar', was the nineteenth-century site where science was marked with gendered credentials.[23] Archivists obviously have been thinking about the nature and history of archives for some time.[24] What marks this moment is the profusion of forums in which historians are joining archivists in new conversations about documentary evidence, record-keeping and archival theory.[25] Both are worrying about the politics of storage, what information matters, and about what should be retained of an archive as paper collections give way to digital forms.[26]

In cultural theory, 'the archive' has a capital 'A', is figurative, and leads elsewhere. It may represent neither a material site nor a set of documents. Rather it may serve as a strong metaphor for any corpus of selective forgettings and collections – and as importantly, for the seductions and longings that such quests, accumulations and passions for the primary, originary and untouched entail.[27] For those inspired more directly by Foucault's *Archaeology of Knowledge*, the archive is not an institution but 'the law of what can be said', not a library of events, but 'that system that establishes statements as events and things, that 'system of their enunciabilities'.[28]

From whichever vantage point – and there are more than these – the 'archival turn' registers a rethinking of the materiality and imaginary of collections and what kinds of truth-claims lie in documentation.[29] Such a 'turn' converges with a profusion of new work in the history of science that is neither figuratively nor literally about archives at all. I think here of: Ian Hacking's studies of the political history of probability theory and state investments in the 'taming of chance'; Steven Shapin's analysis of the social history of scientific truths where he traces the power to predict as one enjoyed by, and reserved for, cultured and reliable men; Mary Poovey's work on how the notion of the 'modern fact' was historically produced; Alain Desrosieres' study (among many others) on statistics as a science of the state and Silvana Patriarca's on statistics as a modern mode of representation; Lorraine Daston's analysis of the development of classical probability theory as a means of measuring the incertitudes of a modernising world.[30] One could also add Anthony Grafton's essays on footnotes as the lines that

Duchein, 'The history of European archives and the development of the archival profession in Europe', American Archivist 55 (Winter 1992), pp. 14–25.

25 See, for example, Richard Berner, Archival Theory and Practice in the United States: An Historical Analysis (Seattle: University of Washington Press, 1983); Kenneth E. Foote, 'To remember and forget: archives, memory, and culture', American Archivist 53, 3 (1990), pp. 378–393; Terry Cook, 'Mind over matter: towards a new theory of archival appraisal' in The Archival Imagination: Essays in Honour of Hugh A. Taylor (Association of Canadian Archivists, 1994), pp. 38–69, James M. O'Toole, 'On the idea of uniqueness', American Archivist 57, 4 (1994), pp. 632–659. For some sense of the changes in how archivists themselves have framed their work over the last fifteen years see articles in The American Archivist.

26 Terry Cook, 'Electronic records, paper minds: the revolution in information management and archives in the post-custodial and post-modernist era', Archives and Manuscripts 22, 2 (1994), pp. 300–329.

27 This metaphoric move is most evident in contributions to the two special issues of History of the Human Sciences devoted to The Archive 11(4), November 1998 and 12(2), May 1999). Derrida's valorisation of 'the archive' as imaginary and metaphor predominates both. On the archive as metaphor also see Allan Sekula, 'The body and the archive', 39 (Winter 1986), pp. 3–64.

28 Michel Foucault, The Archaeology of Knowledge and the Discourse on Language, especially Part III, 'The statement and the archive', pp. 79–134.

29 See, for example, Patrick Geary's Phantoms of Rembrance: Memory and Oblivion at the End of the First Millennium (Princeton: Princeton University Press, 1994), especially 'Archival memory and the destruction of the past', pp. 81–114.

30 Ian Hacking, The Taming of Chance (New York: Cambridge University Press, 1990); Steven Shapin, A Social History of Truth: Civility and Science in Seventeenth-Century England (Chicago: Chicago University Press, 1994); Mary Poovey, A History of the Modern Fact: Problem of Knowledge in the Sciences of Wealth and Society (Chicago: Chicago University Press, 1998); Alain Desrosières, The

lead into moral communities and their claims to truth.[31]

What is it that these all have in common? All are concerned with the legitimising social coordinates of epistemologies: how people imagine they know what they know and what institutions validate that knowledge. None treat the conventions and categories of analysis (statistics, facts, truths, probability and footnotes) as innocuous or benign. All converge on questions about rules of reliability and trust, criteria of credence, and what moral projects and political predictabilities are served. All ask a similar set of historical questions about accredited knowledge and power – what political forces, social cues and moral virtues produce qualified knowledges that in turn disqualified others. To my mind, no set of concerns is more relevant to the colonial politics of archives and their archiving states.

But the archival turn can be traced through other venues as well, suggesting that something resembling ethnography in an archival mode has been around for some time. Carlo Ginzburg's microhistory of a sixteenth-century miller, like Natalie Davis' use of pardon tales in *Fiction in the Archives*, drew on 'hostile' documents to reveal 'the gap between the image underlying the interrogations of judges and the actual testimony of the accused'.[32] Neither was intended as ethnographies of the archive, but both gesture in that direction. In Davis' explicit attention to 'how people told stories, what they thought a good story was, how they accounted for motive', these sixteenth-century letters of remission are shown to recount more than their peasant authors' sober tales.[33] Pardon tales registered the 'constraints of the law', the monopoly on public justice of royal power and the mercy that the monarchy increasingly claimed.[34] Davis' 'fiction in the archives' demonstrated fashioned stories that spoke to moral truths, drew on shared metaphors and high literary culture, and depended on the power of the state and the archived inscriptions of its authority.

While recent participants in the archival turn have been taken with Derrida's contention that 'there is no political power without control of the archive', in fact this insistence on the link between what counts as knowledge and who has power has long been a founding principle of colonial ethnography.[35] Rolph Trouillot's insistence in his study of the Haitian Revolution that 'historical narratives are premised on previous understandings, which are themselves premised on the distribution of archival power' allows him to track the effacement of archival traces, and the imposed silences that people have moved around and beyond.[36] Nicholas Dirk's observation that early colonial historiographies in British India were dependent on native

Politics of Large Numbers: A History of Statistical Reasoning (Cambridge: Harvard University Press, 1998); Silvana Patriarca, *Numbers and Nationhood: Writing Statistics in Nineteenth-Century Italy* (Cambridge: Cambridge University Press, 1996). On the power of 'suasive utterance' in the making of scientific truth-claims see Christopher Norris, 'Truth, science, and the growth of knowledge', *New Left Review* 210 (1995), pp. 105–23.

31 Anthony Grafton, *The Footnote: A Curious History* (Harvard: Harvard University Press, 1997).

32 Carlo Ginzburg, *The Cheese and the Worms: The Cosmos of a Sixteenth-Century Miller* (London: Penguin, 1982), pp. xvii, xviii.

33 Davis, *Fiction in the Archives*, p. 4.

34 *Ibid.*, p. 4.

35 Derrida, *Archive Fever*, p. 4.

36 Michel-Rolph Trouillot, *Silencing the Past: Power and the Production of History* (Boston: Beacon, 1995), p.55.

informants who were later written out of those histories draws our attention to the relationship between archiving, experts and knowledge production.[37] Christopher Bayly's more recent attention to the ways in which the British intelligence service in colonial India worked through native channels, places the state's access to 'information' as a nodal point in the art of governance and as a highly contested terrain.[38] My own work on 'the hierarchies of credibility' that contained colonial narratives in the Netherlands Indies as they constrained what was counted as a plausible plot reads colonial politics off the 'storeyed' distributions of the state's paper production and through the rumours spread by a beleaguered native population that were woven through it.[39]

As Foucault provocatively warned, the archive is neither the sum of all texts that a culture preserves nor those institutions which allow for that record and preservation. The archive is rather that 'system of statements', those 'rules of practice', that shape the specific regularities of what can and cannot be said.[40] Students of colonialism have wrestled with this formulation to capture that which renders colonial archives both as documents of exclusions and as monuments to particular configurations of power in themselves.

Both Gonzalez Echevarria and Richard Thomas follow Foucault in treating the imperial archive as 'the fantastic representation of an epistemological master pattern'.[41] For Thomas that archive is material and figurative, a metaphor of an unfulfilled but shared British imperial imagination. The imperial archive was both the supreme technology of the late nineteenth-century imperial state and the telling prototype of a postmodern one, predicated on global domination of information, and the circuits through which facticities move. Gonzalez Echevarria locates the archive as both relic and ruin, a repository of codified beliefs, genres for bearing witness, clustered connections between secrecy, power and the law.[42] It was the legitimising discourses of the Spanish colonial archives, he argues, that provided the Latin American novel with its specific content and thematic form. For both Thomas and Gonzalez Echevarria, the archive is a template that decodes something else. Both push us to think differently about archival fictions but reserve their fine-grained analysis for literature, not the colonial archives themselves.[43]

Whether the 'archive' should be treated as a set of discursive rules, a utopian project, a depot of documents, a corpus of statements or all of the above is not really the question. Colonial archives were both sites of the imaginary and institutions that fashioned histories as they

37 Nicholas Dirks, 'Colonial histories and native informants: biography of an archive' in Nicholas Dirks, ed., *Colonialism and Culture*, pp. 279–313.

38 Christopher Bayly, *Empire and Information: Intelligence Gathering and Social Communication in India, 1780–1870* (Cambridge: Cambridge University Press, 1996).

39 Ann Laura Stoler, 'In cold blood: hierarchies of credibility and the politics of colonial narratives', *Representations* 37 (1992), pp. 151–189.

40 See Michel Foucault, *The Archaeology of Knowledge*, especially Part III, The Statement and the Archive, pp. 79–134.

41 Thomas, *The Imperial Archive*, p. 11.

42 Echevarria, *Myth and Archive*, p. 30.

43 Thus for Thomas, Hilton's *Lost Horizon* and Kipling's *Kim* are entries in a Victorian archive that was the 'prototype for a global system of domination through circulation, an apparatus for controlling territory by producing, distributing and consuming information about it'.

concealed, revealed and reproduced the power of the state.[44] Power and control, as many scholars have pointed out, are fundamental to the etymology of the term.[45] From the Latin *archivuum*, 'residence of the magistrate' and from the Greek *arkhe,* to command, colonial archives ordered (in both the imperative and taxonomic sense) the criteria of evidence, proof, testimony, and witnessing to construct its moral narrations. 'Factual storytelling', moralising stories, and multiple versions – features that Hayden White ascribes to what counts as history – make sense of which specific plots 'worked' in the colonial archives as well.[46] It was in factual stories that the colonial state affirmed its fictions to itself, in moralising stories that it mapped the scope of its philanthropic missions, and in multiple and contested versions that cultural accounts were discredited or restored.

Viewed in this perspective, it is clear that the nineteenth- and early twentieth-century archives of the Dutch administration in the Indies were not to be read in any which way. Issues were rendered important by how they were classed and discursively framed. Official exchanges between the Governor General and his subordinates, between the Governor General and the Minister of Colonies, and between the Minister and the King, were reference guides to administrative thinking. Organised in folio forms, title pages provided long lists of cross-referenced dossiers and decisions which were abbreviated genealogies of what constituted relevance, precedent and 'reasons of state'. With appended evidence that might include testimonies of experts and commissioned reports, such folios contained and confirmed what counted as proof and who cribbed from whom in the chain of command. Attention to moments of distrust and dispersion, reversals of power and ruptures in contract have been the trademarks of critical political and social history for some time. What has changed is how effectively these moments identify, how, what Richard Thomas has called, these 'paper empires' filed and classified as a part of their technologies of rule.[47]

If it is obvious that colonial archives are products of state machines, it is less obvious that they are, in their own right, technologies that bolstered the production of those states themselves.[48] Systems of written accountability were the products of institutions, but paper trails (weekly reports to superiors, summaries of reports of reports, recommendations based on reports) called for an elaborate coding system by which they could be tracked. Colonial statecraft was built on the foundations of statistics and surveys but also out of the administrative apparatus which produced that information. Multiple

44 This link between state power and what counts as history was long ago made by Hegel in *The Philosophy of History* as Hayden White points out:

'. . . It is only the state which first presents subject-matter that is not only adapted to the prose of History, but involves the production of such history in the very progress of its own being' (Hayden White, *The Content of the Form: Narrative Discourse and Historical Representation* (Baltimore: Johns Hopkins University Press, 1987), p. 12).

45 See Echevarria, *Myth and Archive*, p. 31, for detailed etymology of the term.

46 See Hayden White, *The Content of the Form*, esp. pp. 26–57.

47 On this point see Trouillot, *Silencing the Past*. On the relationship between state formation and archival production see Duchein, 'The history of European archives', cited above.

48 See my 'Racial histories and their regimes of truth', *Political Power and Social Theory* 11 (1997), pp. 183–255.

circuits of communication – shipping lines, courier services and telegraphs – were funded by state coffers and systems of taxation that kept them flush. Colonial publishing houses made sure that documents were selectively disseminated, duplicated or destroyed. Colonial office buildings were constructed to make sure they were properly catalogued and stored. And not unlike the broader racialised regime in which archives were produced, the majority of 'mixed-blood', 'Indo' youths, barred from rising in the civil service ranks, were the scribes who made the system run. Employed as clerks and copyists in the colonial bureaucracy, they were commonly referred to as 'copy machines' and then disdained for their lack of initiative, their poor command of Dutch, and for their capacity to imitate in these constrained roles. Attention to this sort of scaffolding of the colonial state renders an ethnographic reading of the archives very different from what histories of the colonial looked like several decades ago.

ALONG THE ARCHIVAL GRAIN

If one were to characterise what has informed a critical approach to the colonial archives over the last fifteen years it would be a commitment to the notion of reading colonial archives 'against their grain'. Students of colonialism inspired by political economy were schooled to write popular histories 'from the bottom up', histories of resistance that might locate human agency in small gestures of refusal and silence among the colonised.[49] As such, engagement with the colonial archives was devoted to a reading of 'upper class sources upside down' that would reveal the language of rule and the biases inherent in statist perceptions.[50]

The political project was to write 'un-state-d' histories that might demonstrate the warped reality of official knowledge and the enduring consequences of such political distortions. In Ranajit Guha's formulation, colonial documents were rhetorical sleights of hand that erased the facts of subjugation, reclassified petty crime as political subversion, or simply effaced the colonised. The political stakes were put on the analytic tactics of inversion and recuperation: an effort to resituate those who appeared as objects of colonial discipline as subaltern subjects and agents of practice who made – albeit constrained – choices of their own. Within this frame, archival documents were counterweights to ethnography, not the site of it.[51]

But colonial authority and the practices that sustained it permeated more diverse sites than those pursuing this 'romance of resistance'

49 For a more detailed account of these changes in research agenda, see the new preface to my *Capitalism and Confrontation in Sumatra's Plantation 1870–1979* (Ann Arbor: University of Michigan Press, 1995).

50 I discuss some of these issues in 'Perceptions of protest: defining the dangerous in colonial Sumatra', *American Ethnologist* 12, 4, pp. 642–658.

51 For a recent and sophisticated version of this culling project, see Shahid Amin, *Event, Metaphor, Memory: 1922–1992* (Berkeley: University of California Press, 1995).

once imagined. If Marx's insistence that 'people make their own history, but not exactly as they please' informed these early efforts to write histories of popular agency, they also underscored that colonial rule rested on more than the calculated inequities of specific relations of production and exchange. In looking more to the carefully honed cultural representations of power, students of the colonial have turned their attention to the practices that privileged certain social categories and made them 'easy to think'. Not least, we have become more suspect of colonial vocabularies themselves that slip away from their historical moorings and reappear as our explanatory concepts of historical practice rather than folk categories that need to be explained. [52]

Focus in colonial studies on those tensions of empire that were at once intimate and broad has placed sex and sentiment not as metaphors of empire but as its constitutive elements.[53] Appreciating how much the personal was political has revamped the scope of our archival frames: housekeeping manuals, childrearing handbooks and medical guides share space with classified state papers, court proceedings and commissions as defining texts in colonialism's cultures of documentation. Raymond Williams' treatment of culture as a site of contested, not shared, meaning has prompted students of the colonial to do the same. In turning from race as a thing to race as a porous and protean set of relations, colonial histories increasingly dwell on the seams of archived and non-archived ascriptions to redefine colonial subsumptions on a broader terrain.[54] However we frame it, the issue turns on readings of the archives based on what we take to be evidence and what we expect to find. How can students of colonialisms so quickly and confidently turn to readings 'against the grain' without a prior sense of their texture and granularity? How can we compare colonialisms without knowing the circuits of knowledge production in which they operated and the racial commensurabilities on which they relied? If a notion of colonial ethnography starts from the premise that archival production is itself both a process and a powerful technology of rule, then we need not only to brush against the archive's received categories. We need to read for its regularities, for its logic of recall, for its densities and distributions, for its consistencies of misinformation, omission and mistake, along the archival grain.

CIVILITIES AND CREDIBILITIES IN ARCHIVAL PRODUCTION

If colonial documents reflected the supremacy of reason, they also recorded an emotional economy manifest in disparate understandings

52 See the introduction, 'Genealogies of the intimate' in my *Carnal Knowledge and Imperial Power: Race and the Intimate in Colonial Rule* (Berkeley: UC Press, 2002).

53 See my 'Sexual affronts and racial frontiers', *Comparative Studies in Society and History* 34, 3 (1992), pp. 514–551.

54 See *Questions of Evidence: Proof, Practice and Persuasion across the Disciplines*, eds. J. Chandler, A. Davidson, and H. Harootunian (Chicago: Chicago University Press, 1994).

ANN LAURA STOLER

of what was imagined, what was feared, what was witnessed and what was overheard. Such a reading turns us to the structures of sentiment to which colonial bureaucrats subscribed, to the formulaic by which they abided, to the mix of dispassionate reason, impassioned plea, cultural script and personal experience that made up what they chose to write to their superiors and in the folds of official view. Dutch colonial documents register this emotional economy in several ways: in the measured affect of official texts, in the biting critique reserved for marginalia, in footnotes to official reports where assessments of cultural practice were often relegated and local knowledge stored. Steven Shapin's set of compelling questions in his social history of truth could be that of colonial historians as well. What, he asks, counted as credible, what was granted epistemological virtue and by what social criteria? What sentiments and civilities made for 'expert' colonial knowledge which endowed some persons with the credentials to generate trustworthy truth – claims which were not conferred on others?

Colonial archives were, as Echevarria notes, legal repositories of knowledge and official repositories of policy. But they were also repositories of good taste and bad faith. Scribes were charged with making fine-penned copies. But reports on the colonial order of things to the Governor General in Batavia and to the Minister of Colonies in the Hague often were composed by men of letters whose status in the colonial hierarchy was founded as much on their display of European learning as on their studied ignorance of local knowledge, on their skill at configuring events into familiar plots, on their cultivation of the fine arts of deference, dissemblance and persuasion. All rested on subtle use of their cultural know-how and cultural wares. As Fanny Colonna once noted for French Algeria, the colonial politics of knowledge penalised those with too much local knowledge and those with not enough.[55] In the Indies, civil servants with too much knowledge of things Javanese were condemned for not appreciating the virtues of limited and selective familiarity.

Christopher Bayly, in a thoughtful study of the development of an intelligence system by the British in India, argues that the mastery of 'affective knowledge' was an early concern of the British colonial state, which diminished throughout the nineteenth century as that state became more hierarchical and governing became a matter of routine.[56] But I would argue the opposite: that affective knowledge was at the core of political rationality in its late colonial form. Colonial modernity hinged on a disciplining of one's agents, on a policing of the family, on Orwellian visions of intervention in the cultivation of compas-

55 See Fanny Colonna, 'Educating conformity in French colonial Algeria' in Tensions of Empire, pp. 346–370.

56 Christopher Bayly, Empire and Information.

sion, contempt and disdain.

The accumulation of affective knowledge was not then a stage out of which colonial states were eventually to pass. Key terms of the debates on poor whites and childrearing practices from as late as the 1930s, just before the overthrow of Dutch rule, make that point again and again. When classified colonial documents argued against the support of abandoned mixed-blood children – that 'mothercare' *(moed-erzorg)* should not be replaced by 'care of the state' *(staatszorg)*, they were putting affective responsibility at the heart of their political projects. When these same high officials wrote back and forth about how best to secure 'strong attachments' to the Netherlands among a disaffected, estranged and growing European population, 'feeling' is the word that pervades their correspondence. Dutch authorities may never have agreed on how to cultivate European sensibilities in their young, and just how early in a child's development they imagined they needed to do so. But at stake in these deliberations over 'upbringing' and 'rearing' were disquieted reflections on what it took to make someone 'moved' by one set of sensory regimes and estranged from others. Colonial states and their authorities, not unlike metropolitan ones, had strong motivation for their abiding interest in the distribution of affect and a strong sense of why it mattered to colonial politics.

CULTURAL LOGICS AND ARCHIVAL CONVENTIONS

> The archive does not have the weight of tradition, and it does not constitute the library of libraries, outside time and place – it reveals the rules of practice . . . its threshold of existence is established by the discontinuity that separates us from what we can no longer say. (Foucault)[57]

One way to refigure our uses of the colonial archive is to pause at, rather than bypass, its conventions, those practices that make up its unspoken order, its rubrics of organisation, its rules of placement and reference. Archival conventions might designate who were reliable 'sources', what constituted 'enough' evidence and what – in the absence of information – could be filled in to make a credible plot. Conventions suggest consensus but it is not clear what colonial practitioners actually shared. Archival conventions were built upon a changing collection of colonial truths about what should be classified as secrets and matters of state security, what sorts of actions could be dismissed as a personal vendetta or *ad hoc* passion or accredited as a

57 Foucault, *Archaeology of Knowledge*, p. 130.

ANN LAURA STOLER

political subversion against the state.[58] Such conventions exposed the taxonomies of race and rule, but also how skilfully, awkwardly and unevenly seasoned bureaucrats and fledgling practitioners knew the rules of the game.

Attention to these conventions may lead in two directions: to the consensual logics they inscribed but, much more directly, to their arbitrary rules and multiple points of dissension. Political conflicts show up in the changing viability of categories and disagreements about their use. But, as Paul Starr suggests, 'information out of place' – the failure of some kinds of practices, perceptions and populations to fit into a state's ready system of classification – may tell as much or more.[59] Commentaries on European nurseries in the colonies might be expected to turn up in reports on education, but the very fact that they consistently showed up elsewhere – in reports on European pauperism and white poor relief, in recommendations to quell creole discontent – suggest that what was 'out of place' was often sensitive, and that it was children, cued to the wrong cultural sensibilities, who were dangerously out of place.

COLONIAL COMMISSIONS AS STORIES STATES TELL THEMSELVES

As Ian Hacking says of social categories, archives produced, as much as they recorded, the realities they ostensibly only described. They told moral stories, they created precedent in the pursuit of evidence and not least they create carefully tended histories. Nowhere is this history-making work more evident than in the form of the commission of inquiry or state commission. By definition, commissions organised knowledge, rearranged its categories, and prescribed what state officials were charged to know. As the anthropologist Frans Husken notes of Dutch commissions in colonial Java, 'when nothing else works and no decision can be reached, appoint a commission' was a favourite response of colonial authorities'.[60] But commissions were not just pauses in policy and tactics of delay. Like statistics, they helped 'determine . . . the character of social facts' and produced new truths as they produced new social realities.[61] They were responses to crises that generated increased anxiety, substantiating the reality of those crises themselves.[62] By the time most commissions had run their course (or spawned their follow-up generation), they could be credited with having defined 'turning points', justifications for intervention and not least, expert knowledge.

The various commissions produced on the problem of poor whites

58 On the administrative distinctions between the 'political' and the 'private', and the 'criminal' vs the 'subversive' see my 'Perceptions of protest: defining the dangerous in colonial Sumatra', *American Ethnologist* 12, 4 (1985), pp. 642–658, and 'Labor in the revolution', *Journal of Asian Studies* 47, 2 (1988), pp. 227–247.

59 Paul Starr, 'Social categories and claims in the liberal state' in *How Classification Works: Nelson Goodman among the Social Sciences*, eds. Mary Douglas and David Hull (Edinburgh: Edinburgh University Press, 1992), pp. 154–179.

60 Frans Husken, 'Declining welfare in Java: government and private inquiries, 1903–1914' in *The Late Colonial State in Indonesia* ed. Robert Cribb (Leiden: KITLV, 1994), p. 213.

61 Ian Hacking, 'How should we do the history of statistics?' in *The Foucault Effect: Studies in Governmentality*, eds. Graham Burchell, Colin Gordon and Peter Miller (Chicago: Chicago University Press, 1991), p. 181.

62 A good example of what Ian Hacking calls 'dynamic nominalism' or 'the looping effect' in categorisation.

in the Indies between the 1870s and early 1900s, and those carried out in South Africa between the early 1900s and the late 1920s, are exemplary of what I have in mind. There are certain general features they share.[63] Both produced published and publicised volumes: *Pauperism among the Europeans* (published between 1901 and 1902), and *The Problem of Poor Whites in South Africa* (published between 1929 and 1932).[64] Both commissions were about indigent Europeans and their inappropriate sets of dispositions toward work, racial distance, sexual propriety and morality. Each requisitioned administrative energy and expertise, entailed several years of labour, thousands of pages of text, scores of interviewers and hundreds of interviewees. In the case of the Indies, its probing questionnaires on sexual unions, illegitimate children and domestic arrangements sparked the wrath of hundreds of irate colonial Europeans who condemned the Indies government as an 'inquisitionary state'. Both sets of commissions were repositories of colonial anxieties, unsettling testimonies to the insecurity of white privilege, to the ambiguities of membership in the privileged category of 'European' and to the making of a public welfare policy solidly based on race. Both worried over increasing numbers of impoverished whites because they were worried about something else. As stated in the Carnegie Commission, their 'propinquity of . . . dwellings' to 'non-Europeans' tended to bring native and white into contact, 'counteract miscegenation', weaken the colour line and promote 'social equality'.[65]

These commissions could and should be read for their extraordinary ethnographic content, but also for the content in their form. Like other colonial commissions, they marked off clusters of people who warranted state interest and state expense. Two, they were redemptive texts, structured to offer predictions based on causal accounts of exoneration and blame. Three, both sets of commissions were documents to state historiography in the making and monuments to why history mattered to consolidating states. In writing the past, they produced dramatic narrative histories based on select chronologies, crystallising moments and significant events. In defining poverty in the present, they also dictated who later would count as white – and therefore who would be eligible for state aid.

In doing all of the above, they wrote, revised and overwrote genealogies of race. None of these commissions was the first of their kind. On the contrary, they were made credible by how they mapped the past onto prescriptions for the present and predictions of the future. They also showed something more: how practices were histor-

63 I discuss the politics of colonial comparisons elsewhere and therefore will not do so here. I have used the 1902 Indies Pauperism Commission, commentaries around it, and inquiries that preceded it in much of my writing over the last fifteen years on the construction of colonial racial categories. The South African Carnegie Commission and the inquiries that preceded it are compared in a chapter in my forthcoming book Along the Archival Grain. A more general discussion of the politics of comparison can be found in 'Tense and tender ties: the politics of comparison in North American history and (post) colonial studies', *Journal of American History* 88 (December 2001).

64 Students of colonialism could come up with a host of others. For an unusual example of someone who deals with the commission as a particular form of official knowledge, in this case of the South African Native Affairs Commission, see Adam Ashforth, *The Politics of Official Discourse in Twentieth-Century South Africa* (Oxford: Clarendon Press, 1990). Also see Frans Husken's discussion of the Declining Welfare Commission in Java, cited in footnote 59.

65 The Poor White Problem in South Africa, Report of the Carnegie Commission (Stellenbosch: Pro Ecclesia Drukkerij, 1932).

ANN LAURA STOLER

ically congealed into events and made into things; how an increase of unemployment and impoverishment among European colonials became a 'problem' called 'poor whiteism', with attributes of its own. 'Poor whiteism' defined physiologically and psychologically distinct sorts of persons, with aggregated ways of 'being in the world', with specific dispositions and states of mind. Like other colonial commissions, these commissions were consummate producers of social kinds.

Commissions and statistics were features of statecraft in similar ways. Both are eighteenth-century inventions that were consolidated by the nineteenth-century liberal state.[66] Both were products and instantiations of the state's investment in public accountability. But commissions commanded more moral authority, as they purported to scrutinise state practice, reveal bureaucratic mistakes and produce new truths about the workings of the state itself. Moreover, these poor white commissions were quintessential products of 'biopolitical' technologies. Not only did they link the relationship between parent and child, nursemaid and infant, to the security of the state; they sought ethnographic substantiation, eyewitness testimonies from participant-observers that what individuals did – whether they wore shoes, lounged on their porches, spoke Dutch or Malay, or made their children say morning prayers – were practices linked directly to the state's audit of its own viability.

Commissions and statistics were features of statecraft in similar ways. As part of the 'moral science' of the nineteenth century, they coded and counted society's pathologies. While statistics used deviations from the mean to identify deviations from the norm, commissions joined those numbers with stories culled from individual 'cases' to measures gradations of morality. Commissions in turn affirmed the state's authority to make judgements about what was in society's collective and moral good. Both were prescriptive and probabilistic tools whose power was partially in their capacities to predict and divert politically dangerous possibilities.

Like statistics, the commission demonstrated the state's right to power through its will to truth. In the Indies, the Pauperism Commission conferred on the state moral authority by demonstrating its moral conscience and disinterested restraint, its willingness and commitment to critically reflect on its own mishaps, to seek the truth 'at whatever cost'. But its power rested in more than its calculation of the moral pulse of the present and its implications for the future. The Indies commission justified its licence to expend funds, time and personnel in part by rehearsing the past and remembering and reminding

66 Royal commissions have a longer history still. See, for example, David Loades, 'The royal commissions', in *Power in Tudor England* (New York: St. Martin's Press, 1997), pp. 70–82. On statistics and state-building see Alain Desrosières, 'Statistics and the state' in *The Politics of Large Numbers* (1998), pp. 178–209. For the twentieth century see William J. Breen, 'Foundations, statistics, and state-building', *Business History Review* 68 (1994), pp. 451–482.

its readership of its enduring weight. Historical narratives are the architecture of these texts, for these really were stories that deflected the causes of deprivations and inequities away from the present as they rehearsed the enduring burden of earlier policies of administrations past.

Finally, these commissions were quintessential 'quasi-state' technologies, both part of the state and not, at once a product of state agents but constituted invariably by members outside it. If modern states gain force in part by creating and maintaining an elusive boundary between themselves and civil society, as Tim Mitchell has argued, such commissions exemplified that process.[67] Their specific subjects were state-generated but often researched and written by those not in its salary. Both the Indies and Carnegie commissions delegated bodies of experts equipped to assess morality (religious experts), deviance (lawyers, educators) and disease (doctors) and on whom the state conferred short-term and subject-specific voice and public authority. They instantiated the ways in which the state exercised its will to power by calling on 'outside' expert authorities to verify the state's ability to stand in for public interest and its commitment to the public good.

ARCHIVAL SEDUCTIONS AND STATE SECRETS

As archivists are the first to note, to understand an archive one needs to understand the institutions that it served. One needs to understand what subjects are cross-referenced, what parts are rewritten, what quotes are cited, not only about how decisions are rendered but how colonial histories are written and remade. Information out of place underscores what categories matter, which ones become common sense and then fall out of favour. Not least they provide road maps to anxieties that evade more articulate form.

The commission is one sort of archival convention, 'state secrets' are another. States traffic in the production of secrets and the selective dissemination of them. In this regard, the Dutch colonial state was gifted at its task.[68] As Weber once noted, the 'official secret' was a specific invention of bureaucracy that was 'fanatically defended' by it. The designations 'secret', 'very secret' and 'confidential' registered more than fictions of denied entry and public access. Nor did they mostly signal the pressing political concerns of the colonial state. More important, such codes of concealment were the fetishised features of the state itself. State secrets named and produced privileged

67 See Gramsci's discussion of 'state and civil society' in *Selections from the Prison Notebooks*, eds. Quintin Hoare and Geoffrey Smith (London: Lawrence and Wishart), esp. pp. 257–64. and Timothy Mitchell's 'The limits of the state', *American Political Science Review* 85 (1991), pp. 77–96.

68 George Simmel once wrote: 'the historical development of society is in many respects characterized by the fact that what at an earlier time was manifest enters the protection of secrecy; and that, conversely, what once was a secret, no longer needs such protection but reveals itself.' (*The Sociology of George Simmel*, ed. Kurt Wolff [London: Free Press, 1950], p. 331).

knowledge and reminded readers of what was important to know, what kinds of knowledge were coveted, inaccessible and what kind was not. The secreted report, like the commission, created categories it purported to do no more than describe. In the Indies, the classified document was endowed with political weight that called for secret police, paid informants and experts.

Secrets imply limited access but what is more striking in the Dutch colonial archives is how rarely those items classified as 'confidential' (*vertrouwelijk, zeer vertrouwelijk, geheim* and *zeer geheim*) were secrets at all. Some surely dealt with clandestine police and military tactics (such as preparations for troop movements to protect planters against an attack) but far more of these documents were about prosaic, public parts of Indies life.[69] If one could argue that the disquieting presence of European beggars and homeless Dutchmen in the streets of Batavia was 'secret' to those in the Netherlands, it certainly was not to the majority of Europeans who lived in the colony's urban centres.

What was 'classified' about these reports was not their subject-matter – in this case, indigent 'full-blooded' Europeans and their mixed-blood descendants – but rather the conflict among officials about how to act on the problem, their disparate assessments of what was the cause and how many such people there were. Some reports were 'classified' because officials could not agree on whether there were twenty-nine mixed-bloods in straitened circumstances or tens of thousands.[70] In short, documents were classified as 'sensitive' and 'secret' sometimes because of the magnitude of a problem – at other times because officials could not agree on what the problems were. But perhaps what is more surprising is the range of confidentialities that students of colonialism expect them to divulge. State secrets are not necessarily secreted truths about the state but promises of it. State secrets make up a basic feature of the archive, the raison d'être of state institutions charged with producing foundational fictions of concealment and access embodied in content as well as form.

COLONIAL ARCHIVES AS 'SYSTEMS OF EXPECTATION'

To take up Jean and John Comaroff's invitation to 'create new colonial archives of our own' may not only entail, as they rightly urge, attention to new kinds of sources but different ways of approaching those we already have, different ways of reading from those we have yet done.[71] In turning from an extractive to a more ethnographic project, our readings need to move in new ways through archives, along their

69 Algemeen Rijksarchief. Geheim No. 1144/2284. From the Department of Justice to the Governor General, Batavia, 29 April 1873.

70 Algemeen Rijksarchief. Verbaal 28 March 1874, no.47. From the Dept. of Justice to the Governor General.

71 Jean and John Comaroff, *Ethnography and the Historical Imagination* (Boulder: Westview Press, 1992).

fault lines as much as against their grain. De Certeau once defined the science of history as a redistribution in space, the act of changing something into something else. He warns us that our historical labours in the archives must do more than 'simply adopt former classifications'; must break away from the constraints of 'series H in the National Archives' and be replaced with new 'codes of recognition' and 'systems of expectation' of our own.[72] But such a strategy really depends on what we think we already know. For students of colonialisms, such codes of recognition and systems of expectation are at the very heart of what we still need to learn about colonial polities. The breadth of global reference and span of lateral vision that colonial regimes unevenly embraced suggest that an ethnographic sensibility rather than an extractive gesture may be more appropriate for identifying how nations, empires and racialised regimes were fashioned – not in ways that display confident knowledge and know-how, but in disquieted and expectant modes.

72 De Certeau, 'The Historiographic Operation', p. 107.

ANN LAURA STOLER

SECRETARIATE
OF THE STATE SECURITY COUNCIL
PRIVATE BAG/PRIVAATSAK X284
1986 -09- 2 2
PRETORIA
SEKRETARI
VAN DIE STAATSVEILI

H DTG R R 1910358
VAN NATAL GBS
AAN SSVR PRETORIA
INFO H LEER 2   H SAW 2
BT
G E H E I M   NATAL/GBS/400/19 SEP 86
1.   NATAL/GBS/310/1/KARMA/3/1.
2.   MAGTIGING WORD VERSOEK VIR DIE VOLGENDE PROJEK:
A.   PROJEK: ORIENTASIEDAG
B.   TEIEKENGROEP: 80 BLANKE FISIES GESTREMDE LEELRINGE VAN DIE
OPLEUGSKOOL, DURBAN.
C.   DATUM: 14 OKTOBER 1986.
D.   PLEK: KOMMANDEMENT NATAL
E.   DOEL:
I.   OM DIE BEELD VAN DIE SAW ONDER DIE TEIKENGROEP TE BEVORDER
II. OM DIE TEIKENGROEP BEWUS TE MAAK VAN DIE BELANGRIKE ROL WAT
DIE SAW HET OM TE VERVUL IN DIE RSA
III. OM 'N VERTROUENSITUASIE JEENS DIE SAW TE ONTWIKKEL
F.   TEMAS:
I.   ELKE SOLDAAT IS 'N VRIEND
II. DIE SAW IS DIE BESKERMER VAN AL DIE MENSE VAN DIE RSA
III. ONDERSTEUN ONS - ONS SAAK IS REG
IV. SAAM KAN ONS 'N BETER TOEKOMS BOU
G.   FINANSIELE IMPLIKASIES:
I.   KLEINKAS R 60.00 VIR DIE AANKOOP VAN VERVERSINGS.
H.   UITRUSTING BENODIG:
1 X BUFFEL
1 X R 4
1 X R 1
1 X 9 MIL PISTOOL
1 X UZI
. PERSONEEL: LT HALL + 4 KOMOPSWERKERS.
K.   NAVRAE: LT HALL TEL 373421 X 2190
BT
NNNN

LEERHOOFKWARTIER
KOMMUNIKASIESENTRUM
19 -09-1986
ARMY HEADQUARTERS
COMMUNICATION CENTRE

'Secret Document', 1986.

  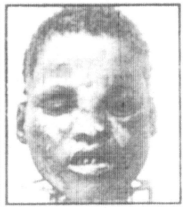

AS can be seen from the photographs, each head has been placed on a metal ring to stop it rolling off the table. On some heads the scars can be seen where the skull has been opened so that measurements can be taken of the brain. (Readers please note we are not publishing these photographs with a view to sensationalism, but simply in the interests of properly documenting our historical past. - Ed)

THE photographs which are on this page show the severed heads of some of the prisoners kept on Shark Island in Luderitz during the 1904-1908 war. History is often unpleasant and some may argue that the reproduction of these photographs is not a useful contribution to the national policy of reconciliation. However, after considerable thought, I decided that the existence of these images should be made public for two reasons:

The first relates to the persistent oral histories that claim that the head of the Kwanyama King, Mandume ya Ndemufayo was cut off after his death. The late Pastor Vilho Kaulinge pointed out that in the Old Testament, David did the same thing after his victory over Goliath. Cutting off the head would provide unchallengeable evidence of victory to doubters. It would also symbolically show that the 'head' of the opposition forces had been removed from power. When an English King defeated the so-called 'Peasant's Revolt' in 1381 he decapitated the leaders and put their heads on poles above the entrance gates to the City of London.

Yet many people say that they can't believe that 'civilised' people would have done something similar in the twentieth century and that the story of Mandume's head must just be a popular, but fictional tale.

Yet there is clear photographic evidence contained in an article published in 1913 (just four years before the attack on Mandume) that a German scientist was willing to cut the heads off dead prisoners of war. Indeed the scientist, Christian Fetzer, wrote detailed accounts of his work on seventeen heads. It is interesting to note that it has also been claimed that one of the heads taken was that of Cornelius Fredericks. Fredericks was one of the southern guerrilla leaders who had a price of 3 000 mark on his head in a proclamation issued by General von Trotha on April 22, 1905.

If true, then surely the choice of Frederick's body for dissection was not incidental, but a southern parallel to the story of the savaging of Mandume's corpse. A postcard reproduced in the Readers' Digest Illustrated History of South Africa (p 287) purports to show the head of Bambatha, a black leader in Natal, whose head, it claims, was removed and displayed after his defeat by British troops. The 'Bambatha Rebellion' took place in 1906, probably the year before the prisoners' heads were removed at Shark Island.

The second reason the existence of these images should be known is the fact that the present is always a product of the past. The 1904-1908 war in Namibia was one of the most extreme racial wars that the world has ever seen. The experiments conducted on the corpses of the prisoners were carried out as part of a project aimed at 'demonstrating' the 'scientific' reasons for the superiority of 'the German race' over black Namibians.

As mentioned in a previous edition of the Picturing the Past it seems likely that the development of racial thought had a significant impact on the development of ideas of racial purity in Germany itself and fed into the development of the ideology of the Nazi Party.

Of course, a great many years have passed since the 1904-1908 war, but ideas are timeless. The question of whether Germany should apologise or pay compensation for acts that took place during the war is a political one, but surely it should at least publicly recognise and reject the extreme racial ideas that enabled some of the more brutal acts of the war to occur. Would not a donation to the National Monuments Council to enable the construction of monuments to those black Namibians that died be a suitable, powerful and praiseworthy gesture?

If the errors of the past are not acknowledged and publicly rejected is there not a danger that they may reoccur? Recent research has shown that genocides (attempts to kill an entire people) have been not by homicidal maniacs, but by ordinary people. Genocide is the ultimate logic of extreme prejudice. Perhaps readers can shed more light on the Shark Island experiments. The photographs of the severed heads reveals the horrific possibilities when one group of people treat another as objects.

* Thanks to Monika Lonker, Atsuko Shibata and Casper Erichsen for the research in this article.

Figure 1: 'Picturing the Past', 9 April 1998

'Picturing the Past' in Namibia: The Visual Archive and its Energies*

Patricia Hayes, Jeremy Silvester and Wolfram Hartmann

A shudder runs through the beholder/viewer of old photographs. For they do not make visible the knowledge of the original but rather the spatial configuration of a moment. (Kracauer)[1]

The nature of photography itself is one of ambiguity and disjunction. It is a medium of fragmentation, of fractured space and stilled time, of shifting meaning and of ambiguity in relating the part to the whole. (Edwards)[2]

'Do you hate me?' The question came at a moment when personal, family and national histories converged for a group of history students. A foreign student at the University of Namibia had just encountered a scientific publication on race[3] during her research in the National Archives. It included photographs of six severed heads of Nama-speaking prisoners-of-war from the big rebellions against German rule in 1904 to 1907.[4] As she was reporting back to her classmates, a second student revealed her discovery of a German diary. This diary named one of the men decapitated for experiments in racial science as Cornelius Fredericks.

Fredericks had been a key leader in the southern Namibian rebellion that followed the German–Herero war of 1904. The German military had put a price on his head when he brought a group from Bethanie into the revolt. After his capture, nothing was known of Fredericks beyond his imprisonment and death on Shark Island, the penal camp off the bleak Atlantic coast of Namibia. As the drama of the possible identification of one of the severed heads in the photographs unfolded in the classroom, a third student, Hermione Smith from southern Namibia, gave events another painful turn. She revealed that Cornelius Fredericks was her great-grandfather. In that dense moment the first student – who was German – turned to Hermione and asked: *'Do you hate me?'*

* This paper is a revised, updated version of an introductory essay entitled 'Photography, history and memory' by the same authors for the volume *The Colonising Camera: Photographs in the Making of Namibian History* (Cape Town, Windhoek and Athens: University of Cape Town Press, Out of Africa and Ohio University Press, 1998). The dynamics of co-authoring when writers are based in Cape Town, Windhoek and New York are complex. The original essay was put together from sections drafted by all three co-authors. This revised version incorporates new material for which Jeremy Silvester and his students are largely responsible; new literature on photography referenced here is largely the work of Patricia Hayes, and the refining of detail concerning (*inter alia*) German photographic practice has been the work of Wolfram Hartmann.

The authors are grateful to those who responded to the newspaper column 'Picturing the Past' and to students at the History Department of the University of Namibia who participated in photographic research and exhibitions detailed in this paper. Thanks to Vilho Shigwedha for his translation of Vilho Tshilongo's text. We are grateful for the suggestions and criticisms received from colleagues at seminars held at the University of the Witwatersrand on 'Refiguring the Archive' in July 1998 and in La Paz on 'Alternative Histories and Non-Written Sources' in May 1999, and from Ciraj Rassool, Leslie Witz and others at the History Department of the University of the Western Cape.

1 Siegfried Kracauer, 'Photography', translated by Thomas Y. Levin. (Originally published in German in the *Frankfurter Zeitung*, 28 October 1927). In *Critical Inquiry* 19 (Spring 1993), p. 431.

2 Elizabeth Edwards, 'Essay' in Jorma Puranen, *Imaginary Homecomings* (Oulu: Pohjoinen, 1999), p. 60.

3 Christian Fetzer, 'Rassenanatomische Untersuchungen an 17 Hottentotten Kopfen', *Zeitschrift fur Morphologie und Anthropologie* 16 (1913-1914), pp. 95–156.

4 The text also relates how the heads were conserved and the condition in which they arrived in Germany for the research. See Fetzer, 'Rassenanatomische Untersuchungen', p. 95.

Picturing The Past: Death On The Rocks

ANYONE travelling to Luderitz will find a causeway that now links a small rocky outcrop known as Shark Island to the mainland. Apparently there is no memorial on the island, nor indeed in Luderitz itself, to record the grim role played by this apparently harmless island in Nambia's history.

The island was used as a prison camp for Herero and Nama captured during the war against the Germans of 1904-1908. Prisoners were transferred to the island from camps at Windhoek and Karibib in about September 1906. The prisoners included Witbooi's troops who had finally surrendered in February (following Hendrik Witbooi's death in October, 1905) and another guerrilla group from Bethanie who had surrendered in March.

However, accounts show that the majority of prisoners were women and children who were included in the labour gangs taken from the island to work on the construction of the railway line between Luderitz and Keetmanshoop. The work was hard, the prisoners weak and undernourished and the climate harsh. Within eight months it was reported that 1032 of the 1795 people kept on the island had died. The bodies of those who desperately tried to swim to freedom were washed up on the shore.

Widespread accounts state that it was common for German soldiers to take women from the camps and rape them. The horror and scale of death on Shark Island makes it unlikely that oral memories of the camp remain. But perhaps readers might be able to identify the sites of the camps at Karibib or elsewhere. The use of prisoners from these camps as hard labour to work on the railway branch to Otavi was another major cause of death and injury. A report compiled by the German authorities themselves calculated that, in all, 7682 prisoners had died in the prison camps by March 1907. Why, one wonders, does there remain such a silence about these events in Namibia today?

RESISTANCE FIGHTER ... An early freedom fighter, Cornelius Fredericks (seated), pictured with unidentified colleagues. Fredericks later died on the notorious Shark Island.

DEATH AND MISERY ... The only known photograph of the prison camp on Shark Island.

* Picturing The Past is a regular column in The Weekender, which features photographs taken from the collection of the National Archives of Namibia. If you have any information about the pictures published today please contact Dr Jeremy Silvester at the History Department, University of Namibia, P/Bag 13301, Windhoek or phone him at (061) 206 3000, or you can leave a message with Audrey at The Namibian (236970) and Dr Silvester will return your call.

New information about the photographs and their historical context will be published in future columns in the interests of building up our understanding of Namibia's past.

Cornelius Fredericks

THE name of Cornelius Fredericks is not prominent in Namibian history books. Until we made a copy for this column, there was no photograph of him held in the National Archives of Namibia.

Yet, Cornelius Fredericks played a significant and important role in Namibian history. He was based in Bethanie and served as a church elder there. However, he fought with Hendrik Witbooi against the Germans in the war of 1894-1895 and was one of the signatories to the peace treaty at the end of the war. After the war he remained a member of the 'Witkamskap' organisation led by Witbooi.

When Witbooi took up arms against the Germans again in 1905, Cornelius Fredericks joined the war with a commando of about 300 men from Bethanie, in defiance of Paul Fredericks (the captain at Bethanie). The commando was seen as particularly dangerous because it threatened the German supply routes in southern Namibia. One measure of his importance was that the Germans put the same price on his head as on that of Hendrik Witbooi (3000 marks). A major effort was made to pursue and destroy his commando, ultimately leading to his surrender in March, 1906. On 16th February, 1907 the name of Cornelius Fredericks was added to the list of those who had died on Shark Island. Ironically it seems that Paul Fredericks was also sent to the island and died there too.

The information for this article was gathered by Leonardus Isaak, a history student at the University of Namibia. But we would be very grateful for any other information that readers might be able to supply about this enigmatic figure from Namibia's past.

Figure 2: 'Picturing the Past', 22 August 1997.

5   Elizabeth Edwards, 'Essay' in Jorma Puranen, *Imaginary Homecomings*, p. 60.

6   The colonial and later 'struggle' photographs at the centre of this study come from the National Archives of Namibia. Many of the photographs formed part of the exhibition *The Colonising Camera: Photographs in the Making of Namibian History*, and the book of the same title. Permission to exhibit and publish photographs for this project was generously granted by the following: National Archives of Namibia; Basler Afrika Bibliographien; Archiv der Vereinten Evangelische Mission (Wuppertal); and the South African Museum. The views expressed about these photographs are solely those of the authors.

It was most of all the photographs, that medium of 'fractured space and stilled time',[5] which placed the two young women amidst a horror that was before their lifetime. The encounter, precipitated by the visual and related texts from the archive, suggests how forcibly such fragments are capable of bridging time. But it is more than that. When the photograph moves out of its stored archive space, it is as if energy is released. This essay cannot possibly disentangle all the reactions and relationships prompted by seeing photographs of the decapitated heads of Namibians who resisted German rule. The attempt here is rather to try to follow more broadly the dialogues created between archival photographs[6] and various audiences who interact

PATRICIA HAYES, JEREMY SILVESTER AND WOLFRAM HARTMANN

with them. These might be in the classroom, at exhibitions, or coming from readers of the fortnightly column 'Picturing the Past' in *The Namibian*, a prominent national newspaper, which acted as a vehicle to publish archive photographs.[7]

What draws our interest here is the trafficking between photography and the archive. There are many levels to this. One is the means by which photographs enter various archives. Then, what happens to photographs as they become encased in the archival filing cabinets – does this make their 'contents invisible' and 'close meanings'?[8] If the photograph 'presents a spatial continuum' as Kracauer says,[9] then his argument here is apt:

> the inert world presents itself in its independence from human
> beings. Photography shows cities in aerial shots, brings crockets
> and figures down from the Gothic cathedrals; all spatial configu-
> rations are incorporated into the central archive in unusual com-
> binations that distance them from human proximity.[10]

Unlike Kracauer, who insists that the meaning of a photograph 'fades with time', we wish to draw on the possibilities for photographs to 'reconstitute the complex spaces which make up and are made by history'.[11] Thus we are concerned with what happens when they are taken out and recirculated to enter (and to make) different spaces at different colonial and postcolonial moments. Our project, in short, is to consider how photographs are brought into new human proximities and become resocialised at distinct points in time: like the moment when Hermione Smith discovered her ancestor's ultimate fate in front of her classmates.[12]

COLONIAL PLATES

At this point we are compelled to talk about colonialism in Namibia. This is so because we think it is important to historicise *the very archive* we have been dealing with and which has been brought to bear on Namibian public audiences, most notably through 'Picturing the Past'. Implicitly we wish to avoid a discussion of the National Archive of Namibia's picture collection as if it were a meta-archive.[13]

Colonialism in the territory could be characterised as a history of overlapping colonial plates, a range of formal and informal influences jostling against each other. Hunt's[14] argument that colonialism 'can no longer be viewed as a process of imposition from a singular European metropole' is highly relevant in this case. The colonialisms

7   The 'Picturing the Past' column is written (or edited) by Jeremy Silvester. In the last three years it has benefited substantially from contributions made by students from the University of Namibia's History Department and by other academic colleagues. We should like to thank the following: Sarafina Biwa, Eugene Maemako, Kassy Nangobe, Vilho Shigwedha, Nehasen Hangula, Z. T. Hilondua ya Makili, Casper Erichsen, Monika Lonker, Atsuko Shibata, Kangumu Kangumu, B. B. Mukanye, Goodman Gwasira, Jeff Gaydish, Werner Hillebrecht, Margie Orford, Patricia Hayes, Dag Henrichsen, Jan Bart Gewald and Heike Becker.

8   Christopher Pinney, Chris Wright and Roslyn Poignant, 'The impossible science. In the photographers' gallery', *The Impossible Science of Being. Dialogues between Anthropology and Photography* (London: The Photographers' Gallery, 1995), p. 10.

9   Kracauer, 'Photography', p. 425.

10 Ibid., p. 435.

11 Edwards, 'Essay', in Jorma Puranen, *Imaginary Homecomings*, p. 61.

12 Besides generating intense discussion amongst fellow students as to the futility of designating all Germans as timeless villains, the material was taken back to senior Fredericks's family members to consider their feelings about the reproduction of the photographs, and the possibilities of taking action or claiming compensation from the German government. Such initiatives by any Namibian group in recent years have met with consistent rejection. The photographs were also run in 'Picturing the Past' (see Fig. 1), though no public feedback has been relayed to the newspaper. Though it is now known he was among the group of bodies used for 'experiment', it is still to be ascertained whether one of the heads photographed is that of Cornelius Fredericks.

13 It is our contention that serious historical ethnographies of the processes of photographing, distributing, collecting, archiving and classifying would greatly strengthen theoretical approaches to South African photographic archives.

14 Nancy R. Hunt, Introduction, *Gender and History* 8, 3 (1996), p. 326.

that Namibians experienced in the twentieth century were indeed 'multiple and distinct', characterised by retreat but continuity (Germany), emergence (South Africa), and the technological and industrial influences and cultures projected from the United States of America, which also became the centre of international politics after the Second World War with the location of the United Nations in New York.

Perhaps the most slippery problem here is that colonial enigma, the South African mandatory state in South West Africa (SWA). This was a marginal colonial state constituted in the wake of the Germans and brokered by the international community after the First World War. South Africa occupied an ambiguous space between its own colonial (later dominion) status under Great Britain, in whose name it occupied Namibia in 1915, and its colonisation and trusteeship of the territory that Randolph Vigne has aptly termed 'Imperialism at one remove'.[15] It displayed insecurities and at times cultural over-statement. Photography by colonisers, whether in the employ of the administration or not, provides particularly striking instances of the effort to project a South African colonial modernity and, frequently and deliberately, indigenous Namibian premodernity or even primi-tivity.[16]

The South African occupation took place with a strong sense of audience. At every stage of South Africa's bid to gain the League of Nations mandate to rule Namibia and to control Namibians, pho-tography was crucial to the politics of representing the place and its peoples. In the attempts to depict, document, normalise and/or pathologise Namibians and to legitimise and memorialise themselves – the colonial version of what Sekula[17] calls the 'double system of rep-resentation' with both repressive and honorific functions – large numbers of photographs were taken and many of them published.

The whole question of photography throws open a number of prob-lems about Namibia's colonialisms. Southern Africa became deeply implicated in metropolitan processes of mechanisation of visual repro-duction from the late nineteenth century. Looking at the way photo-graphy spread through the hinterlands of the subcontinent, following the uneven spread of capitalism and colonialism, a product of industri-al culture that could create new knowledge and easily export it, we can talk of simultaneous processes of colonisation and visualisation of the other. But the 'colonial' photographs in the archive and in publications suggest that, far from dealing with a linear history of colonisation by a single power, there are plural and different colonialisms. And in their

15 Randolph Vigne, 'Imperialism at one remove: Britain and Namibia 1785–1915' in Brian Wood, ed., *Namibia 1884–1994: Readings on Namibia's Society and History* (London and Lusaka: Namibia Support Committee and United Nations Institute for Namibia, 1988).

16 Robert Gordon, 'Backdrops and Bushmen: an expeditious comment' in Wolfram Hartmann, Jeremy Silvester and Patricia Hayes, eds., *The Colonising Camera: Photographs in the Making of Namibian History* (Cape Town, Windhoek and Athens OH: UCT Press, Out of Africa and Ohio University Press, 1998); Michael Bollig, 'Framing Kaokoland' in Hartmann et al., eds., *The Colonising Camera*; Patricia Hayes, 'Northern exposures: the photography of Native Commissioner C. H. L. Hahn' in Hartmann et al., eds., *The Colonising Camera*.

17 Allan Sekula, 'The body and the archive' in Richard Bolton, ed., *The Contest of Meaning: Critical Histories of Photography* (Cambridge MA: MIT Press, 1989).

photographic interactions and encounters with Namibians, each colonialism contributed to the tangled layers of representational politics.

To begin with, much of the early body of photography extant on Namibia comes from the photographers of a defeated colonial power, Germany, whose administration ended during the First World War. This photographic economy encompassed early ethnography, consumer capitalism, political advocacy, evangelical fund-raising, popular memorabilia and much more. The German colonial project was in fact a highly visual one, with the administration in Windhoek opening its first darkroom in 1892[18] and many exhibitions and shows in the metropole forefronting colonial sections with photographs. Moreover, German colonialism left enormously powerful vestigial influences in the form of settler photographers who remained in Namibia after the mandate (or immigrant photographers who left Germany for Africa in the 1920s and 30s), to say nothing of its huge photographic archives.

For the second colonial power, the Union of South Africa, Namibia fulfilled several roles. It offered a new position on the international stage, and it lent its very space for the settlement of poorer whites in the land-hungry 'new South Africa' during a crucial phase of its nation building in the 1910s and 20s.[19] Intellectual initiatives concerning racial science – later than those begun during German rule and very specific – were launched. Namibia offered raw material for the production of knowledge (and images) about 'Bantu' and 'Bushman' which fed into a number of institutional and administrative developments in South Africa itself.[20] Such material on 'natives' now constitutes a great deal of South Africa's own museum[21] and photographic archives, a fact frequently passed over.

In the early days after the 1915 occupation, South Africa's lack of any recent visual archive of the territory and its peoples created problems with regard to the urgent representational needs of the new administration and its international supporters. As a result, incoming South African officials dug into the existing photograph archive and at times plagiarised German photographs – by which we mean photographs were cited in a form that obscured their original provenance.[22] A striking example of this early 'borrowing' was the publication of the visually notorious Blue Book.[23] This circulated a very disturbing vision of how German colonisers incorporated Africans into the colonial economy before 1915. In the Blue Book's appendix with its medical report on German corporal punishment, photographs show African bodies that are emaciated, flogged, chained, tortured and hanging by the neck. Gewald[24] argues that the photographs originat-

18 See *Deutsches Kolonialblatt* 1893, p. 255.

19 Jeremy Silvester, Marion Wallace and Patricia Hayes, 'Introductory Overview' in Hayes et al., eds., *Namibia under South African Rule*.

20 Silvester et al., 'Introductory Overview'; C. Rassool and P. Hayes, 'Gendered science, gendered spectacle: /Khanako's South Africa, 1936–37', paper delivered at the Interdisciplinary Conference on Gender and Colonialism, University of the Western Cape, Cape Town, January 1997; Patricia Hayes, 'South Africa doing African history: bone narratives from Namibia, 1915–1920s' in MacGrath, Jedrej, King and Thompson, eds., *Rethinking African History* (Edinburgh: Centre for African Studies, University of Edinburgh, 1997), pp. 140–143.

21 Martin Legassick and Ciraj Rassool, '*Skeletons in the Cupboard: South African Museums and the Trade in Human Remains, 1907–1917*' (Cape Town and Kimberley: South African Museum and McGregor Museum, 2000).

22 In later years some German photographs also re-emerged in anti-Nazi photomontages appearing in South Africa. See Ciraj Rassool and Patricia Hayes, 'Gendered science, gendered spectacle'; Hartmann et al., eds., *The Colonising Camera* p. 81.

23 Great Britain, 'Report on the natives of South West Africa and their treatment by Germany', HMSO, London (1918).

24 Jan Bart Gewald, 'Mirror images? Photographs of Herero commemorations in the 1920s and 1930s' in Hartmann et al., eds., *The Colonising Camera*.

ed from an official German inquiry into the treatment and corporal punishment of the indigenous inhabitants of its colonies before the First World War, something that is not mentioned in the Blue Book itself. These photographs were, it seems, opportunistically redeployed by British–South African strategists to demonstrate German cruelty and unfitness to retain colonial possessions, and, in turn, to legitimise the South African claim to the award of the League of Nations mandate to govern Namibia.[25]

The 'German' photographic economy, it should be mentioned, has proved very resilient and indeed dense. Despite massive attempts at South Africanisation after the demise of German colonialism, commercial photography for many decades and up to the present has remained largely in German hands. Some of this photography has ensured a visual continuum of the German colonial past. Photo Nink of Windhoek, for instance, which entered its images in the first International German Photography Exhibition in Dresden as long ago as 1909, has a thriving trade in visual memorabilia of German colonialism to this day. Other photographers and studios have ensured the insertion of the remnants of German colonialism into the consciousness of contemporaries and tourists through calendar, coffee-table and postcard photography. Such photographers have also contributed to the specific Namibian landscape genre that constructed the country as a land devoid of people. Thus, while German colonial rule may have ended in 1915, there was a far less dramatic break in some of the dominant photographic traditions in the territory.

But these overtly colonial and nostalgic genres for German-speaking tourist consumption are complicated by the long association of commercial studios with the photography of black Namibians in urban areas. Indeed, such studios or itinerant photographers have facilitated the projection of African modernities since the nineteenth century. The existence of privately held albums and collections of photographs of residents in the African locations and townships – either in commercial studios or by family members – has become increasingly apparent from public responses to 'Picturing the Past'. Namibians were by no means trapped in visual discourses of African tradition and backwardness, a point we shall return to later.

Beyond the German and South African colonial roles in the territory, there is a third outside presence: that of the United States of America (USA), technologically and diplomatically a nascent world power. The cameras of rich safari-goers like President Roosevelt[26] or pseudo-scientific adventurers like Ernest Cadle[27] brought images of

25 A propaganda war between London and Berlin, and between white settlers in Namibia and the South African Administration, rumbled on for nearly a decade until the Blue Book was officially banned in 1926 by demand of the newly constituted Legislative Assembly in Windhoek.

26 Paul Landau, 'Hunting with gun and camera: a commentary' in Hartmann et al., eds., The Colonising Camera.

27 Robert Gordon, Picturing Bushmen. The Denver African Expedition of 1925 (Athens OH, Cape Town and Johannesburg, Windhoek: Ohio University Press, David Philip and Namibia Scientific Society, 1997); Robert Gordon, 'Backdrops and Bushmen: an expeditious comment'.

Africans back to American audiences for various kinds of consumption. More to the point, American camera technology – speeded up by the photographic demands of its own internal colonial expansion westwards – was becoming more popular than that of other producers in SWA even by the 1890s. This made it possible for increasingly sophisticated photography in the most adverse and remote of frontier conditions, such as in Owambo and Kaoko where the Native Commissioner, C. H. L. Hahn, used his Kodak apparatuses to produce incomparable panoramic and other images from the 1910s to 40s.[28]

The figure of Hahn more than any other brought together a mass of photographic record and administrative power, given his three decades of 'indirect rule' and his representation of the vast northern areas to the central administration and to the outside world.[29] This is not to say that photographs of 'natives' comprise the bulk of the collection in the National Archives in Namibia: there are greater numbers of pictures of white settlers in their social settings, and German colonial architecture. In *The Colonising Camera* we chose to focus on the minority of ethnographic and administrative photographs, because these had already enjoyed considerable circulation in official publications and, as genres, seemed to say much more about the construction of colonial relations. In 'Picturing the Past' such photographs were again recirculated, but here the emphasis was towards even more underrepresented kinds of photographs that dealt with social and urban issues for most Namibians, and sought to identify anonymous figures photographed long ago.

Photographic agency was not restricted to white officials, settlers and visitors. While it appears that until the 1960s there were relatively few black photographers or indeed journalists in Namibia[30] compared with South Africa, and especially compared with parts of West Africa,[31] this does not mean that photographic representation in the colonial space of Namibia can be reduced to a one-sided process. Central and southern Namibian elites photographed in the Palgrave album for example appeared in the full idiom of European portraiture; itinerant and studio photographers have been called upon to photograph important occasions, migrant workers, or town-dwellers for probably well over a century. But few such photographs have found their way into the national body of the archive in Namibia. These conceivably represent the making of many cross-cultural spaces.[32] The profundity of John Muafangejo's linocut reinterpretations of published photographs of Kwanyama leaders and colonial officials[33] is an unparalleled deepening of this threshold space in the history of visual

28 Patricia Hayes, 'Camera Africa: indirect rule and landscape photographs of Kaoko, 1943' in Giorgio Miescher and Dag Henrichsen, eds., *New Notes on the Kaoko* (Basel: P. Schlettwein Publishing, 2000).

29 Patricia Hayes, '"Cocky" Hahn and the "Black Venus": the making of a native commissioner in South West Africa, 1915–46', *Gender and History* 8, 3 (November 1996), pp. 364–392; Hayes, 'Northern exposures'.

30 Dag Henrichsen, ed., *A Glance at Our Africa: Facsimile Reprint of the South West News* (Basel: Basler Afrika Bibliographien, 1997); Marion Wallace, 'Looking at the locations: the ambiguities of urban photography' in Hartmann et al., eds., *The Colonising Camera*.

31 Vera Viditz-Ward, 'Alphonso Lisk-Carew: Creole photographer', *African Arts* 19, 1 (1995), pp. 46–51; David Killingray and Andrew Roberts, 'An outline history of photography in Africa to ca 1940', *History in Africa*, 16 (1989), pp. 197–208.

32 Nicholas Thomas, 'Introduction' in Nicholas Thomas and Diana Losche, eds., *Double Vision. Art Histories and Colonial Histories in the Pacific* (Cambridge: Cambridge University Press, 1999), p. 5.

33 Margo Timm, 'Transpositions: John Ndevasia Muafangejo and colonial photographs of King Mandume ya Ndemufayo' in Hartmann et al., eds., *The Colonising Camera*.

cultures in Namibia. It is always possible to colonise the colonising camera, though such subversions come with their own complications. In *The Colonising Camera*[34] and in 'Picturing the Past', we have attempted to set up a photographic paradigm that questions the representational strategies of both 'coloniser' and 'colonised', and shows they are complex, contradictory, at times even blurring into one another. We would argue this is because all parties are mutually engaged in what Hendrickson[35] has called 'a semiotic web whose implications are not completely controlled by any of us'.

REVISITING THE PHOTOGRAPHIC OCCASIONS

There is not necessarily a direct and instrumental link between colonial photographs and colonialism itself. Photographs of empty lands did not necessarily produce hundreds of white settlers;[36] photographs of Africans in 'savage' garb did not necessarily produce military expeditions and conquest.[37] Rather than such a direct causal and positivist link between politics and representation, we wish to suggest that the relationship is far more subtle, problematic and open-ended. It seems crucial to explore the constitutive processes that have gone into the making of such images. Stuart Hall has argued against the old, conventional view that '"things" . . . have a perfectly clear meaning, outside of how they are represented'. Rather, he states that representation enters into 'the very constitution of things'; it is 'as important as the economic or material "base" in shaping social subjects and historical events – not merely a reflection of the world after the event'.[38]

One constitutive process in the making of photographic images was the photographic equivalent of what Pels[39] has termed 'the ethnographic occasion'. These 'photographic occasions' were those 'real' incidents where people or landscapes or animals came before the lens of a camera, and their framed image was transposed on to glass plates or light-sensitive paper and then chemically developed into a print or a plate to produce the photographic analogue of the actual event. There were power relations, administrative contexts and discourses involved in these occasions and let us not forget the possibility of erotic agendas. These were central concerns of the exhibition and book *The Colonising Camera* and indeed of 'Picturing the Past', which also ran key photographs taken by those seeking to constitute a colonial order.

As these colonial photographic occasions are singled out, it becomes clear that there was huge diversity even within one genre.

34 Hartmann et al., eds., *The Colonising Camera*.

35 Hildi Hendrickson, *Clothing and Difference. Embodied Identities in Colonial and Post-Colonial Africa* (Durham and London: Duke University Press, 1996), p. 1.

36 Jeremy Silvester, 'Your space or mine? The photography of the Police Zone' in Hartmann et al., eds., *The Colonising Camera*.

37 We acknowledge that in many cases European publics were prepared visually beforehand for military campaigns (see Annie E. Coombes, *Reinventing Africa: Museums, Material Culture and Popular Imagination* [New Haven and London: Yale University Press, 1994], p.16), but in other cases it appears it was impossible to obtain photographs of African fighters prior to war – for obvious reasons. In the archive of the Thomas Cook travel organisation, for example, photographs and tourist viewing of 'Matabele warriors' in traditional garb were only taken *after* the destruction of Bulawayo and the defeat of Lobengula in the Anglo-Ndebele War of 1893 in present-day Zimbabwe. (See Thomas Cook and Son, travel brochure, *To Buluwayo. Programme of Personally conducted Tour to Buluwayo leaving London, April 14th; returning to London, September 11th, 1894*, London: Thomas Cook, 1894.) Thanks to Leslie Witz for supplying this reference. Numerous photographs of Zulu 'warriors' in the Killie Campbell Library of Africana and the South African Library in Cape Town, for example, were also taken after severe military defeats – not before. For dressed-up, posed Zulu and Xhosa warriors see Karel Schoeman, *The Face of the Country. A South African Family Album 1860–1910* (Cape Town: Human & Rousseau, 1996).

38 Stuart Hall, ed., *Representations. Cultural Representations and Signifying Practices* (London, Thousand Oaks CA and New Delhi, Milton Keynes: Sage, Open University, 1997), pp. 5-6.

39 Peter Pels, 'The construction of ethnographic occasions in late colonial Uluguru', *History and Anthropology* 8, 1–4 (1994), pp. 321–351.

PATRICIA HAYES, JEREMY SILVESTER AND WOLFRAM HARTMANN

There was a vast difference for example in what ethnographic photography produced at different times and in different contexts. When Chapman or Hodgson[40] took pictures of Namibians in what was then called Damaraland in the 1860s and 70s, the portrait figures show fluidity of identity and dress. But when Fourie or Hahn took pictures between 1920 and 30,[41] anthropometric and ethnographic influences become apparent in the attempts to fix identities and appearances. The shifts in convention in photographic representation and their pre-colonial, colonial and postcolonial frameworks need very careful historicisation.

The feedback that 'Picturing the Past' has made possible shows all too clearly the dangers of too-easy contextualisations, and of anchoring colonial photographs to received captions. The latter tends to overdetermine any reading of colonial photographs and certainly oversimplifies the politics of colonial perception. A case in point has been the publication of the Hahn photograph of an elderly man from western Owambo with three younger women, captioned 'Chief Muala of Uukwaluudhi with three of his daughters'. When it was run in 'Picturing the Past',[42] one of Muala's great-granddaughters took the picture to check with her grandmother Kuku Vivi Nangombe, Muala's youngest daughter. She was able to confirm that it was Muala, but none of the females were his daughters – they were simply women present on the photographic occasion who were included with Muala because the photographer considered they were sufficiently picturesque in their 'tribal' gear and had representative hairstyles of that region.[43] The feedback again intimates the deep importance of identification to communities among whom colonial pictures were taken. It also particularises and narrativises an occasion which produced an ethnographic photograph that is not as royal as it seems, and had definite genericising overtones.

The unpredictability of photographs brought out of the archive is also apparent when different academic disciplines are involved in their readings. This in large part arises from the 'messy contingency of the photograph'[44] which means that neither the purpose behind photographs – nor their readings – can be reduced to the inevitable, the instrumental or the functional. A social historian might be expected to privilege 'evidence' and 'context', or the art historian form over content. But photographs cannot easily be contained by disciplines. Even the most rigorous of social history, for example, a commentary by Marion Wallace on urban Windhoek, talks of the photograph that most represents settler fears: an image of black women smoking pipes

40 Silvia Kliem, 'The eye as narrator in the nineteenth-century expedition writing and photography of James Chapman, 1860-1864' (MA thesis, University of the Western Cape, 1995); Karel Schoeman, The Face of the Country.

41 Brent Harris, 'Photography in colonial discourse: the making of "the other" in southern Africa, c. 1850–1950' in Hartmann et al., eds., The Colonising Camera; Hayes, 'Northern exposures'; Michael Bollig, 'Framing Kaokoland'.

42 The Namibian, 30 July 1999.

43 We thank Vivian Nangombe for undertaking the journey to show her grandmother this photograph and providing us with this information (personal communication Vivian Nangombe, 15 September 1999). This feedback was published in the 'Voiceback' in The Namibian of 12 November 1999.

44 Sekula, 'The body and the archive', p. 353.

Picturing The Past

MWAALA GWA NASHILONGO:
Omukwaniilwa Of Uukwaluudhi

VILHO SHIGWEDHA

MWAALE Gwa Nashilongo is believed to have been born sometime between the years 1870 to 1880, during the reign of Niilenge ya Amukwa.

Mwaala's mother was Nekulu Lyaamwaama, a sister of Iita ya Nalitoke who was the ruler of Uukwaluudhi immediately before Mwaala came to the throne.

Mwaala's mother thus belonged to the ruling clan, the Aakwanambwa, and therefore her sons were potential heirs to the throne.

Mwaala had a twin brother called Anghome Nashilongo who died at a young age. In earlier times the birth of twins in the ruling clan was viewed as an omen of bad luck. It is therefore alleged that twins were killed either by forcing sand into their mouths or abandoning them in the bush. By Mwaala's time this tradition was reported to have ended, but there was still a taboo on a twin being able to rule as Aakwaniilwa (plural).

Furthermore, as Dr Williams argues, the mother of twins ". . . would no longer be wife to the king, but would be given to a subject" (Williams, 1991: 188). It is said that at the time of Mwaala's birth it was still the practice for all baby boys who were born to women from the ruling clan to be killed, the idea being to prevent the emergence of aspiring successors who might lead opposition to the Omukwaniilwa. Expectant women would therefore often try to conceal their pregnancies and, if they gave birth to a male child, try all sorts of clever tactics to save their

In a book published in the 1920s this photograph was meant to show 'Chief Muala of Uukwaluudhi and three of his daughters'. However in a recent publication the same photograph bore the caption 'King Tshaanika of Ongandjera with three of his wives'. In the National Archives of Namibia the people are not named at all ! Can readers help us by confirming whether this is really a photograph of Mwaala Gwa Nashilongo ?

sons.

The most common of these was to try and sneak their baby out of Uukwaluudhi and to seek refuge in a neighbouring kingdom where the child might grow up in safety.

Mwaala Gwa Nashilongo was therefore fortunate as, although he was male he was also a twin and so because of the taboo it was believed that he posed no threat and no attempt was made to kill him as a child. Mwaala was able to grow up with his mother and herded cattle at different cattle posts such as Omakongo, Oshini and Ondeka. Mwaala's mother and her sisters developed a great respect for him and organised several secret meetings in which they discussed what they believed to be the injustice of the existing laws in the kingdom of Uukwaluudhi.

The women were particularly unhappy about the power granted to rulers to kill baby boys.

Mwaala's mother and other women from the ruling clan believed that if he became the Omukwaniilwa he would be different and would reform this law. The women made a plan to make sure that Mwaala would succeed Iita ya Nalitoke as Omukwaniilwa. At first they argued with the people that the law that a twin could never lead the kingdom should be abandoned. Next, according to oral accounts, the women secretly plotted - without the knowledge of Mwaala himself - to poison Iita ya Nalitoke. The plan was successful and Mwaala was invited to return from the cattle post and told that he had been chosen to be the new ruler of Uukwaluudhi.

The story around Mwaala's rise to power suggests the ways in which traditional laws were not static, but changed over time. However the conspiracy by the women appears to be a

unique example of women organising themselves to overthrow a ruler and change the laws of a kingdom. Or perhaps readers know of other stories from the past where women also intervened dramatically in pre-colonial politics ?

[Pre-colonial Communities of Southwest Africa: A History of Owambo

Kingdoms, 1600-1920 by Dr F-N Williams, 1991 is available from the National Archives of Namibia and all good bookshops. If you would like to read more of Vilho Shigwedha's account of the history of Uukwaluudhi, based on oral history interviews, it should be available later this year. The *Namibian History Trust will be publishing a set of History Research Papers written by final year history students at the University of Namibia and this will include a paper by Vilho Shigwedha.]*

Figure 3: 'Picturing the Past', 30 July 1999.

together in the Old Location.[45] This settler affect is new territory for historians, a paradigm of the emotions:

> The women in the photograph, dressed in the trappings of 'civilisation' but inhabiting squalid conditions, exhibit a kind of 'dumb insolence' which a white audience would have found unnerving . . . to a colonist in the 1920s, they would have been 'primitives' incapable of becoming fully civilised, carrying within themselves the hidden menaces of disease, disorder and uncleanliness, and all the more threatening for living in such close proximity to whites. This photograph encapsulates, it seems to me, the essence of white fear of the colonised.[46]

This is not to say that this is the only reading possible, or the most authoritative. To a different audience viewing this photograph in a small exhibition about the Old Location set up in a Windhoek shopping centre, it was the politics of naming people that really mattered. Balked by the age of this particular photograph (taken circa 1928) which hampered personal identification, viewers then attempted to read the ethnic markers that would place the women in a specific section of the Old Location and concluded that the dress and pipe-smoking signalled this group to be Damara-speaking.[47]

Different meanings are created by different readers who bring diverse reference systems with them. Readings might shuttle between photography's dual potentialities: between positivism and fantasy, between evidence and enigma, between truth-claims and lies 'that tell a truth', and between photographs that denote and those that connote. Rohde[48] argues that these are the fixed and open readings to which photographs lend themselves. Meaning is derived from the reading of visual imagery at many levels, one of which is almost purely sensate and subjective, harking back to an embodied, nonlinguistic experience of being which is a fundament of perception. This innate ability to lend cohesion to the world of appearances also gives rise to what has been termed elsewhere the optical or ocular unconscious,[49] where meaning, language and vision become conflated. The naturalising tendency of the eye is explained by Kliem[50] as 'the biological ease of vision which naturalises what is in fact a cultural construct'. She argues that the eye of the photographer is socially and culturally conditioned to seeing things in certain ways, thus prompting a particular framing of a scene or people.

How do we then explain the compulsion by the various respondents – from a public starved of images of its past – to put all their reading

45 Wallace, 'Looking at the locations', p. 136.

46 Ibid., p. 136.

47 Thanks to Sarafina Biwa, Ouvrou Dax, Eunice Gustavo and Sylvester Griffiths for their participation in this exhibition at Wernhil shopping mall and their interaction with shoppers.

48 Rick Rohde, 'How we see each other: subjectivity, photography and ethnographic re/vision' in Hartmann et al., eds., *The Colonising Camera*.

49 Walter Benjamin, *Illuminations* (London: Fontana Press, 1973), p. 230.

50 Kliem, 'The eye as narrator', p. 2.

energies into identification above all else? It would seem that audiences seek to give the photographs their own denotations, and fix primarily on the indexical traces. It represents a postcolonial empirical challenge to the system (or non-system) of ordering and identifying the photographs that are emerging from Namibia's colonial archive.

This might be considered ironic when photography is historically embedded in another empiricism. In the late nineteenth century, the 'metrical accuracy of the camera' formed part of a 'truth apparatus'[51] being forged by science and police work in modernising states in Western Europe. In colonial contexts, optical empiricism in the form of anthropometric photography offered a new form of imperial knowledge about colonial peoples.[52] As Landau[53] suggestively puts it, the anthropometric photograph was 'cousin to the police mug shot'. Mofokeng[54] argues that such photographs constituted 'authoritative knowledge', which played 'no small part in the subjection of those populations to imperial power'.

The 'realism' of the photograph has moved in the course of the century, carrying potentially new denotations for viewers which also shift the connotations in relation to the picture. The genericisation and objectification involved in photographing severed heads of prisoners-of-war for ostensible scientific research, or in preparing ethnographic group pictures for government publications in the early twentieth century, are altered when figures can be identified in the late 1990s. These are different agendas of visibility.[55] It seems to be the content of the photograph which draws Namibian viewers, and where this is recognisable it animates the present.[56] As Poignant observes from the Australian context and community she entered with her husband's photographs taken forty years earlier: 'photographs established continuities of self and of family, and seemingly made genealogies visible'.[57]

ON ARCHIVES AND SCOPOPHOBIA

It is not only the observer who brings reference systems, subjectivity and knowledge to looking at archive photographs brought into circulation. There have been many previous sets of filters that have mediated the photographs that have been run before the public in 'Picturing the Past'. Attempts have been made to identify the layers of selection – the inclusions and exclusions – through which the photographs have passed, and the paths along which they have travelled. From the photographer's background, to the photographic occasion in which the

51 Sekula, 'The body and the archive', pp. 352–353.

52 M. Banta and C. Hinsley, *From Site to Sight: Anthropology, Photography and the Power of Imagery* (Cambridge MA: Peabody, 1986).

53 Paul Landau, 'With camera and gun in South Africa: inventing the image of Bushmen, ca 1880–1940' in Pippa Skotnes, ed., *Miscast: Negotiating the Presence of the Bushmen* (Cape Town: University of Cape Town Press, 1996), p. 132.

54 Santu Mofokeng, 'The black photo album/look at me: 1890–1900', *Nka: Journal of Contemporary African Art* (Spring 1996), p. 56.

55 Elizabeth Edwards, 'Essay' in Jorma Puranen, *Imaginary Homecomings*, p. 42.

56 Roslyn Poignant with Axel Poignant, *Encounter at Nagalarramba* (Canberra: National Library of Australia, 1996), p. 15.

57 Ibid., p. 12.

PATRICIA HAYES, JEREMY SILVESTER AND WOLFRAM HARTMANN

picture was taken, to the way photographic subjects presented themselves to the camera, to the technical production of the print, to the private or public circuits into which the image was inserted, to the ultimate fate of the picture – whether as a framed family portrait, a book illustration, part of a forgotten collection that is destroyed or an item in the photographic files of an archive – it is important where possible to contextualise, historicise and theorise the processes by which the photograph has come before the public gaze (or not).

After the technical production of an original print, a wide range of possibilities exists for the reproduction, dissemination, collection and storage of images. During each stage images can be recaptioned, decontextualised and recontextualised. At every level of selection or exclusion, important agendas, needs and desires are at work. One of the most powerful sites of selection and exclusion is, of course, the official body of received photographs from the past in the form of the 'national' or state archive, from which images filter (or do not filter) into the public gaze.

A constant problem encountered in trawling through the emerging literature on visual studies is its Euro- and American-centrism. Most work assumes that the paradigms of the modern state apply, an assumption that needs the kind of interrogation put succinctly by Megan Vaughan:[58] 'Foucault in Africa?' Thus Roberts talks of 'the rigid archival ordering of images';[59] and Sekula's classic essay on Galton's and Bertillon's archives, in London and Paris respectively, takes the order for granted.[60] Such impressive metropolitan archiving allows one to problematise their purpose and – as recent exhibitions and literature show – the contradictions and products of their classificatory systems.[61] But what happens when the photographic archive has not been organised on longstanding bureaucratic principles (as is the case in Namibia) but has been assembled unevenly, haphazardly, anonymously – and is not easily rendered up for scrutiny, not through design but through lack of prioritisation? An entire new historiography has emerged about the metropolitan and imperial archive,[62] but the Namibian case forces us to ask about the nature of the peripheral colonial archive.

A substantial proportion of the photographs in the public picture archive of the National Archives of Namibia did not reach this institution as part of a larger body of images, such as a collection or government's legally regulated deposits. On the contrary, a great many of the images were handpicked and reproduced from private albums, magazines and books. And while these photographs are quite remark-

58 Megan Vaughan, *Curing their Ills: Colonial Power and African Illness* (Cambridge: Polity Press, 1991), p. 8.

59 Chrissie Iles and Russell Roberts, *In Visible Light: Photography and Classification in Art, Science and the Everyday* (Oxford: Museum of Modern Art, 1997), p. 9.

60 Sekula, 'The body and the archive'.

61 Iles and Russell Roberts, *In Visible Light*; Ruth Charity, Christopher Pinney, Roslyn Poignant and Chris White, eds., *The Impossible Science of Being: Dialogues between Anthropology and Photography* (London: The Photographers' Gallery, 1995); Skotnes, ed., *Miscast: Negotiating the Presence of the Bushmen* (Cape Town: University of Cape Town Press, 1996).

62 Michel Foucault, *The Archaeology of Knowledge* (New York: Pantheon, 1972); John Tagg, *The Burden of Representation. Essays on Photographs and Histories* (Amherst: University of Massachusetts Press, 1988); Sekula, 'The body and the archive'; Thomas Richards, *The Imperial Archive: Knowledge and the Fantasy of Empire* (London and New York: Verso, 1993).

able in scope and depth, constituting a significant picture archive of 15 000 items,[63] their route through the institution has often resulted in the destruction of information concerning their provenance.

In fact, there exist two archives of pictures in one official archival institution. The one archive is publicly and directly accessible, catalogued and computerised on a par with the documentary archival holdings. But the other (and bigger) archive is the repository from which the images in the public collection were culled. In theory, access to this repository – mainly private and other acquisitions stored in the archive basement – is not in question. But the form in which these private acquisitions are catalogued does not lead the researcher directly to the photographs. Moreover, even the highly skilled and professional researcher tends to assume that the public collection is the one and only to be consulted for all purposes of visual documentation.

Such transfer as there has been from hidden repository to public photo library has entailed a number of problems. Whereas, in general, great pains are taken to conserve documentary material in its structural, chronological, political and historical context – they are dated and classified according to government department, agency, company or other source – the pictures in this archive are in most cases doubly or trebly removed from such contextualisations. Not only were images actively removed (even torn) from albums or collections for the purpose of professional studio reproduction and frequently not returned to their original place in the acquisitions, but they were also removed from whatever caption or text went with the original print. Then, apart from the inevitable decrease in quality through photographic reproduction of the original, in all cases there is the additional problem of unrecorded format changes: for example, postcards were not reproduced in postcard format, and instances of huge cropping took place. All of the above amounts to a massive dehistoricisation and decontextualisation which, if it had occurred with documents, would create a massive scandal.

To spell out some implications: images travelled in different circuits according to whether they were produced as postcards, for example, or were part of a private collection in a family album. As a postcard or a collectable, many people would have seen the picture and it would have had an impact on public perceptions of a place, an event or the people photographed, especially if there was a caption with the original. Large numbers of Germans, for example, were exposed to a famous postcard depicting the beating of a man[64] because it travelled between Namibia and Germany as a postcard. Mechanisms of exotici-

63 That this collection exists at all is due to the efforts of Christel Stern and Sally Harper who initiated the systematic collection of photographs in the archives in the early 1970s, and whose work was continued by the late Brigitte Lau and fellow staff (especially Everon Kloppers) more recently.

64 Hartmann et al., eds., *The Colonising Camera*, p. 42.

sation and eroticisation relied largely on the construction of images in photography and the percolation of these to the public through postcards, books and magazines. An image culled from a private photo album, however, would have had different audience connotations.

Original captions and locations are crucial in piecing together the dynamics of colonial representation, and the latter's circuits of dissemination and reproduction. It is necessary to trace these processes and, ideally, the archive facilitates this. It is clear that different selections of photographs from the archive have been presented in different collections or albums, and that even the same photograph may have been presented in a variety of ways – like that of Samuel Maherero. The Herero leader posed, while in colonial favour, in a German-style uniform, for a famous photograph 'cited' in several German colonial texts; in 1923 the picture was prominently cited again at Maherero's funeral in Okahandja by his followers, in a remobilisation of 'Herero' identity in the aftermath of war, genocide and exile.[65] The way in which particular photographs have been circulated is a history of selection, distribution and interpretation that has constantly shifted.

The lack of contextual information makes many of the stored images in Namibia's archives, if not worthless, then extremely difficult to assess and evaluate – unless recirculated among an expert or public audience which might recognise certain things or people in them. Very often the name of the photographer, the studio and the place of publication (often the only clue as to the date of a photograph) have been lost in the process of selection and reproduction. These archive processes have simultaneously created the visual archive but also undermined it, engendering a body of visual material but ripping apart the contexts in which it arrived at the institution. Sassoon has outlined a similar problem in Australian visual archives, and explains it in this way:

> [M]any institutions collect and document their photograph collections as image banks of individual items rather than archival collections – that is the image content is seen as the most important feature, above who created it, why it was used or its history of ownership over time. When viewed from the perspective of the mere image, most contextual information surrounding the photograph through its previous lives and at the time that it entered the institution is lost – contextual information which may be seen as ephemeral by some, but which is critical to understanding the ongoing and shifting meanings which surround photographs.[66]

65 Wolfram Hartmann, 'Funerary photographs: the funeral of a chief' in Hartmann et al., eds., *The Colonising Camera*.

66 Joanna Sassoon, 'Writing histories of photographs as a history of multiples: the imaginary picture of Kimberley', paper presented at the African Studies Association Conference 'New African Perspectives', Perth, Australia, November 1999, p. 3.

In general one could argue that this is the result of unthinking scopophobia, so seemingly inherent in academic and official institutions with their privileging of and, indeed, fixation on the word. We use the term scopophobia – literally translated as fear of the picture or fear of the view – to explain the dismissal and neglect with which historians and archivists have viewed photographs as historical documents or resources. History's disciplinary leanings towards positivism and empiricism appear to have encouraged the view that photographs represent *prima facie* evidence only: what is in the picture is seen as a direct and true rendering of reality as it existed at the moment when the camera shutter was operated. This may have tempted archivists and historians alike to define the photograph as a timeless document that, after a minimum of identification, needed no further context, social background or ideological framework to be understood and creatively redeployed. Hence its positioning in the economy of the archive and its merely illustrative use (if at all) by historians.

The problems in the Namibian photograph archive point directly to one of the most interesting broader features of this peripheral territory's colonial history: that processes of producing knowledge here were very strained and ambivalent and did not necessarily feed into the colony itself. For this archive, applying 'Foucault in Africa' is tricky. Sekula's and Tagg's elegant appraisals of the modern state's appropriations of visual knowledge are of limited use to us here: as Stoler[67] argues with regard to Foucault, these analyses are too encapsulated in the European metropoles. The Namibian archive suggests that the circuits of power and knowledge are plainly running on different courses and greatly complicated by the peculiar 'tensions of empire'[68] generated in this part of southern Africa.

Gordon[69] has argued for the outright antipathy of most white settlers in the Namibian context to the acquisition of knowledge about 'the native'. Anti-intellectual tendencies were strong, and created tensions for those few in Namibia who sought to produce a range of knowledges about the territory and its inhabitants. Without the outside audience of the League of Nations, it is doubtful that the little that was published on ethnography and history in the 1920s would have seen the light of day. Moreover, as the South West Africa Administration grasped the importance of publicising the territory and their policies within it for international consumption (and to attract more settlers), the tendency was to fawn over foreign and South African expeditions and scientists and offer support in exchange for Namibia being 'put on the map'. Materials produced by such expedi-

67 Ann Stoler, 'State racism and the education of desires: a colonial reading of Foucault', guest lecture, Interdisciplinary Conference on Gender and Colonialism, University of the Western Cape, Cape Town, January 1997.

68 Ann Stoler and Frederick Cooper, 'Between metropole and colony: rethinking a research agenda' in Frederick Cooper and Ann Stoler, eds., *Tensions of Empire. Colonial Cultures in a Bourgeois World* (Berkeley, Los Angeles and London: University of California Press, 1997).

69 Robert Gordon, 'Vagrancy, law and "shadow knowledge": the internal pacification of colonial Namibia, 1915–1939' in Patricia Hayes, Jeremy Silvester, Marion Wallace and Wolfram Hartmann, eds., *Namibia under South African Rule: Mobility and Containment, 1915–1946* (London, Windhoek and Athens OH: James Currey, Out of Africa and Ohio University Press, 1998).

PATRICIA HAYES, JEREMY SILVESTER AND WOLFRAM HARTMANN

tions did not necessarily make their way into any Namibian archive.

There is, obviously, a direct relationship between the peculiarities of Namibia's visual archive and certain features of South African archives. The presence of large colonial fragments from Namibia – photograph collections deposited in the 'metropole' by officials returning home from service in the territory[70] – often produces a curious result in that visual studies engaging with early photography in South Africa use predominantly Namibian material.[71] Not only has the colonial history of photography in South Africa itself been neglected until recently, but the unquestioned presence of Namibian photographic collections in South African archives has led to a failure to examine the colonial nature of such archiving and, indeed, of some of the scholarship using these collections. The visual archives in South Africa appear to need their own deep ethnographies to disentangle their historical layers and patent displacements, and to complement a current theoretical impetus in visual studies.

The establishment of 'collections' of artefacts, documents and research in Namibia entailed considerable struggle.[72] Some of the most poignant complaints about the lack of a national intellectual effort and a concomitant failure to feed national institutions such as museums and archives came from the territory's Medical Officer in the 1920s, Dr Louis Fourie. Fourie was a dedicated student of ethnography and carried out a systematic anthropometric photography of 'Bushman' groups in eastern Namibia. Fourie lamented the haemorrhage of research material and knowledge out of the territory, which he regarded as the plundering of Namibia's incipient heritage. He was very critical of the opportunism of colleagues and seniors who, it seemed, exploited and plagiarised local intellectual efforts (including his own).[73] It is ironic then that ultimately, like so many of his colleagues, Fourie left his entire collection of papers and photographs to a South African institution.[74]

There appear therefore to be two related sets of questions that might help to bring the Namibian visual archive into focus. One is the colonial problem, or the problem of multiple colonialisms that have extracted materials from the territory for South African, German or other international archives (including the USA), leaving no traces in Namibia or at best inferior copies. Colonial officials themselves were not required to deposit photographs in the same way as documents: with rare exceptions, official photographs tended to survive in Namibia only if they were published. A second set of questions hinges around the application of the metropolitan models of visual regimes, photo-

70 To name a few collections, the Palgrave albums and Chapman's stereotypes are deposited in the South African Library; the Dickman collection and many ethnographic photographs in the South African Museum; the Fourie and other collections in Johannesburg; albums with Resident Commissioner Manning's photographs in the Killie Campbell Africana Library in Durban.

71 This was very striking at the 1999 conference entitled 'Encounters with Photography' held at the South African Museum where most of the nineteenth and early twentieth-century studies were based on photographs from Namibia. See website at www.museums.org.za/sam/conf/enc/index.htm.

72 It was largely to this end that the independent South West Africa Scientific Society was formed in 1925.

73 National Archives of Namibia A450 vol. 4 1/29, Fourie to Hahn, 27 April 1928.

74 Louis Fourie and C. H. L. Hahn, who collaborated in producing *The Native Tribes of South West Africa* (C. H. L. Hahn, Heinrich Vedder and Louis Fourie, *The Native Tribes of South West Africa* [London: Frank Cass, 1928]), are probably the most coherent ethnographic photographers of the first decades of South African rule in Namibia. Photographs by both were used in government publications, Hahn's over a longer period given that he outstayed Fourie in the SWA Administration by many years. Both men kept the main corpus of their photographic output as private collections. Fourie's collection was submitted to the University of the Witwatersrand after his retirement and is now housed in the MuseumAfrica in Johannesburg. Archivists from the National Archives of Namibia persuaded Rodney Hahn in South Africa to lend the bulk of his father's collection to the national institution where it can be found among Hahn's accessioned private papers. We are indebted to Ann Wanless for information concerning the Fourie collection, and to Rodney Hahn, Dag Henrichsen, Carl Schlettwein and the late Brigitte Lau for information concerning the Hahn collection.

graphy and archiving in a marginal colonial region such as Namibia.

The use of 'classic' visual surveillance for social regulation was to be found in the compounds in Lüderitz and other diamond-mining areas to check smuggling, which worked in conjunction with state medical inspection systems and other invasions of the body effected by mining controls from the 1930s at least. But such technologies – especially the panoptical system – seem to have been confined within a contract labour orbit to particular mines. For identification purposes, German colonial law required Namibian workers to wear a metal disc round the neck, and later South African law required all African males in the Police Zone to carry a pass. By the 1950s, passbooks carried fingerprints – but still not photographs. These mechanisms devised for the control of labour and rural–urban movement require much further research.[75]

Beyond this there may well be a collapse of any Benthamite model backed up by a systematic visual archive. What does it mean for instance when the visual *modus operandi* is suggested, not so much by the panopticon, but the panorama? What does it mean when there seems to be an overwhelming visualisation through the panning of a camera lens over vast landscapes with few people in them? There is a sense in which the colonial photographs housed in the archive represent a seeing out over the territory rather than a seeing into its peoples. This is a system of scanning, rather than surveillance: visual appropriations of nature and groups of people rather than effective visual control. Prior to the opening up of political struggles from the 1960s, Namibians were never systematically photographed by the state for identification. At earlier stages, however, select groups of them were photographed for ethnographic and anthropometrical purposes. The making of a body of ethnographic knowledge of a social or ethnic collectivity is not the same as producing citizens with their mug shots in individual identity documents and police records. This creation of collective identities arguably led to Namibians being predominantly subjects rather than citizens – with little access to legal systems and a prevalent experience of indirect rule[76] – though such a conclusion should of course be carefully qualified and debated.

We have already seen how the problem in coming across Namibian photographs deposited in libraries, museums and archives is the way their subjects were constituted as collectivities, representing generic groups with generic qualities. Anonymity or poor identification was often the rule. It is only now that people are beginning to attach names and stories to figures in these pictures.

75 See Silvester et al., 'Introductory Overview' in Hayes et al., eds., *Namibia under South African Rule*.

76 Mahmood Mamdani, *Citizen and Subject. Contemporary Africa and the Legacy of Late Colonialism* (Kampala, Cape Town and London: Fountain, David Philip and James Currey, 1996).

120

'PICTURING THE PAST'

Every fortnight since early 1997, the weekend supplement to the popular Friday edition of *The Namibian* newspaper has run a column called 'Picturing the Past', which features all manner of photographs from the archives. Such initiatives, of course, have many precedents in social history[77] and indeed in the South African media – the *New Nation* for example ran columns with old photographs. But in this most recent Namibian case, the column urged the public to contact the newspaper, or a curator based at the local university, should they have any information or opinion to advance about the photographs. Some of this feedback was in turn printed in the next issue of the series. In a practical sense, this has enabled access to (and made public) those private knowledges that have identified and contextualised a number of photographs in the archive. Thus photographs in the state archive, with captions which literally reduced individuals to representatives of a colonially defined 'type', are acquiring new layers of meaning and, to some extent, being recaptioned.

The implications go much further, however. By shifting the medium, the archive has moved out into a much more public space where, instead of being stored, it circulates along the paths of a national newspaper. The photograph in this medium contributes towards a remembering and an historical awareness on a wide scale, as against the colonial archive, which has dismembered the 'evidence' and put away its component parts into boxes and filing cabinets. The newspaper thus provides an interface between unofficial knowledges and the photographic archive of the past as it is presented in this form, and it offers a site of exchange.

Recognition of people or places in the images (the signs in the representational system) has led to responses. One might say that the photographs trigger 'memory', leading respondents to renarrate the past, often in a form they state they learned from older relatives, particularly when the photographs have featured tragic-heroic figures such as Mandume ya Ndemufayo, the subject of many popular oral histories. There appears to be a very strong connection between visual history and oral history, with the former galvanising the latter in our exercise.

Of course, 'Picturing the Past' is by no means the only vehicle through which images from the archive now travel into different public and private spaces in postcolonial Namibia. In another case, a historian's work started in oral tradition and moved into visual representation. Vilho Tshilongo is a former migrant worker from Uukwambi who has established himself as an important historian of northern

77 Raphael Samuel, *Theatres of Memory* (London and New York: Verso, 1994), pp. 337-340.

78 Interview with Vilho Tshilongo at Elim, Uukwambi, 25 September 1989. We thank Laban Shapange for bringing examples of Vilho Tshilongo's recent work to our attention.

79 This image first appeared in Rossing Uranium Limited, *History Makers. 24 Colourful Characters from SWA/Namibia's Past* (Windhoek: Rossing Uranium Limited, 1983), p. 49.

80 The text with Mandume's picture can be translated as follows:

'Mandume yaNdemufayo. 1. . . . the shape of his ears is like a tray, like Ondjiva woven baskets. 2. He is a forest bird that fears no difficult obstacles. He is Mbangula [a bird with a strong beak that it uses to cut holes in all types of trees] that cuts open trunks of hard wood to seek shelter and protection for its offspring. He is Mbangula yAmekulo yaShekupe yAmukwaya. 3. Mandume take your sword to fight the whites. While you wait for the supply of ammunition. The white men want to dispossess you of your land. They want to take over your throne, the reign of your land that you have rightfully inherited from your predecessor Haimbili, your grandfather. They are not happy that you act in the spirit of those who ruled this land before you, like King Namhadi. 4. This is the land that had never allowed a single white man to overnight on it, except when he was trading liquor. 5. He is an enormous man, full of strength and stamina. Stones shake and tremble to his movements. 6. The sound as if of a knobkerry striking against the ground emerges from the forest, as if Epamba [a bird that produces a type of pounding sound with its wings, similar to when a person strikes a knobkerry hard against the ground] has laid eggs in the forest. 7. He is the force that cracks hard stones, which are believed to be immovable. He is Mandume waKandjibi Hamunyela, waShekupe Hamukwaya [probably Mandume's sisters' names]. When he moves the sound of his movement shakes the unshakeable. 8. He describes his own character by stating that every fig tree is 'Ongete' [a kind of thorn bush very hard to destroy and very resistant to damage caused by soil, termites and water – most oshiKwanyama-speaking people use ongete poles to construct traditional houses because they last longer], every 'Omuve' [a tree that bears sweet yellowish edible fruits the size of groundnuts] is 'Omoonde' [camelthorn],

Figure 4: Tshilongo's leaflet on Mandume ya Ndemufayo.

Namibia, collecting and reproducing praise poems, oral traditions and oral histories from his base as caretaker of a local secondary school.[78] He has moved into visual reproduction of published photographs and hand-drawn copies of photographs, which are then embedded in a one-page history with his typed text. These pages are photocopied, laminated and sold for N$10 (ten rand) with a clip for displaying the picture on walls or noticeboards.

The iconic figure of Mandume ya Ndemufayo is prominent among these. The image of this king is particularly fascinating because the copy Tshilongo published is from a drawing based on an archive photograph of the dead king's body, where the king's physiognomy was redrawn to look as though it were alive.[79] From its base in the mortuary photograph, the hand-traced image takes on an expressive function that repositions and in this case refigures the visual archive, especially through the very wide circulation that Tshilongo's marketing gives this image in northern Namibia today.[80]

In all this, the relationship between memory, oral history and visuality is dynamic and uneven. Memory is not a passive storage system. Nor is the archive, and neither memory nor the archive should be fetishised for the imputed truths they carry: memory's emotional/popular truth, on the one hand, and the archive's objective/bureaucratic truth on the other hand. Samuel writes that memory is conditioned, that it bears the mediated 'impress of experience' and is 'stamped with the ruling passions of its time'.[81] In an even more dense and suggestive vein, Kracauer calls the fragmented assets included in memory the monogram, which 'condenses the name into a single graphic figure that is meaningful as an ornament'.[82]

Both these authors explicitly refer to the ineluctable visuality of memory. Samuel pointedly cites Freud: 'the unconscious mind, splitting, telescoping, displacing and projecting, transposes incidents from one time register to another and materializes thought in imagery'. Kracauer intriguingly compares memory-images with photography, and argues that their visualities are quite opposed:

> Memories are retained because of their significance for that person. Thus they are organized according to a principle that is essentially different from the organizing principle of photography. Photography grasps what is given as a spatial (or temporal) continuum; memory-images retain what is given only insofar as it has significance. Since what is significant is not reducible to either merely spatial or merely temporal terms, memory-images are at odds with photographic representation.[83]

Kracauer insists that from the perspective of memory, 'photography appears as a jumble that consists partly of garbage'. Compared with memory, he states, 'In a photograph a person's history is buried as if under a layer of snow.'[84]

Photography may be no more than a shell compared with the memory-image, but it is enough to hook on to, or provide an association, because it 'conjures up anew a disintegrated unity'.[85] Perhaps it is the very disparity between photography and memory that is at times so productive. It triggers a narrative effort to try to mend the breach between the fragmented parts – between the figure (haunting the memory-image) and the shell (photography) or the effigy (the photographic archive). As Feldman argues, it is in oral history that the

The photograph that allegedly shows South African soldiers displaying Mandume's corpse.

Figure 5: 'Picturing the Past', 20 June 1997.

its thorn-ends like sharpened swords [which could be very harmful in any provocative situation and to barefooted people, especially when handled carelessly]. No guns have been received yet from Naholo's salt pans. White intruders will get us by surprise. It is now high time to reason that we should expect their intrusion soon. Can't we see the dark cloud of dust over Nambala's house? We must learn from Martin kaDhikwa's mistakes, the King of Ondonga. He allowed the whites to settle in Ondonga, unchallenged, because he was caught unaware.'

Translated and annotated by Vilho Shigwedha, History Facilitator, University of Namibia Oshakati campus.

81 Samuel, *Theatres of Memory*, p. x.

82 Kracauer, 'Photography', p. 426.

83 Ibid., p. 425.

84 Ibid., p. 426.

85 Ibid., p. 431.

fragments are reassembled, that a new body is woven through language.[86] The juxtaposition between photograph and stored knowledge of the past sets in motion a process of re-cognition, materialising as language: a narrative release suffused with intellect and emotion.

It is what photography does with time (as well as space) that also hooks the viewer. 'Picturing the Past' is frequently positioned in the newspaper facing another page of contemporary photographs called 'Seen Around'. In the random assemblage from recent weddings, birthdays and parties, each person is individually identified. The juxtaposition of this column with 'Picturing the Past' seems to heighten the reader-viewer's sense of the anonymities of the archive pictures and to power the motivation of those contacting the paper to position, absorb and articulate these old faces within a framework of memory.

We have made reference earlier to Freud's contention that memory materialises language and thought as images, and to Kracauer's argument that memory-images congeal around *the figure*. Because the shell of the figure is in the photographs, it is possible to look for *the figure* in the archive – to mine its visual holdings which have different bearings on the processes of people's memories than written documents. To address visual holdings is not so much to refigure the archive: it is literally to *figure* it.

RECONSTITUTING THE SPACES: WINDHOEK'S OLD LOCATION AND THE CASSINGA MASSACRE

Editions of 'Picturing the Past' which have dealt with Windhoek's Old Location have produced a series of complex, ongoing responses. When images of the Warmgat Band and others appeared in stages, readers telephoned the History Department at the University of Namibia to urge the publicisation of more Old Location material.[87] Students in the Department's History Society responded by setting up a display of over one hundred photographs for two different public audiences in Windhoek: shoppers at the busy Wernhil mall on a Saturday morning (mentioned above), and the congregation of Bethel church in Katutura on a Sunday afternoon (a congregation that included many former residents of the Old Location). At both sites the students elicited and recorded the comments of those who came forward to view the uncaptioned images. Texts were provided by the viewers, who suggested their own personalised captions: 'This was my first boyfriend'; 'That is the house where I grew up. I used to walk down this road to school.'[88]

86 Allen Feldman, *Formations of Violence: The Narrative of the Body and Political Terror in Northern Ireland* (Chicago: Chicago University Press, 1991), p. 10.

87 The Old Location in Windhoek shared the fate of many similar black urban settlements in neighbouring South Africa when it was demolished in 1959–68 and its residents forcibly removed.

The first feedback on Old Location pictures published in 'Picturing the Past' came from Peter Katangolo and Victoria Uukunde, especially concerning the Warmgat Band, during interviews with Jeremy Silvester, Windhoek, 1997.

88 Sarafina Biwa, Ouvrou Dax, Eunice Gustavo and Sylvester Griffiths deserve special acknowledgement for their work on this Old Location project and for recording viewers' comments.

PATRICIA HAYES, JEREMY SILVESTER AND WOLFRAM HARTMANN

The column's tendency to highlight themes and spaces that are visually underrepresented in the photograph library of the National Archives has encouraged people to come forward with photographs from their private archives. Families living in the black townships of Namibia have kept their own collections of studio portraits, townscapes (notably Swakopmund) and informal family shots. A set of pictures depicting the 'old location' in the coastal town of Swakopmund during the South African period has now been deposited in the National Archives, whose existing collection had dwelt exclusively on the German buildings of the town. Another collection of over forty photographs of Windhoek's Old Location was donated by a German photographer, Otto Hinrichs, who had served as a photographic apprentice in the city during the crucial years of 1959–1960.

It is the publication of colonial images in the newspaper that has led to people communicating information about these private holdings. Until this point, few such images made their way into the National Archives. From their unofficial sites they have begun to challenge the assumption of a colonial or settler monopoly of photographic history. Thus the process of airing the archives has in itself begun to generate a new archive and shift the nature of 'national' holdings. Putting this accumulating new archive into such circuits offers the possibility of a new urban heritage, however preliminary or fragile.

The photographic material that has appeared in response to a series of articles on Windhoek's former 'locations' then furnished a larger, new exhibition held in Windhoek in 1999. This commemorated the fortieth anniversary of the Old Location shootings on 10 December 1959 in which thirteen people died and over forty were wounded. The exhibition, located in the hallways of the municipal offices in central Windhoek, presented people with a series of visual colonial analogues as they queued to pay their rates and bills. Viewers can gaze upon photographs showing people paying their bills and having their pass books stamped in the former municipal offices in the heart of the Old Location, where during the shootings police took cover and opened fire on a crowd gathered in the space outside. The municipal walls are intended to provide 'new human proximities' for the photographs.

Many of the photographs of the Old Location, barring personal or group portraits taken by commercial studio photographers, were taken at a high point in documentary photographic practice in the region. Official documentary photographs in 1950s colonial Namibia attempted to portray social conditions of both urban and rural Africans for the purposes of international publicity and United

Nations publications. Criteria were fed to the Visual Section of the State Information Office in Pretoria as to what South African and American publics for example most needed to see. We have described elsewhere how the resulting pictures glossed over worsening conditions for Herero-speaking dairy producers for example or, *Drum*-style, celebrated Old Location social life even while forced removals were known to be imminent.[89] Unlike particular American documentary projects like that of the Farm Security Administration to foster support for New Deal relief programmes for the 'worthy poor',[90] it would be difficult to argue that these documentary photographs taken in Namibia were reformist in intent.

'Documentary' photography – a most intensively debated area of photographic theory – is held by Solomon-Godeau to be 'part of a larger system of visual communication, as both a conduit and agent of ideology, purveyor of empirical evidence and visual "truths."'[91] It draws on what Barthes called the effect of the real, as well as an identifiable range of subject matter. But clearly the 'real' can be read in

Above:This photograph allegedly shows some of the rocks and boulders thrown into the Municipal Offices by the crowd.

Right: Pictured here is the hatch into the Municipal Office where people used to come to pay thei. 'kop' tax. Police took shelter in the office during the attack.
* All photos courtesy of the National Archives Of Namibia

89 Hartmann et al., eds., *The Colonising Camera*, pp. 5 and 18.

90 Abigail Solomon-Godeau, *Photography at the Dock. Essays on Photographic History, Institutions, and Practices* (Minneapolis: University of Minnesota Press, 1991), p. 176; see *inter alia* Agee and Evans (1941).

91 Ibid., p. 170.

many ways, and the repositioning of documentary photographs among different audiences opens them to multiple evidential debates. One particular photograph taken after the Old Location shootings – a police photograph submitted to the Hall Commission of Enquiry – has recently been subject to divergent forensic readings.[92] It shows the inside of the municipal office on the morning of 11 December 1959. The legs of a man can be seen on the right of the frame and the floor is covered with huge boulders (see Fig. 7).

Before appearing in 'Picturing the Past' the photograph had already circulated in several different settings. It served forensic purposes as evidence in the Hall Commission, the official inquiry into the Old Location shooting. Chief Justice Hall used the photograph to support his findings that the crowd had launched a deadly attack on the encircled policemen in the building. The same photograph was used by the state as evidence in an unsuccessful case brought against 11 residents of the Old Location accused of 'public violence' after the attack.

In 1992, a community-based history group, consisting largely of

N WEEKENDER

SPECIAL FOCUS

EVENTS TO MARK THE 40TH
Anniversary Of the Old Location Shooting:

A competition for schools is being sponsored by the Namibian History Trust. The Old Location Shooting is part of the Grade 10 syllabus. Schools teaching history in that grade are invited to submit up to two entries to the competition. Each entry should consist of a drawing AND a written account of life in the old location. Learners are encouraged to seek out elders in their communities who have direct knowledge of the Old Location to obtain eye-witness accounts. Prize money to the value of N$1 000 has been provided by the Namibian History Trust to reward the best entries. Deadline: October 11. Entries should be submitted to Ms Prudence Egumbo, History Department, Unam, Private Bag 13301, Windhoek. Enquiries: Ms. Egumbo on 206-3000.

An exhibition on Windhoek's Old Locations is being assembled by Unam History Department and Unam History Society and will go on show in November this year. The History Department is keen to speak to former residents of the Old Location and those who have strong memories of the events that took place in December, 1959. We would also like to locate more photographs, documents (such as pass books) and objects which could help recreate the atmosphere of the Old Location. If you can help us than please contact Dr Jeremy Silvester on 206-3000

or Werner Thaniseb on 293 - 4435.

Improvements to the Old Location Graveyard. Drivers will have noticed that the National Monuments Council has already started work on a new wall to protect the Old Location Graveyard. Further improvements are planned.

A special event is being planned to mark the 40th anniversary of the Old Location Shooting on December 10 at a site near to the Old Location Graveyard. It will include a dramatic representation of the shooting set in a partial reconstruction of the Old Location itself. Enquiries: Ms Eva Neels on 270-7279.

It is hoped that a night vigil to remember those who died during the Old Location Shooting will also be organised. If your church is interested in participating they should initially contact Werner Thaniseb on 293 - 4435. It is hoped that there will be a number of special features during the coming months on the television and radio to help mark the anniversary. If you are planning an event and would like to publicise it than please contact Ms Kandi Iihuhwa at the Windhoek Municipality on (061) 290 2911.

* Jeremy Silvester is a lecturer in the History Department of the University Of Namibia.

Figure 6: The Namibian Weekender, 16 July 1999.

92 The theme of urban removals has opened up a new branch of the visual archive to students of Namibia's history. Court records constitute one of the most overlooked deposits of visual history. Whilst albums donated to the National Archives were harvested of their images for the photograph library, rich nodes of forensic photographs lie entombed and uncatalogued within their neglected court files.

survivors of the shooting, came across this photograph in the archive. According to their reading, the evidence pointed to a lack of credibility in the official explanation for the shootings by police. How could the alleged crowd have thrown such large rocks through the windows of the municipal office while being fired at by armed policemen? The photographic evidence suggested instead the complete unreliability of the state version of events.

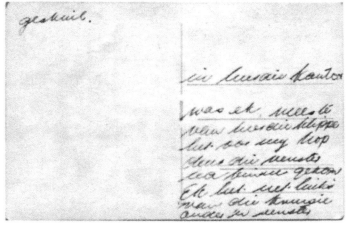

Figure 7: Original photograph with comment: inside the office. 'I was in this office, most of these stones came over my head, through the outside window. I hid under the window, just left of the cross.'

The photograph appeared in 'Picturing the Past' in 1999.[93] The column editor received a phone call from a retired policeman, who recalled being posted to Windhoek after graduating from the Police College in South Africa a few days before the shooting.[94] During the ensuing interview, the elderly policeman produced a personal photograph album in which he had assembled the images representing moments he regarded as the most significant in his life. Enclosed among these private pages was the set of photographs from the original court case, including its most contested picture. On this photograph, the policeman had inscribed a cross to show the place where he

93 *The Namibian*, 16 July 1999.

94 Interview with W. O. by Jeremy Silvester, Windhoek, 6 August 1999.

PATRICIA HAYES, JEREMY SILVESTER AND WOLFRAM HARTMANN

had sheltered under a window (see Fig. 7). As he pointed to the photograph on its album page, he described his own physical and mental terror: ammunition was running low and people climbed on to the roof of the municipal office to tear off the light corrugated-iron sheets and drop boulders on the heads of those inside.

The biographical detail sedimented the photograph with new meanings, adding a new surfeit to the repeated recontextualisations in

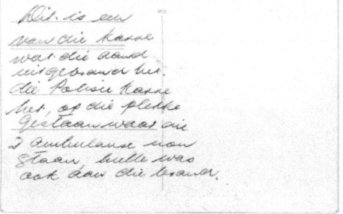

Figure 8: Original photograph with comment: outside the office. 'This is one of the cars that burnt out that evening. The police cars were parked on the spot where the two ambulances would have parked; they were also burning.'

different legal and historiographical episodes. The last speaker's combination of visualisation and personal narration, especially his inscription of the photograph, reconstituted a space of history that was also a space of violent exchange and conflict. The opening of the archive – in this case the court record that held this picture and its publication in 'Picturing the Past' – has not only effected a production of new histories, but also a series of exchanges. New narrations and new photographs (or new copies of the same photograph) have been forthcoming: a series, not simply of new historic turns, but of new historic turns and returns in an expanding economy of visual history.

The medium of the newspaper itself precipitated the evolution of the column as the site of growing dialogue and at times confrontation between the past and the present, going beyond the column to the creation of new exhibitions and wider public dialogues. This happened not only around people's responses to Old Location photographs, but even more strikingly around visual representations of the Cassinga massacre of 1978. The Cassinga affair has been commemorated annu-

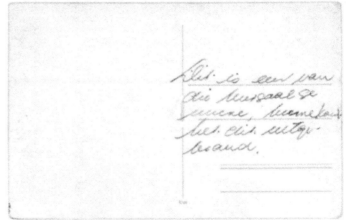

Figure 9: Original photograph with comment.
'This is one of the walls of the hall; the interior was completely burnt.'

ally in 'Picturing the Past', usually with a full page or more of photographs and text. These photographs derive from recent deposits in the National Archives of Namibia which are intended to do photographic justice to the country's liberation struggle.

Publication of these Cassinga photographs escalated energies around visuality and history and resulted in a full-scale exhibition in 1999, 21 years after the South African aerial and ground attack on Namibians in the southern Angolan camp that resulted in hundreds of deaths.[95] This exhibition incorporated not only all the photographs of the attack and its aftermath now lodged in the National Archives, but

95 Estimates of the dead range from 610 to 871. See *The Namibian* 9 May 1997; Annemarie Heywood, *The Cassinga Event* (Windhoek: National Archives of Namibia, 1994).

PATRICIA HAYES, JEREMY SILVESTER AND WOLFRAM HARTMANN

Remembering Cassinga

This is an extract from an interview with RUUSA NAANGO-SHAANIKA, who was sixteen at the time of the South African attack on Cassinga, having arrived at the camp a few days before May 4. The events are described in her own words.

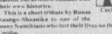

Ruusa Naange-Shaanika

A Sister Who Died Too Young

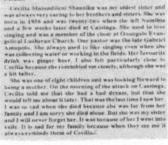

Cecilia Mulundileni Shaanika

Figure 10: 'Focus on Cassinga', 30 April 1998.

Figure 11: Ruusa's photograph of Cecilia. Reverse side shows inscription of her name, date of birth and date of death.

also feedback from readers of 'Picturing the Past' concerning Cassinga from previous issues. Ruusa Shaanika for example had come forward in 1998 with a photograph and obituary for her young sister Cecilia who was killed in the attack, and described her own memories of the day.

A strange twist of photographic fate occurred at the opening of the 1999 Cassinga exhibition in the Katutura Community Hall in Windhoek. A Cassinga survivor who had been invited to open the exhibition, Tina Hipandulwa, was startled to discover a photograph of herself on display of which she had been unaware. It showed her receiving treatment in a hospital bed after being wounded in the South African

PICTURING THE PAST   BY JEREMY SILVESTER

Cassinga Revisited

WHEN Tina Hipandulwa spoke at the opening of the Cassinga Exhibition in Katutura last week she revealed a surprise. One of the photographs on display showed a young girl in a hospital bed after the attack. The photograph had been found in the National Archives with a vague caption, but Hipandulwa recognised herself lying in hospital recovering from the serious injuries that she sustained during the South African attack on Cassinga on May 4 1978.

The opening featured liberation songs performed by 'Bazooka' and an extract from a new play about Cassinga produced by Banana Shikupe as well as accounts of the attack given by Hipandulwa and Ellen Namhila, another survivor of the attack.

The exhibition gathered together a great deal of information about the attacks on Cassinga and Vietnam base (that took place on the same day) and provided some new insights on an event which has become a symbol of the sacrifices made by many ordinary Namibians during the liberation struggle.

The exhibition (or sections of it) will be available to travel to other venues in Namibia and a number of groups have already requested to see it. If you would like to suggest a place where the exhibition could be shown please contact Ms Betty Hango-Rumuukainen at the National Museum of Namibia on 293-4353 or Dr Jeremy Silvester at the History Department of the University of Namibia on 206-3000.

Research for the exhibition has included a number of fresh interviews with survivors of the attacks and these have started to help clarify some of the confusion that has surrounded existing accounts of the operation. One puzzle has surrounded the fact that a delegation from Unicef who visited Cassinga a month before the attack reported that (on the basis of counting those lined up at a parade in their honour) there were 11 000 - 12 000 residents in the camp. Whilst this figure may reflect the gathering of some people from neighbouring camps for the occasion it now seems clear that there was also a partial evacuation of the camp before the attack on 4th May. The number of people in the camp at the

A bus destroyed during the attack on Cassinga. Was this the bus that had been captured and taken from Namibia a few weeks earlier ?

time of the attack is now commonly agreed to have been between 3- 4 000.

A Cassinga survivor recalled: "There was a proposal to move the people from the camp because South African reconnaissance planes were detected in the area. However there was a problem which prevented us from implementing this motion immediately. We had a shortage of food at that time. The little food we had could not be divided among those who would reach the destination first, those on the way and those who would remain to follow later. We were waiting for a fresh food supply so that we could move out of Cassinga. An attempt was made to move out the groups most at risk - women, children and the aged. We could not move them far away from the camp because of the food shortage. We settled them at a place called Camp No. 2 that was only 400-500 metres away from the main camp.

"Cassinga was a transit camp for the people who came straight from home. It was made mainly to accommodate women, children and the aged. It was fortunate that when the enemy attacked the main camp, it did not know Camp Number 2, therefore the comrades who were there were safe."

The existence of this second camp would explain the apparent contradictions that exist about the size of the camp at Cassinga. We would be particularly interested to hear from any other witnesses who could shed further light on the timing and organisation of the transfer of people to this second neighbouring camp.

A further point that has clearly emerged from the interviews that we have carried out so far is that there was a clear gap (of about an hour) between the initial bombing of the camp and the arrival of the South African troops that were dropped by para-

chute. The delay was due to a mistake that meant that many of the paratroopers landed far from their intended drop zones. While the aeroplanes continued to attack the camp it clearly provided an opportunity for an evacuation of some of those who had survived the devastating early morning attack on the camp residents assembled on the parade ground.

A Swapo official interviewed shortly after the attack claimed that they were able to evacuate about two-thirds of those remaining at Cassinga, while the defence unit of the camp tried to delay the advance of the South African troops. The interviewees identified particular individuals whose actions helped them to survive. For example, Ellen Namhila recalled the bravery of a 'Captain Kanhana' who helped both her and an injured baby across the swollen river to safety. As further interviews are carried out it will be possible to identify other individuals whose acts of bravery should be remembered as part of Cassinga Day.

SADF documents obtained by the Truth and Reconciliation Commission (TRC) in South Africa reveal that one of the primary objectives of the attack on Cassinga was the death or capture of the Plan commander, Dimo Hamaambo. It is clear that whilst Hamaambo had a house and even fields at Cassinga, he spent much of his time at the Plan Headquarters at Lubango. The TRC concluded that the South African army did seem to believe that Cassinga was a legitimate military target. However they also concluded that the use of fragmentation bombs at Cassinga in the knowledge that the camp contained civilians was "an indiscriminate and illegitimate use of force and a violation of Protocol 1 to the Geneva Conventions of 1949. The foreseeable killing of civilians at Kassinga was therefore a breach of humanitarian law".

The camp commander responsible for the day-to-day running of Cassinga was 'Comrade Mbelondondo' whilst Justus Uubulu Uushona and Greenwell Matongo a so seem to have played s gnificant roles. It is hoped that it will be pos-

sible to expand on these as more oral history is gathered.

The total number and names of those who died at Cassinga still remains a mystery, although slowly new names are being added to the list as further interviews are carried out. The reason for this the fact that the population of the camp was constantly changing as new people arrived and others moved on, but also due to the difficult circumstances under which the dead were buried. As one survivor recalled - "On the third day, May 6, the Cuban aeroplanes came. They brought food and other assistance. We remained there to bury the dead and collect some of the remaining belongings. There were some trenches which were dug to serve as storage for some of our belongings. We used those trenches as mass graves of the comrades killed. First, we put them in the two

Unexploded fragmentation bombs whose use at Cassinga was judged a breach of the Geneva Convention by the South African Truth and Reconciliaton Commission.

trenches on one side and when they were full, we went to put them in another trench on the other side. We did not count them when we laid them down in the trenches as the situation was still very tense."

The list of those who died at Vietnam is even more incomplete. It is hoped that as more people view the exhibition others will come forward to add to the list of the dead that

forms a central feature of the exhibition. It seems unfortunate that NBC television have not covered the exhibition as this would have helped ensure that a larger audience was aware of this important objective. It is hoped that as the exhibition travels and prows it will help ensure that the young generation understand the significance and symbolism of the annual public holiday that is Cassinga Day.

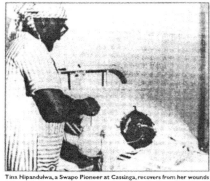

Tina Hipandulwa, a Swapo Pioneer at Cassinga, recovers from her wounds in hospital.

One of the buildings at Cassinga destroyed during the attack. Do any readers remember what this building was used for?

Figure 12: 'Picturing the Past', 7 May 1999.

attack. The photograph was unexpected and not something she remembered. Injured, hospitalised, stunned after the bombing and killing at the camp, she had no memory of the presence of the camera. It seemed a case where the photograph showed her history 'buried as if under a layer of snow'.[96] The caption inserted by the co-curator of the exhibition, Betty Hango-Rumakainen, was simply 'A wounded refugee in hospital'. Now, a further caption was written by hand under the photograph after the nameless refugee recognised herself: *Tina Hipandulwa*.

As cited earlier, Poignant writes of the 'continuities of self' that are perceptible to those audiences looking at photographs that bear on their histories. The inscription of Tina Hipandulwa's name on the photograph, in her presence – instating her identity – is an act that revokes the anonymity and to some extent the victimhood of the figure photographed after the Cassinga massacre. Poignant also writes of the continuities of family that the figures in photographs might evoke, and the way in which genealogies are made visible.[97] These affinities seem to be of crucial importance to Namibian interested parties who have reacted to the expanding publication and exhibition of archive photographs, and have brought out their own pictures, collections or albums to shift the nature of the extant visual archive. But there is something beyond such direct relationships that causes a movement, 'a shudder', a ripple, among those exposed to photographs.

In the case of Tina Hipandulwa's photograph, it is the juxtaposition of the survivor with her picture.[98] It is like having two streams of time running together, the past and the present, with the sudden insight that memory is part of the present. For the audience, the scars of history are immediately exposed. They share an intense moment in someone's life: it is the thing and its shadow at the same time, the source and its index. They are no longer viewers but participants. The wounded refugee in the picture is a stranger no more.

In a preternatural response to Tina Hipandulwa's identification of herself in the Cassinga photograph, members of the audience crowded into the frame with the survivor to have repeated new photographs taken with her underneath the picture. The kinaesthetics of this reaction to seeing a survivor with her past, so close to death during the episode that epitomised South African brutality to Namibians, argues not so much the continuities of genealogy but of broader public solidarities. Perhaps, too, it was an indication of that contemporary and compulsive relationship we have with photographs, of which Kracauer wrote: 'That the world devours them is a sign of the *fear of death*.'[99]

Figure 13: Tina Hipandulwa stands in front of a photograph taken 21 years earlier after the attack on Cassinga.

96 Kracauer, 'Photography', p. 426.

97 Poignant, *Encounter at Nagalarramba*, p. 12.

98 A similar effect emerged at the opening of the Robben Island Museum Exhibition entitled *Cell Stories* on 8 November 1999, where ex-prisoners were at times encountered in their former cells and were recognisable from their photographs on the walls.

99 Kracauer, 'Photography', p. 433.

5 March 1963.

The Director of Archives,
PRETORIA.

RESEARCH ON PONDOLAND.

1.   I have today had in the Reading Room of this depot a
Mrs. Arenstein, who has described herself as a "journalist",
and who is doing research on the history of Pondoland.

2.   It occurred to me that this person might be connected
with the Mr. R. Arenstein who has been judicially debarred from
entering Pondoland and, I understand, placed under other
restrictions in the Durban area.

3.   The Security Branch of the Durban South African Police
have confirmed telephonically that the person who is doing
research here is, in fact, the wife of Mr. R. Arenstein.

4.   Mrs. Arenstein has been, for the time being, given
printed publications which, presumably, available elsewhere.
To date it has not been necessary to produce any official
records.

5.   At short notice I am unable to state whether there is, in
fact, information in the records of this office which should
be withheld from such a person.

6.   I have thought it wise to report this matter to you in
case you deem it necessary to issue any instructions in regard to
the matter.   This letter has been sent Express post, together
with other confidential matter of a less urgent nature, in order
that there might be the minimum of delay caused.

CHIEF: NATAL ARCHIVES DEPOT.

The Archival Sliver: A Perspective on the Construction of Social Memory in Archives and the Transition from Apartheid to Democracy *

Verne Harris

Introduction: Mapping a perspective

Understanding of and feeling for a concept are shaped inevitably by the weighting of experience. In my case, both as a South African and as a practising archivist, experience has been dominated by the drama of South Africa's transition from apartheid to democracy. This drama has absorbed the complex elements of personal experience, and has transcribed my thinking around the word 'archives' into an indelible metaphor – 'the archival sliver'. As process, the transcription probably began in the late 1980s, when I did volunteer work for an organisation providing support to political detainees, trialists and prisoners. At the time we needed no documentary evidence to demonstrate that organs of the state were conducting a dirty tricks campaign against opponents of apartheid. We knew they were. Now, as the Truth and Reconciliation Commission (TRC) unfolds the details of that campaign,[1] it is oral rather than documentary evidence that carries the story. The archival record, both oral and documentary, is but a sliver of social memory, and the archival residue in documents is but a sliver of the documentary record. Between 1996 and 1998 I represented the National Archives in a TRC investigation into the destruction of public records.[2] This investigation exposed a large-scale and systematic sanitisation of official memory resources authorised at the highest levels of government. Between 1990 and 1994 huge volumes of public records were destroyed in an attempt to keep the apartheid state's darkest secrets hidden.[3]

One must be wary of delineating general patterns from extreme circumstances. However, I would argue that in any circumstances, in any country, the documentary record provides just a sliver of a window into the event. Even if archivists in a particular country were to preserve every record generated throughout the land, they would still have only a sliver of a window into that country's experience. Of course, in practice, this record universum is substantially reduced through deliberate and inadvertent destruction by records creators and managers, leaving a sliver of a sliver from which archivists select what

* This essay draws heavily on four articles by me published previously: 'Towards a culture of transparency: public rights of access to official records in South Africa', *American Archivist* 57, 4 (1994); 'Redefining archives in South Africa: public archives and society in transition, 1990–1996', *Archivaria* 42 (1996); 'Transforming discourse and legislation: a perspective on South Africa's new National Archives Act', *ACARM Newsletter* 18 (1996); and 'Claiming less, delivering more: a critique of positivist formulations on archives in South Africa', *Archivaria* 44 (1997). I am grateful to Ethel Kriger (National Archives of South Africa) and Tim Nuttall (University of Natal) for offering sometimes tough comment on an early draft of the essay. I remain, of course, fully responsible for the final text. It was prepared originally for a book *Archival Truths and Historical Consequences* edited by the Canadians Terry Cook and Joan Schwartz. I am grateful to them for permission to use an adapted, shorter version for this book.

1   The 17-member Truth and Reconciliation Commission was established in 1995 with a four-fold mandate: to establish as complete a picture as possible of the causes, nature and extent of gross human rights violations committed in South Africa between 1960 and 1994; to facilitate the granting of amnesty to perpetrators of gross human rights violations associated with a political objective; to recommend appropriate reparation for the victims of gross human rights violations; and to compile a report of its activities, findings and recommendations. The Commission's final report was submitted to President Mandela in October 1998. However, the work of the Commission's Amnesty Committee proceeded and is anticipated to continue through 2001.

2   The work of this investigation is reflected in the following sections of the final report (*Truth and Reconciliation Commission of South Africa Report*, Cape Town, 1998): vol. 1 ch. 8, and vol. 5 ch. 8, paragraphs 62, 66, 67, and 100 to 108.

they will preserve. They do not preserve much.[4] Moreover, no record, no matter how well protected and cared for by archivists, enjoys an unlimited lifespan. Preservation strategies can, at best, aim to save *versions* of *most* archival records. So archives offer researchers a sliver of a sliver of a sliver.[5] If, as many archivists are wont to argue, the repositories of archives are the world's central memory institutions, then we are in deep, amnesic trouble.

A notion common in archival discourse is that archives reflect – or provide an image of – process, the event. Stated more crudely, the idea is that archives, mirror-like, reflect reality. My archival 'sliver of a window' offers a direct challenge to this metaphor. Of course, the assumption that there is 'a reality' capable of reflection in records is debatable from several perspectives. This full-frontal attack I shall forgo, offering instead three outflanking manoeuvres. First, even if there is 'a reality', ultimately it is unknowable. The event, the process, the origin, in its *uniqueness*, is irrecoverable. As Jacques Derrida has pointed out: 'The possibility of the archiving trace, this simple *possibility*, can only divide the uniqueness.'[6] Secondly, while it is self-evident that the record is a product of process, it must be acknowledged that process is shaped fundamentally by the act of recording. Thirdly, if archival records reflect reality, they do so complicitly, and in a deeply fractured and shifting way. They do not act by themselves. They act through many conduits – the people who created them, the functionaries who managed them, the archivists who selected them for preservation and make them available for use, and the researchers who use them in constructing accounts of the past. Far from enjoying an exteriority in relation to the record, all these conduits participate in the complex processes through which the record feeds into social memory. The view that the record lies inert from its creation until it is used by researchers is patently untenable. While researchers release energies – and generate new energies – through usage, the record is always already a space in which energies dance. This is seen, for instance, in the simplest archival intervention – by adding related records to a record in archival custody, and extending descriptive tools accordingly, the archival window is recast.

To return to my 'sliver of a window' metaphor, the window is not only a medium through which light travels; it also reflects light, transposing images from 'this side' and disturbing images from the 'other side'. In this paper I explore the connections – a fractured, shifting play of light – between the archival sliver and social memory in the context of the transition from apartheid to democracy.

3   The National Intelligence Service headquarters, for instance, destroyed an estimated 44 tons of paper-based and microfilm records in a 6–8-month period during 1993. *TRC Report*, vol. 1, ch. 8, p. 219 (par. 60).

4   The appraisal programme of the National Archives of South Africa, for instance, aims to secure the preservation of 5 per cent of records generated by the state.

5   This sliver of a sliver of a sliver is seldom more than partially described.

6   Jacques Derrida, *Archive Fever: A Freudian Impression* (Chicago and London: University of Chicago Press, 1996), p. 100.

Through four decades the apartheid system demonstrated an extraordinary capacity to secure the support of most white South Africans as well as the acquiescence or collaboration of significant sections of the black population. A key element in this exercise of hegemony was the state's control over social memory, a control that involved both remembering and forgetting. The public service, managed largely by English-speaking whites in 1948, was rapidly 'Afrikanerised'. The educational system, particularly at primary and secondary levels, was secured within the framework of 'Christian National Education'. Radio and, from the 1970s, television were controlled directly by the state. A powerful Afrikaner nationalist presence was built in the press. The network of state-funded libraries, museums, art galleries, monuments and archives was shaped profoundly by an apartheid imprint. By their silences and their narratives of power, their constructions of experience, apartheid's memory institutions legitimised apartheid rule. A vast, simmering memory of resistance and struggle was forced into informal spaces and the deeper reaches of the underground. Outside the country, the liberation movements and their support networks documented their own activities and gathered – both formally and informally – the memories of exiles and those remaining in South Africa.[7] Many prominent anti-apartheid activists and researchers deposited archival materials with institutions located in Europe and the United States of America.[8]

Apartheid's huge bureaucracy, which reached into almost every aspect of citizens' lives, generated a formidable memory resource. Control over racial classification, employment, movement, association, purchase of property, recreation and so on, was documented by thousands of government offices. This was supplemented by the record of surveillance activities by the security police and many other state intelligence bodies, and by large quantities of records confiscated from individuals and organisations opposed to apartheid. Obscenely, registries and record strongrooms converted the abnormal into the normal. As Michel-Rolph Trouillot has observed, 'Built into any system of domination is the tendency to proclaim its own normalcy.'[9] Bureaucratic memory, of course, was tightly controlled. While all governments are uncomfortable with the notion of transparency, in apartheid South Africa government secrecy was a *modus operandi*. Interlocking legislation restricted access to and the dissemination of information on vast areas of public life.[10] These restrictions

7 During the 1980s, for instance, the Popular History Trust in Zimbabwe collected oral history and other documentation related to the struggle in South Africa. Julie Frederikse, 'We look back to move forward: making oral history popular and accessible', *Innovation* 14 (1997).

8 Ibid., p. 18.

9 Michel-Rolph Trouillot, *Silencing the Past: Power and the Production of History* (Boston: Beacon Press, 1995), p. 84.

10 These included *inter alia* the Archives Act, Criminal Procedure Act, Disclosure of Foreign Funding Act, Inquests Act, Internal Security Act, Nuclear Energy Act, Official Secrets Act, Petroleum Products Act, Protection of Information Act and Statistics Act.

were manipulated to secure an extraordinary degree of opacity in government, and the country's formal information systems became grossly distorted in support of official propaganda. This obsessive secrecy was served not only by legislation but also by a range of judicial and executive tools. The most effective tool, ultimately, was the selective destruction of public records. In the introduction to this essay, I referred to the large-scale destruction exercises of the 1990–1994 period. The selection of records for archival preservation (and concomitant identification of other records for destruction) by state archivists are addressed below.

Record destruction by the state embraced not only public records. The TRC investigation referred to earlier revealed that all the records confiscated by the security police from individuals and organisations opposed to apartheid were destroyed before the 1994 General Election.[11] The state also destroyed many other non-public records during raids on and bombings of anti-apartheid structures and premises both inside and outside the country. A story that still awaits telling is that of the impact of apartheid on the record-keeping practices of anti-apartheid individuals and organisations, in particular the reluctance to commit certain types of information to paper and the readiness to destroy records rather than allow them to fall into the hands of state operatives.[12] More chilling processes of memory erasure were also utilised widely by the apartheid state, with many thousands of oppositional voices being eliminated through such means as media censorship, various forms of banning, detention without trial, imprisonment, informal harassment and assassination.

Until the late 1970s and 80s, which saw a flowering of small non-public collecting institutions, the South African archival terrain was dominated by the State Archives Service (SAS). By 1990 SAS had facilities in seven cities across the country, including six archives repositories and five records centres. From its formal establishment in 1922, SAS's custodial mandate embraced the archives of central and provincial government offices. In 1962 this was extended to incorporate all local government offices.[13] In addition, from the outset SAS enjoyed a mandate to supplement its public record holdings by collecting non-public records. Its functions *vis-à-vis* public records still in the custody of government offices – its records management functions – remained modest and purely advisory until 1953. Thereafter, especially after the passing of the 1962 Archives Act, SAS developed a significant records management capacity sustained by wide-ranging regulatory powers. Apartheid's public archives system was made up by

11 *TRC Report*, vol. 1, ch. 8, pp. 217 (par. 50) and 236 (par. 105).

12 For instance, I remember the Pretoria Black Sash Branch destroying its records in 1988 after one of its members was detained. See also *TRC Report*, vol. 1, ch. 8, p. 205 (par. 17).

13 Excluded from this mandate were the South African Defence Force, the homelands, and so-called 'offices of record'. The last were defined as offices 'responsible for documents which require special treatment in order to ensure that the authenticity and legality of the contents cannot be questioned'. State Archives Service, *Handbook* (Pretoria, 1991), pp. 15–35.

the South African Defence Force Archives and the various bantustan (or homeland) archives services.[14]

Throughout the apartheid era SAS suffered the consequences of isolation. Denied membership in the International Council on Archives (ICA) and shunned by most other countries, particularly during the cultural boycott of the 1980s, SAS was largely excluded from the international exchange of professional ideas and resources. Within the country, anti-apartheid organisations and individuals active in the arena of social memory shunned SAS. Isolation fostered a 'laager mentality' resistant to new ideas and enthralled by an outmoded professional discourse.[15] Even exchange and joint endeavour with other establishment-aligned institutions were rare.

Apartheid realities and SAS's status as an organ of the state combined to ensure that many of its services were fashioned into tools of the apartheid system. Three examples illustrate this. First, although user services were open to all and offered free of charge, black South Africans made up only a small proportion of the users. Systemic barriers – low educational standards, high rates of illiteracy, physical isolation from city centres, competency in languages other than the official Afrikaans and English – ensured that most South Africans enjoyed only nominal access to public archives. SAS did very little to overcome these barriers. Outreach endeavours were modest, uncoordinated and targeted at white users. Service provision was geared to supporting white users and, until the 1980s, specifically white academics.[16] Secondly, SAS's records management functions – designed in the first instance to identify and safeguard public records with archival value, but also to support administrative efficiency – in effect oiled the wheels of apartheid bureaucracy. Thirdly, in its relationships with the bantustan archives services, SAS was placed in a classic apartheid dilemma: cutting them loose professionally would have meant reinforcing bantustan underdevelopment; providing comprehensive support would have meant buttressing grand apartheid policy. In practice, SAS's approach fell uncomfortably between the two stools, thus at once supporting apartheid objectives and restricting bantustan access to scarce archival resources.

Another dilemma confronted SAS in the form of powerful state organs obstructing its legitimate activities and flagrantly ignoring or defying its legal instruments. Given the apartheid system's disregard for accountability and SAS's junior status within government,[17] SAS was poorly positioned to resist. Again, three examples serve to illustrate this dimension. First, many government offices persistently

14 Although excluded from my analysis it should be noted that the SADF Archives and the homeland archives services, in both conception and administration, faithfully reflected apartheid logic. Under a system that awarded inordinate power and autonomy to the military, it is not surprising that the SADF Archives, although legally subject to the professional supervision of the State Archives, in practice sustained an independent operation. Nor is it surprising, in the context of apartheid homeland policy, in particular the inadequate professional and administrative assistance made available by central government, that the homelands either neglected public archives entirely or maintained only rudimentary services.

15 Almost every area of thinking and practice was dominated by a discourse cemented in the 1950s and 60s. Primary influences were the 1898 *Manual for the Arrangement and Description of Archives* by Samuel Müller, Johan Feith and Robert Fruin (as late as the 1980s, new archivists were given a copy of the *Manual* as their fundamental training text), later Dutch literature (Afrikaans-speakers are usually comfortable readers of Dutch), the English archivist Sir Hilary Jenkinson (particularly his 1937 *A Manual of Archive Administration*) and the American T. R. Schellenberg.

16 Academic users were predominantly historians. Even today, the discipline is dominated by white males, with South Africa in 1997 possessing less than twenty black History PhDs. G. Cuthbertson, 'Postmodernising history and the archives: some challenges for recording the past', *South African Archives Journal* 39 (1997), p. 13. From the 1980s the State Archives Service began shaping its user services around the needs of its largest clientele grouping – genealogical (almost exclusively white) researchers.

17 In the 1980s the senior public servant in a government department held the rank of a director-general. As a director, the head of the State Archives Service was three levels lower.

18 Notable examples were the Department of Foreign Affairs and the National Intelligence Service.

19 An incident from my own experience illustrates this. When I and some of my colleagues in the State Archives Service discovered in 1993 that state offices were destroying classified records in terms of a Security Secretariat authorisation we pushed the Director of Archives to intervene urgently. When he did not do so, I leaked the authorisation first to the press, then to Lawyers for Human Rights. The latter challenged the authorisation in court and secured an out of court settlement in which the state agreed to manage the disposal of classified records strictly in terms of the Archives Act.

20 Unrestricted access was withdrawn to records less than fifty years old of six government offices, and to all post-1910 records of a further four offices. According to the 1962 Archives Act, unrestricted access applied to records more than thirty years old, unless the responsible minister imposed restrictions on the grounds of 'public policy'. These restrictions were lifted in 1991, and in practice constituted only a minor infringement of public access to the records concerned. State Archives Service records indicate that between 1980 and 1990 requests for permission to consult 2 381 items in the archives of these offices were received and access was denied to only nine items.

21 By 1990 not one professional post in the State Archives Service had been occupied by a black person. In 1990 the Service's professional staff comprised seventy people. All were white, with 39 women and 31 men.

22 In 1990 only one of the twelve most senior officials was not an Afrikaans-speaking male – she was an Afrikaans-speaking woman.

23 From 1963 reading room supervisors were under instruction from the Director of Archives to report the presence of any banned person (Circular instruction of 5 June 1963). The evidence suggests that this information, together with details of the records being consulted by such persons, was passed on to the security police.

24 For accounts of this programme, see my 'Exploratory thoughts on current State Archives Service appraisal policy and the conceptual

refused to subject their records systems to design analysis and archival appraisal or to co-operate in the transfer of records into SAS's custody.[18] Secondly, in the 1990–1994 period of mass records destruction by state offices, SAS intervention achieved nothing. SAS's leadership was intimidated by the security establishment and lacked the will to act decisively.[19] Thirdly, in the 1980s SAS was forced by its political masters to withdraw unrestricted access to certain records in its custody.[20] This incident contributed to a perception of SAS as a willing collaborator in state-imposed public amnesia.

Not that willing collaboration with the apartheid system was not a powerful dynamic in SAS. Indeed, I would argue SAS was moulded as an institution by apartheid and absorbed apartheid bureaucratic culture. Until the mid-1980s, public service legislation laid down that only whites could be appointed to professional and many administrative posts.[21] As in the rest of the bureaucracy, senior positions were dominated by white, Afrikaans-speaking males.[22] SAS's structure was rigidly hierarchical and its management ethos was authoritarian. Transparency and broad participation in decision-making were given short shrift. Official language policy was implemented, with Afrikaans dominant except in isolated lower reaches of the organisation. Much core policy documentation was produced only in Afrikaans. Language usage also impacted on SAS's interface with users and the public generally, as did SAS's provision of racially segregated reading-room and toilet facilities until the 1970s, and the collaboration of SAS staff with the security police in spying on reading room users.[23]

The absorption of apartheid bureaucratic culture and, at a deeper level, of apartheid ideology shaped SAS's functions and left indelible marks on SAS's contribution to social memory. Its archival appraisal programme, fashioned in the 1950s, was characterised by incoherence in both theory and methodology.[24] In practice, appraisers made decisions around one central question: does this record possess actual or anticipated usefulness to researchers? Of course, the researchers served by appraisers were white. Moreover, researchers were conceptualised in a hierarchy of importance in which 'the serious researcher' – the academic scholar, the historian – was on the top of the pile. Until the 1970s blossoming of social history and revisionist historiography began to impact on the programme in the late 1980s, SAS's fashioning of appraisal into a tool for historians resulted in the experience of apartheid's marginalised and oppressed communities being poorly reflected in the public records chosen for preservation. The fact that most of SAS's appraisers were taught as undergraduates by establishment-aligned Afrikaner historians was an important contributory factor. In addition, the public records chosen for preservation reflected apartheid power relations and carried the reductionist constructions of process typical of any bureaucracy.

A more fundamental skewing of social memory is evident in SAS's collections of non-public records. With the exception of Boer resistance to British imperialism, they documented poorly the struggles against colonialism, segregation and apartheid. Black experiences were also poorly documented and in most cases were seen through white eyes. Similarly, the voices of women, the disabled, and other marginalised people were seldom heard. This is partially explained by the difficulty experienced by SAS in securing donations of records from sources other than those that were establishment-aligned.[25] But the heart of the issue was a collecting policy that quite deliberately directed archivists away from grassroots experience towards society's pinnacles and eschewed the documentation of orality. A more blatant ideological intervention was demonstrated by SAS's official history project, which involved the production of a multi-volume official history of a central event in Afrikaner memory, the South African War of 1899–1902.[26] 'It was', according to historian Albert Grundlingh, 'the Afrikaner's answer to the British *Official History of the War* and *The Times History of the War*.'[27] Ideological considerations also informed the selection of theses for publication in SAS's *Archives Year Book for South African History*. Introduced in 1938, the series became an important vehicle for Afrikaner nationalist historiography, with the legitimisation of white rule and the exclusion of oppositional voices being key objectives in selection policy.[28]

Characterisation of apartheid's archives system as one controlled by whites, preserving records created by whites, and providing services to whites, is an oversimplification. It misses the specificities of shifting class alliances in apartheid's dominant section. It misses the role played by black bureaucrats, including archivists, in the bantustan administrations and, from the 1980s, in black local authorities' 'own affairs' administrations and other branches of the state.[29] It misses the increasing numbers of black users of archives in apartheid's twilight years. It misses the emergence in the 1980s and early 90s of institutions dedicated to 'giving voice to the voiceless' through archival collections. But it captures the essential character of the system.

During the 1980s an increasing number of anti-apartheid organisations and individuals prominent in the struggles against apartheid

foundations of macro-appraisal', *Archives News* 37, 8 (1995) and 'Appraising public records in the 1990s: a South African perspective', *ESARBICA Journal* 16 (1996). Between 1926 and 1953 the appraisal of public records was the function of the Archives Commission, a statutory body appointed by the responsible minister. Thereafter the function was assumed by the State Archives Service, although the Commission retained the power to authorise destruction until 1979.

25 Verne Harris and Clive Kirkwood, 'The State Archives Service and manuscript collections: some thoughts on policy and practice', *Archives News* 37, 12 (1995), p. 7.

26 The project was initiated in 1959 and continued into the 1990s.

27 Albert Grundlingh, 'Historical writing and the State Archives in a changing South Africa', *South African Archives Journal* 35 (1993), p. 81.

28 Albert Grundlingh, 'Politics, principles and problems of a profession: Afrikaner historians and their discipline, c. 1920 – c.1965', *Perspectives in Education* 12, 1 (1990), pp. 11–13. Theses were selected by the Archives Commission, on which the State Archives Service was represented by the director.

29 In 1984 the apartheid government introduced a House of Parliament for 'Indians', the House of Delegates, and the House of Representatives for 'coloureds'. Each was supported by a similarly racially-defined 'own affairs' administration.

began depositing archival materials with collecting institutions, particularly university libraries. Significant accumulations were collected by *inter alia* the Cory Library (University of Rhodes), the Killie Campbell Africana Library (University of Natal), the University of Cape Town Library, the University of South Africa Library and the William Cullen Library (University of the Witwatersrand). Several universities initiated projects for the collection of oral history and oral tradition. A significant development was the establishment of the South African History Archive under the auspices of the United Democratic Front and Congress of South African Trade Unions.[30] After 1990 these and newly established archives acquired significant quantities of records documenting anti-apartheid struggles, from both within and outside the country.

TRANSFORMATION

The apartheid regime was not overthrown. The revolution fought for by the liberation movements over nearly three decades did not happen. Instead, between 1990 and 1994 the apartheid government and its political allies negotiated a transition to democracy with the opponents of apartheid. Although the African National Congress won a sweeping victory in South Africa's first democratic general election in 1994, it would manage at least the first five years of democracy-building through a Government of National Unity. Crucial to the success of this process was the efficacy of the major players on the ideological terrain in shaping a new national identity. This identity coheres around the notion of a rainbow nation united in its diversity and finding reconciliation through the confronting of its past. Its most powerful symbolic embodiment is in the person of Nelson Mandela.[31] The nature of the transition to democracy meant that there would be no dramatic dismantling and reconstruction of the apartheid archival system. Rather, the new would be built out of the old through a process of transformation.

A transformation discourse quickly emerged after 1990, informed by the assumption that archives required redefinition, more precisely reinvention, for a democratic South Africa. Participants in this discourse, unlike those in many other spheres, had very little to build on. They were confronted by a paucity of revisionist thinking and debate, and in the early stages of transition were forced to rely on ideas from international archival literature and from more broadly-based debates around social memory within the country.[32] These

30 See Razia Saleh, 'The South African History Archive', *Innovation* 4 (1992).

31 For a brilliant account of the Mandela myth, see David Beresford, 'Mandela's greatness is from being here', *Mail and Guardian*, 7–13 November 1997, p. 30.

32 A survey of pre-1990 South African archival literature, for instance, reveals a predominance of work positioned comfortably within the status quo. The only significant exception was Jill Geber's 1987 University of London dissertation, 'The South African Government Archives Service: past, present and future', which attempted an historical analysis of the State Archives Service and offered a vision for public archives in a post-apartheid South Africa. This seminal work marked the birth of transformation discourse, but its immediate impact was slight.

debates had gathered momentum in the 1980s and informed a burgeoning praxis of oppositional memory construction. In a fundamental sense, resistance to apartheid in this period was a struggle of remembering against forgetting. Engagement by the liberation and broader democratic movements in cultural practice had become ever more vigorous. Activists and academics collaborated in conceptualising a 'people's education' in opposition to the apartheid educational system. The radical historiography that had emerged in the 1970s became more influential both in the academy and in public space. 'Struggle literature' and 'struggle theatre' – a discourse of opposition in fiction – flourished. 'Alternative' publications and publishers, running the gauntlet of state censorship, provided an ever-shifting space for oppositional voices. A growing number of art galleries, libraries and museums began to question long-established orthodoxies. As mentioned above, projects for the collection of oral history and oral tradition were sustained by universities.

Since 1990 there has been a flowering of non-public institutions committed to filling apartheid-fashioned gaps in social memory. They have contributed significantly to transformation discourse and have played an important role in demonstrating an alternative archival practice.[33] Crucially, they have been at the forefront of endeavours to bring back to South Africa archives generated by the experience of exile or located outside the country as a result of the exigencies of struggle. The records of the African National Congress and the Pan Africanist Congress, for instance, are being brought from around the globe to the University of Fort Hare. A large accumulation of International Defence and Aid Fund (IDAF) records have been deposited with the Mayibuye Centre at the University of the Western Cape. More recently, the National Archives (see below) has secured the credibility to participate in this endeavour. In 1999 agreements were forged by it to acquire IDAF and Christian Fellowship Trust records. Bringing the hidden, the marginalised, the exiled, the 'other' archive, into the mainstream, allowing that archive to trouble conceptualisations of the 'mainstream', has created powerful currents in transformation discourse.

In 1996, transformation discourse delivered the National Archives of South Africa Act, which established the National Archives out of SAS and provided the legislative framework for the development of a new national archival system.[34] It would be premature for me in this essay to attempt an analysis either of the nature or the efficacy of this system. The Act only came into operation on 1 January 1997 – most

33 For instance, the African National Congress Archives at the University of Fort Hare, the Alan Paton Centre at the University of Natal, the District Six Museum, the Gay and Lesbian Archives, the Mayibuye Centre at the University of the Western Cape and the Robben Island Museum.

34 For an analysis of the Act as a product of transformation discourse, see my 'Transforming discourse and legislation'.

of the transformation programmes defined by it are still in their infancy, and many of the system's elements are not yet operative. For instance, only two of the envisaged nine more or less autonomous provincial archives services – in most cases to be fashioned out of ex-SAS and bantustan archives structures – have been established. Interrelated legislation is still not fully in place – the Legal Deposit Act only became operative in 1998, national heritage legislation in 1999, the Promotion of Access to Information Act in 2001, and by 2001 only two provinces had passed any legislation.[35] The non-public archives, established after 1990 specifically to fill apartheid-fashioned gaps in social memory, are only beginning to establish themselves and link into the national system. What I propose to offer is an account of what I regard to be the core issues in transformation discourse; the issues that give the discourse its fundamental shape. While in each instance the focus is heavily on public archives – the main target for transformation – the ground being contested, I would suggest, is the very identity of archives.

In my view, the defining idea, the leitmotif, of transformation discourse is that archivists, far from being the impartial custodians SAS liked to portray, are active documenters of society and shapers of social memory. Exploration of this idea's implications has occupied centre stage, developing several strands and generating fierce debate. Perhaps the least contested argument is that the stranglehold enjoyed by whites over the archival profession needs to be broken. It matters – in terms of power relations, in terms of the construction of social memory in archives – that whites control archival institutions and dominate transformation discourse. It matters that only Western epistemologies have been deployed in the re-imagining of South African archives. The drive for representivity in the public service since 1994, facilitated by affirmative action policies, has begun to effect meaningful change in this crucial area.[36] Significant numbers of black archivists have also been employed by non-public institutions. Another argument enjoying wide acceptance is that archives, because of both their role as active documenters and their apartheid legacies, must be subject to high levels of transparency and accountability within a framework of professional autonomy. The apartheid model for public archives – answerable only to the state, with operations largely opaque – has been firmly rejected. Debate has revolved around mechanisms for achieving transparency and accountability, as well as the question of how an appropriate balance of accountability to the users of archives, to society and to the state is to be achieved. The National

35 The Legal Deposit Act makes the National Film, Video and Sound Archives (a component of the National Archives) a place of partial legal deposit for audiovisual publications. National heritage legislation ties the National Archives and other archival bodies into a broader national heritage structure. The Promotion of Acces to Information Act legislates, *inter alia*, the new Constitution's recognition of the right to information and the right to the protection of private information.

36 By July 1998 the National Archives had 18 black professional staff members.

VERNE HARRIS

Archives of South Africa Act accords the National Archivist full managerial and professional responsibility, but in the context of a delicate balance of power and accountability with parliament, the national cabinet minister responsible for archives, and the National Archives Commission. The role of the last-mentioned is crucial – appointed by the minister through a process of public nomination, it is the minister's and society's watchdog over the National Archives. Mechanisms for the exercise of state control over non-public institutions, with two exceptions, have attracted little support. The role of the state is seen as one of co-ordination, support and advice rather than of control. The National Archives of South Africa Act gives just such a role to the National Archives and the National Archives Commission. The two exceptions to this voluntary model relate to access provisions and the disposal of records. The Promotion of Access to Information Act legislates the constitutional right of access to records held by private bodies.[37] And there is consensus on the need for state control over the disposal of records in non-public archival custody: the National Archives of South Africa Act makes it an offence to destroy, export from South Africa, or otherwise dispose of records recorded on a National List by the National Archives Commission without the Commission's approval.

In the formative stages of transformation discourse, influential voices expressed the view that the shaping power of archives should be harnessed by the state to promote particular narratives, for instance, that of reconciliation and nation building. Mercifully this view has been in decline since 1994. History is littered with examples of states – not least the apartheid state – controlling their public archives to manipulate social memory. In 1993 Albert Grundlingh warned against it by raising the spectre of SAS being '. . . called upon to provide a legitimising historical project for the new state. Will that', he went on to speculate, 'involve the appointment of an official state historian . . . to narrate the anti-apartheid struggle in the same way that Breytenbach started some thirty years ago to chronicle the Afrikaner struggle against the British Empire?'[38] This has not happened, and appears unlikely to happen. However, there has been a strong emphasis on the active promotion of archives as a tool in the interrogation of South Africa's past. Heavy use has been made of archival holdings by bodies such as the TRC, the Commission for the Restitution of Land Rights, the Investigation Task Unit and Attorney-General's offices. There is poetic justice in the use of records of the apartheid state, which documented so densely and so obscenely the state's con-

37 South Africa's new Constitution recognises the right of access to 'any information that is held by another person and that is required for the exercise or protection of any other rights' (Section 32[1][b]).

38 Albert Grundlingh, 'Historical writing and the State Archives', p. 83.

trol over citizens' lives, to unfold the intricacies of oppression, expose the perpetrators of human rights violations, support the claims of the dispossessed to restitution, and prosecute those who refuse to ask for, or who fail to get, amnesty from the TRC.

Similar questions have permeated discussion of those core 'shaping' functions of public archives, appraisal and collecting.[39] With the former the focus has been on appraisal as an institutional process: Who should be responsible for appraisal? To whom should appraisers be accountable? How transparent should the process be? How reliable are the appraisals done during the apartheid era? These questions are rooted in an intense distrust of SAS's appraisal practice, which was characterised by an unrelenting opacity. Some have gone as far as to recommend that the appraisal function be taken from public archives and given to independent boards comprising academics and other 'stakeholders'. The intensity of this distrust was illustrated in November 1995, when South Africa's National Cabinet imposed a moratorium on the destruction of all public records – irrespective of whether they had been appraised by SAS – until the completion of the TRC's work. By 1995, however, debate had yielded substantial agreement that appraisal is an archival function and archivists should be responsible for it. Nevertheless, democratic imperatives demand that levels of transparency be high, that public account of appraisal decisions be given, and that there should be some measure of public participation in the decision-making. These positions are reflected in the National Archives of South Africa Act, which charges the National Archives with the appraisal of public records, subject to approval of its overarching appraisal policy and monitoring of the policy's implementation by the National Archives Commission.

Debate around the theoretical and methodological underpinning of appraisal practice has been less widespread but equally vigorous. Located mainly within SAS (later National Archives) structures, the debate has pitted defenders of SAS's established practice against advocates of macro-appraisal.[40] Macro-appraisal theory is built on the assumption that records have meaning within the contextual circumstances of their creation and contemporary use. Records are the product of processes involving complex interactions between creators of records, socio-historical trends and patterns, and clients/customers/citizens. All these elements constitute the dynamic contextual milieu in which records are created. The purpose of appraisal is to secure an appropriate documentary window into this milieu. Moreover, macro-appraisal contends that archival value is located, in the first instance,

39 There is no clear conceptual distinction, of course, between appraisal and collecting. Active documenting is an integral part of appraisal and collecting presupposes appraisal decisions. But in South African archival discourse and practice the distinction has been made firmly, with appraisal a function related to public records and collecting to non-public records. The National Archives' new appraisal programme is beginning to break down this distinction.

40 Macro-appraisal first became an issue in South African archival debate during Eric Ketelaar's visit to the country in 1992. His account of the Dutch PIVOT Project was received with scepticism within the State Archives Service. However, subsequently, the writing of Terry Cook on appraisal and the Canadian macro-appraisal approach raised considerable interest. This was the primary consideration behind the State Archives Service's invitation to him to visit the country in 1994. His explosive impact led directly to the Service's establishment of an Appraisal Review Committee, which in 1996 recommended the adoption of macro-appraisal.

not in records but in the processes that underlie their creation. First the appraiser must identify the key elements of the contextual milieu (appraisal of processes), and then seek to document them (appraisal of records). The methodology demanded by this approach is founded in broad-based research and strategic planning.[41]

Not surprisingly, SAS's appraisal practice – outlined earlier in this essay – has proved an easy target for advocates of macro-appraisal who question the validity of its intellectual foundation and its appropriateness to the realities of the 1990s. Macro-appraisal, they argue, provides an explanation of archival value rooted in the archival bedrock of provenance, which, unlike the idea of usefulness, secures a workable yardstick and meshes with a methodology appropriate to modern records environments. Moreover, it displaces the notion of the appraiser as a neutral handmaid to users of archives and replaces it with the view of the appraiser as an active documenter of societal processes. In 1996 SAS formally embarked on a macro-appraisal-inspired overhaul of its appraisal programme, which has been inherited and developed by the National Archives.

SAS's collecting function – also outlined earlier in this essay – has proved an equally easy target. Its critics have developed broad consensus on the defining characteristics of an alternative vision for collecting by public archives, one deeply influenced by the concept of 'total archives'. Policy, it is asserted, should direct archivists not only to society's pinnacles but also, firmly, to grassroots experience and the full gamut of experience in between. Policy should accommodate the complementing of official holdings but be directed primarily at filling its gaps. Collecting should be driven by the post-apartheid imperative to give voice to the voiceless. Public archives should not compete with the country's many non-public collecting institutions for material that would be more appropriately preserved by the latter. This vision has already found expression in the National Archives of South Africa Act, but two key questions remain unresolved. First, to what extent, if at all, should the collecting function be subordinated to the management of official holdings?[42] Secondly, what should public archives' involvement be in the collection of oral tradition and history? In South Africa, with its strong oral traditions and high rates of illiteracy, 'giving voice to the voiceless' will require a strong commitment to the collection of oral sources. Still being debated is whether public archives should collect oral tradition and history themselves, acquire oral sources collected by experts in the field, facilitate access to oral sources by means of a national register,[43] co-ordinate and pro-

41 For a fuller account of macro-appraisal, see my 'Appraising public records in the 1990s: a South African perspective', *ESARBICA Journal* 16 (1996).

42 The State Archives Service subordinated the collecting function firmly – in 1995 non-public records made up 5,4 per cent of the Service's total holdings.

43 In 1998 the National Archives launched an automated National Register of Oral Sources.

mote the collecting of oral testimony, or be invested with a combination of these functions. In 1999 the National Archives launched a national oral history programme which is positioned within the last-mentioned conceptualisation.

Debate around the use and availability of public records has followed numerous streams. Much attention, for instance, has been paid to the question of public rights of access, with substantial cross-fertilisation taking place between the archival debate and the wider public debate on freedom of information.[44] However, the defining issues in transformation discourse have hinged, in my view, on the assertion that it is not enough for public archives to ensure equal access to their holdings, even if they do so in terms of constitutionally entrenched rights of public access. They must go beyond being merely servers of records users. They must become creators of users; or, in the words of the popular slogan, they must 'take archives to the people'. From the outset this position formed one of the dominant streams in transformation discourse, and quickly secured hegemony, even within SAS. Its proponents pointed to the array of systemic barriers to access raised by the apartheid system, the alienation from public archives of most South Africans, and the urgent need to utilise public resources in addressing the huge inequalities and imbalances inherited from apartheid. Public archives, in short, should be transformed from a domain of the elite into a community resource. This position has found expression in the National Archives of South Africa Act, which requires the National Archives to 'make known information concerning records by means such as publications, exhibitions and the lending of records . . . with special emphasis on activities designed to reach out to less privileged sectors of society . . .'

CONCLUSION: AN ENCHANTED SLIVER

Apartheid's sterile archival discourse has been vanquished by a successor born of and connecting assuredly with South Africa's new societal dynamics. Although in the ascendancy and possessing a remarkable coherence, this transformation discourse is open-ended, accommodating sometimes intense debate. Moreover, it is characterised by many consensus positions arrived at by compromise – reflecting, I would argue, the contours of South Africa's political terrain. The discourse, then, is distinctively South African. Nevertheless, it has been influenced by and meshes with recent developments in international archival discourse, which in turn reflects the post-1990 ending of

44 The National Archives of South Africa Act reduced the restricted access period on public records in archival custody from thirty to twenty years. The new Constitution's recognition of the right of access was legislated for by the Promotion of Access to Information Act (Act 2 of 2000).

VERNE HARRIS

South Africa's isolation.

At the start of a new millennium, South Africa is set apart from most other nations by its embrace of a future through the negotiating of its past. In the academy, in memory institutions, school classrooms, courtrooms, the media, people's living rooms and, crucially, the TRC, South Africans are searching for meanings in myriad narratives of the past. Sadly, for most – and this criticism has been levelled at the TRC itself – the search is for closure – the closing down of meaning – rather than for a releasing of meanings. For some the meanings are borne by 'facts'; the 'truth' of what happened. For others 'fact' and 'fiction', 'history' and 'story', coalesce in imaginative space. In her account of two years as an investigative reporter covering the TRC, Antjie Krog for instance concedes that 'I have told many lies in this book about the truth'.[45] The writer André Brink argues that 'the best we can do is to fabricate metaphors – that is, tell stories – in which, not history, but imaginings of history are invented'.[46] Others occupy a middle ground, believing that story adds texture to the text of history, fills its gaps: 'the lacunae in the archives are most usefully filled through magical realism, metaphor, and fantasy . . .'[47]

This negotiation of the past, which is unfolding many new dimensions in social memory and generating huge quantities of archives, constitutes the ground on which the transformation of archives is being played out. I would argue, however, that transformation discourse is failing to engage the realities of this ground fully, or to utilise all the space this ground provides, because it remains wedded to a positivist paradigm rooted in the nineteenth-century birth of 'archival science'. In this paradigm the meanings of words like 'archives', 'archivist', 'record' and a host of others are simple, stable and uncontested. There is little attempt to address the new realities being fashioned by technological revolution and postmodernist epistemologies. The positivist paradigm posits archival records as providing a reflection of 'reality'. There is no space in it for the 'sliver of a window' concept that I explicate in the introduction to this essay. While it is true that transformation discourse has substituted the notion of archivists as impartial custodians with the view of them as active shapers of social memory, the discourse still defines archival endeavour in terms of custodianship, conceptualises archives in terms of physical things and places of custody, and proposes a (narrower) shaping of the record as the carrier of memory rather than a (broader) participation in the processes of memory formation. South Africa's transformation project in archives is interpreted in triumphalist terms, with the notion of archives holding

45 Antjie Krog, *Country of My Skull* (Johannesburg: Random House, 1998), p. 281.

46 André Brink, 'Stories of history: reimagining the past in post-apartheid narrative' in Sarah Nuttall and Carli Coetzee, eds., *Negotiating the Past: The Making of Memory in South Africa* (Cape Town: Oxford University Press, 1998), p. 42.

47 'Introduction', *Negotiating the Past*, p. 3. The editors mistakenly identify André Brink as a proponent of this view.

the collective memory of the nation muscling out my image of a fractured, shifting archival sliver.

In my view, then, while South African archivists have successfully re-imagined what they do and who they are in a post-apartheid South Africa, they have been less successful in engaging technological revolution and the conditions of postmodernity. Furthermore, they have not begun to allow space for, less explore, the contribution offered by what has been called 'African' or 'indigenous' epistemologies. It is not enough for black South Africans to establish a representative presence in the archival profession and its discourses. What is needed is voices in these discourses employing conceptual frameworks for meaning construction that are rooted in South African societal realities and pasts. Archivists, then, cling to outmoded positivist ideas that underpin inappropriate strategies, distorted notions of their role and inflated accounts of their accomplishments. I offer four examples to illustrate this. First, in pressing to reach out to users and to create new users, archives are too frequently opting for the neatly packaged information product rather than the rich contextualisation of text. In doing so they are contributing to what Jean-François Lyotard has called the 'commodification of knowledge'.[48] Knowledge as commodity carves a gulf between knower and known, provides answers rather than stimulating questions, encourages closure rather than opening. Moreover, much of archival outreach provides little or no space for competing narratives. We adopt the language of meta-narrative too easily, using our exhibitions, posters, pamphlets and so on to tell the story of, for instance, the struggle against apartheid, or of nation building, or of transformation. The counter-narratives, even the sub-narratives, too frequently are excluded, and so we deny our audience the very space in which democracy thrives. Secondly, both in the work done and in the planning of future projects related to oral history and tradition, there is a worrying tendency to underestimate, or simply not to grasp, the problems of converting orality into material custody. There are two aspects to this: a determination to view and to utilise recorded oral history as 'source' for historiography rather than as 'history' in its own right; and a failure to understand the extent to which oral history, in the words of Isabel Hofmeyr, 'live[s] by its fluidity'.[49] Thirdly, among archival appraisers there persists the notion that their appraisal work is simply about the building of a coherent reflection of 'reality' through the jigsawing of individual appraisals. There is little perception of the fact that the appraiser participates in the processes, the 'reality', which the

48 Jean-François Lyotard, *The Postmodern Condition: A Report on Knowledge* (Minneapolis: University of Minnesota Press, 1984), pp. 5, 45 and 51.

49 Quoted by Carolyn Hamilton, '"Living by fluidity": oral histories, material custodies and the politics of preservation', paper presented at the conference 'Words and Voices: Critical Practices of Orality in Africa and African Studies', Bellagio, Italy, February 1997, p. 17.

VERNE HARRIS

archival record 'reflects'. The appraiser's values, quality of work, perspectives, interaction with the records creating agency, engagement with the policy s(he) is implementing, and so on, all shape and are reflected in the appraisal. The appraiser is not simply identifying records with archival value; s(he) is creating archival value. This participation becomes part of the broader context to the text that is preserved. So the archival record provides a window into the appraisal process as much as it does into anything else. This demands an approach that embraces the individual appraisal as a record, a text with a very specific ontological status. Fourthly, in the contextualisation of text, which is central to all archival endeavour – whether it be in appraisal, the preparation of finding aids, exhibition commentaries or direct user support – most South African archivists remain wedded to the notion that their objective is the detaining of meaning, the resolving of mystery, the closing of the archive. There is little awareness of the imperative for contextualisation to reveal the multiple layers of construction in text, or of the need to disclose archival contextualisation as yet another layer. Such awareness would transform archival endeavour into an exercise in releasing meanings, tending mystery, opening the archive. It would foster passion for the different, the wholly other (Jacques Derrida's *tout autre*), the impossible.

The archival record, I have argued, is best understood as a sliver of a sliver of a sliver of a window into process. It is a fragile thing, an enchanted thing, defined not by its connections to 'reality', but by its open-ended layerings of construction and reconstruction. Far from constituting the solid structure around which imagination can play, it is itself the stuff of imagination. Another metaphor is provided for it by Ouma, a character in André Brink's novel *Imaginings of Sand*: 'I am a very ordinary person in most respects . . . But in one respect I know I am extraordinary. My memory. You're right. I have an amazing memory. At times I even surprise myself. I can remember things that never happened.' [50] The archival record, like all repositories of memory, is an extraordinary creation of remembering, forgetting and fantasy. Only when it is understood as such, treasured as such, will its enchantment be fully released to enrich South Africa's negotiation of the past.

50 André Brink, *Imaginings of Sand* (London: Minerva, 1997), p. 4.

Extracts from transcripts of Truth and Reconciliation Commission hearings

GOBODO-MADIKIZELA, CLOSING STATEMENT, BOLAND HEARINGS, 25 June 1996

Ms Gobodo-Madikizela: We have heard moving testimony this morning and indeed this afternoon since ten minutes ago. We were taken back to the early 1960s a period which marks the changes or the gradual and very slow changes that we have now witnessed recently. It was a very painful long process in which many people died . . . literally and figuratively when people like Mr Mkhabile and Mr Makhubalo, old stalwarts of the struggle in our fight for liberation, come to testify to this Commission and I am one of the people sitting here listening to their stories of endurance, of suffering – of humiliation, of important anger – sense of helplessness which continued in a struggle over the years over the 70s and the 80s.

I am really very humbled by some of the stories that have been shared here this morning, older men who are much older than many of us in this room. Parents, husbands, sons, the humiliation that they all suffered. We are grateful that we have been taken back to that period.

We've also heard how people have died – Petronella and her mother-in-law Ms Ferus told us about the endurance that their son and husband suffered. I think it's very important to note that one of the things that Ms Ferus said is how her son had repeatedly said to her, that mamma I will one day tell the public – tell South Africans how I have suffered – one day I will stand in a – in public in front of an audience and share with them how much I have suffered and how they have tortured me and how much they have tortured others.

And today Ms Ferus and Patti celebrated that vision of their son and husband to share that suffering with us, we [are] privileged to have been part of that audience, which that stalwarts of the liberation struggle in South Africa dreamt about. It's very special that we were part of that hope that he had and [we are] privileged that you came to share it with us.

Ms Joseph has just recently shared with us the senseless death of her son, and the inexplicable way in which he died and only to be told I am sorry Ms Joseph, sorry is such an inadequate term and for somebody to say I am sorry, without any explanation to the killing, even the sense in which we are told that stones were thrown – these people threw stones, how could we ever use live ammunition when people are just throwing stones – what if they are throwing stones – is there sufficient reason for them to be shot at with live ammunition – never mind the fact that the consequences were death?

It seems this became a pattern in this area – in the Boland region – the Boland – much as it is a rural region, it is perceived as a rural region, where the media very rarely comes unless something very big happens – where high profile leadership doesn't frequent the struggles of the areas – although they know about them. Where people really feel that they are forgotten, they are in the back of beyond – in spite of that, we have listened today and in the week to ordinary people – ordinary people, ordinary in the sense that nobody know about them. All these people we heard today, all these people we've heard in the week, nobody knows about them – and yet they were the most extraordinary people – they were involved in the most courageous acts of suffering, perseverance and enduring the pain and humility to their personhood, to their manhood, to their womanhood in the most unbelievable way. We are not able to comprehend the extent to which all these people have suffered.

I think it is particularly important for us to remember how courageous women of this area have been as well. In spite of the fact that they were also subjected to a particular kind of humiliation for women to be abused and for them to have their womanhood thrown about or reduced to an unimaginable level – is something which many of us would never fully comprehend and would never fully understand what it means for those woman to have been reduced to the level in which they were pulled down by the Security Police and all the police who were torturing them.

Theirs was a multiple kind of suffering, suffering the torture as in the physical torture but also suffering what Patti earlier on, Patti Esterhuizen referred to as an inner pain – these were very special people, they were very special women. I think also it was important for us to relate to their kind of leadership that came out of this little Boland which is supposed to be the back of beyond. We are extremely touched by it and we are humbled and we share the pain that all of you have suffered. . . .

Mr Williams: So what happened is this, I was in Kamalunga as an Engineering Instructor, well I was popular among the trainees cadres. As all these Instructors and the rest in fact they, the, most of the Instructors were genuine you see, we knew who was innocent and we knew the sell-outs and some of the sell-outs were Security men and they were appointed above us but we knew that but we couldn't speak, so in fact there was this boiling that was taking up in the camps, you know, it was this swelling that was supposed to burst you see, so the guys, some Comrades were taken to fight UNITA, they refused. When they refused Joe Modise called them half-baked soldiers, cowards and so on and yet the Comrades explained that 'Listen, it is not that we are scared to fight, their bosses want to fight the Boers not UNITA. If we fight UNITA we are going to die here in Angola. We want to go inside South Africa and die in South Africa fighting', so what happens is that they were kept in this camp far away from the trainees, they were understood to be having a bad influence. Well I continued there in Caculama and this mutiny thing started. The Comrades in Kamalunga, they mutinied over through the Administration, well they told them this 'Listen you guys are simple puppets, they are not going to kill you – we don't want you to go to South Africa and fight.' They disarmed the Administration and the Security, they took the trucks, the whole armament, they went to some other, it was called the Eastern Front, of which we didn't recognise it, because it was not in South Africa, it was in Kapuso, another town in Angola, the UNITA had overrun that town, taken it and we went there we pushed UNITA out of that town and was supposed to guard that town, because it was said our logistics used to pass through there. Our argument was that we were able to secure our trucks to and fro with logistics, even if we die at no point had we failed to secure our trucks, especially the June 16 detachment, because it was well trained. Right, OK. This mutiny went to Kapuso, at Kapuso the authorities there, they wanted to resist, they were overrun, trucks and armament was also taken there. The mutiny or mutineers grew – the number they became strong it was most the whole detachment now that was in that thing, in Angola except the Security and another transit camp that was called Vienna. We were prepared to go to Vienna, we knew that the Security would try to fight there and we were prepared to shoot them out and disarm them. I was still at Kamalunga. Another man who was in that thing, in the June 16 uprisings, Bongani came to me, he was a friend of

mine, he was also a Military Engineer, he came to me and told me that . . . (intervention)

Mr Sandi: Could you please confine yourself to the question of the Human Rights Violations to yourself. Especially what happened to you during the ANC camps so that we should not take long with peripheral issues, we would like you to tell us of yourself, tortures and experiences. Just a small reminder for you to confine yourself to the things that have happened to you and what you did, especially when you came back to the country in 1985. What steps did you take to raise your complaints with the Organisation concerned?

Mr Williams: Thank you Sir. First, I was demoted without any reason given, secondly, that was in Kamalunga and then in Caculama, in 1983 while I was that thing – head of Engineering Department I was punished, I was punished, I had to carry a sack on my back, doing tactics. . . .

Mr Sandi: Yes, you have already mentioned that, how you were punished . . .

Mr Williams: I didn't mention that Sir. I just said the punishment was like this, I am trying to confine now the whole thing to myself.

Mr Sandi: Mr Williams, you have come to the Commission to say that you were a victim of gross Human Rights Violations by an Organisation which you have mentioned. The request by the Commission is that you should confine yourself to those issues that deal with your ill-treatment or maltreatment whilst you were in exile and what did you do when you came back to the country.

Mr Williams: So I was punished, I carried this sack for six hours. I was running doing tactical exercises, that is crawling, jumping up immediately with a sack on what weighed more than 30kg because it was wet and it was sand and it was cold, I ran with this sack for 24 rounds around the grounds and then some of the people, the perpetrators who did this to me, 'No, this one looks very tough, he didn't have enough', they said he must have some more tactics. They took me to a – that thing – a rivulet, there was a rivulet in Caculama, they said I must, they took some of these things from ZAPU from ZIPRA where Selous Scouts, you see people who were working for the Rhodesian Armed Forces were infiltrated ZIPRA where harassing and frustrating ZIPRA Comrades so they did, they did this also to us, I was put in this rivulet, I mean I am hot now, very hot after doing many rounds and tactics, put in this rivulet to stay there with my head under the water, I was told not to come up, if I come up I will be battered with an automatic rifle – that is an AK – will be beaten, and I had to suffer this, all along I told myself that I wish the Lord gives me the power to survive. I prayed all along, and indeed the Lord did answer. I survived this. I stayed there, when the mutiny was at Vienna, Bongani came, he said to me, listen we know what happened to you, you can't stay here, join us, let's be a force, let's challenge these corrupt authorities so that we can go to South Africa. I said OK, wait, my time has not come.

Mr Sandi: I'm sorry, Mr Williams, can I interrupt you. Besides what you have said so far, are there any other forms of brutality to which you were submitted – and if one, what is your instruction to the Commission, what are you asking us to do, do you understand, do you say that we should take this up with the ANC?

Mr Williams: Thank you. There are so many. In Kapuso, I was done the same thing by a man who we knew was a sell-out, was an informer, was known 'Green' in Kapuso – that Eastern Front. I was taken to the Eastern Front because the ANC was beginning to be feel UNITA. So we were taken there because we were fighters, real fighters. We went there, we tried to put a check on UNITA and after that I was punished, once more again for being given a party by Soviet Comrades, you see they called me to a party and then I was punished that I am having parties and so on, without seeing the authorities and I get drunk, while I am supposed to be . . .(intervention)

Mr Sandi: I am sorry Mr Williams, can I ask you once more what is your, your request to the Commission, all in all before I hand over to the Chairperson.

Mr Williams: OK. Let me go on. So there was this mutiny, at Kakuso I was re-called back to Kathlawa and then I stayed in Caculama. Later on I ran away from Kakuso to the mutiny –

Mr Sandi: You have mentioned the mutiny already, I asked you if there is any other form of brutality to which you were subjected to?

Mr Williams: Yes sir. As mutineers, we were rounded up – excuse me, I would the Commission to try and protect me also – because you see I am a determined person. When I stand for a principle, I stand for it, I don't think anybody or anyone – that's why I was able to survive up to this point. And that's why the 16th couldn't break me – including the National African Congress itself.

Mr Sandi: Could you please switch off please. Mr Williams you are well protected, we have afforded you longer time than any other witness that has come before us up to this

stage. We wish that you bear in mind that there are six more witnesses which we still have to take. Could you please in summary form as the person is asking you who is leading you. Give us Human Rights Violations which were done to your by the ANC on those camps and give us your requests to the Commission.

Mr Williams: As I said as a mutineer, we were rounded up and we were put in a concentration camp we were 21, and the ANC had a concentration camp.

Mr Sandi: Mr Williams, I am trying to protect you and I am doing my best, could you come to the Human Rights Violations – call them by name so that we can record them and come to the request that you would like to put to the Commission.

Mr Williams: I was in the concentration camp in Paola – where some of the mutineers were put there, for what was so-called rehabilitation – we didn't need rehabilitation, we were well rehabilitated. We were put here to hew, to hew wood and draw water. Simply that. And it was said we are being reorientated, with being given politics – we were just fed food, food that we didn't even trust, some of us didn't want the food and were asked many questions. I was called upon one day and I was told that I was going to be roped up to a tree by 'Green' – this 'Green' was a chief of staff at Paolo, we knew him to be an informer, former police spy – so-called tender – revolutionary – Green said to me 'Listen, for your defiance we are going to rope you up to a tree, and you are going to stay overnight', there I said 'No, it would never happen to me', and he started to box me, to hit me, I parried him, the Commissar went in, he said 'What are you doing, are you fighting against the Chief of Staff'. I said 'No, I am not fighting, I am just blocking him, I haven't yet started fighting, if I start fighting, I will hit him very hard'. The Commissar said . . .(intervention)

Mr Sandi: Mr Williams, sorry, I am afraid I think we, we have given to very close to an hour – can we go onto your instructions or your requests to the Commission. What are you asking the Commission to do – in a nutshell, can you say that very, very briefly please?

Mr Williams: No, excuse me Sir. You see there are more Human Rights abuses that happened to me, these are just petty ones, being roped up to a tree overnight, they are petty – what about refusing to be chained to a tree – I was taken to Quattro.

Mr Sandi: Please elaborate on your recent statement after you have testified, there is no problem about that. But can we now ask you, to ask exactly what are you asking the

Commission to do? I see in your statement here you are saying the Commission should get the ANC to have you compensated for the years spent in exile preparing to fight for liberation of your country. Is there anything more you want to say in addition to that?

Mr Williams: That one is not important Sir. What is important is that I will request, because you see, when I am here, I am not simply here.

Mr Sandi: You also say in your statement you tried to get what you call 'demobilisation packages' at the ANC offices but nobody seems to want to cooperate with you in regard to that. Is there anything more you want to say in addition to that?

Mr Williams: Yes.

Mr Sandi: In the interest of time, I must emphasise this – in the interest of time.

Mr Williams: What I would like to request the Commission to do for the sake of the people of South Africa, especially for the sake of those fathers and mothers who had their children killed in exile without any reason – that the African National Congress, if it's prepared to face the truth, to cleanse itself it should come up at least with all the names who died in exile and along each name an explanation be attached or be given that this one died of malaria at such and such an hour. This one died at the hands of UNITA, at such and such an hour. This one died because he was resisting the ANC security or whatever, or this one died because the Security killed him – for this reason or that reason. Or this one committed suicide.

Mr Sandi: OK. The long and the short of it is as I understand you is that the ANC should provide a list of names of all the people who died in exile in whatever circumstances, whatever the circumstances may have been. That is what you are saying in a nutshell. . . .

AMNESTY HEARING, JOHANNESBURG, 11 April 1997

Mr Black: Now, the evidence of Mr Ndlovu was that when he entered that house, he after he spent some time in that house trying to persuade the occupants of that house, to evacuate that house and he explained what they intended to do to the house and that is why you must all get out. His evidence was that he – it wasn't just a brief time, he explained over, he made several attempts to get you out of the house before setting the house alight, did that happen?

Mr Masupa: No, Sir, that is not true.

Mr Black: Did he make any attempt that you saw to go into the house to get the children out of the house, persuade any other of the occupants to remove themselves from the house?

Mr Masupa: No, Sir, they didn't waste time after they arrived in the house. They didn't waste time. They just came and did what they intended to do. They didn't even give us a chance to go out. If they gave us a chance to go out, we could not have been injured.

Mr Black: Yes.

Judge Wilson: Who were they who came into the house, you say they didn't waste time?

Mr Masupa: My late sister who told us the saying Vusi, which means it is Vusi is the one who is called Absalom Gobela. That is the one whom my sister called his name, that is the one I was able to identify.

Judge Wilson: Do you remember you gave evidence at the trial?

Mr Masupa: That is true, Sir.

Judge Wilson: And there you said there were two people who came into the house, Vusi and Phineas.

Mr Masupa: That is true, Sir.

Judge Wilson: Well, now you've told us the only one you know was your sister called us Vusi? Which is the correct . . .

Mr Masupa: The truth is that she called Vusi because she said to Vusi what do you want, let us talk. Phineas at that time was with him, there were two people who were in the house.

Judge Wilson: Well, did you see him?

Mr Masupa: Phineas?

Judge Wilson: Yes.

Mr Masupa: Yes, Sir.

Judge Wilson: Why did you a few minutes ago say that you didn't, that the only person that you saw there, the only person you could identify as being there was Vusi because your sister called out his name, that is how I understood your evidence?

Mr Masupa: She called Vusi's name and Phineas was together with him, she didn't call Phineas, but they were two. She didn't say Vusi, Phineas, she said Vusi, but they were together.

Adv de Jager: Would it be correct if I say you didn't know Phineas' name before or did you know his name?

Mr Masupa: Phineas?

Adv de Jager: Yes.

Mr Masupa: Yes, he grew up in the area, I know him.

Adv de Jager: So you knew him? Were you in fact able to see him there?

Mr Masupa: Do you mean Phineas?

Adv de Jager: When were you able to see him, weren't the lights out? When did you recognise him?

Mr Masupa: When they entered the house, they entered when it was dark and when they said Mantha, it is when they switched on the lights, then Mantha called his, Vusi's name.

Ms Khampepe: But Sir, when you got to the kitchen, you saw two people and you were able to remember that one of them was Vusi because Mantha called his name. Were you able to recognise Phineas Ndlovu, who grew up in front of you?

Mr Masupa: Yes.

Ms Khampepe: And you can today say with certainty that he was in the kitchen on that night, that him and Phineas, no Phineas Ndlovu and Vusi Gobela were in the kitchen on the 2nd of July, that night?

Mr Masupa: Yes, both of them were in the kitchen.

Ms Khampepe: Did you perhaps make a mistake during the trial when you only mentioned Vusi and you failed to mention Phineas.

Judge Wilson: He mentioned Phineas in the trial.

Ms Khampepe: You only mentioned Phineas Ndlovu.

Judge Wilson: He mentioned both of them at the trial.

Ms Khampepe: He did, oh?

Judge Wilson: He mentioned both of them in the trial, he didn't mention Phineas before us today.

Ms Khampepe: Oh, okay. Sorry, I thought it was the other way around, I thought my Committee member had said that you had not mentioned Phineas Ndlovu at the trial.

Judge Wilson: You mentioned Phineas at the trial, you did not mention Phineas earlier in your evidence, is that not the position? Here today you did not mention Phineas until I began questioning you.

Mr Masupa: I was explaining to the Committee that both of them entered the house. Vusi is the one who was being called by my sister and Phineas was with him.

Judge Wilson: Carry on.

Ms Khampepe: Did you perhaps mention Vusi because Mantha had called Vusi by name?

Mr Masupa: That is true, Ma'am.

Mr Black: Right, Mr Masupa, you were satisfied and you testified at the trial that there were at least these two people in the kitchen, is that correct?

Mr Masupa: That is true, Sir.

Mr Black: Okay. But did you go to the kitchen?

Mr Masupa: Yes, I went to the kitchen.

Mr Black: At what stage did you go? At what time did you go to that kitchen? Did you go into the kitchen?

Mr Masupa: Yes, I went to the kitchen whilst Mantha said the petrol, we are smelling petrol in the kitchen.

Mr Black: Okay, so you heard her say that and then you went to go and investigate, is that correct?

Mr Masupa: That is true.

Mr Black: Now, the important point is at no time did any of those two people who had entered your house, attempt to persuade you or any other member inside that house, to vacate the house before the petrol was set alight, is that correct?

Mr Masupa: That is correct, they never gave us time to be out of the house.

Mr Black: Yes, okay. Now, you suffered extensive burn injuries, you've lost the sight of your eye. What about personal belongings inside that house, what happened to them?

Mr Masupa: The property was damaged in the house and the house was also burnt.

Mr Black: When you say damaged, what do you mean? Completely burnt out?

Mr Masupa: We couldn't use them any more, they were completely burnt.

Mr Black: Okay. Now there are one or two other issues I just want to clear up with you. As far as Mantha or Christina, your late sister is concerned, was she a political activist and a student?

Mr Masupa: That is correct.

Mr Black: And was she regarded as a comrade?

Mr Masupa: Yes, she was regarded as a comrade.

Mr Black: And as far as – what standard was she in then?

Mr Masupa: She was doing standard 9.

Mr Black: Standard 9, right. You've heard the evidence of Mr Ndlovu and it has been explained to you that we will get an opportunity to ask him questions on that, further questions. But Mr Ndlovu says that he was also in standard 9 and at Davey High School. Do you know if he was at school? He was your neighbour.

Mr Masupa: I will briefly explain to this Committee about Mr Ndlovu. He grew up at his mother's place, that is in the Sotho section and they moved to our area and he came to be our neighbours.

Mr Black: When was . . .

Mr Masupa: He didn't go to school at that time.

Mr Black: Okay, but now how old – when – you must be a bit, we don't know the times and the dates or the year you are talking about. When was this, in the same year?

Mr Masupa: They arrived in 1985 to be our neighbours, that is Phineas Ndlovu.

Mr Black: And his mother?

Mr Masupa: Yes.

Mr Black: Was he attending school then?

Mr Masupa: No, he was not schooling.

Mr Black: Did he attend school at any time after 1985?

Mr Masupa: After 1985, there were riots until in 1987 when they were arrested.

Mr Black: Yes . . . (tape ends) and I understand Hendrik Masupa who has been mentioned, is he – he is your younger brother, is that so?

Mr Masupa: That is correct.

Mr Black: Did he sleep at that house?

Mr Masupa: No, it was years of not sleeping at home.

Mr Black: And we are talking about the house that was burnt down now. And where did he sleep?

Mr Masupa: He used to sleep at my grandfather's shop.

Mr Black: Is this the shopping complex which was referred to earlier on in the evidence of Mr Ndlovu?

Mr Masupa: That is correct, that is the same store, Sir.

Mr Black: Right, and as far as, if I may refer to him as Hendrik, is concerned, was he attending school?

Mr Masupa: Yes, he was schooling.

Mr Black: What standard was he in at the time this happened?

Mr Masupa: He was doing standard 8.

Mr Black: And what school was he attending?

Mr Masupa: Davey Senior Secondary School.

Mr Black: Okay. As far as Phineas Ndlovu and his family is concerned, was there any difficulties or problems between your family and his family?

Mr Masupa: There were not problems at all between the two families.

Mr Black: Was there any reason whatsoever to your knowledge why Mr Ndlovu and his friends arrived at your house, your mother's house and set it alight with everyone inside?

Mr Masupa: I do not bear any knowledge up to now, Sir.

Mr Black: They did not give you any reasons when they entered the house?

Mr Masupa: No, Sir.

Mr Black: And your knowledge of Mr Phineas Ndlovu's activities, he claims that he was a scholar and that he also was a comrade. What is your knowledge of his activities in that area?

Mr Masupa: I can testify before this Committee that he was not schooling. The comradeship that he referred to was the comradeship of robbing people, of stealing cars from people, of taking food from the delivery vans in the township. That he was a comrade, a real comrade, I do not want to testify to that effect.

Mr Black: What do you mean by that, was he regarded, was he regarded, was he considered in the community to be a comrade?

Mr Masupa: No, Sir.

Judge Wilson: What do you mean by comrade?

Mr Masupa: A comrade is a person involved in politics. That is my understanding.

Ms Khampepe: Mr Masupa, were comrades in your area not involved in stopping delivery trucks?

Mr Masupa: No.

Judge Wilson: Did you know anything about a people's court?

Mr Masupa: There is nothing I know about the people's court, Sir.

Adv de Jager: During those days, everybody was almost politically active, wasn't it so? And your sister Mantha was also a comrade and a political activist?

Mr Masupa: Yes.

Adv de Jager: Who was the leader of Mantha and her comrades' group?

Mr Masupa: I know a person called Aubrey.

Judge Wilson: Do you know him as the leader of Mantha's group?

Mr Masupa: I know him very well, he used to frequent our home.

Judge Wilson: Was he the leader of Mantha's group? Was he connected with the group that Mantha associated with, the comrades?

Mr Masupa: That is correct.

Ms Khampepe: Was he a scholar?

Mr Masupa: Yes, he was also at Davey Senior Secondary School.

Adv de Jager: The people – on entering the house – was there only one speaker or did both of them or more of the people entering the house, address you and speak out?

Mr Masupa: I couldn't understand, I couldn't hear well what they said, but there was talking in the kitchen.

Ms Khampepe: Mr Masupa, how soon after you had heard people coming into the kitchen, did you go to the kitchen to join them?

Mr Masupa: I went to the kitchen when the deceased, Mantha, said we are smelling petrol.

Ms Khampepe: Was it after some time or was it immediately after you had heard people coming into the kitchen?

Mr Masupa: That was after they called her name, Mantha.

Judge Wilson: Was the talking in the kitchen before they called Mantha's name?

Mr Masupa: No.

Judge Wilson: Well, when did it happen – the talking, you said there was talking in the kitchen but you couldn't hear what they said.

Mr Masupa: They called Mantha, Mantha went to the kitchen and she said to them Vusi, what do you want, talk and she said I am smelling petrol.

Judge Wilson: Yes, but a moment [ago] you said to us I could not hear well what they said, but there was talking in the kitchen. What did you mean by that?

Mr Masupa: I mean they were talking, but they were not shouting. There was no noise.

Judge Wilson: When were they talking?

Mr Masupa: They came into the house, they called Mantha, she went to the kitchen.

Judge Wilson: And they talked then, did they?

Mr Masupa: It means they talked to her because she replied. Because she went on to say I am smelling petrol.

Ms Khampepe: Was your mother present when Mantha went to the kitchen, was she there?

Mr Masupa: Yes, she was in the kitchen.

Ms Khampepe: Do you still want to lead, Mr Black?

Mr Black: Yes, I thought there was still . . . Mr Masupa, as far as Mr Ndlovu is concerned, his activities, you say you know him well, is that correct?

Mr Masupa: I know him very well.

Mr Black: Alright. Do you know anything – did you know Mr Sibisi?

Mr Masupa: Yes, I know Mr Sibisi.

Mr Black: Now, how do you know him?

Mr Masupa: He was staying at the next street from my grandfather's shop and he had a car.

Mr Black: Yes, and what do you know about that now? Did Mr Ndlovu know Mr Sibisi, do you know anything about it, could you please just tell us what . . .

Mr Masupa: Mr Phineas Ndlovu and them were troubling Mr Sibisi because he had a car. They always wanted to use his car, if there was anything they wanted to do, they would go to him and he couldn't bear it any more. He said I am leaving this area, these boys are troubling me every time they come to my place and they take my car with force.

Mr Currin: Sorry Mr Chairman, is this not hearsay evidence and what is its relevance? If it is hearsay, I do object to it. Are you going to call Mr Sibisi to say that this is what he has been saying?

Mr Black: It is not hearsay in the sense that Mr Sibisi told him, told him and this is – no . . .

Judge Wilson: Isn't hearsay clearly what somebody tells you?

Mr Currin: It is hearsay in the sense of what allegedly these people did, but he, Sibisi gave him a reason for leaving the area. That is it, whether it is true or not, it is immaterial.

Adv de Jager: Mr Currin, since we've practised, I believe the Act has been changed. Hearsay evidence can be allowed; whether it has got any value, that is another thing.

Mr Currin: Just in the spirit of the nature of cross-examination for the purposes of this Committee, I would suggest that maybe this evidence is really not relevant.

Mr Black: Well, I don't want to get embroiled at this stage.

Judge Wilson: Well, I think it is finished now, hasn't it, so let's go on.

Mr Black: Now you heard Mr Ndlovu testify yesterday, he addressed you and the family at length asking for forgiveness for what he had done. What is your attitude towards, what do you feel about that?

Mr Masupa: I will never forgive Mr Ndlovu. If it were possible for him to raise my dead sister, I would forgive him, but I am not in a position to forgive him now. I am not referred to as – people don't refer to me with my name, they call me a burnt person and I don't want to pretend that I will forgive him. God please forgive me, I don't have forgiveness in my heart. We are here to speak the truth, to reconcile, but I am sorry, I cannot.

Mr Black: Did you at that time, Mr Masupa, regard the actions of Mr Ndlovu and his friends as acts carried out by comrades? Is that what you expected comrades to do, let's put it that way?

Mr Masupa: No, Sir. I never expected the comrades to burn the house. Comrades are fighting for truth and justice.

Mr Black: Just to clarify one little issue. You were asked about certain political activities that took place in the township, were you working during say the year of 1987?

Mr Masupa: Yes, I was working.

Mr Black: Were you working on a full time basis?

Mr Masupa: Yes, I used to go to work at seven and knock off at four.

Mr Black: Were you in any way involved in any political activities in the sense of . . .

Mr Masupa: No, Sir, I was not involved in any political activities.

Mr Black: Okay I have nothing further to add, thank you, Mr Chairman.

NO FURTHER QUESTIONS BY **Mr Black**.

Ms Khampepe: Mr Masupa, I will only ask you one question pursuant to what has been led by Mr Black. To your knowledge did the comrades not burn down houses of people who were perceived to be informers in your area?

Mr Masupa: I don't remember of such an incident. That – our house was the first to be burnt, that is according to my knowledge.

Mr Currin Just two questions for clarification.

Mr Black: Mr Chairman, may I – before, there was one question I omitted to put to the witness.

Judge Wilson: You may go on.

FURTHER EXAMINATION BY **Mr Black:** Thank you. Mr Masupa, do you know whether the comrades in that area that you knew, approved of the fact that your house had been burnt down?

Mr Masupa: No, Sir.

Mr Black: Why do you say that?

Adv de Jager: Mr Black, you are asking whether he knows whether they approved. He said well, I don't know, so I presume the answer would mean he doesn't know whether they approved or disapproved.

Mr Black: Mr Masupa, do you know whether the comrades in that area said that it was the right thing to do, did they approve of the burning of your house or not? Did they approve of it or did they not approve of it?

Mr Masupa: No, they didn't approve it. Because even when we were at the hospital, the comrades came to visit us. Aubrey and them came to visit us at the hospital.

Mr Black: Yes, but when they came to visit you did they say that it was the right thing or the wrong thing that was done?

Mr Masupa: They were telling us about the thugs that attacked us in the house. They told us how they arrested some of them, they got hold of them all. After we were burnt in the house, the comrades went out searching for them and they found them.

Mr Black: Yes, so are you saying that it was made clear to you by comrades there that they did not approve of this act?

Mr Masupa: Yes, they were totally against the burning of our house. They came to see us at the hospital.

Mr Black: Yes, thank you.

...tlya	BD	7581J	Molamka	714

Top-left table

NAME	CAUSE
umale,E	HA
umalo,J	HA
umalo,8	DD
...mazul,P	KA
...G...	KA
...eale	KA
...koon	DD
...00	DD
...	DW
...letsh	DW

Top-middle table

BODY NO.	PLACE	NAME	CAUSE
157...	...A	J Molaca	KA
2142		C. Molheli	KA
X002	Zimb	Molife, D	DD
92011	Zimb	Molamia, K	KA
X157	SWA	Kalete	
2413	8WA	Pfeile, E	DD
4091	Fr	McKlet	DW
9710	Fr	Hadson	DW
0...	F	Gill	DW
104	F	Dorla	DW
101	F	Shula	DW

Top-right table

DEAT...
BODY NO.
11485
2517
2897
98563
7151
1256
915...
95...
9168

Middle-left table

NAME	CAUSE
...mazul, A	KA
...mazul, F	KM
...u, F	KA
...ed, K	
...l, R	KA
...ea	F
...eno	DW
...ile	KA

Middle-middle table

BODY NO.	PLACE	NAME	CAUSE
12300	Gr	Mullins	KA
721X	Gr	Rivea	KA
X01	191	Noyes	KA
7X...	G	Niteri	KA
740	G	Nickesh	KA
1297	G	Gratum	KA
21817	G	Old	KA
7869	G	Little	KA
2861	FC	Mitting	KA
9766	G	Jamut	KA

Middle-right table

BODY NO.
X214
701
7666
9606

Bottom-left table

	CAUSE
...and, E	KA
...lay, V	D.D
...ll, V	D.D

Bottom-middle table

BODY NO.	PLACE	NAME	CAUSE
X01	Viet	Frances, T	KA
X27	Viet	Digle, O	KA
394	Viet	Bugdet	KA
...	Viet		

Bottom-right table

DEA...
BODY...
X212

The Archive, Public History and the Essential Truth: The TRC Reading the Past*

Brent Harris

At a lecture presented in London on 5 June 1994, Jacques Derrida discussed the complexities of the meaning of the archive. He described the duality in meaning of the word 'archive', in terms of temporality and spatiality as a place of 'commencement', and as the place 'where men and gods *command*' or the '*place* from which *order* is given'.[1]

As the place of commencement, '*there* where things *commence*',[2] the archive is ambivalent. It houses what could best be described as 'traces'[3] of particular aspects of the Past[4] in the form of documents. These documents were produced in the Past and are subjective constructions with their own histories of negotiations and contestations. Their preservation in the archive represents a moment of the end of epistemological instability. They are the outcomes of negotiations and contestations over knowledge and the effects of power in this outcome. Yet, as a container, as a depository of evidence the archive represents a second moment in ending instability, in creating stasis and the fixing of meaning and knowledge when the evidence it houses is deployed in historical narratives.

This is because the archive has long been the hallmark for and of the production of history, particularly in the academy. Students of history have been taught that, to do research, they have to go to the archive to 'read' the primary sources located there. The process, in historical research, of discovering 'new' areas of research had tended to close the past contained in the archive.[5] For decades most researchers were not inclined to go back to the documents that preceding researchers had consulted, privileging not only the previous researcher's discovery of the documents but also that researcher's interpretation of those documents. This was partially due to a once dominant argument and assumption that history was a science and to a related assumption that research could and should be done objectively. In this event, the documents housed in the archive were taken to be neutral and were endowed with the power to speak the truth. Hence, they were thought of as representing 'open windows' to the Past.

These assumptions have been challenged for quite some time and from many quarters, and in some quarters they have even been dismissed.[6] It is more prevalent nowadays for subsequent researchers to

*This essay has benefited tremendously from extensive comments on earlier drafts by Dr Leslie Witz, Dr Gary Minkley, Premesh Lalu and Dr Patricia Hayes of the History Department, Dr David Bunn of the English Department at the University of the Western Cape and Adam Sitze of the Cultural Studies and Comparative Literature Department at the University of Minnesota, as well as from comments and interventions from the editors of this volume. They are not, however, held responsible for the arguments or errors contained herein.

1 Jacques Derrida, *Archive Fever: A Freudian Impression* (Chicago and London: University of Chicago Press, 1996), p. 1. Emphasis in original.

2 Derrida, *Archive Fever*, p. 1. Emphasis in original.

3 The term 'traces' is taken from Keith Jenkins, *Re-thinking History* (New York: Routledge, 1991) and is preferred to terms such as 'information', 'sources' or 'evidence' as these are embedded in positivist and objectivist claims that deny the subjective construction of 'information' and 'evidence'. My usage of the term 'evidence' elsewhere in this essay should be read as a miming of positivist and objectivist claims that this essay criticises.

4 The Past with a capital 'P' refers to a pre-narrative and pre-textual reality, and differs from the past as contained in the archive and in historical narratives.

5 This has partly been the effect of research-funding policies and postgraduate studies' requirements at most universities, the effect, as it were, of power in the production of knowledge.

go back to the archive to reread the documents that previous researchers have consulted. Through these practices, the past, as contained in the archive, is typically revisited, reread, reappraised, reinterpreted, revised and rewritten. In this regard, the archive does become the place from which the past commences, despite the past contained in the archive being incomplete as the archive can only hold certain traces of certain aspects of the Past.

From its establishment, the Truth and Reconciliation Commission (TRC) was seemingly presented in opposition to the Derridian sense of the archive as the place of 'commencement'.[7] Instead, those involved in the TRC and a number of politicians presented it as 'shutting the book on the country's past', as coming to 'terms with our dark past *once and for all*' and as closing 'a horrendous chapter in the life of our nation'.[8] In discursive statements, the TRC's role was often referred to as that of 'uncovering' and 'unearthing' the Past, with functions of exhumation and reburial, rather than revisiting and reinterpreting the past. With the added function of assembling an archive, the TRC represented an attempt, however (un)successful, at the fixing of knowledge, both in the sense of correcting misunderstandings and in the sense of ending the instability of the meanings attached to the Past.

The second implication that Derrida identified in the word 'archive' is more closely related to the production of knowledge. In his lecture he alluded to the role of the superior magistrates, or the *archons*, in ancient Greece. '[T]he *archons*', Derrida said,

> were considered to possess the right to make or to represent the law. On account of their *publicly recognised authority*, it is their home, in that place which is their home . . . that official documents are filed. The *archons* are first of all the documents' guardians. They do not only ensure the physic security of what is deposited and of the substrate. They also accord the hermeneutic right and competence. They have the power to interpret the archives. Entrusted to such *archons*, these documents in effect speak the law: they recall the law and call on or impose the law.[9]

Those prominent in the discursive space created around the TRC conferred upon it the role of the *archon* of the 'new' South Africa. Indeed, a number of eminent commissioners claimed for the TRC the 'publicly recognised authority' and power to interpret the archive that it was entrusted to establish. They claimed this authority on the basis of representing and being representative of the nation, and permitted the Past to speak and called upon it to speak by inviting the nation to

6   See, for example, Hayden White's 'The burden of history' in White, *Tropics of Discourse: Essays in Cultural Criticism* (Baltimore and London: Johns Hopkins University Press, 1985), pp. 27-50. Also see Keith Jenkins, *Re-thinking History*; Carlo Ginzburg, 'Checking the evidence: the judge and the historian' in James Chandler, Arnold I. Davidson and Harry Harootunian, eds., *Questions of Evidence: Proofs, Practices and Persuasion across the Disciplines* (Chicago and London: University of Chicago Press, 1991), pp. 291-303; and Joan Scott, 'The evidence of experience' in Chandler et al., eds., *Questions of Evidence*, pp. 363–387.

7   The TRC had been established in 1995 by parliamentary decree to 'uncover and acknowledge' human rights violations that were committed by various parties during the struggle for and against apartheid and to facilitate the granting of amnesty to the perpetrators of those violations.

8   Final Clause of the Constitution of the Republic of South Africa Act, No. 200 of 1993 quoted by Dullah Omar in 'Justice in transition', *The Truth and Reconciliation Commission* (Cape Town: Justice in Transition, ca 1996), p. 2; and Desmond Tutu quoted in *Weekend Argus*, 'Commission "must heal nation": true reconciliation main aim, says Tutu in first address', Sunday, 16/17 December 1995. Emphasis added. These undoubtedly referred to the Past.

9   Derrida, *Archive Fever*, p. 2. Emphasis in original.

recall and recollect the Past at the TRC's public hearings. In this way, *they* recalled and imposed history.

Here a tension existed in the work of the TRC: the Commission was established through the Promotion of National Unity and Reconciliation Act (Ponura) to 'uncover' 'as complete a picture as *possible* of the nature, causes and extent of gross violations of human rights' that occurred during the last three and a half decades of the apartheid era in South Africa.[10] Yet the impression was created that through the work of the TRC the Past could be known 'once and for all'. This impression was reinforced by the institutional nature of the TRC as a parliamentary commission, by the TRC's public hearings at which elements of the Past were presented to and for the nation, and by the TRC's function of gathering and consigning evidence of the Past for the archive. In this sense the work of the TRC was self-referential. It archived the evidence it required to support the history that it produced and, by archiving its evidence, it guaranteed the veracity of the history it produced.

The process of archiving evidence, of gathering information together for an archive, is associated, Derrida suggests, with 'the function of unification, of identification, of classification'. This process, he adds, 'must be paired with . . . the power of consignation'.[11] For Derrida, consignation refers to two related processes: one is the 'act of consigning through *gathering together signs*' into 'a single corpus, in a system or a synchrony in which all elements articulate the unity of the ideal configuration';[12] and the other 'involve[s] classification and *putting into order*'.[13] Thus, while the archive does not, and cannot, house the complete Past, its consignation creates the illusion of unity, of being a co-ordinated and ordered corpus.

The TRC was established by governmental decree to fulfil particular, predefined objectives. As such, the government defined, or at least presented, the rudimentary framework by which the TRC would 'order' the archive it was entrusted to consign. Here the TRC was assigned the task of 'uncovering' the Past in order to provide 'a historic bridge between the past of a deeply divided society characterised by strife, conflict, untold suffering and injustice, and a future founded on the recognition of human rights, democracy and peaceful co-existence for all South Africans'.[14]

The TRC was also established to facilitate nation-building through reconciliation. As such, it was required to shape the past into an 'ideal configuration', 'to effect an ethically responsible transition from present to future'.[15] TRC commissioner Pumla Gobodo-

10 Promotion of National Unity and Reconciliation Act, No. 34 of 1995, 3(1)(a); hereafter abbreviated 'Ponura'.

11 Derrida, *Archive Fever*, p. 3. Emphasis added.

12 Derrida, *Archive Fever*, p. 3. Emphasis in original.

13 Derrida, *Archive Fever*, p. 4. Emphasis in original.

14 As proclaimed in Ponura.

15 White, *Tropics of Discourse*, p. 49.

16 Pumla Gobodo-Madikizela, HRVC Hearing, Paarl, Wednesday, 16 October 1996. Emphasis added.

17 Ponura, 3(1).

18 In his analysis of South African commissions of inquiry into 'the native question', Adam Ashforth arrived at the conclusion those commissions were 'not just modes of scientific investigation' but were simultaneously 'performances which served to authorise a form of social discourse'. See Adam Ashforth, *The Politics of Official Discourse in Twentieth Century South Africa* (Oxford: Clarendon Press, 1990). Emphasis added. Also see George E. Marcus, 'The official story: response to Julie Taylor', in Michael Ryan and Avery Gordon, eds., *Body Politics: Disease, Desire and the Family* (Boulder, San Francisco and Oxford: Westview Press, 1994), pp. 207–208.

19 Ponura defined 'gross violations of human rights' as the actual or attempted 'killing, abduction, torture or severe ill-treatment of any person . . . by any person acting with a political motive'. See Ponura, 1, 1, (1), (ix).

20 See Steven Robins, 'TRC must look at "ordinary" apartheid', *Cape Times*, Tuesday, 5 August 1997 and Robins, 'No-name people who kept cogs of apartheid oiled', *Cape Times*, Wednesday, 6 August 1997.

21 The TRC did, however, attempt to incorporate some of these processes into its field of investigation by holding workshops, notably at Oudtshoorn, in which some of the psychological aspects of apartheid oppression were addressed, and by holding 'sector' hearings to investigate the activities of the media, the business sector and religious bodies, among others, during apartheid. However, these sector hearings presented the media and the business sector with a subject position from which to speak and from which to represent its version of, and its position in, the past. See, for example, 'Ill-prepared TRC fails to press business for atonement', *Cape Times*, Monday, 17 November 1997; 'The truth: business's moral omissions', *City Press*, Sunday, 16 November 1997; 'Now even acceptability is a commodity', *Weekend Argus*, Sunday, 15/16 November 1997. Also see Sam Shilowa, HRVC Hearing, Johannesburg, Thursday, 13 November 1997 and Jay Naidoo, HRVC Hearing, Johannesburg, Thursday, 13

Madikizela made this quite explicit at the end of the public hearings of the TRC's Committee on Human Rights Violations (HRVC) at Paarl when, in response to the TRC's critics 'who continue to say that we should not be doing this work because we are opening up old wounds', she said that 'if you want to move into the future we [*sic*] should reflect on the past', and asked, 'how do you look *into* the future without exploring what happened in the past?'[16]

The TRC was thus essentially a commission of inquiry that was grounded in the present and was designed to 'promote' a future nation that would be characterised by 'unity'.[17] It was not left, however, to define the discourse that would promote this national unity. Instead it served as a mechanism that authorised and legitimised the government's discourse on nation, nationalism, patriotism and the conflicts of the anti-apartheid struggle.[18] Indeed, Ponura, which governed the TRC, restricted the Commission's scope and delimited the nature of the archive it was to consign. The Act placed limitations on the TRC: it restricted the TRC to a specific period of oppression and a specific phase of resistance to that oppression in South Africa. Through the phrase 'gross violations of human rights', Ponura restricted the TRC's field of inquiry to particular patterns of oppression and resistance and to particular forms of suffering, victimhood and perpetration,[19] as Steven Robins indicated.[20] The TRC could thus not investigate with any rigour the exploitative economic policies, discriminatory provision of education and other services that were part and parcel of apartheid, or the psychological effects and suffering caused by detention without trial and solitary confinement, where these were not accompanied by acts of torture, poisoning, maiming or death while in detention or police custody.[21]

For Derrida, the archive contains a third implication, related to the consignation of the archive. The archive, he said, is not only the place 'where things commence' and the place 'from which order is given' but is also the place where memory is deposited so that, as George Marcus states, '[a]s long as the archive is there, the memory exists as stored information' that remains 'publicly available'.[22] It is, however, not a repository of 'spontaneous memory, as *mnémé* or *anamnesis* [but] of *hypomnéma*',[23] not of memory that resides in one's mind but of memory that has been preserved and remains 'publicly available' through inscription.

As a repository of memory Derrida suggests the archive is simultaneously related to the process of forgetting – of forgetting that which 'operates in silence' and consequently that which 'never leaves its own archive'.[24] The process of silence and forgetting in the consignation of the archive, he continues, is not innocent. The archive itself produces silences. It frames what is consigned in the archive as a unified whole and represses what is left outside the archive, denying its existence and consigning it to oblivion. But the archive, like the exergue, 'serves . . . to lay down the law and give the order'.[25] This Derrida describes as 'the violence of the archive'[26] and is of significance because, as he suggests, the archive is always consigned and ordered ethically, 'as anticipation of the future'.[27]

I find Derrida's discussion of the archive and his discussion of the archival implications of the establishment of the Freud Museum useful in describing the epistemological relationship between the archive, evidence and history and in thinking about the TRC as a metonym for this relationship. In this essay I use the TRC as a model for exploring some of the intricacies of this relationship. I argue that the reconciliatory processes of the TRC relied upon the recent Past and that those processes required the creation of a collective social memory of that Past which would be applicable, it was hoped, to all South Africans. This, I argue, was an important feature of the TRC and entailed re-imagining the South African people as a new nation and making a clean break with the Past. Much of the debate around the TRC, prior to its establishment, centred around the issue of addressing human rights violations, restoring the dignity of the victims, healing the society, and ensuring that such violations were not to be repeated in the future.[28] These human rights violations were, however, read and cast by many protagonists of the TRC as symptomatic of a lack of national unity. In this view, the political conflicts of the Past had resulted in the polarised memories of a 'deeply divided society' and, in the belief that social memory and social identity are interrelated, the social memory of the Past has to be made 'whole', it has to be made to constitute a 'single corpus'[29] to be relevant to the new nation. The TRC institutionalised this Past by consigning it into an archive, by exposing it in public and by producing an official Report. This Past, I suggest, was made to represent itself, to speak itself, and was represented as a real and objective history precisely through its correspondence in the archive. By setting up its own archive, the history that the TRC produced became self-referential as the TRC assumed the authority of the *archon* to interpret the archive that it assembled.[30]

For the TRC to assume the authority of the *archon*, to call on the Past to speak and to permit the Past to speak, and because the archive it consigned was a national archive, the TRC needed to define and

November 1997.

22 Marcus, 'The official story', p. 208.

23 Derrida, *Archive Fever*, p. 11.

24 Derrida, *Archive Fever*, p. 10.

25 Derrida, *Archive Fever*, p. 7.

26 Derrida, *Archive Fever*, p. 7.

27 Derrida, *Archive Fever*, pp. 16–18.

28 See the articles in Alex Boraine, Janet Levy and Ronel Scheffer, eds., *Dealing with the Past: Truth and Reconciliation in South Africa* (Cape Town: IDASA, 1997) and Alex Boraine and Janet Levy, eds., *Healing the Nation?* (Cape Town: Justice in Transition, 1995).

29 The former Chilean National Commission for Truth and Reconciliation commissioner José Zalaquett argued, for example, that '[a] society cannot reconcile itself on the grounds of a divided memory. Since memory is identity, this would result in a divided identity.' See José Zalaquett in Boraine et al., eds., *Dealing with the Past*, p. 13.

30 Like the archive, this essay creates the illusion of constituting a single corpus but unlike the archive I attempt to perform this failure by acknowledging it. Furthermore, in this essay I critique the use of the archive and evidence to construct a history that creates the impression of reality yet this essay is itself an archive of sorts and uses evidence to construct an argument. In essence, this essay employs the same conventions that it seeks to critique. As such, it is an epistemological failure – for I cannot use the conventions that this essay requires for its success – and a cognitive failure – for the conventions that destabilise historiographical practices have not and possibly cannot be imagined other than against existing conventions in which case it becomes anti-historiographical. Thus, trapped in the form of historical argument, I cannot illustrate *and* counter the deployment of evidence in history. I cannot argue against the referential and rhetorical use of evidence as reality in historiography, and remain within the confines of historiography, without deploying evidence in the same manner. (I am greatly indebted to Adam Sitze for his assistance in formulating this note more clearly. I, however, bear full responsibility for adopting this position.)

constitute the nation in relation to which it positioned itself. Hence, from its inaugural meeting in December 1995, the Commission set about facilitating nation-building and re-imagining of the nation as 'new', an official process that had originated during the Convention for a Democratic South Africa (Codesa)[31] negotiations of the early 1990s.[32]

The TRC, however, differed from Codesa in numerous ways. The latter convention occurred largely away from, and without the direct input of, the public. It was a process that occurred between political leaders who rallied their supporters in 'rolling mass action' to place pressure on their rivals at the negotiating table, and who in turn were pressurised by their supporters to arrive at particular settlements, particularly with regard to the issue of political prisoners.[33] The processes that characterised the TRC, on the other hand, occurred to a large extent within the public sphere. Here the 'public' was invited to participate in the making of a new nation through the telling and the witnessing of the nation's Past at the TRC's public hearings. Thus, while the nation was being rethought and discussed by politicians at Codesa, at the TRC hearings the public was invited to participate in the rethinking of the nation. They were not, however, invited to influence or shape the imagining of that nation. The nation had already been imagined as one, as united, and as comprising 'all South Africans, black and white'.[34] The TRC thus served to authorise the notion of South Africa as a 'new nation' by making it part of the public sphere and part of public discourse. Not that this process was without opposition. At Codesa the opposition was dramatically displayed by the attempts of the right-wing *Afrikaner Weerstandsbeweging* (AWB) to disrupt the negotiations process, under the leadership of Eugene Terre'Blanche. This opposition was further demonstrated by the withdrawal of the Conservative Party (CP) and the Inkatha Freedom Party (IFP) from the process, as well as by the CP's rejection of the 1994 general elections. At the TRC, the shaping of the nation as well as the processes of reconciliation through contrition was opposed by the Afrikaner community, most notably in the Afrikaans press, and by the IFP.

Despite this, the TRC had articulated South African society in national terms since its inception. It had referred to South African society in the single collective – as 'us' and 'we' – and to South Africa as 'our land'. As in the 'rainbow nation' espoused by the TRC's chairperson, Archbishop Desmond Tutu, the nation was thought of as simultaneously multifaceted and divided. This notion of a 'rainbow nation', influenced perhaps by the international discourse on 'multi-

31 Codesa saw the coming together of the various parliamentary and extra-parliamentary political movements in the early 1990s and had as its objective a peaceful settlement of the political conflicts in South Africa.

32 Before Codesa, South African society did not figure as a unified nation in the official discourses of the state. Instead the state thought of South African society in terms of separate and distinct nations or peoples, as *volke* rather than *nasies*. A similar use of the concept 'nation' was employed by the liberation movements at least until the establishment of the United Democratic Front (UDF) in the 1980s. The UDF was an unofficial space in which South African society was imagined as one nation.

33 This occurred most noticeably at the ANC's Consultative Conference in December 1990. See Steve Clark, ed., *Nelson Mandela Speaks: Forging a Democratic Nonracial South Africa* (New York, Montreal and Sydney: Pathfinder, 1993), pp. 69–74.

34 This understanding of the nation as a duality is expressed most noticeably by Thabo Mbeki cited in the *Weekend Argus*, 'Mbeki slams SA's party-poopers: Deputy President says opposition parties are not committed to nation building', Saturday, 30/31 May 1998; *City Press*, 'Rainbow nation – two worlds in one', Sunday, 31 May 1998; *City Press*, 'SA a country of two nations – Mbeki', Sunday, 31 May 1998; and *Cape Argus*, 'Mbeki: We must end race divide: Equal "only in theory"', Friday, 29 May 1998. It is, however, also evident in the ANC's Freedom Charter, see Raymond Suttner and Jeremy Cronin, *30 Years of the Freedom Charter* (Johannesburg: Ravan Press, 1986), as well as in the thinking of the UDF.

culturalism' and by American civil rights activist Jesse Jackson's 'Rainbow Coalition', both emphasised unity – as *the* rainbow nation – and implied separateness and disunity. It thus appears to have vindicated the 'separate cultures, separate nations' policy, advocated and implemented by the apartheid state, but also to have qualified the discourse of reconciliation and the TRC's use of the metaphor of a nation, fragmented under apartheid, to be reunited in post-apartheid South Africa by the TRC.

Having in this way defined the nation as one but divided, the TRC established its authority to interpret the nation's Past, to call on the nation's Past to speak, to recall the nation's Past, and ultimately to speak the Past for the nation. It did this by casting itself as representative of the nation and as representing the nation.

At the Commission's inaugural meeting in Cape Town on 16 December 1995, Tutu emphasised the TRC as representing the nation, and as having authority on that basis, when he stated:

> By and large, and remarkably so, the composition of this commission has found general and *favourable acceptance*. It means we have *credibility* and we must do all we can to enhance that credibility. We hope through some of the appointments to the Committee on Human Rights Violations and the Committee on Reparations and Rehabilitation to make the commission *even more representative* and inclusive.[35]

Indeed, when the TRC's commissioners were appointed in November 1995, two people were added to the names that had been chosen through a selection panel. These two were added 'in order to enhance, in the opinion of the president and cabinet, the resonance of the Commission across the various divides of South African society'.[36]

Just over a year later, the Commission's deputy chairperson, Alex Boraine, was to reiterate the idea that the TRC represented the 'various divides' of the nation. Following a dispute within the Commission itself, which resulted in some 'black TRC officials' alleging that they were being 'marginalised' and that the Commission was practising racial discrimination,[37] Boraine explained that the TRC 'is a microcosm of South Africa, which is itself experiencing enormous tensions as it recovers from a period of desperate conflict' and, hence, 'it would be surprising if there were no tension in the TRC'.[38]

At the same time, the TRC claimed to be representative of the nation as a whole rather than as comprising a collection of representatives of its divides. The most significant inference of this was con-

35 Tutu quoted in the *Weekend Argus*, 'Commission "must heal nation,"' Sunday, 16/17 December 1995. Emphasis added.

36 Gerwel quoted in the *Cape Times*, 'Mandela names Tutu to head Truth Commission', Thursday, 30 November 1995. Similarly, the TRC's Reparations and Rehabilitation Committee (R&RC) was expanded in February 1996 to ensure that the Eastern Cape Province had a representative on the R&RC. See Alex Boraine quoted in the *Argus*, 'Eastern Cape wins Truth forum voice', Tuesday, 6 February 1996.

37 *Sowetan*, 'TRC to discuss internal tensions', Wednesday, 22 January 1997. Also see Gaye Davis, 'On a wing and a prayer', in *Siyaya* 3 (Spring 1998), pp. 6–9.

38 Boraine quoted in *Sowetan*, 'TRC to discuss internal tensions', Wednesday, 22 January 1997. Also see Wendy Orr quoted in Davis, 'On a wing and a prayer', pp. 8–9.

39 Wilhelm Verwoerd, 'Continuing the discussion: reflections from within the Truth and Reconciliation Commission', *Current Writing*, 8, 2 (October 1996), p. 66. Verwoerd responded here to a range of critical questions posed by participants and papers at 'The Future of the Past: The Production of History in a Changing South Africa' held at the University of the Western Cape, 10–12 July 1996.

40 Verwoerd, 'Continuing the discussion', p. 68.

41 This was reiterated by Archbishop Desmond Tutu at the end of the hearing into the disappearance of Siphiwe Mtimkhulu and Topsy Madaka. At this hearing Tutu affirmed that the Commission was established by the nation through parliament and was ordered by 'our president' to fulfil certain tasks. See Tutu, HRVC Hearing, Port Elizabeth, Wednesday, 26 June 1996.

42 This was partly the consequence of the artificial but practical separation of victim and perpetrator hearings and the demographic effect of the struggle for and against apartheid that had resulted in the victims being mainly black, and mainly the victims of apartheid atrocities, and the perpetrators being mainly white and having acted mainly in accordance with apartheid.

43 The TRC was to endorse this declaration. See *TRC Report*, vol. 1, p. 94.

44 *TRC Report*, vol. 5, pp. 212–13, 222.

45 *TRC Report*, vol. 5, pp. 212–13, 218–22.

46 Tutu cited, 'Tutu: Ex-govt exquisitely cruel', *Citizen*, Wednesday, 24 April 1996.

47 *TRC Report*, vol. 5, p. 239.

48 See, for example, Manthata, HRVC Hearing, Duduza, Tuesday, 4 February 1997.

49 Tutu cited, 'Need for strong opposition shown – Boraine', *The Star*, Friday, 26 April 1996. Also see Tutu, HRVC Hearing: NP Second Party Submission, Cape Town, Thursday, 15 May 1997.

tained in an article by Wilhelm Verwoerd, a member of the TRC's Research Department. In this article Verwoerd responded to academics' 'critical questions', posed at a conference in June 1996 that he had attended, challenging 'the nature, scope and legitimacy of the TRC'.[39] He suggested in his response that academics had no representative legitimacy from which to criticise – rather than critique – the TRC, particularly as 'the nature of the TRC' was 'uniquely democratic'.[40] Since the TRC had been established *constitutionally* through the enactment of the Promotion of National Unity and Reconciliation Bill, in parliament, by the members of parliament, he pointed out, and since its commissioners were appointed by the State President, the TRC was *de jure* representative of the nation by proxy.[41]

Once it had claimed the authority of the *archon* to bring the Past to speak, the nature of the past that was to be 'uncovered' became important. The TRC required a past that would foster a non-racial nationalism; it required national subjects that could speak this past; and it required a national audience that would hear and bear witness to the speaking past. The TRC thus sought to expose a past that would bridge the existing racial divisions in South Africa.

The imagining of the nation as 'new', constructed at the TRC through the accumulation of individual memories into a body of collective memory, was designed to overcome the narrowly defined, racial divisions of the Past and to build a future society based on a reconstruction of the Past. The TRC aspired to expand a sense of community and a sense of collectiveness, purportedly founded on the oppression, hardship and injustices of apartheid, and to make it applicable to 'the new nation'. In so doing, it emphasised individual memories and experiences of the struggle against apartheid, and cast them as of national significance, applicable to all South Africans.

This was an ethical decision, for while the TRC 'uncovered' a multiplicity of positions as well as a multiplicity of political conflicts of the recent past, it tended to reduce these to two positions: one that resisted apartheid and another that defended apartheid. The TRC presented the position against apartheid as legitimate and just, and elevated the moral significance of that position while vilifying the other as unjust and illegitimate.[42]

Archbishop Desmond Tutu's reaction to former State President F. W. de Klerk's testimony at the National Party's second party submission to the TRC, and the subsequent media coverage it received, are illustrative of this and were in line with the United Nations' declaration of apartheid as a crime against humanity and the Kairos

Document. Indeed, the TRC was to endorse this declaration,[43] and was to find that the apartheid state, 'through its security and law enforcing agencies', was 'the primary perpetrator of gross human rights violations in South Africa, *and* from 1974, in Southern Africa'.[44] The Commission added that particularly under the rule of P. W. Botha some of the apartheid state's violations were of a 'criminal nature'.[45] Some TRC commissioners also described the previous government as 'exquisitely cruel'[46] and 'callous' and implied that the struggle against apartheid was a 'just war'. Indeed, the TRC was to 'endorse the position in international law . . . that both the ANC and PAC were . . . conducting legitimate struggles' against apartheid. It also acknowledged the 'comparative restraint with which the ANC conducted its armed struggle'.[47] Furthermore, when those involved in the anti-apartheid struggle during the 1980s were cited as perpetrators of gross human rights violations, TRC members often referred to them as having 'vitiated all the noble efforts of the liberation struggle'[48] or their victims as having been 'caught in the crossfire'.[49]

One implication of this moral positioning was that the emphasis on the extent of the 'cruelty' and 'callousness' of apartheid caused the atrocities that occurred in the struggle against apartheid to seem justifiable, and made it possible for some to argue that because the ANC's armed struggle was a 'just war', it was not necessary for those engaged in the legitimate activities of armed struggle to apply for amnesty.[50]

The TRC thus chose to emphasise what Richard Rorty would call a South African 'community of solidarity',[51] supposedly fostered and established during the conflict of the apartheid era, particularly in the 1980s. During this period, internal resistance politics was dominated by multiracial organisations such as the United Democratic Front (UDF) and the Congress of South African Trade Unions (Cosatu). The TRC appears to have adopted the concept of nation contained in the discourse of these anti-apartheid movements, particularly that of the UDF, 'the most popular internal opposition movement' to apartheid during the 1980s.[52] At that stage the UDF had

> envisioned a 'national liberation struggle' that included all the nation's peoples, white and black, opposed to continued minority domination. The only criterion for inclusion in its . . . concept of nation was opposition to apartheid and 'voluntary adherence' to the broad principles of nonracial democracy.'[53]

For the TRC, this sense of solidarity had developed among the oppressed communities in South Africa, a perception expressed at the

50 Deputy President Thabo Mbeki also contended that the ANC's armed conflict, and the deaths and injuries arising therefrom, were justified as 'the former government systematically closed off to its major opponents all avenues for peaceful political activity, eventually leaving them with no choice but to resort to violent struggle in pursuit of justice and freedom' (Editorial, *Cape Argus*, 5 November 1996). Mpumalanga Premier, Mathews Phosa, extended this to his argument that the ANC should not be required to apply for amnesty for 'legitimate acts against apartheid'. See Mathews Phosa cited in the *Sunday Weekend Argus*, 2/3 November 1996; and in *Sowetan*, 5 November 1996. Also see the *Sowetan*, 'ANC to explain"just war"', Thursday, 6 March 1997; *Cape Times*, 'Old foes at loggerheads over war', Wednesday, 7 May 1997; and the *Weekend Argus*, 'Struggle not terrorism but a just war – Mbeki', Sunday, 24/25 August 1996. Another implication not explored here is that apartheid then becomes the historical source of all evil in South Africa, potentially trivialising the colonial moment in South African history. Ironically, just prior to the release of the *TRC Report* in October 1998, high-ranking members of the ANC government, with the notable exception of President Nelson Mandela, criticised the TRC for equating the struggle against apartheid with apartheid in its report, though they had not raised such concerns before that moment.

51 See Richard Rorty, *Contingency, Irony and Solidarity* (Cambridge: Cambridge University Press, 1989), pp. 189–98.

52 Anthony W. Marx, *Lessons of Struggle: South African Internal Opposition, 1960–1990* (Cape Town: Oxford University Press, 1992), p. 14.

53 Marx, *Lessons of Struggle*, p. 15.

HRVC hearings at Ashton, on Tuesday 25 June 1996, when the TRC claimed that 'in 1990 the coloured community of Oukamp and the black residents of Zolani united to fight racism in Ashton'.[54] This was not a fictitious claim; many activists engaged in the struggle in the 1980s had rejected the terms of identity 'coloured' and 'black', preferring instead the prefixed description 'so-called coloured' and 'so-called black'. Indeed, this solidarity in the resistance against apartheid was proclaimed in struggle poetry and slogans, such as *'Ons is almal in die struggle, die Mammies and die Pappies, die Oumas en die Oupas, die honde en die katte'*.[55] Although this slogan did not mention racial identities, it did indicate a unity that transcended differences of race, gender and generation.

However, the non-racial national ideal of the UDF did not become a reality. The South African society of the 1980s remained fraught with contradiction. First, not all South Africans, and significantly not all oppressed South Africans, had taken up the struggle against apartheid. Certain members of 'the oppressed' served on, and supported, the apartheid state's security structures. They were, thus, not seen by the UDF and its supporters as part of the oppressed but became seen as traitors, sell-outs, police informants and collaborators.[56] The community councillors of the black local authorities, black police officers, *kitskonstabels*,[57] police informants and Inkatha supporters of the time remained outside the UDF's 'nation' as they did not subscribe to the tenets of the UDF's 'national liberation struggle'. Secondly, other internal political movements, such as Inkatha and the Azanian People's Organisation (Azapo), competed with the UDF's ideological tenets and fostered exclusively ethnic and racial identities respectively. Thirdly, the internal liberation movements were also involved in internecine conflict. These internecine conflicts did come to the attention of the TRC, as they were referred to at a number of hearings.[58] Despite these contradictions, the TRC spoke of a past during which a 'community of solidarity' existed, and sought to transfer this 'solidarity' to the 'new nation'.

The TRC attempted to do this by exhibiting the personal memories of the victims of apartheid and by casting these victims as innocent and without agency. The TRC then sought to expand the boundaries of inclusion into this community of solidarity, elevating those memories to the level of supranational significance, so that all South Africans, regardless of race, could partake in it. Here the TRC appeared to vindicate Kader Asmal, Louise Asmal and Ronald Suresh Roberts' assertion that 'for the new South Africa to abandon accurate

54 'Many hurt in "senseless shooting spree by police,"' *Argus*, Wednesday, 26 June 1996. This conclusion was attributed to the TRC's research department. Also see Pumla Gobodo-Madikizela, HRVC Hearing, Ashton, Tuesday, 25 June 1996.

55 Afrikaans for: 'We are all in the struggle, the mothers and the fathers, the grandmothers and the grandfathers, the dogs and the cats.'

56 See, for example, 'Family of councillor tells of "merciless" township killing', *Argus*, Wednesday, 26 June 1996; Malinge Zweni, HRVC Hearing, Ashton, Tuesday, 25 June 1996; *TRC Report*, vol. 2, pp. 384–392; *TRC Report*, vol. 3, pp. 108, 475–479.

57 *Kitskonstabels* was the colloquial name for the special constables deployed in the African townships from 1986. They were called *kitskonstabels*, which can be loosely translated as 'instant constables' because of the short amount of training they had to undergo. Initially their training was only six weeks long but was later extended to three months.

58 See, for example, Marx, *Lessons of Struggle*, pp. 170–176; Rejoice Mlungisi Kungwayo and Vuyo Mfutwana, HRVC Hearing, Port Elizabeth, Wednesday, 26 June 1996. Also see *TRC Report*, vol. 3, pp. 96-106, 108–112, 475, 669–670.

remembrance in these early years of its birth would be the most cruel self-slaughter', and that the 'Truth and Reconciliation Commission will prevent that'.[59]

For Asmal et al., the 'new South Africa' was an objective reality that existed in physical, rather than abstract, mental spaces in the mid-1990s. They suggested that the 'new South Africa' did exist; all that the 'new South Africa' required was a mechanism to ensure that it would neither forget nor mis-remember its past. They furthermore claimed that the 'new South Africa' had one essential Past.[60]

For the TRC, however, the 'new South Africa' existed between physical and abstract reality. The 'new South Africa' did exist as certain elements of it were tangible enough for the TRC to address and represent the 'new South African nation'. In this respect, post-apartheid South Africa was equated with the 'new South Africa'. The full expression of a 'new South African' nationhood, however, remained an abstraction, but one that could be fulfilled through re-conciliation and the re-imagining of the South African nation as one. Hence, in his opening address at the HRVC's hearings at Worcester on 24 June 1996, Alex Boraine 'reminded' those present that the Commission was 'dedicated to the search for truth in the hope of the contribution towards the reconciliation which we all long for and are working towards but have yet to realize fully in our country'.[61]

In terms of reconciliation, the place of truth and its relation to the Past were perceived as crucial to the working of the TRC. Before its establishment in 1995, a number of interlocutors had already affirmed the basic assumption that '[u]nless a society exposes itself to the truth, it can harbour no possibility of reconciliation, re-unification and trust. For a peace settlement to be solid and durable, it must be based on truth.'[62] Perhaps the most daunting reference to the truth and the Truth Commission was put forward by Mary Burton, then a prominent member of the anti-apartheid movement Black Sash, and subsequently appointed a TRC commissioner. In 1994 she suggested that a South African truth commission

> must gather in stories to reach that truth which is, in a way, already widely known and accepted. But we need to make it legitimate through that process. We need to tell and record and validate that truth. We need to acknowledge the wrongs, not only in terms of justice and hurt, but also the terrible loss.[63]

Two years later the TRC began to 'validate' the 'already known truth' through the movement of sources from the oral to the written, and

59 Kader Asmal, Louise Asmal and Ronald Suresh Roberts, *Reconciliation through Truth: A Reckoning of Apartheid's Criminal Governance* (Cape Town: David Philip and Mayibuye Books, 1996), p. 12.

60 See Asmal, Asmal and Roberts, *Reconciliation through Truth*, pp. 12–13.

61 Boraine, Opening Address, HRVC Hearings, Worcester, Monday, 24 June 1996. Emphasis added.

62 Roberto Canas in Boraine et al., eds., *Dealing with the Past*, p. 54; Zalaquett in Boraine et al., eds., *Dealing with the Past*, p. 13; and Patricio Aylwin in Boraine and Levy, eds., *Healing the Nation?*, p. 42. Also see Juan Mendez in Boraine et al., eds., *Dealing with the Past*, p. 89; Asmal in Boraine et al., eds., *Dealing with the Past*, pp. 138–139; Boraine in Boraine et al., eds., *Dealing with the Past*, p. 153; and Asmal in Boraine and Levy, eds., *Healing the Nation?*, p. 29.

63 Mary Burton in Boraine and Levy, eds., *Healing the Nation?*, pp. 122–123.

through the 'gathering in' and institutionalisation of this movement in the production of a Commission report and the consignment of a national archive. This movement occurred primarily at two moments in the TRC, at the moment of statement taking and at the moment of transcribing testimonies. These two moments were governed by two different sets of practices. The moment of statement taking was just that – the instantaneous taking down or recording of witnesses' statements onto paper.[64] The moment of transcribing testimonies was completely different. It was not an instantaneous moment and did not merely entail the taking down of the witnesses' statements but also the recording of an interaction between the witnesses and the Commission in an audiovisual format that was later transcribed onto paper by Veritas Transcription Services, a private company contracted for this purpose by the TRC, and the print media. That both the audiovisual, or at least the audio, recording and their transcripts were to be deposited in the archive is a testament of the TRC's self-referentiality. Here the audio recordings are the measure of the accuracy of its transcriptions of the Commission. But the public presentation of testimonies was also the moment of what Mary Burton called the 'telling' and 'acknowledging' of the truth. Thus, the audio recordings and the transcripts housed in the archive constitute the accuracy, the reality and the truth of the history presented by the TRC through its public hearing and in its report.

It was argued that for purposes of reconciliation these testimonies would be most fruitful if they were presented and circulated in public. As such, these testimonies became elements in a public display and a public history, at the same time that they were being 'gathered in', 'gathered together' and archived. The public was thus invited to attend the TRC hearings and to 'bear witness' to the past that was put on display through the TRC. In this event, the TRC became an official body at which the public history, history and the archive were cast in correspondence.

The public attended the TRC hearings as spectators who witnessed the unfolding of the past. As spectators, they contributed to the epistemological project of the making of meaning, which the state, through institutions like the TRC, was embroiled in. The public did not judge the testimony laid before it as evidence, but expressed its acknowledgement of the testimony as evidence of the Past through its reactions to the testimony and the orator, acknowledging these testimonies emotionally. At the HRVC hearings this reaction was often sympathetic and served to affirm the testimonies as the 'essential

64 This was, however, not a neutral process. It relied heavily on the selectivity of memory, which I will discus in the next few pages, and was influenced by the statement taker's attitude to the deponent. The TRC Report indicates that statement takers were instructed to be sympathetic to the deponents. See TRC Report, vol. 1, pp. 138, 140.

truth' while at the Amnesty Committee (AC) hearings the audience's reactions were either hostility shown toward members of the previous state's security forces, or disbelief. These reactions were captured on film by the ever-present media cameras and microphones and were relayed daily to a wider television, radio and newspaper audience, which for the TRC was part of its audience and part of the public.

The TRC's reference to 'public' hearings was illustrative of the Commission addressing the nation, because for the TRC the public that attended its hearings was a synecdoche of the nation. Thus, during his opening address at the HRVC's hearing into the Trojan Horse incident, Archbishop Desmond Tutu proclaimed that 'the nation acknowledges the victims' awful experience and, in a way, the nation is saying sorry'.[65] Similarly, at the HRVC's first round of hearings in Cape Town, on Monday 22 April 1996, Alex Boraine acknowledged to Nomakula Evelyn Zweni that she had 'come a very very long way' and that 'we'd like you to tell your story to all of us now, and not only to those in this room, but of course to many, many others who are listening on the radio, or perhaps will watch the television or read about it in the newspapers. You have a story that we all need to hear.'[66] At the HRVC special hearing that dealt with the fates of Tobekile 'Topsy' Madaka and Siphiwe Mthimkulu, Boraine reiterated this, when he said that the hearing was 'very special for all the people from New Brighton, from Port Elizabeth and so many others who will be listening on the radio and watching and reading about you and your son and the suffering and pain that you've endured',[67] while Tutu thanked 'the electronic and print media for helping to tell . . . the stories' of the victims of gross human rights violations.[68]

The TRC thus laid claim to an extended audience – to the audience present at the hearings and to a remote media audience. Essentially, the members of this extended audience were related, not in a 'language-field',[69] but in an ethically and morally defined field of interest, and 'formed, in their secular, particular, visible invisibility, the embryo of the nationally imagined community'.[70] In this sense, and through the TRC, the public and the nation became synonymous.

Here the usage of 'the public' differed from Jürgen Habermas' notion of the public sphere, yet the TRC exemplified a Habermasian public sphere. For Habermas, the public sphere is not the aggregate of the citizens of the nation state but includes all those who might join in a discussion of issues raised by the state. The participants in this discussion include agents of the state and 'private citizens'.[71] The public sphere is thus a space of potential interactive discourse where neither

65 Tutu, *The TRC Special Report*, SABC 1, Sunday, 25 May 1997. Tutu was speaking at the opening of the HRVC's event hearing concerning the Trojan Horse incident in which policemen killed three youths on 15 October 1985. In this infamous incident, policemen had been concealed in the back of a South African Railways truck that had driven through an unrest flashpoint in Athlone with the expectation that the vehicle would be stoned and that the police would open fire on the protesters. Indeed, the vehicle drove through the area twice, not having been stoned on the first occasion.

66 Boraine, HRVC Hearing, Cape Town, Monday, 22 April 1996.

67 Boraine, HRVC Hearing, Port Elizabeth, Wednesday, 26 June 1996.

68 Tutu, Closing Address, HRVC Hearing, East London, Thursday, 18 April 1996.

69 Benedict Anderson, *Imagined Communities: Reflections on the Origin and Spread of Nationalism* (London and New York: Verso, 1991), pp. 41–43.

70 Anderson, *Imagined Communities*, p. 42.

71 Jürgen Habermas cited by Craig Calhoun, 'Introduction: Habermas and the public sphere', in Craig Calhoun, ed., *Habermas and the Public Sphere* (Cambridge, MA and London: MIT Press, 1992), p. 8.

participation nor the nature of the discussion nor its occurrence is important, but where there is potential for a number of people to participate in the discussion, which implies knowledge of, and exposure to, issues raised by the state. The TRC was, essentially, such a discursive space. It was an official body at which the official history and the public history of the recent past were cast in correspondence, for, while the TRC 'gathered in' stories of the past and consigned them in the archive, it publicly displayed elements of the archival body under construction. In so doing, it enabled the public circulation of issues raised on behalf of the state, creating further discursive potential.

The public was thus invited to participate in the official process of imagining the nation through the production of meaning and truth from the evidence of the nation's new history that was presented to the nation at the TRC hearings. In this respect, the TRC called on the private citizens to recall the past through testimony, from the subjective positions of witnesses of the Past. Simultaneously, the national recollection of the 'already known truth' was facilitated through the public telling of testimonies at the TRC hearings.

These testimonies were, however, mainly concerned with the fate of the victims of apartheid atrocities, primarily those that suffered their victimisation in the 1980s. More significantly, these testimonies, while having been presented mainly by black women, were concerned with the black male victims of the security forces. These victims were represented through the TRC as 'voiceless'. Indeed, the TRC came to be represented as a public space and an official institution at which the memories of a category of people that had been described and regarded as 'voiceless' could be 'given voice'. This process of 'giving voice to the voiceless' was aptly stated by Alex Boraine, when in his introduction to Mthimkulu HRVC hearing, he said to Joyce Mthimkulu, the mother of Siphiwe Mthimkulu:

> You travelled to East London [to appear at the HRVC's first public hearings in April 1996]. You and your husband were excited, at last you were going to have a chance to talk to a presidential commission, to the nation at large about [the poisoning and disappearance of] Siphiwe. This was denied you by a court interdict. You had no chance. We met with you and you very graciously agreed that you will come to the Port Elizabeth hearing [in May 1996] and you came, you sat over there and we waited and once again you were muzzled [by a court interdict], you couldn't speak. All of us were very angry and very upset, but you were remarkable. You

too were upset, but you understood, because you knew that one day you would have an opportunity, and today is that day.[72]

For Boraine, the condition of voicelessness was measured not in terms of inability to speak, but in terms of inability to speak *and* be heard by those in power. The TRC thus 'gave voice' through its capacity as an official, 'presidential commission'. However, most of the victims emphasised through the HRVC hearings and through the media were not ordinary or voiceless in two senses. First, as Steven Robins indicated, the TRC 'privilege[s] the experiences of a relatively small number' of anti-apartheid activists 'by concentrating on issues of murder, kidnapping, detention and torture',[73] and secondly, most of the victims of the apartheid security forces were clearly targeted by the strategies of identification, isolation, victimisation and/or 'elimination' of prominent and leading activists in the struggle against apartheid. As leaders, therefore, they were not 'voiceless' in terms of not being able to speak and be heard in their own communities, although they were not heard in official state discourses. They were often prominent local political activists engaged in local struggles against apartheid, but were framed as 'voiceless' through the rhetoric of, and around, the TRC.

By casting the stories of prominent and 'known' local figures in the struggle against apartheid as the stories of the 'voiceless', the TRC located them within the national struggle for liberation. They were thus no longer local but teleologically part of a national struggle for liberation. This fulfilled the TRC's notion of 'uncovering' a 'hidden' history, of 'unearthing' a suppressed Past and making that Past part of the new history of the nation. In so doing, the TRC provided prominent activists with a subject position from which to speak to, and of, the nation while denying others the same opportunity[74] and implied that because those who appeared at the HRVC's hearings spoke from experience, they spoke with authentic voices. These (eye-) witnesses and their experiences of pain and trauma became the TRC's primary sources; they were the TRC's 'open windows' to the Past and formed the core of the TRC's public history and its archive.

As such, these testimonies hold implications for the new South African past and for the TRC's archive. To begin with, testimonies were based on first-hand experience, the use of which as 'uncontestable evidence', as Joan Scott has argued, is problematic, for it 'takes as self-evident the identities of those whose experiences are being documented and thus naturalise[s] their' identities.[75] At the TRC, the experi-

72 Alex Boraine to Joyce Mthimkulu, HRVC Hearing, Port Elizabeth, Wednesday, 26 June 1996.

73 Steven Robins, 'True national reconciliation is imperilled: TRC highlights the plight of the few, but the masses go begging', *Cape Argus*, Monday, 17 February 1997.

74 At the HRVC hearing into the poisoning and disappearance of Siphiwe Mthimkulu and disappearance of Topsy Madaka, for example, Mthimkulu's mother speaks, along with the prominent comrades that were his contemporaries. These prominent comrades included Lulu Johnson who was a former president of the Congress of South African Students. Indeed, Boraine did not mention Topsy Madaka in his introduction nor was the hearing concerned with Madaka except for his disappearance alongside Siphiwe Mthimkulu. The hearing thus pieced together a biography of Mthimkulu, focusing on his involvement in the struggle against apartheid. No biographical sketch of the life of Topsy Madaka was entered into. See HRVC Hearing, Port Elizabeth, Wednesday, 26 June 1996.

75 Scott, 'Evidence of experience', p. 367. Also see Michael Pickering, *History, Experience and Cultural Studies* (London: Macmillan Press, 1997), pp. 217–236.

ences displayed publicly were those of the black victims of apartheid, yet, by looking at the experiences of victims of apartheid abuses, the TRC did not uncover the ideological mechanisms that apartheid employed in assigning the identity of blackness and enabling its internalisation by those so assigned, nor was the TRC overtly aware of its role in assigning the identities of victims, survivors and perpetrators.[76]

In addition, memory, for this is where experiences are stored, is unstable. It is 'inherently revisionist' and is 'never more chameleon-like when it appears to stay the same'.[77] This is particularly the case with personal memories that underlie the individual's sense of self and the individual's social identity. This form of memory, which Endel Tulving defines as 'episodic' memory,[78] exists in a dialectic relation with social identity. It shapes social identity and is constantly shaped by social identity.[79] It is unstable largely because of this constantly fluctuating dialectical relationship. This instability can, however, be overcome through its textualisation and preservation in written form.[80] Furthermore, its validity can only be assessed intertextually, through reference to other testimonies and to written documents. However, when this intertextual referentiality is lacking, memory is often treated with scepticism. Thus, when Bokvela Phulula recollected an experience of 1963 when he was tortured by police in Cape Town after being arrested for being in the urban area without a pass, his testimony drew some scepticism. At the end of his hearing, Archbishop Desmond Tutu voiced this scepticism when he spoke for the Commission and said that the TRC

> hope[s] that you have taken your oath seriously, when you were giving your statement here. We hope that what you are telling us today is the truth. Like we have said before, we are going to investigate. We have said even the same thing to the others before you. But we are going to try and we are going to try by all means, but it is going to be very difficult when everybody who can bear evidence of what you are telling us, is now all dead.[81]

The TRC's archive and the new South African history that it produced exist in a relationship similar to what Roland Barthes described as a 'referential illusion'. This, Barthes argued, is the positivist relationship between a 'real' Past and 'objective' history. He suggested that while historians claim to 'uncover' a 'real' Past, they can only construct the past discursively. In other words, he argued that the practice of history does not facilitate the understanding of the Past empirically or functionally but is, as narrative, modes of signification

76 Indeed, it became quite difficult for 'victims' to talk of their own activities in victimising others and of themselves as 'perpetrators'.

77 Raphael Samuel, *Theatres of Memory. Volume 1: Past and Present in Contemporary Culture* (London and New York: Routledge, 1994), p. x. Also see Raphael Samuel and Paul Thompson, 'Introduction' in Raphael Samuel and Paul Thompson, *The Myths We Live by* (London and New York: Routledge, 1990), p. 7; James Fentress and Chris Wickham, *Social Memory* (Oxford and Cambridge, MA: Blackwell Publishers, 1992), p. 15.

78 Endel Tulving divides memories into two 'memory systems' – a 'semantic memory system', which is responsible for knowledge of things and events that are not part of the individual's field of experiences, and an 'episodic memory system' that underlies the individual's sense of self and their identity by organising memories of personal experiences. Endel Tulving cited in Fentress and Wickham, *Social Memory*, p. 20.

79 See, for example, Jacques le Goff, *History and Memory*, translated by Steven Rendall and Elizabeth Claman (New York: Columbia University Press, 1992), pp. 3–4; and Fentress and Wickham, *Social Memory*, p. 7.

80 Fentress and Wickham, *Social Memory*, p. 9.

81 Tutu, HRVC Hearing, Umtata, Wednesday, 19 June 1996.

through which meanings of its referent, the Past, are established. By claiming that history is objective and real – making it *History* – historians imply that the narratives of the Past that they produce mirror the Past, in so doing denying the signified and 'claim[ing] to let the referent speak for itself'.[82]

The archive compounded this 'referential illusion' for the TRC as it produced not only the new history of the new South Africa, but also the archive upon which that past is constructed, making the archive conform to its public history. In this form the 'violence of the archive' was brought to bear on the Past. Here the violence did not merely involve memory and forgetting, inclusion and exclusion, but also occlusion - the obstruction of the recording of, and for, memory. This was most evident at the HRVC's Umtata hearings on Tuesday 18 June 1996, when Teddy 'Mwase' Williams appeared before the Commission. Williams recounted his experiences gained at an ANC camp in Angola in the early 1980s and the sexual abuse experienced by newly arrived female recruits at the hands of senior ANC camp commanders. The 'picture' he presented was not one the Commission wished to 'uncover' at that stage, hence he was kindly requested to

> please confine yourself to the question of the human rights violations to yourself, especially what happened to you at the ANC camps so that we would not take long with peripheral issues. We would like you to tell of yourself, tortures and experiences. Just a small reminder for you to confine yourself to the things that have happened to you and what you did.[83]

Thus, by being occluded from the archive, the parts of the Past that were not consigned to the past by the TRC cannot be visited, read, interpreted, let alone revisited, reread, reinterpreted. As such, the Past cannot be kept open. The TRC archive is thus not the place where the occluded Past can begin but is the place where it does not exist for memory because, for whatever reason, it has not been deposited in the archive. This is precisely because the archive is the hallmark for and of history. The archive or, rather, written documents, still figure in history as the basis of verification. Written sources are still privileged as evidence over oral sources, with the latter often being utilised only when they can be verified by the former.[84] This prejudice is, however, not a function of inclusion, exclusion and occlusion, nor is it one of orality versus textuality. Rather, it is a function of the 'reality effect' in the production of History, whether that History is written in the form of an essay, a book or an archive.

82 Roland Barthes, *The Rustle of Language* (Oxford: Basil Blackwell, 1986), pp. 128–133.

83 Ntsiki Sandi, HRVC Hearing, Umtata, Tuesday, 18 June 1996. The TRC has subsequently attended to the abuses suffered by women at a special hearing at Johannesburg on Monday, 28 July 1997 and Tuesday, 29 July 1997. It also held hearings on the abuses suffered at the ANC's detention camp, Quattro, in Angola. It did not, however, bring to light the sexual abuses alluded to by Williams. See HRVC Special Hearing on Women, Johannesburg, 28–29 July 1997.

84 See, for example, Charles van Onselen's use of 'documentary evidence' and other interviews to 'check' the accuracy of Kas Maine's interviews. See Charles van Onselen, *The Seed is Mine: The Life of Kas Maine, A South African Sharecropper, 1894–1985* (Cape Town: David Philip, 1996), pp. 10–11.

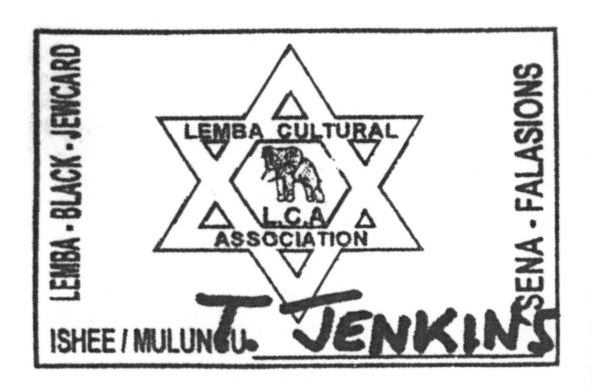

Figure 1: The name card given to Trefor Jenkins when he attended a gathering
of the Lemba Cultural Association.

The Human Genome as Archive: Some Illustrations from the South*

Himla Soodyall, Bharti Morar and Trefor Jenkins

INTRODUCTION

Humans have pondered their origins for as long as they have existed. This is reflected in the many myths and creation stories. We need only think about the Judaeo-Christian Garden of Eden for an example. Indeed, such stories seem to be a nearly universal feature of human cultures.

The most direct account of our past is inferred from the fossil record. Skeletal remains have been instrumental in establishing the evolution of human ancestors in Africa, and they have also provided important information about the evolution of modern *Homo sapiens*. However, the fossil record is fragmentary and many critical gaps remain.

The genetic variation found among living peoples offers another way of studying human evolution. Genes are blueprints or biochemical instructions that determine inherited traits. They consist of sequences of building blocks of deoxyribonucleic acid (DNA). Genes are collected together to make up the larger chromosomes of which humans have 23 pairs. We inherit half the complement of chromosomes from our mothers and the other half from our fathers. Chromosomal DNA is found in the nucleus of the cell and is referred to as nuclear DNA (Fig. 2). As well as nuclear DNA, the mitochondria, the energy-producing organelles in the cytoplasm of all cells, also contain DNA, which is referred to as mitochondrial DNA (mtDNA). MtDNA is inherited only from our mothers, and only females can pass it on to their children (Fig. 3). The Y chromosome that is found in the nucleus is also uniparentally inherited, and is transmitted exclusively from father to son. Together, nuclear DNA and mtDNA carry the information needed to synthesise all eighty thousand or so proteins in our bodies. The code is determined by the order of nucleotide bases, many thousands of which go to make up a single gene. The total genetic complement, or genome, of humans contains some three billion of these bases in different combinations, controlling the development and functioning of the organisms and producing the genetic variation among humans.

When it became possible to study genetic variation in humans,

* This paper is dedicated to the memory of the late Dr Margaret Nabarro, who encouraged us to pursue genetic studies on the Lemba. The authors would like to express their gratitude to all participants who donated blood samples that made this study possible; and to Paul Stidolf and Bruce Dangerfield for their invaluable assistance with fieldwork in Zimbabwe. Support for this research was provided by the South African Institute for Medical Research, the University of the Witwatersrand and the South African Medical Research Council.

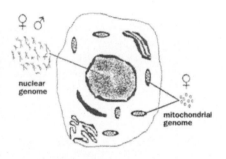

Figure 2: Schematic diagram of a human cell showing the biparental inheritance of nuclear genomes from both males (♂) and females (♀), and the uniparental inheritance of mitochondrial genomes from females (♀) only.

biologists began to use the data to assess the affinities and origins of the various populations that go to make up humankind. Major demographic events (population migrations, bottlenecks and expansions) leave imprints, in the form of altered gene frequencies, on the collective human genome. Because these imprints are transmitted to succeeding generations, the modern human genome contains an indelible record of our evolutionary past. As more genetic loci are examined in populations throughout the world, our evolutionary history should be largely decipherable.

Thus, by studying human variation at the molecular level, we can learn more not only about our evolutionary history, but also about the genetic contribution to health and disease. The body, more specifically the DNA found in every nucleated cell, harbours the 'blueprints' that determine our individuality. We would contend, therefore, that the body, through its DNA, constitutes an archive, with a narrative of our prehistory and evolutionary past. Brenner claims that research in molecular genetics 'has become so directed toward medical problems and the needs of the pharmaceutical companies that most people do not recognise that the most challenging intellectual problem of all time, the reconstruction of our biological past, can now be tackled with some hope of success'.[1]

TYPES OF DNA MARKERS

We can use both nuclear DNA and mtDNA to examine variation at the molecular level. Nuclear DNA is packaged in 22 pairs of autosomal chromosomes (autosomes) and one pair of sex chromosomes (two Xs in females and one X and a Y in males). The pseudoautosomal region of the Y chromosomes, the X chromosomes and the autosomes undergo recombination or crossing over during meiosis (the type of division that occurs when sperm and egg cells are produced). Recombination results in exchange of DNA segments between the chromosomes, thereby introducing new variation into every individual so produced. The recombined chromosome therefore carries genetic material from many different ancestors. Since there have been multiple recombination events in several regions of the nuclear genome, it is difficult to reconstruct the history of any segment of DNA to a single ancestor. Haploid or uniparentally inherited genomes, like mtDNA and the non-recombining region of the Y chromosome, are ideal for the purpose of studying the transmission of genes or segments of DNA to a point of common ancestry. In this essay, we exploit

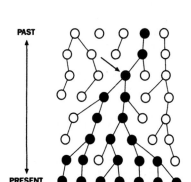

PAST

PRESENT

Figure 3: An illustration of the principle that all contemporary mtDNA types must trace back to a single ancestor. The solid circles indicate the path of descent from the ancestor (arrow) to the present generation (or, alternatively, the path of coalescence from the present population of mtDNA types to the ancestor); empty circles represent mtDNA types that went extinct. While the contemporary mtDNA types ultimately trace back to a single ancestor, note that other individuals co-existed with the mtDNA ancestor, and that the mtDNA ancestor also had ancestors. The same principle applies to Y chromosome inheritance transmitted exclusively by males.

1   S. Brenner, 'The impact of society on Science', *Science* 282 (1998), p. 1412.

the unique properties of mtDNA and some Y-chromosome DNA markers to this end, and emphasise their value in reconstructing human history.

MtDNA

The human mtDNA genome consists of about 16 500 base-pairs of DNA, or about 0.0006 per cent of that of the human nuclear DNA genome. Several properties of mtDNA make it useful for evolutionary studies. First, mtDNA is present in high copy number in human cells. The average somatic cell has just two copies of any given nuclear gene but hundreds to thousands of copies of mtDNA.[2] This property of mtDNA, along with its extra-nuclear cytoplasmic location, makes it easier to obtain for analysis, and also makes it the molecule of choice for analyses of ancient DNA, that is, the DNA in bones, hair and teeth.

Secondly, mtDNA is perhaps the best-known eukaryotic (organisms possessing a nucleus in their cells) genome, with the complete sequence and gene organisation known in many species including humans.[3] Knowledge of the complete sequence initially made it possible to construct detailed restriction enzyme fragment patterns that could be predicted from knowledge of the published sequence. More recently, the advent of polymerase chain reaction (PCR) technology makes it possible enzymatically to amplify any small DNA segment for which the flanking sequence is known.

The third property of mtDNA is that it is strictly maternally inherited, with no paternal contribution or recombination.[4] This means that the mutations found in contemporary humans can be reconstructed to some point back in time to a common ancestor (Fig. 3). The final property of mtDNA of evolutionary interest is that it evolves rapidly, five to ten times faster than the average segment of nuclear DNA.[5] This means that mtDNA will be most useful for comparisons involving closely-related species or populations of the same species, as a sufficient number of mutations will have accumulated over even a short evolutionary timespan, thus permitting an assessment of population relationships.

By making use of these properties of mtDNA, initial studies of human mtDNA variation led to what has become popularly known as the 'African Eve' hypothesis.[6] There are three aspects to this hypothesis: first, all mtDNA types in contemporary humans trace back to a single ancestor (Fig. 3); secondly, this ancestor probably lived in Africa; and thirdly, this ancestor probably lived about two hundred thousand years ago.[7]

2   E. D. Robin and R. Wong, 'Mitochondrial DNA molecules and virtual number of mitochondria per cell in mammalian cells', *Journal of Cellular Physiology* 136 (1988), pp. 507–513.

3   S. Anderson, A. T. Bankier, B. G. Barrell, M. H. L. de Bruijn, A. R. Coulson, J. Drouin, I. C. Eperon, D. P. Nierlich, B. A. Roe, F. Sanger, P. H. Schreier, A. J. H. Smith, R. Staden and I. G. Young, 'Sequence and organisation of the human mitochondrial genome', *Nature* 290 (1981), pp. 457–465.

4   U. Gyllensten, D. Wharton, A. Joseffson and A. C. Wilson, 'Paternal inheritance of mitochondrial DNA in mice', *Nature*, 352 (1991), pp. 255–257.

5   M. D. Brown, M. George and A. C. Wilson, 'Rapid evolution of animal mitochondrial DNA', *Proceedings of the National Academy of Science, U.S.A.* 76 (1979), pp. 1967–1971.

6   R.L. Cann, M. Stoneking and A. C. Wilson, 'Mitochondrial DNA and human evolution', *Nature* 325 (1987), pp. 31–36.

7   M. Stoneking, 'DNA and recent human evolution', *Evolutionary Anthropology* 2 (1993), pp. 60–73; M. Stoneking, 'Mitochondrial DNA and human evolution', *Journal of Bioenergetics and Biomembranes* 26 (1994), pp. 251–259; M. Stoneking and H. Soodyall, 'Human evolution and the mitochondrial genome', *Current Opinion in Genetics and Development* 6 (1996), pp. 731–736.

Y chromosome

As the paternally transmitted counterpart of the mtDNA, the non-recombining portion of the Y chromosome has attracted great interest.[8] Unlike mtDNA, the mutation rate of the Y chromosome is very low, and variation has been exceedingly difficult to find. The recent development and implementation of new technologies like denaturing high-performance liquid chromatography (DHPLC) has resulted in the identification of over 150 new variable sites.[9] Some of these markers show transcontinental distribution and indicate vestiges of ancient common heritage, while more recent and localised mutations define subsequent regional differentiation. These markers, together with short-tandem repeat (STR) markers, are being used widely to examine population relationships and human evolution.

THE HUMAN GENOME AS ARCHIVE

We have made use of both mtDNA and Y-chromosome markers to study population relationships and to reconstruct population history. By taking advantage of the archival information in the genes we were able to test and/or refine theories put forward on the basis of the historical, linguistic, cultural and archaeological archival data. We present in this paper two examples of the value of the genetic archive. In the first example, we make use of mtDNA to trace the mtDNA types found in the present-day inhabitants in Tristan da Cunha, to verify the genealogical information compiled from the historical data. In the second example, we examine the validity of the cultural archive claiming a Jewish historical connection of the Lemba people using both Y-chromosome DNA and mtDNA.

TRACING THE FOUNDING FEMALES OF TRISTAN DA CUNHA

Tristan da Cunha is an island of volcanic origin, situated in the South Atlantic Ocean roughly half way between Cape Town and Rio de Janeiro (Fig. 4). It spans an area of approximately 38 square miles, of which only some three square miles are suitable for settlement and agriculture. Tristan da Cunha was first discovered by the Portuguese in 1506. Thereafter it was used by sailors as a stopover for replenishing supplies. In 1816 the British established a garrison on Tristan to prevent the French from rescuing Napoleon Bonaparte, who was in exile on St. Helena some 1 350 miles to the north. In 1817 the garri-

8   M. F. Hammer, A. B. Spurdle, T. Karafet, M. R. Bonner, E. T. Wood, A. Novelletto, P. Malaspina, R. .J. Mitchell, S. Horai, T. Jenkins and S. L. Zeruga, 'The geographic distribution of human Y chromosome variation', *American Journal of Human Genetics* 145 (1997), pp. 787–805; M. F. Hammer, T. Karafet, A. Rasanayagam, E. T. Wood, T. K. Altheide, T. Jenkins, R. C. Griffiths, A. R. Templeton and S. L. Zegura, 'Out of Africa and back again: nested cladistic analysis of human Y chromosome variation', *Molecular Biology and Evolution* 15 (1998), pp. 427–441.

9   P. A. Underhill, L. Jin, A. Lin, S. Q. Mehdi, T. Jenkins, D. Vollrath, R. W. Davis, L. L. Cavalli-Sforza and P. J. Oefner, ' Detection of numerous Y chromosome biallelic polymorphisms by denaturing high-performance liquid chromatography (DHPLC)', *Genome Research* 7 (1997), pp. 996–1005.

son on Tristan was judged inconsequential to the security of Bonaparte on St. Helena and the British withdrew.

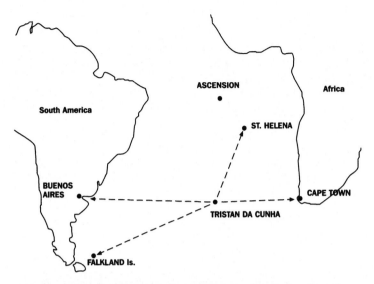

Figure 4. Map of the South Atlantic showing the relationship of Tristan da Cunha to neighbouring islands and land masses.

On withdrawal of the garrison, Corporal William Glass, his wife (M. L.) and two children, plus two other men (John Nankivel and Samuel Burnell), were granted permission to remain on Tristan. This was the start of the first permanent settlement on the island. Of the four original settlers, only Glass and his wife contributed to the gene pool of the current population; the other two men left Tristan for Cape Town to sell the island's produce and did not return.

Subsequently, both male and female immigrants arrived on Tristan, and the genealogy of the islanders has been reconstructed from family and church records. Altogether, the current gene pool can be traced to twenty-two ancestors, including seven females and fifteen males. However, only seven surnames (Glass, Swain, Green, Rogers, Hagan, Repetto and Lavarello) remain in use among the 297 members of the population.[10] According to the historical records, the other eight men contributed to the gene pool but subsequently left the island, taking their surnames with them.[11]

During the course of its history, fifteen women contributed genes to the population, but since some of these women and their descendants died or left the island, the nuclear gene pool of the present population is derived from only seven women. According to the historical records, the first woman to arrive was M. L., who came from Cape

10 *Statistical Yearbook*, 39th issue, United Nations, 1994, p. 42.

11 P. Munch, *Sociology of Tristan da Cunha*, Det Norske, Videnskaps-Akademi (Oslo, 1945); D. F. Roberts, 'The demography of Tristan da Cunha', *Population Studies* 25 (1971), pp. 465–479.

Table 1

MtDNA types found in contemporary Tristan islanders traced to the founding female

Founding female	N	Variant positions compared with the reference sequence 1
S.W	22	16086T, 16129A, 16324C, 73G, 199C, 263G
M.W.	16	16223T, 1629ST, 16362C, 73G, 146C, 199C, 263G
E.S & A.S.	14	152C, 263G
M.L.	9	16129A, 16223T, 16230G, 16243C, 16311C, 73G, 146C, 152C, 195C, 247A, 294A
S.P	14	16223T, 16263C, 16311C, 73G, 152C, 195C, 204C, 263G

[1]Anderson et al. (1981)

N=Number of individuals sequenced with identical mtDNA sequence

Town in 1816. Subsequently, three women, among them two 'sisters' (M. W. and S. W.) and one mother and daughter pair (M. W. and My. W.) arrived from St. Helena in 1827. S. P., also from St. Helena, arrived in 1863 and the second pair of sisters (E. S. and A. S.) of Anglo-Irish descent arrived in 1908. Little is known about the women from St. Helena and Cape Town, but it has been suggested that they were of mixed ancestry.

Since mtDNA is maternally inherited and does not recombine, it is possible to use the mtDNA types found in the present-day Tristan da Cunha population to trace their ancestry to the founding female ancestors. Using the transmission of mtDNA from mother to off-spring pairs, we traced the mtDNA types found in 161 extant individuals to five female founders (Table 1). Although the historical data claimed that two pairs of sisters were among the founding females, mtDNA data showed support for only one pair of sisters. It is possible that the other pair of 'sisters' could have had the same father but different mothers, accounting for their different mtDNA types. Since genetic material was not available from the 'father', we could not verify whether paternal inheritance had contributed to this discrepancy. It is also possible that 'sisters' in this instance is a kinship term with non-Western meaning, and may have no biological meaning.[12]

In the nearly two hundred years following the permanent settlement of Tristan da Cuhna detailed records of the demography of the islanders and historical events have been maintained. However, genetic studies uncovered a discrepancy with some of the historical information. This study emphasises the value of genetic markers in reconstructing history without biases introduced from cultural data or information gleaned from oral traditions.

12 D. F. Roberts and H. Soodyall, 'Population ancestry on Tristan da Cunha: the evidence of the individual' in A. J. Boyce and C. G. N. Mascie-Taylor, eds., *Molecular Biology and Human Diversity* (Cambridge: Cambridge University Press, 1996), pp. 196–204; H. Soodyall, T. Jenkins, A. Mukherjee, E. du Toit, D. F. Roberts and M. Stoneking, 'The founding mitochondrial DNA lineages of Tristan da Cunha Islanders', *American Journal of Physical Anthropology* 104 (1997), pp. 157–166.

Origins of the Lemba

The Lemba population of southern Africa constitutes a group of Bantu-speakers who claim Jewish ancestry.[13] According to Mathivha (leader of the Lemba Cultural Association of South Africa):

> First we Lemba are Jews. There are many of us. Maybe one hundred thousand in South Africa and Zimbabwe . . . But these are the signs: like the Jews we practise circumcision; we bury our dead like the Jews; we offer animal sacrifices like the old Jews; like the Jews the first day of the moon is sacred; like the Jews the seventh day of the moon is sacred; . . . like the Jews we keep kosher . . . We cut the throat of animals like the Jews; like the Jews we keep ritual purity; like the Jews we do not marry the *wasenzhi* – the gentiles.[14]

Figure 5: Lemba leader wearing prayer shawl and yarmulkah.

Historically, the Lemba were distinguished from their Bantu-speaking Negroid neighbours, the Venda, by their means of livelihood, physical appearance, customs and rituals,[15] although some of these cultural traits are evident in other neighbouring populations like the Sotho. Several historical facts set them apart from other Bantu-speakers: they are highly skilled metal workers (including iron, copper and gold) and skilled potters; the men wear long cotton garments and they practise a religion that embraces many extraordinary rituals and laws. Among these cultural practices, the Lemba practise male circumcision – boys are initiated at about the time of puberty – and they have adopted stringent food laws based on Jewish custom, for example, abstinence from consuming pork and mixing meat and milk products.[16]

Dear Prof. Trefor Jenkins,

Greetings! Thank you very much for your e-mail. It was kind of you. Yes, I do have some thoughts about what you asked. For so long the Lembas were stating facts about their origin, religion, and culture, but it was thrown away because it was not something documented. The worst about it was the fact that what they claimed to have was gone and they had nothing to prove it. What was left at their disposal were religious and cultural doctrines drilled in their minds by their parents. They knew for sure that they were not Moslems as they were mistakenly if not wrongly identified. The contributing factor was that they were very secretive because of their past experience, namely persecution, rejection, etc.

Most of their rejection was based on their failure to prove scientifically who they were. Now that genetic science brought something to confirm what was stated by the Lemba folk, they find themselves being able to collect things together. The problem now is to de-syncretise their religion and culture. This is because there are many things which were adapted because of the influence of the environment. The study of genetics gave more confidence to the Lembas to tell it openly that they knew Yahweh before the coming of the early European missionary enterprise. ...

Sincerely yours,
Rabson

Rabson Wuriga is a member of the Hamisi clan of the Lemba people settled in Zimbabwe.

13 M. E. R. Mathivha, *The Basena/Vamwenya/Balemba* (Môrester: Toyandu, 1992).

14 T. Parfitt, *Journey to the Vanished City. The Search for the Lost Tribe of Israel* (London: Phoenix, 1997), p. 40.

15 N. J. van Warmelo, 'The classification of cultural groups' in W. D. Hammond-Tooke, ed., *The Bantu-speaking Peoples of Southern Africa* (London: Routledge and Kegan, 1974), pp. 56–84.

16 A. B. Spurdle and T. Jenkins, 'The origins of the Lemba "Black Jews" of southern Africa: evidence from p12F2 and other Y-chromosome markers', *American Journal of Human Genetics* 59 (1996), pp. 1126–1133.

According to oral tradition,[17] the Jewish ancestors of the Lemba were traders around the seventh century BC who migrated from the 'North' to the Yemen, where they established both a large community at Sena (Sa'na) and several trading posts along the eastern African coast. The Jewish community of Sena, called 'Basena' by Mathivha,[18] was later expanded by exiles escaping the Babylonian destruction of Jerusalem in 586 BC. At some later stage 'trouble broke out between the Basena and the Arabs', resulting in the migration of some Basena to Africa. Here the group split into two: one moving westward to settle in Ethiopia (the Ethiopian Jews, formerly called 'Falashas' by their Christian neighbours, or 'Beta Israel' as they preferred to call themselves), the other (the Lemba) moving southward, finally to establish communities in southern Africa.

There are several contradictory claims about the origins of Ethiopian Jews. According to their oral traditions, they believe that they came from Egypt via the Sudan after the destruction of the First Temple around 486 BC.[19] Other scholars claim that they came from the Yemen during the sixth century.[20] From 1830 onwards, the 'Beta Israel' people came under attack from Protestant missionaries, resulting in many of the 'Black Jews' fleeing to Israel from about 1862 onwards.[21] Then, during a dramatic airlift from the Sudan, known as 'Operation Moses', over 6 500 Ethiopians were taken to Israel between 1984 and 1985.[22] Since then the population of Ethiopian Jews in Israel has increased to about twenty thousand.[23]

Genetic studies conducted by Batsheva Bonne-Tamir and colleagues on Ethiopian Jews living in Israel revealed that there is a strong Caucasoid-Mediterranean and African genetic contribution to the gene pool of present-day Ethiopian Jews.[24] In addition, these data revealed that the African contribution was introduced primarily by females whereas the Caucasoid contribution was introduced primarily by males.

It is estimated that there are about forty thousand Lemba living in South Africa and about fifteen thousand spread among other southern and central African countries. The Lemba did not retain their own language but adopted that of the Mbire-Shoko people among whom they lived south of the Zambezi at Sena, in present-day Mozambique.[25] By the time they became settled in various small isolated groups, they were speaking the language belonging to the people among whom they live: the Lemba of the Northern Province speak Venda, and in Zimbabwe they speak one or other of the western dialects of Shona. But even today, there are still Lemba in the Venda region who can

17 Mathivha, *The Basena / Vamwenya / Balemba*.

18 Ibid.

19 H. Rosen, 'Ethiopian Jews: an historical sketch', *Israel Journal of Medical Science* 27 (1991), pp. 242–243.

20 Ibid.

21 Ibid.

22 Ibid.

23 Ibid.

24 A. Zoossmann-Diskin, A. Ticher, I. Hakim, Z. Goldwitch, A. Rubinstein and B. Bonne-Tamir, 'Genetic affinities of Ethiopian Jews', *Israel Journal of Medical Sciences* 27 (1991), pp. 245–251.

25 Van Warmelo, 'The classification of cultural groups', pp. 56–84.

recall much of the language spoken by their ancestors from before the end of the seventeenth century when they migrated south of the Limpopo.[26]

Not all researchers agree that the Lemba (also referred to as the Remba in Zimbabwe) have Jewish origins. Ruwitah argues:

> My research experience among the Mberengwa, Masvingo and Manicaland Remba has not been able to reveal any particularly unique physical, linguistic and religious features that would differentiate them from neighbouring ethnic communities. Nor does the large admixture of Semitic blood or a definitely Semitic origin argument appear to be based on sound scientific judgement as it reflects what the authors think they see rather than empiricism.[27]

In fact, Ruwitah strongly believes that

> the attachment of a tag to the Remba which gives them a foreign character was a deliberate crusade to rob the indigenous people of any semblance of technical know-how and civilization. This conveniently created fertile ground for the development of Eurocentric views of the Zimbabwe culture and civilization, nurtured and enthusiastically propagated by early European travellers and pseudo-archaeologists, as well as men of Western religion.[28]

There have also been some suggestions in the literature that connect the Lemba to Arabic origin.[29] After reviewing the various accounts put forward by other ethnographers, Mandivenga concludes:

> We take the view that the Semitic cultural traits among the Lemba are Islamic (traceable to Arabs, Persians, mixed breeds, including Swahili as well as Islamised Sena and Shona); and that these influences originated in South East Africa in general where Muslims are known to have flourished for a number of centuries. In some cases the geographical origin may be traced to Sena and Tete on the Zambezi where the last known settlements of Muslims were located. Our conclusion is that the Semitic influences among the Lemba are Islamic, and not Jewish.[30]

After months of research and travelling through Africa and Yemen in search of the geographic origins of the Lemba, Tudor Parfitt, author of the book *Journey to the Vanished City: The Search for a Lost Tribe of Israel*, wrote: 'Most of the evidence then suggests that the past of the Lemba was connected with the Arab world. Ethiopian or

26 Ibid.

27 A. Ruwitah, 'Lost tribe, lost language? The invention of a false Remba indentity', *Zimbabwea* (1997), p. 57.

28 Ibid., p. 56.

29 T. Baines, *The Gold Regions of South Eastern Africa* (London: Edward Stanford, 1877); H. A. Stayt, 'Notes on the BaLemba (an Arabic-Bantu tribe living among the BaVenda and other Bantu tribes in the Northern Transvaal and Rhodesia)', *Journal of the Royal Anthropological Institute of Great Britain and Ireland* 61 (1931), pp. 231–239; E. Mandivenga, 'The history and "re-conversion" of the Varemba of Zimbabwe', *Journal of Religion in Africa* 19 (1989), pp. 210-212; T. Parfitt, *Journey to the Vanished City*; A. Ruwitah, 'Lost tribe, lost language?'

30 Mandivenga, 'The history and "re-conversion" of the Varemba of Zimbabwe', p. 108.

Indian antecedents seemed to be based on far more flimsy evidence. But that being the case the question still remains: where was the original Sena? Somewhere no doubt in the Arabic speaking world. But where?'[31]

The late Dr Margaret Nabarro had become convinced of the Semitic connection of the Lemba from her unpublished ethno-musical studies as well as her deep knowledge of Lemba traditions. It was she and her husband, Professor Emeritus Frank Nabarro, who encouraged one of us (T. J.) to pursue genetic studies on the Lemba. As a guest of Professor Mathivha, head of the Lemba Cultural Association, T. J. attended the annual festivals in 1987 and again in 1988 at Blue Waters, near Elim in the Venda region of what is today the Northern Province. Professor Mathivha was enthusiastic about the genetic studies on the Lemba, which he believed would corroborate the beliefs of the Lemba about their origins as reflected in their oral history. Thus, during the two visits made to Venda, T. J. collected blood samples from approximately one hundred volunteers; these have been used for both the mtDNA and Y-chromosome studies discussed below.

In our earlier studies we made use of mtDNA restriction fragment length polymorphisms (RFLPs) to examine the mtDNA diversity in the Lemba people. Restriction enzymes recognise specific nucleotide sequences and then digest DNA at specific sites. By making use of six restriction enzymes, *Hpa*I, *Bam*HI, *Hae*II, *Msp*I, *Ava*II and *Hinc*II, we were able to derive mtDNA types by combining the restriction enzyme patterns observed for each of the six enzymes in the order given above. These studies revealed that mtDNA types found in the Lemba are indistinguishable from the Venda and other south-eastern Bantu-speakers.[32] Analysis of mtDNA types using phylogenetic methods reveals that mtDNA types found in the Lemba are very closely related to those found in other south-eastern Bantu-speaking groups (unpublished) and not to the Israeli Arabs and Israeli Jews studied by Bonne-Tamir et al.[33] Thus, mtDNA data reveal that the female contribution to the gene pool of the Lemba was of African origin.

More recently, we screened for length variation in the intergenic region between the genes coding for cytochrome oxidase II and transfer RNA for lysine, commonly associated with a deletion of one of two 9-bp repeats. The 9-bp deletion is not associated with any pathological condition, but is common in some central and southern African populations. We found that the deletion occurs at a frequency of 27 per cent in the Lemba, 22 per cent in the Venda, and from 5 to 20 per cent in south-eastern Bantu-speaking groups.[34] Sequencing data re-

31 Parfitt, *Journey to the Vanished City*, p. 315.

32 H. Soodyall, 'Mitochondrial DNA variation in southern African populations' (Ph.D. Thesis, University of the Witwatersrand, 1993).

33 B. Bonne-Tamir, M. J. Johnson, A. Natali, D. C. Wallace and L. L. Cavalli-Sforza, 'Human mitochondrial DNA types in two Israeli populations: a comparative at the DNA level', *American Journal of Human Genetics* 38 (1986), pp. 341–351.

34 H. Soodyall, L. Vigilant, A. V. Hill, M. Stoneking and T. Jenkins, 'Mitochondrial DNA control region sequence variation suggests multiple independent origins of an "Asian-specific" 9-bp deletion in sub-Saharan Africans', *American Journal of Human Genetics* 58 (1996), pp. 595–608.

affirms the African contribution of mtDNA associated with[35] and without (unpublished) the 9-bp deletion.

However, when Y-chromosome markers were used, Spurdle and Jenkins[36] established that approximately 50 per cent of the Y chromosomes present in the Lemba appeared to be of Semitic (Jewish or Arab) origin, 36 per cent of Negroid origin, and the ancestry of the remaining 14 per cent could not be resolved by the methodology used at the time. This study sparked a great deal of interest among researchers interested in the origins of the 'Black Jews' of South Africa.

With the discovery of additional markers on the Y chromosome, Skorecki et al.[37] made use of two Y-chromosome markers and constructed haplotypes (or chromosome patterns) for 188 male Jews. These authors showed that a particular Y-chromosome haplotype was common among the priestly caste, the Cohanim, who ,according to the Bible and Jewish tradition, are male patrilineal descendants of Aaron, the brother of Moses. The descendants of Moses are known as the Levites, and all other Jewish people who were not descendants of the Cohanim or the Levites are referred to as Israelites.[38] By extending the Y haplotype to include another five markers, Thomas et al.[39] found a specific haplotype in the Cohanim that they termed the Cohen Model Haplotype (CMH). The CMH is found in members of the Jewish priesthood (45 per cent in Ashkenazi and 56 per cent in Sephardic priests) and at moderate frequencies (3 to 5 per cent) in the major Israelite Jewish populations, both the Askhenazi and Sephardic.[40] Goldstein and co-workers did not find the CMH in non-Jewish populations they examined (Yakut, Mongolian, Nepalese, Greeks) and it was found at low frequency in Palestine Arabs. They inferred from the distribution of this haplotype that the CMH may have been a constituent of the ancestral Jewish population and estimated that it arose about 106 generations or 3 180 years ago (assuming a generation time of 25 years).

Goldstein and co-workers also examined a sample of 136 South African Lemba and found that approximately 9 per cent of the Lemba had the CMH, but the CMH was absent in a mixed group of 77 Bantu-speaking individuals examined. The frequency of the CMH in the Lemba is similar to those found in major Jewish populations. Since the CMH is rare or absent in all non-Jewish populations tested so far, these findings strongly support the Lemba tradition of Jewish ancestry. (The findings of this paper were also reported in the *New York Times* of 9 May 1999.)

We have expanded on the study initiated by Spurdle and Jenkins[41]

35 Ibid.

36 Spurdle and Jenkins, 'The origins of the Lemba "Black Jews" of southern Africa', pp. 1126–1133.

37 K. Skorecki, S. Selig, S. Blazer, R. Bradman, N. Bradman, P. J. Waburton, M. Ismajlowicz and M. F. Hammer, 'Y chromosomes of Jewish priests', *Nature* 385 (1997), p. 32.

38 M. G. Thomas, K. Skorecki, H. Ben-Ami, T. Parfitt, N. Bradman and D. B. Goldstein, 'Origins of Old Testament priests', *Nature* 394 (1998), pp. 138–140.

39 Ibid.

40 David Goldstein and co-workers, 'Signature haplotypes and the history of Jewish populations', paper presented at the Human Evolution Meeting, Cold Spring Harbor Laboratory, USA, 21–25 April 1999.

41 Spurdle and Jenkins, 'The origins of the Lemba "Black Jews" of southern Africa', pp. 1126–1133.

and made use of four STR markers (a subset of the markers used by Goldstein and colleagues) in conjunction with the Y Alu insertion polymorphism (YAP) to construct Y haplotypes in Lemba males from Venda and in Remba males from Zimbabwe. In addition, the same markers were used to derive Y-chromosome haplotypes in South African Jewish, Indian and other Bantu-speaking groups for comparative analyses. From these studies we found that the CMH is found in 1/41 Lemba from Venda, 4/56 Remba from Zimbabwe, 10/36 South African Jews and 2/50 South African Indians. By showing the relationship of the different Y chromosome types on a network (Fig. 6), and assuming a single-step change between any two types linked on the network, we were able to determine the derivatives of the CMH in the Lemba (Fig. 6). We then used the CMH and their derivatives to define Semitic Y chromosomes and then estimated the proportion of Y chromosomes in the Lemba derived from Semitic origins. We found that 51 per cent of Y chromosomes in the Lemba from Venda are derived from Semitic ancestry and 44 per cent from African ancestry, while the ancestry of the remaining 5 per cent could not be resolved. However, the Semitic and African contributions in the Remba from Zimbabwe were estimated to be 73 per cent and 27 per cent, respectively. The two groups of Lemba share five haplotypes, which may be assumed to be due to a recent common ancestry. We did not detect any of the Semitic Y chromosome types in 46 Venda and 382 Bantu-speakers from South Africa (unpublished data). These data reaffirm a significant Semitic contribution to the Y chromosomes found in South African Lemba and Zimbabwean Remba.

Figure 6. Partial network showing the relationship of Y chromosome haplotypes and the distribution of the Cohen Model Haplotype (CMH) and its derivatives in Lemba from Venda and Zimbabwe, South African Ashkenazi Jews and South African Indians. Haplotypes were constructed using alleles at four Y chromosome short tandem repeats in the order DYS393, DYS19, DYS390 and DYS391.

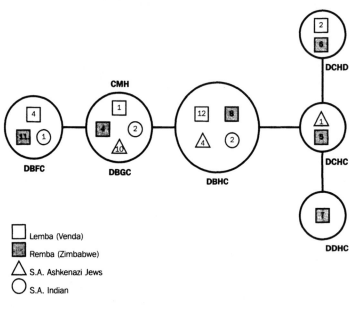

Conclusions

Both examples discussed above emphasise the value of genetic markers in discriminating subtle differences that occur at the molecular level. In the first example, we had a small population from Tristan da Cunha with known ancestry and a complete genealogy compiled from historical information. The reliability of this historical information has been called into question by the power of resolution of mtDNA studies, reinforcing the idea that the human genome is a resourceful archive for testing historical data.

In the second example, genetic data show that a significant proportion of Semitic males contributed to the founding of the Lemba people of southern Africa, those living among the Venda of South Africa, as well as those living among the Shona of Zimbabwe. However, mtDNA studies which trace the contribution of females to the gene pool of a population provided no evidence of a Semitic female contribution. This study reveals that males and females have contributed differently to the gene pool of the Lemba and that their nuclear DNA and mtDNA are derived from different sources. It is also interesting that while the Lemba claim Jewish ancestry, their cultural and biological identity has been transmitted via males. According to Jewish law, Jewish identity, cultural as well as biological, is transmitted through the mother.

As human biologists, our reading of ethnography would suggest that anthropologists and social scientists seem not to be very interested in the genetic relationships of different populations. Similarly, biologists emphasise genetic relationships, often neglecting the valuable resource provided by other archives. This paper emphasises the value of the genome archive in refining and/or testing theories based on historical, anthropological, archaeological and cultural data.

A5.9.1   Eric Walkey Gillett   9 files   1925-1979   (Embargoed)

Letters to C.T.W. from Edgbaston, Birmingham, and Lincoln College,
Oxford to his death in 1979. Their close relationship, travels, his
marriage to Joan Edwards, the birth of his son Anthony, to whom C.T.W.
was godfather, their travels together, his life in Singapore as
Professor of English Literature at Raffles University, the estrangement
from his wife, his return to England, his wife's death and remarriage
to Nancy Miller, his ventures into publishing and broadcasting, editor
for the National Institute for the Blind. He became an author and
critic and until his late 70's student counsellor on the staff of the
Royal College of Music. He died at the age of 85, in 1979.

Figure 1: Extract from inventory of Canon Wood collection.

Archival source: Church of the Province of South Africa (CPSA) archive, Department of Historical Papers, University of the Witwatersrand.

'The History of the Past is the Trust of the Present':
Preservation and Excavation in the Gay and Lesbian Archives of South Africa
Graeme Reid

INTRODUCTION

In 1980, the University of the Witwatersrand received a substantial bequest from an Anglican priest, Canon C. T. Wood. Through the intervention of Wood, the Department of Historical Papers became home to a substantial collection of Church of the Province records and in the wake of his death the Department welcomed a wealth of additional church material as well as Wood's personal papers. These included diaries, lectures, articles, memoranda, notebooks, photographs, sermons and letters addressed to Wood. In addition, the University received a cash sum, which still sustains many special archival projects to this day.

In 1978 the University Librarian, Professor R. Musiker, supported by Professor Garson, then head of History, motivated for an honorary degree for Canon Wood. The motivation concluded aptly:

> Without any formal archival training, Canon Wood has, as an
> enthusiastic amateur, made an enormous contribution to scholar-
> ship by preserving original source material, which is used not
> only by students of church history but by historians from both
> South Africa and overseas researching social and political topics.
> He has truly lived up to his own words 'The history of the past is
> the trust of the present'.

It was a trust that, in the case of Canon Wood, was betrayed when a university archivist of the time decided to place an indefinite embargo on his collection of personal letters (see Fig. 1) and to destroy some articles in his collection. The letters were written by priests and laity from various parts of the world and some of them allude to 'our condition' in veiled and coded ways. A number of letters mention literary texts, by Gide and Wilde, for example, or refer to others who were openly gay at the time. Some of the recent letters are more frank about matters of sexual orientation. On reading the embargoed letters I was surprised that the archivist had been so thorough as to have read these letters, recognised the coded gay subtext and decided to embargo them. Her explanation was that there had been other, more explicit letters and a series of photographs that she, in consultation with a senior member of the library administration at the time, had decided to destroy in order to protect the reputation of Canon Wood.

Canon Wood was himself an archivist – would he have donated material to the University Archives that he did not intend to be in the public domain? In his will no restriction is placed on any aspect of the collection. Twenty years later his wishes will be met, when the embargo is lifted on his collection of personal letters. The changing social and legal status of lesbians and gay men and the creation of the Gay and Lesbian Archives has led, ironically, to the reinstatement of this particular collection of letters in the public domain. The photographs and other letters deemed unsuitable to his memory are, sadly, lost forever.

This incident concerning the destruction of material and the unrequested embargo placed on part of the collection illustrates some important points. Archivists are susceptible to the social mores and moral codes of the time. Homosexuality and, in particular, homosexuality in the church was sufficiently taboo to allow for a radical departure from archival principles of preservation. It also serves to demonstrate two key aspects of the work of the Gay and Lesbian Archives, namely the provision of an institutional home for the preservation and protection of existing records and documents relating to lesbian and gay experience, and the excavation of material in other archives.

EXCAVATION

Where do lesbian and gay lives appear in the public record and how are these lives and experiences represented? Of course, how lesbians and gay men appear in the public record is not unrelated to where they appear. Echoes of gay and lesbian lives are to be found in legal records, in police and military archives, in church commission reports, and in the records of psychiatric and social welfare departments. The way in which lesbians and gay men have been perceived is reflected in the way in which lives and histories have been constructed and documented within the archival holdings of public institutions. Records from the criminal justice system, church records and psychiatric records provide evidence from three powerful social institutions and demonstrate the importance of excavation.

Notes from the criminal justice system
Between the hours of nine and ten o'clock at night on the first day of February 1827 Hugh Robertson, according to the Court of Justice

Records, 'had the appearance as if he was having an unnatural and criminal connection with his said comrade'. Charged with attempted sodomy, he was banished to Robben Island and subsequently sent to New South Wales for 14 years.

If the court had been able to prove that he succeeded in his attempt, the sentence would not have been so lenient. At the time it was common practice for sodomites to be sentenced to death. For example, this was the sentence handed down to Adam January by the Swellendam Circuit Court in 1852 for having 'a venereal affair with Jan Korasie, a cattle herd'. His denomination was listed as 'Bastard Hottentot' – clearly the authorities did not expect him to be redeemed even in the hereafter.

The first recorded case of sodomy in South Africa

Occasionally court records include personal statements that have survived to this day. One of the most remarkable is that of Klaas Blank (ca 1705–1735). Through his personal statement and the documents that accompany it, the extraordinary story of interracial same-sex love in the early days of Dutch settlement is preserved in the VOC records housed at the National Archives Repository in Cape Town.

Klaas Blank, a Khoi youth, was sentenced in 1718 to fifty years' imprisonment on Robben Island for reasons that remain unknown. He became the first recorded instance of someone sentenced to death for sodomy in Cape Town. He was executed by drowning in Table Bay in 1735 together with his co-accused, Rijkhaart Jacobz (ca 1700–1735) of Rotterdam, when both were in their mid-thirties. Evidence was led that they were seen committing sodomy as early as 1724 on Dassen Island, where they had been sent by prison authorities to collect seal blubber. The sergeant in charge on Robben Island was, according to the court record, informed of these acts, but turned a blind eye. He was relieved of his post partly for this reason. His replacement was less tolerant and through severe beating obtained a confession from Jacobz relating to other occasions on which he and Klaas were seen having sex together. These confessions were confirmed in court, leading to their conviction and execution. Their case was not an isolated one. Between 1705 and 1792 more than two hundred men were tried, under Dutch law, in 150 sodomy trials conducted by the Court of Justice in Cape Town. Sentences were determined by the nature of the crimes – the death sentence for actual sodomy, and milder punishments, such as flogging, banishment and forced labour, for the crimes of attempted sodomy and other sexual misdemeanours.[1]

1   I am indebted to Jack Lewis for this description, based on the translation of the original Dutch records. R. Aldrich & G. Wotherspoon, eds., *Who's Who of Gay and Lesbian History from Antiquity to World War II* (London: Routledge, 2001), p. 55.

Police surveillance

More recently, in the late 1960s, lesbians and gay men across South Africa were the subject of a nationwide police investigation.[2] The police records, recently recovered from a confidential series of files kept at the South African Police Services Archive in Pretoria and transferred to the custody of the National Archives, reveal the surveillance strategies employed by the police as well as official attitudes to homosexuality at the time. Police commissioners from seven provinces and two 'homelands' submitted reports to Pretoria on homosexual activity in the areas under their jurisdiction. The reports included lists of names, addresses and occupations of known and suspected homosexuals throughout South Africa. Photographs, intercepted mail, correspondence from spies (see Fig. 2) and lists of car registration numbers noted from vehicles outside homosexual 'bottle parties' (see Fig. 3) are some materials contained in these files.

The reports are characterised by a degree of suspicion and ignorance that, in retrospect, sometimes makes for amusing reading. One senior police official believed that he had uncovered a homosexual conspiracy operating in John Orr's, a well-known department store. Evidently a shop assistant was suspected of selling carpets at reduced prices to his circle of homosexual friends and acquaintances in order to assist them in decorating their fashionable inner-city apartments!

2   In 1999 I was granted access to six police files at the South African Police Services Archive in Pretoria that included background material that was subsequently compiled into a police report submitted to the Parliamentary Select Committee investigation into homosexuality in 1968. In response to a request from GALA these files have now been transferred to the National Archives of South Africa.

Figure 2: Invitation to Rupert and Ashley's Bottle Party, showing typed text addressed to Brig. Joubert at the South African Police Force.
Archival source: National Archives of South Africa.

GRAEME REID

Hidden leaves of the church record

The Church of the Province of South Africa (CPSA) Archive forms part of the collections housed in the Department of Historical Papers at the University of the Witwatersrand. One of the index terms in this collection is 'homosexuality', which refers non-specifically to 'homosexuality – Commission' (see Fig. 4). A note to the index card for this particular component of the CPSA collection reads: 'This will be embargoed unless permission obtained from Church Archivist.' Historian and former theological scholar Nicholas Southey gained access to this church commission report on homosexuality and recorded his responses in an article entitled 'Confessions of a gay ordinand: a personal history'.

Southey describes his 'chance discovery in the CPSA archives at the University of the Witwatersrand of a document of enormous relevance'. The collection consists of the records of a 1977 commission appointed by the Archbishop of Cape Town 'to determine a Christian understanding of homosexuality particularly pertaining to the ordained ministry'. Southey quotes from sections of the report to demonstrate church attitudes to homosexuality: 'Students tend to be highly manipulative of situations, generally devious, and form a sort of network of homosexuals . . . They are seldom penitent, and their ability to rationalise their own excesses, when these do take place, is brilliant.'[3]

3   N. Southey in P. Germond and S. de Gruchy, eds., *Aliens in the Household of God. Homosexuality and Christian Faith in South Africa* (Cape Town: David Philip, 1997), p. 54.

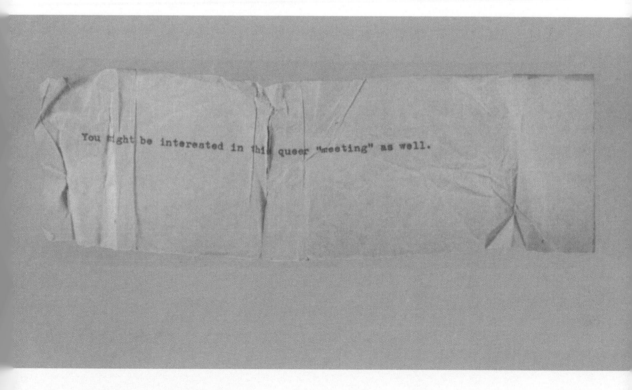

Psychiatric reports

Seven months prior to the publication of the Kinsey Report, on 29 March 1956, C. J. P. was admitted to the Komani Mental Hospital. Facing charges of 'sodomy and crimen injuria', he wrote an eleven-page handwritten statement, which can be read with hindsight as a powerful personal testimony and as a carefully worded defence against the charges that he was facing. In the statement he creates a self-portrait that constructs his effeminacy and passivity in sexual relations with other men. In concluding, he reflects on the act of writing:

> I began these pages for myself and my doctor in order to think out my own individual balance of life – I had that feeling that my experience was different from other people's. Many men I thought, are content with their lives as they are . . . But I have talked to many others who like myself had their own problems their own desire to be what I wanted to be.

It is a story that contrasts with the observations of the patient by the psychiatrist, who charts his employment history and comments on his behaviour in the ward, by recounting what had been told to him:

> Dit word rapporteer dat hy baie vroulike eienskappe in die afdeling openbaar. Hy rangskik die blomme in die afdeling en hou

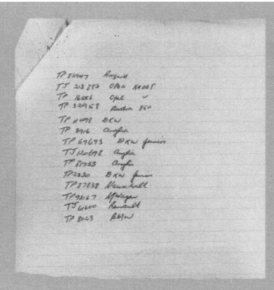

Figure 3: List of car registration numbers from police files.
Archival source: National Archives of South Africa.

homself die hele dag besig met huiswerk. Hy wil net met die kos werk, eiers bak en die hele afdeling netjies hou. Hy werk selfs beter en flukser huiswerk as die verpleegsters.[4]

On 12 April 1956 the psychiatrist noted, 'Niks nuut te rapporteer nie.'[5] And C. J. P. was discharged to the police on the same day.

C. J. P.'s statement gives us some insight into the life of a sexual outsider in the 1950s. It also gives us a sense of the tenacious ways in which he was constructing a defence against the charges that he was facing. An argument unfolds that is implicit in his statement – namely that as a passive, effeminate man who wanted to be a woman, he could not possibly be guilty of sodomy or crimen injuria.

These examples demonstrate the way in which the lives of sexual outsiders are typically represented in the formal institutional archives' documentary record. These institutional records are often (as in the case of early colonial history) the few documentary records that do provide some historical traces of same sex relationships.

These records, while rare, demonstrate institutional practices and social attitudes and occasionally give remarkable insight into the lives of lesbians and gay men. Karen Martin, archivist and researcher, has questioned the assumption that lesbian lives are easier to excavate in the private rather than the public realm. Reflecting on the material contained in the records of a police disciplinary hearing into a lesbian

4 'It is reported that he displays many feminine characteristics in the section. He arranges the flowers in the section and keeps himself busy with housework the whole day. He just wants to work with the food, fry eggs and keep the whole section neat. He works even better and harder than the nurses.'

5 'Nothing further to report.'

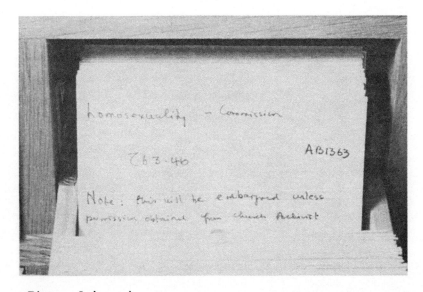

Figure 4: Index card.
Archival source: Church of the Province of South Africa (CPSA) archive, Department of Historical Papers, University of the Witwatersrand.

relationship, she remarks:

> The cold, formal and ruthlessly intrusive enquiry reveals in painful detail the course of the relationship and allows the reader access to the most intimate parts of it, including the pet names they called each other and the number of phone calls it took to resolve one or other disagreement. I was appalled and fascinated, and as an archivist have had to interrogate my assumption that women's lives are best documented in material from the private realm – letters, journals and so on.[6]

Material on homosexuality that exists in formal institutional archival repositories provides information and allows researchers to revisit social attitudes towards homosexuality at various points in time. Voices of lesbians and gay men are also present, albeit in a mediated form. These records, although often reflecting bias and prejudice, are valuable archival sources deserving of protection, preservation and serious academic engagement.

In deciding what is included and what left out of the public record, archivists wield considerable power. It is a power that impacts considerably on groups who are marginalised or oppressed by the dominant social order. In the words of the director of the Khama III Memorial Museum in Serowe, Botswana, 'If history and culture are important for any community, they are even more important for a once-colonised society or for people that have lived under a form of domination.'[7] Information on homosexuality in existing archives is so scarce that whatever does exist, albeit biased, inaccurate or moralistic, remains valuable simply because it is so rare.

The 'sin, crime or disease' model of homosexuality evident in the archives of the church as well as state institutions illustrates the need for an independent archive devoted to the collection and documentation of different narratives and memories. For example, no institutional archive in South Africa collected the organisational records of lesbian and gay groups that resisted the various forms of legislation that governed their lives. There was also no place for the letters, diaries and photograph albums that give a sense of lives lived under varying degrees of social condemnation and legal constraint.

Why a Gay and Lesbian Archive?

The Gay and Lesbian Archives of South Africa (GALA) were established, in part, to address this absence from, or biased representation

6 Karen Martin, 'Lesbian biography and oral history in gay and lesbian archives of South Africa', *South African Archives Journal* 40 (1998).

7 Scobie Lekhutile, 'Community participation', *South African Archives Journal* 40 (1998), p. 16.

within, the formal institutional archives of church and state. The source of this gap in the archival record is described by Joan Nestle of the Lesbian Herstory Archives (LHA) in these terms:

> The roots of the Archives lies in the silenced voices, the love letters destroyed, the pronouns changed, the diaries carefully edited, the pictures never taken, the euphemized distortions . . . But I have lived through the time of willfull deprivation and now it is time to discover and to cherish and to preserve.[8]

Jack van der Wel of Homodok outlines a process of exclusion that led to the creation of a specifically *Queer Thesaurus*:

> . . . existing retrieval systems have pretentions of being universal, neutral and comprehensive, but information on gay men and lesbians is hard to find and disappears into the oddest categories.[9]

The Lesbian Herstory Archives and Homodok

In order to bring together two different perspectives on lesbian and gay archival theory and practice, GALA decided to invite representatives from these two international archives, namely the Lesbian Herstory Archives in New York and Homodok in the Netherlands, to participate in the 1998 Refiguring the Archives seminar series. Lesbian Herstory Archives co-ordinator and veteran volunteer, Maxine Wolfe, presented a paper entitled 'The Lesbian Herstory Archives: a passionate and political act'. This paper examined the background and origins of the Lesbian Herstory Archives, reflecting on how the policies and practices of this community archive have evolved since its establishment in 1973.[10] In his paper entitled 'The realisation of the *Queer Thesaurus*', the director of Homodok, Jack van der Wel, explained the construction of subject categories and discussed the implications of these for archival practice.

These papers, like the archives from which they emerge, can be characterised as representing two streams within lesbian and gay archival experience: one is a steadfastly community archive, driven by the premise of 'radical archiving';[11] the other, also serving a particular community, has created new institutional categories that represent the mainstreaming of gay and lesbian cultural identity. The Lesbian Herstory Archives (LHA) is an entirely community-driven enterprise. It is housed in a building bought from donations by lesbians in the United States of America and is staffed entirely by volunteers. The LHA's acquisition policy is based on the premise that individual lesbians or lesbian organisations decide what should be preserved. It is

8   Joan Nestle, as quoted in Judith Schwarz, 'Living herstory', *Off Our Backs* (May 1978). Reprinted in *Gay Insurgent* (Spring 1979)r

9   Jack van der Wel, 'The Realization of the *Queer Thesaurus*', paper presented at the Refiguring the Archives seminar series, 29 September 1998.

10 Maxine Wolfe, 'The Lesbian Herstory Archive: a passionate and political act', paper presented at the Refiguring the Archives seminar series, 29 September 1998.

11 The principles of 'radical archiving' devised by the Lesbian Herstory Archives are as follows:
   1. All lesbian women must have access to the Archives; no academic, political or sexual credentials may be required for usage of the collection; race and class must be no barrier to use or inclusion.
   2. The Archives will collect the prints of all our lives, not just preserve the records of the famous or the published. Every woman who has had the courage to touch or desire another woman deserves to be remembered here.
   3. The Archives shall be housed within the community, not on an academic campus which is by definition closed to many women, and shall be curated and maintained by lesbians.
   4. The community should share in the work of the Archives.
   5. The Archives shall be involved in the political struggles of all lesbians.
   6. Archival skills shall be taught, one generation of lesbians to another, breaking the elitism of traditional archives.
   7. Funding shall be sought from within the communities the Archives serves, not from the government or mainstream financial institutions.

run on the principle that 'every woman who has had the courage to touch or desire another woman deserves to be remembered here'. Or, in the words of Maxine Wolfe, 'the community defines what is important about their lives'.

Homodok was founded in 1978 in response to pressure exerted by academics and students at the universities of Amsterdam and Utrecht to include lesbian and gay studies in the curricula. The library and documentation centre was housed at the University of Amsterdam until 1999, when it merged with the lesbian archive and resource centre, the Anna Blamanhuis, and moved to new premises in Amsterdam. A joint project of the Anna Blamanhuis and Homodok was the development of the *Queer Thesaurus*, which informs and influences archival theory and institutional practice. It informs, by providing a myriad index terms in order to create a standard reference text for archivists working with lesbian and gay material. It influences, in that through the process of naming and categorising the thesaurus will leave an indelible stamp on archive repositories. The stated aim of the *Queer Thesaurus* is to

> provide all lesbian, gay, bisexual and transgender archives, libraries and documentation centres, as well as those persons or organisations wishing to set up such an archive, library or documentation centre, with a ready-to-use international thesaurus of gay and lesbian index terms.

Through the compilation of a manual of index terms, described as 'a controlled vocabulary to index and search information about gay and lesbian existence, and gay and lesbian studies',[12] the *Queer Thesaurus* marks an important moment of institutionalisation for gay and lesbian archives internationally. In the *Queer Thesaurus*, an area of human experience that has either been left out of the institutions of public culture by remaining unnamed or is present in the form of generalised categories like 'homosexuality' and often derogatory terms such as 'deviance' or 'perversion' becomes subject to a proliferation of terms reminiscent of the 'incitement to discourse', a concept developed by Foucault in *The History of Sexuality*. In contrast with the repressive hypothesis, Foucault maintains that, from the eighteenth century onwards, 'around the apropos of sex, one sees a veritable discursive explosion'.[13] The *Queer Thesaurus* contains an extraordinary list of terms that in turn are refined and elaborated to capture all possibilities that may fall under the broad rubric 'homosexuality'. Significantly the word 'homosexuality' as an index term is absent in the *Queer*

12 Ko van Staalduinen, Anja Jansma, Henny Brandhorst and Afke Bruin, translated by Henny Brandhorst, *A Queer Thesaurus: An International Thesaurus of Gay and Lesbian Index Terms* (Amsterdam: Homodok/Anna Blamanhuis, 1997).

13 Michel Foucault, *The History of Sexuality: An Introduction* (London: Penguin Books, 1981), p. 17.

GRAEME REID

Thesaurus, as every term in the thesaurus refers in some way to homosexuality, while the term 'heterosexuality' does appear. In a reversal of conceptual norms, the *Queer Thesaurus* assumes homosexuality as normative and thereby the word itself becomes redundant. The range of terms contained in the thesaurus highlights the processes of exclusion that take place when descriptions and finding aids fail adequately to reflect sexual diversity.

These two archives, Homodok and the LHA, encompass both radical archival practice and processes of institutionalisation. Whereas the LHA emphasises difference in the form of radical practice, by its very existence it embodies a degree of institutionalisation, even on the level of acquisition, arrangement and housing of materials in a way that is accessible to a broader public. Homodok was established in order to serve a particular community, and at the time of its inception was considered particularly radical in the international academic arena. GALA is based at an academic institution, the University of the Witwatersrand, and attempts to provide a service to gay and lesbian communities in South Africa. GALA thus attempts to fulfil two roles, as a community archive[14] responsive to the needs of an admittedly ill-defined 'community', and as an academic resource based in an established and relatively well-resourced university. The archive strives to establish a professional research node for lesbian and gay studies in southern Africa while at the same time, through the acquisition policy and a proactive outreach and dissemination programme, to remain responsive to community needs.

Mainstreaming gay and lesbian experience

For Homodok, the creation of a new set of index terms was an intervention made to address the problem of invisibility, or inappropriate referencing: '[t]he absence of such an index was seen as the principal reason for the lack of indexing of gay and lesbian materials and information about gay and lesbian existence'. The LHA has its origins in the lesbian-feminist movement of the 1970s and sought to establish an independent archive, based on the principles of 'radical archiving', a vision described by Joan Nestle on the opening of the new premises: 'The Archives is living proof that a radical, lesbian-feminist, socialistic, independent grass-roots community based organization, run by an all-volunteer collective and based on consensual decision making, not only can survive but can be successful.'

Brenda Marston, writing in her capacity as the human sexuality archivist at Cornell University's Department of Manuscripts and

14 The archive attempts to fulfil its community function through a range of outreach activities. The university is not always the most accessible environment for the casual browser, for example. These projects have included collaborating on documentary film productions, notably *The Man who Drove with Mandela* and *Apostles of Civilised Vice* and a proposed new documentary on the life of Simon Nkoli. GALA commissioned a theatre project in which individuals conducted research and workshopped a theatre production that has toured community venues in the Gauteng region and travelled to various parts of the country. Another means of fulfilling the community functions is through exhibitions at community events, such as the annual Gay and Lesbian Pride Parade, and at organisational meetings and conferences. The Gay and Lesbian Library also falls under the auspices of the archives and operates as a lending library, with some fifteen hundred titles and a small collection of videos.

University Archives and paraphrasing the intentions of the patron of the collection, David B. Goodstein, makes a powerful argument for the inclusion of lesbian and gay material within a broader category of human sexuality:

> to discourage a perception that gay and lesbian experiences are completely separate from heterosexuals' lives; to discourage defining lesbians and gays exclusively in terms of their sexuality; and to emphasize the relevance of such a collection to all people.[15]

The Equality Clause: an international precedent

The specifics of South African history have shaped the nature, form and location of GALA. Since May 1996, when South Africa adopted a Constitution that included 'sexual orientation' in the Equality Clause of the Bill of Rights, the legal status of lesbians and gay men has changed dramatically. It is this broader political context, the inclusion of the 'sexual orientation' clause and the history that precedes this international precedent, that has informed and influenced, not only the establishment of GALA, but where it is housed and the kinds of interventions that the archive seeks to make. In a recent exhibition curated by Karen Martin and Catherine Mooney, the Gay and Lesbian Police Services Network was included in a display reflecting changing police attitudes to homosexuality in South Africa. A massive police raid of a gay party in 1966 and a commission of inquiry into the conduct of two lesbian police officers in the 1980s were contrasted with the poster produced for the South African Police Services stall at the 1996 Lesbian and Gay Pride Parade, announcing the benevolent presence of 'Priscilla'.

In contrast to the 1977 report on homosexuality commissioned by the Anglican Archbishop of Cape Town, the National Coalition for Gay and Lesbian Equality collection includes a copy of a letter written by Archbishop Desmond Tutu, who in 1996 wrote to the Constitutional Assembly:

> It would be a sad day for South Africa if any individual or group of law-abiding citizens in South Africa were to find that the Final Constitution did not guarantee their fundamental right to a sexual life, whether heterosexual or homosexual.

The location of GALA was influenced by this unique political history. GALA forms part of a conglomeration of archives: included under the broad umbrella of the Department of Historical Papers at the University of the Witwatersrand are the Church of the Province

15 Cal Gough and Ellen Greenblatt, *Gay and Lesbian Library Service* (Jefferson, North Carolina: McFarland & Company, 1990), p. 66.

Archive, the South African History Archive (SAHA), and GALA. GALA is constituted as an independent project of SAHA, which was formed in the 1980s with the aim of documenting and preserving the records of the anti-apartheid struggle, including the trade union movement. As such it was an archive that was subject to state harassment and threat. Records, pamphlets, minutes of meetings, posters, T-shirts and ephemera were sometimes moved from safe house to safe house and a number of documents were sent out of the country for safe-keeping. In the post-apartheid era, the South African History Archive has undergone its own process of institutionalisation by becoming part of the collections located at the University of the Witwatersrand.

The presence of GALA within the broader collections of SAHA is appropriate as it reflects the political processes that led to the inclusion of sexual orientation in South Africa's Constitution. It is unique in the history of African anti-colonial struggles that the South African liberation movement eventually included 'sexual orientation' as part of its agenda. The sexual orientation clause was not achieved by a gay and lesbian movement working in isolation; rather it was through a strategic alliance between lesbian and gay anti-apartheid activists and organisations and the broader liberation movement within South Africa and in exile. The democratic dispensation that recognises lesbians and gay men as full citizens also created a new space for the lesbian and gay community in South Africa. The adoption of the Constitution thus provided the context in which a gay and lesbian archive became possible. The establishment of GALA is both a response to the changing political situation and part of an ongoing social movement in South Africa.

This perspective is also reflected in the nature of GALA's collections. The most comprehensive set of collections housed within GALA is organisational records from the 1960s to the 90s that document the fledgling gay and lesbian movement during this period of South African history. These collections from organisations and individuals document this complex political process which, through eventual inclusion in the broader transformation process, distinguishes the gay and lesbian movement in South Africa from many of its counterparts in the Western world. It is the international precedent set by the inclusion of 'sexual orientation' in South Africa's Constitution and the legal reform process that followed in its wake, which have led to an unprecedented research interest both within South Africa and abroad.

The archive is a place of safe-keeping, preserving and imagining. In its broadest sense, the archive provides the source material for the creative arts. It is the repository, not only of documents and records, artefacts and memorabilia, but the place where all that is important and special and valuable is stored and preserved for posterity.

I will use one example of a submission made by an individual to the parliamentary Select Committee hearings in 1968, to make a point about the way in which public and official perceptions shape individual self-imagining:

> I am a homosexual. Due to shyness on my part and great discreetness on the part of other homosexual men, I have never had the opportunity to become a practising homosexual . . . None of my friends or family suspect my condition . . . I attach copies of testimonials which I feel sure will assure you that I am considered a good character and a diligent employee, and not a degenerate sort . . . I hope I shall be forgiven addressing this letter to you. I feel this matter so nearly threatens my future and that of so many others like me that I had to write.[16]

This letter has a particularly poignant tone, but throughout the submissions made to the parliamentary Select Committee opposing the proposed new draconian legislation, the arguments forwarded are medical, legal and moral. Individuals argue that they are not a menace to society, that they should be left alone, that they cannot be cured. One writer goes as far as to say that while homosexuality is regrettable, the government should refrain from tightening up on existing legislation as many 'of South Africa's most valuable and useful citizens will be driven from their homeland if conditions were made untenable and intolerable for them'. He combines the racial ideology of the time with his opposition to the proposed legislation:

> Can South Africa afford to lose only one of her white citizens, let alone possibly tens of thousands because of archaic and outmoded legislation which has it's [sic] roots in ignorance, superstition and bigotry?

The submissions of 1968 contrast with the hundreds of letters sent to the Constitutional Assembly in 1995–1996 when the demand for equality was couched in terms of the discourse of inclusivity and human rights that characterised the period. In the words of

16 Archival source: Library of Parliament.

MaWilliams, a political activist from Vosloorus, who addressed a letter to the Constitutional Assembly as the mother of a lesbian:

> All of her friends I want them to sign the partition of being proud to be known as lesbians and gays and list their names and addresses I want to tell you my house was always an office for political organisations meetings and now it is open for lesbians and gays meeting the democracy allows me.[17]

Alpha Rasekhala, a gay Christian, made the following statement: 'I believe as a South African citizen I've the right to be respected. As I am a man who loves other men.'

The contrast between these two submissions and the tone and content of those made in 1968 echoes something of the changing nature of the social fabric in South Africa. The same institution that allowed the destruction and restriction of material deemed to be unsuitable, now houses a national collection of lesbian and gay material; and in the words of the then Vice-Chancellor of the University, Colin Bundy, 'Without gay history there can be no gay pride.'[18]

17 Archival source: Gay and Lesbian Archives.

18 GALA Dinner, 25 November 1998.

'Living by Fluidity': Oral Histories, Material Custodies and the Politics of Archiving*

Carolyn Hamilton

INTRODUCTION

In 1992, in a dramatic address to the American Association of African Studies, the pioneering figure in the study of African oral traditions, Jan Vansina, identified what he considered to be a major challenge to African history which, if not met, would condemn African history to mediocrity and irrelevance in Africa itself.[1] It consisted of two parts: the wholesale transfer of European concepts into Africa around issues of no concern to Africans and a postmodernist attack on historical methodology. Remarking on the 'irrelevance' of Luise White's study of prostitution in Nairobi when Kenyan historians were involved in heated debate about the Mau-Mau, Vansina also criticised White's interview techniques and what he termed her 'sample selection', as well as the sampling done by Belinda Bozzoli in her study, *Women of Phokeng*. Citing instances of 'hasty' and 'shoddy' work he went on at length about the neglect of methodology. Vansina repeatedly addressed the work of David William Cohen, depicting it too as irrelevant, and as a profoundly foreign mode of inquiry[2] that both abandons the existing rules for the interpretation of evidence and eschews the possibility of historical truth. In 1995 an amplified version of Vansina's address appeared as a review article, 'Some Perceptions on the Writing of African History, 1948–1992'.[3] The piece revealed more of the thinking that lay behind the seemingly gratuitous criticisms voiced at the annual meeting three years earlier.

In the article Vansina emphasised how, until the 1950s and the pioneering efforts of Oliver and Fage, and later himself, it was widely believed outside Africa that Africans did not write and that there were no sources for the reconstruction of African history. The great advance of that decade then was the recognition that 'written sources were not uncommon in half the continent, and that oral traditions were to give the insider's view on the past'.[4] Academic historians of Africa were charged with the task of locating these sources, preserving them and 'enriching' them.[5] With that came the 'transformation of a fledgling field into a professional speciality'[6] within history, as well as the beginnings of a commitment to the creation of oral archives. In much of the article, Vansina was concerned to chronicle the advances made in African history in the 1960s, 70s and early 80s. Ruing the neglect of precolonial history in the later part of this period, he nonetheless

*Thanks are due to Nessa Leibhammer, Verne Harris and Isabel Hofmeyr, who commented on an earlier draft of this essay, as well as to the participants at the International Conference 'Words and Voices: Critical Practices of Orality in Africa and African Studies' held in Bellagio, 1997, where this essay was first presented.

1   My title is adapted from a key phrase in Isabel Hofmeyr's wonderful study, *'We Spend Our Years as a Tale that is Told': Oral Historical Narrative in a South African Chiefdom* (Johannesburg: University of the Witwatersrand Press, 1993), p. 54.

2   Vansina was here echoing Martin Chanock's comments reproduced as part of the 'Afterpiece' appended to D. W. Cohen and E. S. Atieno Odhiambo's *Burying S. M.: The Politics of Knowledge and the Sociology of Power in Africa* (Portsmouth NH: Heinemann, 1992).

3   J. Vansina, 'Some perceptions on the writing of African history: 1948–1992', *Itinerario* (1995), pp. 77–91. See also his 'Lessons of 40 Years in African History', *International Journal of African Historical Studies* 25 (1992).

4   Vansina, 'Writing African history', p. 79.

5   Ibid.

6   Ibid., p. 81.

209

celebrated new advances in knowledge of the African past, while indicating his anxiety about the 'triumph of theory'.[7]

For Vansina a turning point occurred around 1985 and was identified most closely with David William Cohen, whom Vansina described as 'the foremost champion of postmodernism'[8] in African studies and as the promoter of the notion that 'culture and history are perpetually "invented"' in the present. For Vansina, Cohen's work amounts to a denial that the writing of history is possible and an ignoring of 'elements other than the contemporary in the make-up of historical evidence and consciousness, a point too obvious to me', Vansina noted ambiguously, 'to belabor it'.[9] When he refers to such a perspective as a 'cul-de-sac' in the very next paragraph it suggests that rather than thinking that Cohen's point was too obvious to be worth making, Vansina considered the arguments in opposition to Cohen's position to be so self-evident as to preclude any need for reiteration.

The debate between Vansina and Cohen has a long history that dates back to the 1977 publication of Cohen's study *Womunafu's Bunafu*.[10] In that book, Cohen stressed the significance for precolonial studies of less formal oral texts than those on which Vansina's 1961 path-breaking study in oral historical methodology focused. Cohen pointed out that in Busoga, Uganda, there were no specialists charged with the responsibility for preserving historical information. Rather, '[t]o some extent everyone was involved in the preservation and transmission of historical information, though not necessarily consciously'.[11] Cohen's study showed that historical information flows not merely along the orderly chains of transmission identified by Vansina, but also 'through the complex networks of relationship, association, and contact that constitute social life'.[12] These networks suggested a form of historical knowledge quite different from the formal historical accounts marked by highly distinctive oral characteristics that Vansina had identified. What Vansina viewed as 'distortions' Cohen conceptualised as the essence of processes of historical memory. Vansina has since taken account in significant ways of some of the issues raised by Cohen, but continues to focus on the identification of the 'rules' that govern the formation of oral sources.[13]

More recently, Cohen has widened his critique beyond the consideration of oral memories of precolonial Africa to look at the popular production of history in other contexts. This trajectory culminated in his position paper prepared for the Fifth International Roundtable in Anthropology and History, held in Paris in 1986. Entitled simply 'The Production of History', the paper argued that the processes of the pro-

7   Ibid., p. 87.

8   Ibid., p. 89.

9   Ibid., p. 90.

10   David William Cohen, *Womunafu's Bunafu: A Study of Authority in a Nineteenth-Century African Community* (Princeton: Princeton University Press, 1977).

11   Ibid., p. 8.

12   Ibid., p. 9.

13   J. Vansina, *Oral Tradition as History* (Madison: University of Wisconsin Press, 1985).

duction of historical knowledge extend into areas well beyond those normally considered by historiographers, and posited the existence of multiple locations of historical knowledge. The corollary of this kind of perspective, Cohen indicated, is an interest in what is silenced or forgotten.[14] Cohen focused on 'the rich and awkward commotion' of the production of history, and 'the contests which produce, reproduce and change historical knowledge'.[15] For Vansina this approach adds up to a position that holds that history and culture are simply invented in the present moment and only have meaning in the present,[16] and it was this position that Vansina was moved to reject so vehemently.

Vansina's former student, and editor of the gatekeeping journal of methodology in African studies (*History in Africa*), librarian David Henige, for one, did choose to belabour the point concerning the 'role of the contemporary'. In a review article published in the *Journal of African History*, scathingly entitled 'Omphaloskepsis and the Infantilizing of History',[17] Henige offered an extraordinarily vitriolic review of Cohen's 1994 book, *The Combing of History*,[18] which extended and developed the arguments of the position paper. Like Vansina, Henige identified Cohen's work as 'postmodernist'. The article is interesting for the vituperation evident in the reviewer's use of language. The 'postmodernism' is 'cant', to which Cohen is depicted as making 'obeisance'. The tone of the book is 'self-congratulat[ory]', Cohen's sources are 'cats' paws', his explanations 'gymnastics', and his readings (in this case of the Leakey postcard) 'so personalized, trivial, and wrong-footed as to constitute self-sabotage'. Above all else, as the article's title indicates, Henige expressed scepticism of the value of what he dubbed Cohen's navel-gazing. Discerning the nub of Henige's criticism is difficult above the din of the grinding axe, but seems to come down to a claim that Cohen's attempt to think anew about the way in which history is produced is nothing more than, as Henige put it at one point, a reinvention of the epistemological wheel without any advance in technique or construction. '[T]he proposition that historians (and other scholars) never thought much about the idea of examining themselves in and around their work is pretentious; a myriad of prefaces and prologues since Thucydides illustrate this beyond cavil', remarked Henige.[19]

Many books are published every year that improve little on their predecessors but few such mundane efforts draw criticisms so lengthy and so sharply and explicitly denigratory as Henige's assessment of *The Combing of History*. If the real problem is not the reflexive turn, then the fear that Cohen's book inspires in the reviewer stems from what Henige believes to be its advocacy that any interpretation is as valid as any other,

14 A version of this essay was subsequently published in David William Cohen, *The Combing of History* (Chicago and London: University of Chicago Press, 1994).

15 Cohen, 'The production of history', position paper prepared for the Fifth International Roundtable in Anthropology and History, Paris 1986, pp. 25, 64.

16 Vansina, 'Writing African history', pp. 89–90.

17 D. Henige, 'Omphaloskepsis and the infantilizing of history', *Journal of African History*, 36 (1995).

18 Cohen, *The Combing of History*.

19 Henige, 'Omphaloskepsis', p. 316.

and its capacity to relieve 'the historian of the tedium of grappling with sources in serious combat'.[20] In short, Henige's spleen was vented in response to a perceived threat of Cohen's work to the professional production of history by experts trained 'to be true to the evidence'.[21]

My essay takes this conflict as a starting point and seeks to explore the possible significances of the fact that this debate assumes so heated a form amongst scholars renowned for their work in the use of oral sources for the study of Africa, and their longstanding concern with Africa's precolonial past. My object in engaging in this exercise is to consider the implications of these kinds of debates for historical practice in South Africa today and, more particularly, for the possibility of preserving, archiving and promoting knowledge about the remote past. The essay thus shifts of necessity between taking Africa-wide perspectives and a more narrow focus on developments in southern Africa. It proceeds in three parts: the opening section offers a short historiographical overview of the way in which oral accounts have been drawn on in the production of African, and more specifically southern African, history; the middle section examines some recent developments in the understanding of the interfaces between the oral, written and material or physical; while the final section tries to draw out the implications of these developments for contemporary archival, museological and academic historical practice concerning the African past.

HISTORIOGRAPHICAL SUMMARY

For the last half-century or so, a great weight of scholarly endeavour in the field of African history has been devoted to the recording and analysis of oral accounts of the past. A number of problems have been regarded as typical of oral sources. Transmitted by word of mouth, oral accounts have been considered by scholars to be notoriously open to accretions over time, to selective adaptations, and to be permeable to the orientations, biases and even manipulations, of their narrators. These problems have been understood to be compounded by the vagaries and deficiencies of memory. Oral accounts have been considered typically to lack clear chronological organisation and to focus on the history of rulers at the expense of that of ordinary people.

The 1961 publication of Jan Vansina's seminal study on the methodology of oral traditions (translated into English in 1965) was the first indication that these problems could be dealt with by academic historians. Vansina's approach, with its attention to features thought to characterise oral accounts such as the 'hour-glass effect' in historical narratives

20 Ibid., p. 317.

21 Ibid.

CAROLYN HAMILTON

and the 'floating gaps' typical of dynastic histories, offered historians of Africa a new set of methodological tools with which to tackle these problems.[22] The Vansina toolkit held out the promise that, if used rigorously, it would enable historians to write, for Africa, histories very similar to those produced for Europe and America. An era dawned in which it began to be believed that oral sources would redeem the project of African history, permitting periodisation and filling in the details of the precolonial and colonial past where written sources were either absent or biased in favour of literate, often alien, conquering élites. As the editors of the recent volume of essays in honour of Vansina put it, this methodological breakthrough was seen as marking the beginning of the lifting away of Africa's veil of imagined 'darkness'.[23] In the late 1960s and 70s, students of Africa, predominantly from a handful of universities in the United States of America and Europe, with Vansina's handbook tucked away in their knapsacks, busied themselves with the collection, usually on tape, of African oral histories. Typically these were transcribed, translated into English or French, and then used to augment scanty written sources in the reconstruction of the African past. Many a funding proposal from this time was prefaced with the claim that the oral traditions of a particular area were in danger of extinction as the older, knowledgeable generations died out. It was assumed that what was needed was to get their testimony onto tape as soon as possible, preferably transcribed into English or French, and safely stowed away in an archive where it would be free from further intervention.

As is well known, an important factor shaping African studies in this period was the rapid decolonisation of the continent and a concern with the empowerment of Africans, of 'rehabilitating Africa by recovering its past'.[24] An ethic emerged among certain scholars in terms of which the deposit of the recorded oral materials at their universities or in the national archives, or an equivalent body, of the country of their origin was deemed desirable.[25] Likewise, some scholars, far fewer in number, elected to publish the oral materials in translation or, still more rarely, in the languages in which they were originally recorded. [26] Still others engaged in the production of textbooks for the newly independent states, which sought to give the ex-colonial subjects access to their own histories.

A further dimension was added to the project of African history when social historians – many of them Marxist in orientation and mostly, though not exclusively, concentrated in South Africa – began to turn their attention to the history of the black working class.[27] Drawing on the work of E. P. Thompson and inspired by the endeavours of the History Workshop in Britain, these scholars began to look

22 See also J. Vansina, 'Comment: traditions of genesis', *Journal of African History*, 15 (1974).

23 R. Harms, J. Miller, D. Newbury and M. Wagner, eds., *Paths Towards the Past: African Historical Essays in Honor of Jan Vansina* (Atlanta: The African Studies Association Press, 1994), p. 5.

24 Harms et al., *Paths Toward the Past*, p. 6.

25 See for example, P. L. Bonner, *Kings, Commoners and Concessionaires* (Cambridge: Cambridge University Press, 1983); J. B. Peires, *The House of Phalo* (Johannesburg: Ravan, 1981).

26 David William Cohen's *Historical Traditions of Busoga*, published in the vernacular, was path-breaking in this regard.

to oral histories as important sources for the reconstruction of the history of the working class. Oral histories were seen as a means to derive categories of explanation that catered for human agency and that provided a view 'from below'.[28] The Wits History Workshop, established in 1978, for example, explicitly sought to promote the history of the underclasses, to promote the collection of oral histories and, as they put it, to 'offer ordinary South Africans a different vision of their past'. [29] A formidable range of oral history projects sprang up, motivated by these kinds of concerns, and animated for the most part by varying degrees of commitment to empower thereby the people concerned.[30] As with oral traditions, one of the guiding ideas was that the recording of oral histories in written form would protect sources that were otherwise in danger of being lost and, by preserving them for posterity, would provide the underclasses with continued access to their own history. Life histories, usually elicited in response to researchers' interviews, were also seen as a means of getting around the problem of having only the accounts of élites and leaders. By the mid-1980s, even oral traditions, typically concerned with chiefly history, were being subjected to new modes of analysis that enabled scholars to make them yield up data pertinent to past political struggles and subaltern histories.[31]

Vansina's enormous effort in attempting to develop a formal methodology constitutes an extended definition of oral tradition. David Henige has sought a more curtailed definition in terms of an account's adherence to a given cultural design or template.[32] Many academic historians, without always being explicit about their practice, have tended to define oral traditions and oral histories in relation to each other. At one level the difference has been seen to lie in the period referred to: thus oral accounts that purport to discuss events prior to the life of the narrator and usually refer to the history of a social group, an account of which was received by the narrator from at least one other party and possibly as part of a longer 'chain of transmission', have been labelled 'oral traditions'. The term 'oral histories', by way of contrast, has tended to be reserved for first-hand, often autobiographical, life histories of individuals speaking about their own experiences.[33] In an article published in 1991, entitled 'Oral History and South African Historians',[34] Paul la Hausse noted that oral traditions have been less drawn upon by South African historians than by their colleagues further north and suggested that this is because oral traditions among local African communities 'bore traces of written historical sources to a degree seldom encountered elsewhere in Africa', one of the 'intractable problems associated with oral traditions'.[35] Oral history or

27 For a detailed review of these developments, see C. Saunders, *The Making of the South African Past: Major Historians on Race and Class* (Cape Town and Johannesburg: David Philip, 1988).

28 B. Bozzoli and P. Delius, 'Radical history and South African history' in J. Brown et al., *History from South Africa: Alternative Visions and Practices* (Philadelphia: Temple University Press, 1991), p. 21.

29 B. Bozzoli, 'Intellectuals, audiences and histories: South African experiences, 1978–88', in Brown et al., *History from South Africa*, p. 211.

30 See Bozzoli's comments, 'Intellectuals, audiences', p. 214; see also S. Jeppie, 'Briefing: Western Cape Oral History Project', University of Cape Town, 1988.

31 C. A. Hamilton, 'Ideology and oral traditions: listening to the "voices from below"' *History in Africa* 14 (1987).

32 D. Henige, *Oral Historiography* (New York: Longman, 1982).

33 For a more sustained discussion of the ways in which oral traditions and oral testimonies have been distinguished from one another, and for a critique thereof, see Hamilton, 'Ideology and Oral Traditions'.

34 P. la Hausse, 'Oral history and South African historians' in J. Brown et al., *History from South Africa*.

35 Ibid., p. 344.

'testimony' on the other hand, La Hausse argued, has a 'rich potential' for the recovery of 'the subjective popular experiences of social change wrought within living memory'.[36] In these terms, then, replete with notions of contamination and authenticity, the views of the remote past held by 'ordinary people' are dismissed as faulty and tainted, while their 'experiences' are considered valuable data for the historian to work with. In insisting on the subjectivity of oral 'testimony', the 'ordinary' person's processes of reconstruction of the past are contrasted implicitly with the objectivity of the academic historian, who is allowed, indeed expected, to use both oral and written sources.

Thus oral accounts have come to be seen as an important 'source' for historians,[37] allowing academics to reconstruct the worldview of Africans. La Hausse showed how academics use oral accounts but ignored how 'ordinary people' use them, thereby asserting that only academics are the 'historians' of his article's title. Oral projects were evaluated by La Hausse in terms of their capacity to augment archival holdings and to generate 'particularly useful documentary material'. [38] La Hausse's description of historians' aims 'to recover unwritten histories' [39] implied that what is not written is lost. The notion of 'lost' here comes perilously close to proposing that the dynamic existence of such accounts in oral form from which they are to be recovered is no existence at all. The use of the term 'unwritten' rather than 'oral' suggests that for histories truly to exist, they must dispossess themselves of the negative prefix and lose the lack connoted by the 'un-'.

Underpinning these kinds of approaches to oral history was a set of implicit assumptions about who the producers and consumers of history were, respectively academics and 'ordinary people'. Thus Bozzoli described the History Workshop as promoting 'the writing of *academic* studies of "hidden histories", the preparation of accessible histories for non-academic *"audiences"* and the provision of training to non-academics for the *writing* of their own histories'.[40] In short, this view asserted that real history is produced by academics or by ordinary people following academic procedures, occurs in written form and is published. Oral histories, then, are relegated to the status of sources; they are not really 'histories' and they are consigned to archives. Oral sources are further regarded as being different from written ones, and as different from and 'softer' than the kinds of data generated from a range of scientific bases like environmental analysis, demography and household surveys.

Professional academic historians do indeed do different things from what local oral historians do. But to assume that what academics write is 'history' and that what local historians narrate is not, is to

36 Ibid., p. 345.

37 Ibid.

38 Ibid., p. 348.

39 Ibid., p. 349.

40 B. Bozzoli, 'Intellectuals, audiences', pp. 210–211. All emphases mine.

draw a distinction of dubious validity that automatically privileges the academic historian as a master craftsperson, the writer of real history. La Hausse's claim that 'oral history' in South Africa is 'still in its early stages',[41] when it is by far the oldest form of historical practice in the region, plays straight into this assumption.

One way of trying to think about the differences between what it is that academics and so-called 'ordinary people' do might be to argue that academics may not be concerned so much with simply reconstructing the past, as with deriving theories explaining human action; a task, some might argue, that is larger and more ambitious than the average person's need of 'history'. At pains to stress that oral histories were drawn on by the revisionists not simply to fill in interpretative frameworks with colourful detail, Bozzoli and Delius, in a review in 1991 of radical South African scholarship, emphasised the aim of deriving 'categories of explanation which catered both for human agency and for structured reality'.[42] Relatively little work has been done to explore the extent to which 'ordinary people' use history as means of thinking about the nature of the world, but it is certainly sufficient to cause us to hesitate before accepting the proposition that such activities are the special preserve of the academics.[43] Conversely, oral materials have been used by historians to do extensive service in filling in colourful detail and in making accounts of the past 'come alive'. To what extent they have given rise to categories of explanation of the kind described above remains to be demonstrated, while data drawn from 'harder' sources prove to be the preferred bases for the construction of past realities.

RECENT DEVELOPMENTS

Increasingly in the late 1980s and early 90s all of these claims about the strengths and weaknesses of oral accounts, and about the status of non-academic historians, were challenged. Where Vansina's early work suggesting that oral traditions were viable historical sources that needed their own distinctive methodology for utilisation constituted an extended definition of oral tradition, and where his revised version produced in 1985 modified the definition by accepting more fully the impact of the present time of narration on the tradition, David William Cohen was arguing for the 'undefining of oral tradition' in 1989.[44] Cohen's article emphasised how historical knowledge in diverse forms is deeply engaged in everyday social processes, and resists bifurcation into 'close experience' and 'general experience', or first-hand testimony

41 La Hausse, 'Oral History', p. 350.

42 Bozzoli and Delius, 'Radical history and South African history', p. 21.

43 Especially germane to the discussion in this essay is the work of D. W. Cohen and E. S. Atieno Odhiambo, *Siaya: The Historical Anthropology of an African Landscape* (London: James Currey, 1989), on Luo uses of history in order to understand society and culture.

44 D. W. Cohen, 'The undefining of oral tradition', *Ethnohistory* 36, 1 (1989).

CAROLYN HAMILTON

and relayed tradition. Cohen also challenged the idea that oral traditions had become 'a casualty' of the delving into written sources by
local historians.[45] In short, where Henige regarded oral traditions as
becoming infected with 'the disease of writing',[46] Cohen was pointing
to long-established roots of revisionism in societies with oral traditions,
which existed before the advent of writing and still exist as part of 'the
working intelligence of daily life that sits at the base of the knowledge
past',[47] in both oral and written texts, in formal and highly informal
settings, in special texts and in everyday forms of knowledge.

If Vansina in his revised work on oral tradition methodology was
prepared to acknowledge the effect of the present on a narrated text,
the methodological tools that he had pioneered continued to be vaunt-
ed and refined so as to deal with the problem. But the effectiveness of
the toolkit depended on the recognition of oral traditions as a formal
genre, subject to particular rules. Cohen's act of 'undefining' unsettled
the founding assumption of the methodology. Taken with a separate
but highly influential body of work on 'the invention of tradition', the
possible implication of Cohen's work was that oral forms of historical
knowledge were subject to such complex processes of creativity that
the academic historian could never establish a method guaranteed to
recover 'the historical meaning of a text'.[48]

Another development of the late 1980s was the growing recognition amongst professional historians that many of the points considered so distinctive of oral historical accounts were characteristics
shared by written sources and by historical writings. By this time, historians were becoming ever more alive to the way in which written
texts could be every bit as subjective as oral ones and not at all imper-
vious to change.[49] Scholars began to see in written sources precisely
the same kinds of alterations and biases that were deemed the special
characteristics of oral accounts. The porousness of oral and written
texts to materials from one another became apparent. In short, the
work of a number of scholars demonstrated that the division between
the oral and the written was blurred.[50] An adjacent development was
a growing challenge to the assumed benefits of writing history. Some
commentators noted the place of writing as a key cultural institution
of colonialism, control and inscription, others viewed writing as an act
of violence, while Isabel Hofmeyr's observation that writing separates
the utterer from the word[51] raises the issue of how writing cloaks subjectivity with the apparent neutrality of the (absent) author.

In her study of the telling of oral historical narratives in a South
African chiefdom, Hofmeyr is herself cautious about presenting the spo-

45 At much the same time as Cohen was
engaging in this debate with historians using
oral traditions, scholars of other forms of oral
texts were also challenging the idea of a clear
division between the oral and the written, and
an unproblematic shift to the written. The
'Introduction' to Hofmeyr, 'We Spend Our
Years' provides a useful overview of these
developments.

46 'The disease of writing' is the title of
Henige's essay in Miller, ed., The African Past
Speaks.

47 Cohen, 'The undefining of oral tradition', p.
15.

48 The phrase is cited by Henige in
'Omphaloskepsis'.

49 Peter Novick's That Noble Dream: The
'Objectivity Question' and the American
Historical Profession (New York: Cambridge
University Press, 1988), was perhaps the
benchmark study in this regard.

50 Hofmeyr's study 'We Spend our Years',
offers a useful review of this process of
'blurring' (Introduction). See also her own work
on the blurring, especially in Part Four.

51 Hofmeyr, 'We Spend Our Years', pp. 53–4.

ken word in writing, pointing out the extent to which oral history 'live[s] by its fluidity'.[52] The shift of perspective involved in the recognition that fluidity is a core strength of oral accounts, rather than their fatal flaw, is perhaps the most significant of the recent developments, but it is one with its roots in literature and performance studies, and it continues to be little taken up by historians. In contrast to the many Africanist historians who point to the vulnerability and ephemerality of oral texts, Hofmeyr, although concerned with what leads to the demise of oral storytelling, describes orality as 'an extremely tenacious resource'.[53] These kinds of points, highlighting the fluidity and strength of oral accounts, resonate strongly in a large and influential body of scholarship about succession disputes and indigenous law in Africa.

John Comaroff's work on political processes in a Tswana (Tshidi) chiefdom is a case in point. Comaroff demonstrates that succession 'rules' are not so much prescriptions able to determine a clear succession, but represent rather a code through which the complexities of political competition are ordered and comprehended.[54] Where many earlier studies of succession practices pointed to apparent contradictions between stated prescriptions and everyday processes, and regarded this as a 'problem', Comaroff's study shows that such anomalies are not unusual or exceptional: 80 per cent of all cases of accession to the Tshidi chiefship represent such 'anomalies'. To put his point in Hofmeyr's terminology, this 'fluidity' is fundamental to the indigenous political system designed to allow necessary strategic political manipulation. Comaroff shows how the prescriptive rules of succession, derived from agnatic ranking principles, are clear and known to all. 'A chief, in formal rhetoric, is born, never elected.'[55] He goes on to demonstrate how the accession 'rules' nonetheless 'provide a systematic basis for ongoing political competition and a means of imposing order on it'.[56] His basic point is that the rules are not addressed to the content of the ruler's functions, but concern rather the means by which the affairs of the chiefdom are conducted. Comaroff shows that genealogical claims are not simply fabricated, but that genealogical alterations occur according to a strict code designed to expedite good government. 'The anomaly', he concludes, '. . . is a function of etic methodological perspective, not of Tshidi political history as they understand it',[57] and '[i]n this sense, achievement and ascription may be seen as two levels of one reality, rather than as opposed principles'.[58] What Comaroff shows so well is the encompassing logic of a system in which the transmission of power, its ongoing negotiation and its coding are articulated elements in a constant (political) process, mediated by the properties of a specific set of rules.

52 Ibid., p. 54.

53 Ibid., p. 15.

54 J. L. Comaroff, 'Rules and rulers: political processes in a Tswana chiefdom', *Man* 13 (1978).

55 Ibid., p. 3.

56 Ibid., p. 4.

57 Ibid., p. 15.

58 Ibid., p. 16.

CAROLYN HAMILTON

It is precisely this essential 'fluidity' that the codification of customary law and the work of the government ethnologists in recording genealogies obliterated in an attempt to systematise and fix indigenous systems. That point is well recognised when such recording activities occurred in the context of the exertion of colonial power. The possibility that the recording of oral traditions in postcolonial times, with the aim of preserving histories, may have similar effects, should perhaps give pause to historians, archivists and custodians of heritage.

The example of customary law is not merely suggestive as to how we might want to think about the preservation of oral traditions. The two matters are linked in a more fundamental sense: indigenous law and the role of traditional authorities have gained constitutional recognition in South Africa. A complex exercise is now required in this country both to unpick the colonial and apartheid administrative legacies in which indigenous laws and rights are enravelled and to revitalise those features in ways that can be effective in the modern world.[59] This involves, at least in part, an attempt to show how particular, possibly erroneous, constructions of indigenous law emerged, an exercise that asks historians also to consider what precolonial legal systems may have entailed. Such questions may drive legal historians back to oral sources. But, as we have noted, oral sources are themselves characteristically just as fluid as indigenous laws and rules. In addition, Cohen's emphasis on the production of history draws attention to what might be thought of as yet another form of fluidity that any student of indigenous law would need to take into consideration, namely the contests that produce, reproduce and change historical knowledge. (Ironically, then, the chief characteristic of Cohen's own scholarship, his emphasis on how historical knowledge is produced in different ways in different settings, in its concern with such fluidity, is more akin, than it is alien, to the fluidity identified in the indigenous forms!)

Recognition of the centrality of fluidity as a core characteristic of oral traditions raises questions about the appropriateness of the acts of recording or fixing that the use of the 'toolkit' requires. Whereas La Hausse's article took for granted that taping, transcription, translation, cataloguing and ultimately archiving is a 'good thing', these perspectives begin to show how the fixing of oral accounts may undermine their resilience and disempower precisely those people who are deemed to have the greatest need of the history that the oral accounts contain.

Interestingly, lawyers concerned with issues of customary law have begun to negotiate solutions to these dilemmas: Heinz Klug, for example, has argued that the reinvigoration of indigenous law requires

59 H. Klug, 'Defining the property rights of others: political power, indigenous tenure and the construction of customary land law', *Journal of Legal Pluralism and Unofficial Law* 35 (1995).

the institution of a process whereby communities committed to the recognition of indigenous law 'contribute directly their shared understandings and accepted intra-community practices as sources'.[60] The implication of this move for historians is: can we envisage a situation where instead of recording (or only recording) to preserve oral traditions, we seek to facilitate their reinvigoration by creating conditions where, to paraphrase Klug, communities committed to the recognition of oral traditions contribute directly their shared understandings and accepted intra-community practices as sources? In assessing this proposal, many questions require consideration: do people still have understandings and practices to contribute; what criteria might be used to distinguish 'good' knowledge of the past from 'poor' knowledge; and if there is 'good' knowledge available for contribution, how might this be facilitated on an ongoing basis?

La Hausse's dismissal of South African oral traditions as contaminated by their contact with written sources must be reassessed critically in the light of Hofmeyr's recent work on the conditions of survival of oral historical narrative in the Valtyn chiefdom and the larger body of work that informs her approach. Hofmeyr shows how certain oral historical narratives have remained coherent and animated, while others have become dishevelled and empty.[61] Hofmeyr contends that it is not contact with written texts that corrupts the oral accounts, but the breakdown of the physical and institutional contexts that determine correct transmission and reception, which threatens their integrity. She examines closely the changes that traditions undergo primarily through the lens of the changing household shape, particularly the shift from cluster-style homesteads to grid-plan villages implemented under apartheid. Hofmeyr posits that the disappearance of the *kgoro* (the courtyards where men discussed the business of the chiefdom or community), previously the primary site for the telling of and listening to oral historical narrative, and the disappearance more generally of the everyday physical world of the chiefdom, constituted the loss of both the site of the practice of oral narration as well as of the powerful physical mnemonics for historical memory. Hofmeyr notes that when people lose access to the topography that helps to enfold memory it may wither and die or get taken up by bricoleurs becoming, in the process, farce.[62]

Hofmeyr's observations about the connections between topography and historical memory are strongly borne out by the work of the Swaziland Oral History Project (SWOHP),[63] a research effort still more squarely focused on oral accounts pertinent to precolonial times. Like Hofmeyr's research, the accounts collected by SWOHP from areas

60 Ibid.

61 Hofmeyr, 'We Spend Our Years', p. 172.

62 See also I. Cunnison, 'History of the Luapula: an essay on the historical notes of a Central African tribe', *Rhodes Livingstone Papers* 21 (1951), for an early instance, and Cohen and Odhiambo, *Siaya: The Historical Anthropology of an African Landscape*, for a more recent instance, of the recognition of the way in which history is embedded in landscape.

63 This University of the Witwatersrand project, originally concerned with only materials from southern Swaziland, has widened its ambit to include materials pertinent to an area that today includes southern Mozambique and northern KwaZulu-Natal (Bonner and Hamilton, 2 vols., in preparation).

CAROLYN HAMILTON

where chiefdom politics remain important, and where narrative occasions persist, retain significant coherence and integrity. Perhaps even
more strongly than Hofmeyr's materials, these accounts make use of a
range of mnemonics located in the landscape, in landmarks such as
gravesites and battlefields, and in items of material culture.[64] The
SWOHP accounts were, however, as often collected from narrators
physically displaced from the places referred to as they were from narrators present within the landscape being discussed, but in all instances
the importance of establishing the modern location of sites was
stressed.[65] In some instances, place references were densely compressed
into the praises attached to family names (*tinanatelo*/*izitakazelo*) that
were simultaneously both highly valued and considered amusing
because of their high level of esoteric content. Places that could not be
located by the tellers in a modern geography were the object of active
investigation. Thus the late Swazi king, Sobhuza II, sent search parties
into the Lubombo mountains to interview the inhabitants of the mountain chiefdoms in an effort to locate the sites named in the royal praises and in narratives of Swazi origins, while aspects of the infamous
Ingwavuma land deal between Sobhuza and the South African government, nearly concluded in the early 1980s, concerned the return of
Swazi ancestral sites located inside South Africa, such as the Rock of
Ngwane. Likewise, in 1994, local Ndwandwe historian Bongani
Mkhatshwa journeyed from Swaziland into South Africa carrying an
ancestral Ndwandwe staff, in an effort to locate Ndwandwe grave sites,
and there with the aid of the staff to address those lost ancestors.[66] For
the Swazi king and the ardent Ndwandwe nationalist, the sites constituted a valued form of proof of the integrity of the oral histories.

The role of places and objects in stimulating oral historical narration and in constraining the form and extent of change they undergo
is widely attested to in Africa,[67] but one instance of this recognition
that bears special address is provided by the work around memory in
relation to the material culture of the Luba peoples of southern Zaire.
The exhibition *Memory: Luba Art and the Making of History*, at The
Museum for African Art in New York, explored the role of objects as
mnemonics for historical narratives.[68] The exhibition focused on
memory boards, ancestor figures, royal staffs, divination instruments
and a range of other items of material culture that work as mnemonic devices, and it probed the role that objects play in the making of
Luba histories of kingship and centre/periphery political relations.
Interestingly, Jan Vansina, in the catalogue foreword, notes that symbolic signs marked on objects that are aids to memory 'are not writ-

64 Using materials collected by the Swaziland
Oral History Project, Ronette Engela is
conducting archaeological research in northern
KwaZulu-Natal which focuses on the
relationship between historical memory and
landscape. See her paper, 'Remembered
landscapes: origins of Ndwandwe identity in
the northern KwaZulu-Natal landscape',
presented to the conference on New
Theoretical Approaches to Interpreting Past
Landscapes, University of Cape Town, 1997.

65 While the SWOHP materials seem to stand
in some contrast to the *oriki* discussed by
Barber, in which the emphasis is on metaphor,
on 'absent, other places', and a metaphysical
idea of location, Barber's work is suggestive of
the extent to which stories create the
landscape as much as the landscape may
prompt the story. (K. Barber, 'The secretion of
oriki in the material world', *Passages* 7
[1994].)

66 Mkhatshwa was invited to join a research
party convened by SWOHP because he had
long expressed the ambition to undertake such
a mission.

67 See the essays presented to the workshop
on 'Texts in Objects' held at the Institute for
Advanced Study and Research in the African
Humanities, Northwestern University,
reproduced in *Passages* 7 (1994).

68 *Memory: Luba Art and the Making of
History*, organised and presented by The
Museum for African Art, New York (1996). See
also the catalogue of the same title edited by
Mary Nooter Roberts and Allen F. Roberts.

ing, because they are not univocal: a sign does not correspond to either a single sound or a meaning'.[69] But Vansina goes on to claim that this multivocality refers to many subjects at once, 'only one or a few of which may relate to such historical narratives as the coming of kingship to the main Luba kingdom'. Thus while acknowledging that the scope for various interpretations is thus great, greater, he says, than in the case of writing, and that the scope is not infinite ('it can tell a common historical narrative'), Vansina continues to look for the common and constant 'core', trying to overcome the fluidity 'problem'.

As much as the SWOHP work shows that the loss of direct access to the topography associated with oral accounts is not inevitably destructive of the oral narrative, so too do a number of other studies demonstrate that opaque or fragmented historical accounts are not necessarily so corrupted that they have no intellectual content. In her study of *mregho* sticks and the material of memory on Kilimanjaro, Kerner, for example, notes that in some instances oral accounts may seem incomprehensible because they are embedded in a 'deep language, esoteric and secret', which is designed to hide its meaning from strangers and the uninitiated, and that this language is often linked to objects.[70] The work of Steven Robins on the recuperative role of memory in Namaqualand provides yet another perspective on the status and significance of historical materials that survive in a fragmentary and inconsistent form.[71] The process of revitalising a Nama identity that took place in the Northern Cape in the late 1980s amongst people labelled 'Coloured' under apartheid has been described by anthropologists as a self-consciously instrumental performance in pursuit of land by people who had previously resisted attempts to link them to any form of indigenous Khoisan ancestry. Robins' study offers two important qualifications to this view: he notes that the invocation of the historical identity of Nama was not simply a traditionalist response by people claiming to be the descendants of the Nama. It was characterised rather by an intense engagement with the legal and bureaucratic discourses and institutional practices of the modern state. Nama cultural brokers were not seeking to revive or preserve a historic culture, but were attempting to connect ideas about Nama tradition with modern political and legal strategies. These ideas, he notes, were fragmentary, hybrid and inconsistent. They had this character not because of a failure of oral memory, or even the collapse of old institutional frameworks, but because they 'constitute the subaltern condition'.[72] It is Robins' contention that the devastation of colonial conquest and domination renders those claiming the Nama heritage today incapable of producing the coherent and totalising

69 Catalogue, p. 12.

70 D. O. Kerner, 'The material of memory on Kilimanjaro: mregho sticks and the exegesis of the body politic', *Passages* 7 (1994).

71 S. Robins, 'Transgressing the borderlands of tradition and modernity: identity, cultural hybridity and land struggles in Namaqualand (1980–1994)', *Journal of Contemporary African Studies* 15, 1 (1997).

72 Ibid., p. 26.

CAROLYN HAMILTON

narratives required by historians. 'This condition', he suggests, 'reflects and *contains* the traces and embodied knowledge of Nama historical experience.'[73] Robins goes on to point out how 'fragments of Nama memory' inhabit the marginal spaces of everyday social practices and places, such as the *matjeshuise* (mat huts) at the *veeposte* (stock posts), the remnants of Nama language still used, family genealogies and practices of body marking such as the removal of part of a finger. In court cases and land contests these details are recovered, given a new logic, and re-enter the public sphere. This, Robins suggests, is not instrumental manipulation, but 'an act of recuperation and memory'.[74]

Hofmeyr's identification of the role played by spaces and social situations of narration, SWOHP's emphasis on the location of narratives in landscape and physical landmarks, the Kilimanjaro material of memory, the Luba attaching of history to items of material culture, and the fragments of Nama memory reshaped into land claims, all show us that the 'fluidity' in oral accounts is far from arbitrary and not simply opportunistic, but is closely circumscribed. Culture and history are not 'invented' by the historians who narrate accounts of the past. As Kerner put it, the carvings on the *mregho* stick are a form of 'hard text' that could remain obscure and timeless, while the 'soft text', the narratives embedded on the *mregho*, remained open to commentary and revision.[75]

Attention to the link between words and objects is not only of significance to scholars seeking to know more about the precolonial past. Focus both upon the transience of the spoken word and the longevity of objects creates a demand for new kinds of archives. It further opens up new ways of thinking about social memory and its role in the construction, maintenance and transformation of social identities. One of the primary sites concerned with objects – as opposed to documents that are more usually housed in archives – though by no means the only one, where the activities of academics and cultural brokers dealing in social memory come together, is in museums. The final section of this essay considers some of the implications of the link between words and things for the politics of preservation.

PRESERVATION PRACTICES AND POLITICS

In 1996, the South African Minister of Arts, Culture, Science and Technology finally tabled a White Paper on Arts, Culture and Heritage, which outlined a programme for the transformation of heritage policies in a manner designed to correct the imbalances of apartheid history preservation and associated resource distribution and skills develop-

73 Ibid., p. 26, my emphasis.

74 Ibid.

75 Kerner, 'The material of memory on Kilimanjaro: *mregho* sticks'.

ment. The White Paper recognised the need to extend the definition of heritage to include what it terms 'living heritage'. 'Means must be found to enable song, dance, story-telling and oral history to be permanently recorded and conserved in the formal heritage structure.'[76] The emphasis in the document was on activities of recording, conserving and inventorying. The White Paper effectively proposed to subject 'living history' to the archiving practices and controls developed for document preservation, and ultimately thereby to the expertise of archivists and university-trained historians familiar with such procedures. In short, some of the very people whom the writing down of historical traditions is meant to protect or empower may lose any capacity they might have had of exercising control over their materials. The White Paper was also devoid of any vision as to how to revitalise 'living history'.

The White Paper was followed in 1998 by the promulgation of the Cultural Institutions Act, which made provision for the restructuring of the national institutions but did not make any fundamental changes to museum policies and practices. The 1999 National Heritage Resources Act, however, promotes a more 'integrated and interactive system for the management of the national heritage resources'. The definition of heritage resources in the Act is broad, encompassing everything from rock art and archaeological material remains, through living heritage (here defined to include cultural tradition, oral history, performance, ritual, popular memory, skills and techniques, indigenous knowledge systems and a holistic approach to nature, society and social relationships), to graves, monuments, significant sites, places, landscapes and natural features. Significantly, the definition excludes the holdings of the National Archives, which are covered by a separate piece of legislation, the National Archives Act of 1996.

The discussion in the preceding sections of this essay may offer some useful pointers as to how preservation practices appropriate to 'living history' might be developed, and how this aspect of heritage might be invigorated. The core of the argument that follows is that the oral and performative aspects of living heritage are inextricably and fundamentally linked to material objects, places, sites or landscape features in ways of which current legislation and policy is not sufficiently cognisant. One implication of the discussion is that preservation efforts may need to be concentrated on the mnemonics and on the creation of structured opportunities, spaces and places for the telling and reception of oral historical narratives. Robins' study, for instance, shows that fragments of memory may be embedded in highly hybrid forms that could not have been exhumed by researchers

76 See chapter 5 of the White Paper.

CAROLYN HAMILTON

working under apartheid. They required changed social conditions and public occasions to draw them out and make them available for 'preservation'. Such a shift of emphasis is predicated on a recognition that history is always located in a social and political universe.

A great deal has been written recently about museums, archives and monuments commissions as institutions rooted in nineteenth-century knowledge practices designed to underpin colonial dominance. It is widely recognised that the transformation of these kinds of institutions in South Africa today will require fundamental changes. A concern with the preservation of the mnemonics and the reanimation of situations for the relay of oral historical accounts may hold within it the seeds for germinating radical institutional transformation of the kind aimed for in the White Paper and the subsequent National Heritage Resources Act. The capacity for the material and physical to invite multiple historical interpretations, while constraining the extent of historical 'invention', when transported into the museums and monuments that house or preserve the material and physical, questions the long-held authority of the heritage institutions without conceding a complete relativism. It presents a challenge to archives to move away from their strong documentary bias, and demands that they do not simply expand their concept of document to include the transcribed oral text. At the same time, indigenous ideas about the custodial role of the material or physical may add new dimensions to the institutions' custodial charters. Such perspectives begin to suggest that the project of 'living history' is not simply to augment written 'white' sources with recorded oral 'black' sources within old institutional frameworks now maintained by increasing numbers of black personnel. Rather, it may entail the redefinition of the charters and spheres of work of archives, museums and monuments bodies. The collection of written documents, and increasingly oral recordings in archives, and their separation from objects, considered the preserve of the museums, require reassessment, as does the separation from both archives and museums of monuments, Western histories' 'mnemonics' *par excellence*.

Such a shift of emphasis holds the potential of giving new substance to African intellectuals' needs to reclaim their pasts, and to use them to revise what are described as Western forms of epistemology. Likewise, it has the potential to assist the development also of the academic study of the past: few scholars today subscribe to a positivist absolutism and the focus on fluidity offers a fresh perspective on what has been the dominant view of history as the truth about the past. Significantly, recognition of the need to preserve mnemonics rather than simply recording particularly 'good' texts would set in motion a process of preservation predicated on the idea that the purpose of conservation is not to obtain a single definitive knowledge of the past.

The emphasis in this essay on fluidity and processes does not constitute a rejection of the value of recordings and of the preservation of such recordings for posterity. Nor is it meant to suggest that the academic work on the remote past is doomed to drown in perpetually swirling waters. It does constitute a claim that recording is insufficient on its own, and that academic pursuit of knowledge of the remote past cannot proceed without due acknowledgement of the multiple fluidities involved in the production of historical knowledge. Likewise, while the essay draws attention to the custodial role of the material and the physical and to the 'evidence' inscribed in the material world, it does not constitute a claim that the material stands free of interpretation. In so far as historical narratives are attached to the material world they can give shape and meaning to the material as much as the material may contribute to their composition.

CONCLUSION

It is possible to read Cohen's work in a way that is by no means incompatible with Vansina's own more formal approach and that suggests that the scholar of the past has plenty of work to do. Where Vansina's methods require the historian to examine the accretions and distortions to which an oral account has been subject, and where possible, to reconstruct an archetype, Cohen's position demands a still larger project: the historical reconstruction of the circumstances of the production of historical knowledge, including the disorderly processes that lie beyond the tradition itself. In their study, *Siaya: The Historical Anthropology of an African Landscape*, Cohen and Odhiambo challenge the assumption of a clear distinction between the two parties to an investigation, the observer and the observed, and foreground the existence of 'evidence that "other cultures" have been busy producing their own anthropologies and their own histories, discoursing on their own identities and constitutions, producing their own introspections',[77] and, in effect, their own historiographies, the very things conventionally deemed to be historians' 'sources'.

The nub of the debate between Vansina and Cohen stands revealed not as an argument about whether historical knowledge is possible as Vansina would have it, but rather it is focused on the status of oral texts: are they historiographies as Cohen would insist, or are they, to

77 Cohen and Odhiambo, *Siaya*, p. 2.

CAROLYN HAMILTON

use the term introduced by Vansina, 'historiologies'.[78] Historiographies, following Cohen, need to be set in the social and historical contexts of their own production. The Nama land claim, for example, is part of such a historiography, and requires such contextualisation. The scientific suffix to 'historiologies' directs us to the formal analysis of their components and form. To recognise the status of oral traditions as historiographies is not to throw out all formal analysis. Drawing on literary theory, Hofmeyr manages to combine attention to the formal properties of oral historical narratives with a concern with their sociology, while SWOHP employs tools from both Vansina's kit and what might be termed the 'production of history' approach. This is neither the 'triumph of theory' nor the relinquishment of the attempt to know more about the precolonial past. It is, however, a demand for a radical reconceptualisation of the status and nature of oral traditions with significant repercussions for the practices and politics of their preservation and archiving. Where David Henige fears that the 'infantilizing' of history may stem from excessive self-reflexivity and flexibility ('magpie history' with 'no characteristics, no definition, no boundaries'), Hofmeyr shows how infantilisation and the diminishing of oral narrative result rather from the breakdown of the institutional contexts of narration and a loss of flexibility.[79]

This essay seeks to resist the shape being taken by the current debate over the status of oral traditions as a source for the African past as consisting of two opposed positions, one arguing for the mining of well-preserved oral traditions for nuggets of historical data, using well-honed tools; the other suggesting that all historical accounts, and particularly oral traditions embroiled in modern political contests and filled with ideas drawn from written sources, are inventions and hence have little or nothing to offer those interested in pursuing knowledge of the past. The essay suggests that closer attention to the relationship between oral accounts and associated material objects or places may begin to free the debate from the polarities of 'historical truth' versus 'historical invention'. At the same time the essay suggests ways that aspects of indigenous heritage practices may be used to transform old apartheid and colonial heritage institutions in a form that benefits both academic historians and other producers of historical knowledge, now and in the future. It posits the necessity of a new mode of archiving oral traditions and living heritage that is cognisant both of their fixed and their flexible elements: the connections between the oral text and associated physical materials or sites, and their contextual fluidities.

78 Vansina, *Oral Tradition as History*, p. 196.

79 Hofmeyr, *'We Spend Our Years'*, p. 54. Her comment on p. 54 about infantilisation is made with specific reference to fantastical stories, but the substance of the argument at this point of her study is that the fixing of these stories in school primers robs them of their flexibility and contributes to the process of infantilisation, and as such is almost the exact reverse of Henige's anxiety.

albino -
abi - marble
Alf - Alfred, Alpheus (abr.)
ambaag - trade; skills
awthi - young man; sometimes it is a boyfriend e.g (cherrie - opp.) (pron. awty)
synonyms - jita; mjita; cangusha; cangushi; mthakathi; mpintshi; bhaab, sbali etc
ayas - cap; usually with an average beak; usually plain or in a check
banda (uku) to be afraid (ukusha, ukugwaja - synonyms)
badi - see awthi
bhaketa - bargain
bhamama - more than the usual scale of anything that can be handled with
two or one hand; nkibinkibi (synonym).
biza - he who shares the same name with you
bhla - friend, mthakathi; mpintshi; cangushi, cangusha, sbali, bhaab, mkhulu, clien
bhambha - fat person, especially men.
Bhizat - Boy; any young man who is feared and usually troublesome in any given area.
bhiza - boy; male servant in any given business.
bhenda - train
bhani - bicycle
bhathi - shoe(s) (synonym - sbhathu; skoender)
biggie - blanket
bhabbi - bhabhalaz; hangover, stlamaflama
bhaya - bioscope
bhifo - bioscope
bhra - big brother (opp. nwana)
blem - hang around
bhosera - tight long pants
borotho - stolen goods
buaja - beautiful teenage girl
bhteza - orenhwood stick
bhabhoza - bees with brainly some times
bo-blash - deemers/thick and expensive
bhari - someone who does not seem to know and understand anything
bhakabhaka - Bus, Orlando Pirates
bhambino - baby
boodskap - message
bhangai - badi
bhathta - hijack

Orality and Literacy in an Electronic Era

Phaswane Mpe

At Naudé, who had a wireless set, came into Jurie Steyn's voorkamer, where we were sitting waiting for the railway lorry from Bekkersdal, and gave us the latest news . . . We listened for a while to what At Naudé had to say, and then we suddenly remembered a marathon event that had taken place in the little dorp of Bekkersdal – almost in our midst, you could say.[1]

Oral historians and archivists in South Africa are extremely committed people. In the apartheid days some of them, working for the National Archives and other similar institutions, would have been committed to archiving material in ways that were of positive use to the separatist, discriminatory ideology. To acknowledge this is not to brand them racist. Rather, one is acknowledging that there were forces behind what they did, forces like the state, whose power neither they, nor anyone else, could simply overlook. After the April 1994 general elections and the establishment of the Truth and Reconciliation Commission, this commitment assumed a new face: rather than collect and document data and narratives for the apartheid government, these materials are now archived for other political purposes. Not only is the focus now on democratic governance and politics, it is also, as Verne Harris observes, 'oral rather than documentary evidence [in this case the preserve of the apartheid state and its agents] which carries the story'.[2] One sees in 'democratic governance' and the 'Truth and Reconciliation Commission' a conflation of terms: democracy and truth go hand in hand in a rather unproblematised manner. It is as if now that the general public has access to channels of communication that the Truth and Reconciliation Commission can afford, the truth about numerous hitherto unexplained incidents and events that happened during the apartheid period will come to the fore, thanks to the fact that people can now literally *speak* for themselves. I am suggesting here that many people who want to hear it from the horse's mouth, as it were, tend to believe that the horse's mouth is a more *reliable*, more *authentic* source of information than written testimony. This authenticity of oral testimony is also often assumed to exist in oral

1 Herman Charles Bosman, 'A Bekkersdal Marathon' in *Herman Charles Bosman at His Best* culled by Lionel Abrahams (Cape Town and Pretoria: Human & Rousseau, 1965).

2 Verne Harris, 'The archival sliver: a perspective on the construction of social memory in archives and the transition from apartheid to democracy', paper presented at the Refiguring the Archive Seminar Series (University of the Witwatersrand, 1998), p. 1.

literature, where some observers tend to associate oral literature like poetry with closeness to nature and greater closeness to culture than the written arts. It is for this reason that we need to pause and reflect on what goes on in oral history and literature projects. Who tells the story? Why is the story told in the first place? And how is it told?

In suggesting at the beginning of this essay that oral historians and archivists are extremely committed people, I was alluding to an important point, namely that, as Terry Eagleton would have put it, they are committed to *irony*.[3] Much of the irony lies in the fact that their concern with and commitment to truth are not always accompanied by keen reflection on how what is supposed to be the truth comes about. Professional oral historians and archivists ordinarily interview their oral sources of information or data on a specific historical event. A translator mediates between the historian or archivist (often these professionals tend to be people unable to speak the language of interviewees proficiently), and later there is a process of transcribing and editing the provided material. Indeed, as Isabel Hofmeyr phrases it, '[O]ne of the great ironies of oral historiography in South Africa (over the years) is how little direct listening in fact occurred – notwithstanding the many metaphors on "voices" whether "lost," "hidden" or "from below." Instead what we have had is people listening to translators, waiting for written transcriptions and translations and then poring over these written texts.'[4]

In the process of transcription and editing, bits and pieces that are perceived as irrelevant get thrown out the window, despite the fact that the interviewee mentioned them because he/she thought them to be important. It is for this reason that one needs to use as many media as possible for the preservation of information or data.

In research that Derrick Nielsen engaged in from 1994 to 1996, in which I participated as a translator, I had an opportunity to glimpse the value of the often ignored aspects of oral testimony. Nielsen was researching some of the events that had led to a battle between the Sepedi-speaking people of Moutse and the Ndebele-speaking people of KwaNdebele in January 1986. At stake was the fact that the people of Moutse were rejecting the impending incorporation of the area into KwaNdebele by the central government.[5] One of the respondents, an old man, explained that they had rejected the incorporation because the people of Moutse did not want to lose their language and culture. He mentioned that when Bophuthatswana was formed, small non-Setswana-speaking groups were put to a disadvantage when the president of the homeland, Lucas Mangope, made Setswana an official

3   Terry Eagleton, 'Nationalism: irony and commitment' in Seamus Deane, ed., *Nationalism, Colonialism and Literature* (Minneapolis: University of Minnesota Press, 1990).

4   Isabel Hofmeyr, '"Wailing for purity": oral studies in Southern Africa', *African Studies* 54, 2 (1995), p. 25.

5   According to Nielsen's findings, 'the story of the establishment of KwaNdebele suggests that the South African government was never, despite its rhetoric, primarily concerned to consolidate an ethnic "unit." KwaNdebele's establishment and its consolidation were not driven by an ethnographer's vision or even by a divide-and-rule plan. Although elements of each were involved, the creation of an Ndebele homeland was an attempt by government to manage the effects of emerging economic and political dynamics in the region. Following its creation, ethnic criteria were similarly downplayed in planning for the fledgling bantustan's growth and development. Through a series of government commissions and internal departmental proposals the "separate development" ideal of a "national unit" was increasingly ignored in favour of geographical, administrative and developmental concerns. The unstated, but clearly discernible, shift in government policy culminated in the government's forced incorporation of Moutse into KwaNdebele.'

As Nielsen observes later, the '"relevant factors" cited by the government (for wanting to incorporate Moutse into KwaNdebele) were administrative and material in nature, including Moutse's integrated road network, the Philadelphia hospital, and its many schools and clinics'. See Derrick Nielsen, ` "Bringing together that which belongs together": the establishment of KwaNdebele and the incorporation of Moutse' (unpublished seminar paper presented at the Institute for Advanced Social Research, University of the Witwatersrand, 11 March 1996), pp. 3, 24.

language, and other languages could not be spoken and written in homeland schools. Here 'Bophuthatswana' becomes a tool employed by the history of the Sepedi speakers of Moutse to think through the possible consequences of incorporation into KwaNdebele, in much the same way that At Naudé's radio news about nonstop or marathon dancing in Europe, in Herman Charles Bosman's short story, becomes a historical template through which Oom Schalk Lourens and his fellow Afrikaners can remember and reflect on their own history of breaking records, without knowing it, in singing marathons. Simultaneously, this 'Bophuthatswana-as-a-tool' was remembered because of the very existence of the threat of possible incorporation. When the incorporation finally happened, some people felt extremely angry that proper channels of communication had not been followed in informing them about the day from which the incorporation would be officially effective.

One respondent actually told us how he and many others got to know about the incorporation. He remembered distinctly that the news was first broken to them by Radio Lebowa,[6] as Thobela FM was then called, on the eve of the incorporation. This respondent even expressed his hatred for Frans M. Sethosa, the Radio Lebowa broadcaster who read the news at the time. For those unacquainted with him, Sethosa was an energetic news reader who was also given to joking, with the result that his news reading and subsequent cracking of jokes (it was not clear that the jokes related, either directly or indirectly, to the incorporation), when there were such grave matters at stake, were not welcomed by this particular respondent. In addition, the respondent felt bitter that the government had not had the decency to send a messenger to inform them about the final decision.

It must be mentioned here that other, scribal sources seem to suggest that the government, represented in this case by ministers Piet Koornhof and sometimes Chris Heunis, had become weary of negotiations with the representatives of the people of Moutse, as, in the view of the government, these negotiations were dragging. So, for the government, radio was a quick, useful way of making the announcement. But then the people of Moutse did not have access to this mass medium and could not therefore provide their views on the disagreeable incorporation. One such view suggested that Cedric Phatudi, the then prime minister of Lebowa, had sold Moutse for oranges.[7] Earlier on, the government had indicated its preparedness to give Zebediela orange farms to Lebowa, to which Moutse belonged at that time, in exchange for Moutse.[8] Although it is on record that in the late 1980s

6   Derrick Nielsen and Phaswane Mpe, Interviews, Moutse (1994–1996).

7   Ibid.

8   Department of Foreign Affairs, cited in Nielsen (1994), p. 24.

Lebowa objected explicitly to the excision of Moutse from the home-land,[9] the people of Moutse had a reason to remain suspicious of Phatudi. Since, as the incorporation approached, Phatudi was meeting government representatives very often, and the people of Moutse were not always sure that this was in their best interests as some of their chiefs and other representatives occasionally got excluded from the meetings,[10] the view that Phatudi sold them for oranges was not total-ly unfounded. This notion of people being sold for oranges is crucial: *oranges* (and not the land) became a useful metaphor for remembering the incorporation, so that the indignity of knowing one's fate uncere-moniously and at the same time as everyone else in the country, through the radio, was reinforced by the lightness with which the homeland of Lebowa, like the central government, is perceived to have treated the matter.

The incorporation finally happened, with effect from 1 January 1986, as the proclamation by the State President made clear on 31 December 1985. Radio, in such a context, while it was in a way a source of information, was also a site from which the government could exercise and stage its own power, an exercise whose repercus-sions were to prove disastrous when those without access to radio, except in their capacity as audience, resorted to physical action. Of course, this resorting to physical action was also in part a direct response to the violent intimidation that the people of Moutse were suffering at the hands of the Ndebele, whose assertion of authority over Moutse was not only orally announced, as most respondents re-iterated. Feeling harassed by both the Ndebele and the state, Moutse residents concluded that their only viable option in such difficult times was to fight those whom they could fight, namely the Ndebele.

This role of the radio is crucial to understand because some respondents do not mention it at all, although it is likely that it is where they too would have heard the first news of the official incor-poration of the land into KwaNdebele. Others would no doubt have learned this news through gossip: those who heard it on the radio then circulated orally the newsworthy but sad radio report. Authenticity in cases like this becomes a misleading term since one of the transmitters of the people's own history was a radio station whose control lay with the state and its agents.[11] Similarly, while the Truth and Reconcili-ation Commission attempts to draw out detailed information and data on certain happenings – uncovering some hitherto unknown ones in the process – it is true that, as members of the general public, we learn about these proceedings in crudely condensed forms on the radio and

9   Nielsen (1994), p. 18.

10   Ibid., p. 21.

11   Those interested in reading about the media and their role as propaganda tools might like to read Henriette J. Lubbe, 'The myth of the "Black Peril": *Die Burger* and the 1929 Election', *Southern African Historical Journal* 37 (1997), pp. 107–132. Lubbe's investigation concerns itself with the way in which *Die Burger* had served as a propaganda machine for the National Party before and around the 1929 elections. A significant part of this propaganda entailed the dissemination of the notion of black South Africans as a danger to the political as well as economic interests of Afrikaners. The Afrikaner interests were also seen as threatened, to a lesser but nevertheless worrying extent, by the presence of the 'brutal British' in the country.

television and through print media like newspapers. Thus what we get to know are the highlights, as perceived, selected and re-narrated by journalists, and not the crucial but apparently mundane details. In other words, oral historians and archivists may have to think carefully not just about how they collect data, but also about how they store it, and, if it should come to the point, how they transmit it to other people. Their modes of transmission can have far-reaching consequences, as the anger sparked by the radio announcements in Moutse shows. In the historians' and archivists' case the consequence can be one of constructing a popular memory founded on highlights and not on a proper understanding of events and the processes of their narration.

I have already mentioned in passing the question of storage of data. In this regard, I would like to share our research experience in September 1993, when seven of my fellow BA Honours students and our course leader, Isabel Hofmeyr, went on a trip to the Acornhoek area to collect some oral poems.[12] We did not just try to collect the poems, we also interviewed some of the poets about their works. We recorded the proceedings on video. Because of our position as students, one respondent indicated that he would recite a few poems for us to record. But he felt that, going around with Isabel Hofmeyr as we were, we should have a little money with which to buy him a *sekala* ('scale'), a word referring to a one-litre bottle of home-brewed sorghum beer. He disrupted the interview several times to remind us that we could have induced a bit more out of him had we made an appointment, brought the necessary money and organised more time. Oral poetry, he insisted in his way, was something that, depending on who its collector was, should help its practitioners to earn their daily bread or, shall we say, beer. Here was a view of oral poetry that was similar to the way publishers see their literature and other books. But this particular respondent was telling us all this because he believed strongly that the University of the Witwatersrand must have lots of money, and that Hofmeyr also must have some of it. While in talking about oral history and archives many observers suggest that there are unequal relations of power, often meaning that the researcher has power over the researched, in this case one was seeing an instance where the interviewee was conscious of his own power: the power to refuse to give us as much poetry as we had hoped for. Also, he would not go into details about the historical context of the poems because, again, he felt that if he told us much we might not come back – with money, of course. If one were to translate and transcribe the material

12 Isabel Hofmeyr et al., A Collection of Oral Poems and Interviews from Acornhoek on Video Cassette (Department of African Literature, University of the Witwatersrand, September 1993).

derived from this interview, it is likely that the poems and bits of historical context of the poems would be put down on paper, whereas the politics of money would be left out. However, as the respondent made clear, oral poetry and history are useful commodities.

In viewing the video of these interviews, I came to realise how important electronic storage mechanisms could be. Through them poems and narratives are kept as intact as can be, compared to transcripts, in that one does not fiddle with them. Of course, given financial, storage and other constraints, a professional archivist and oral historian would probably want to edit such material and eliminate that which is apparently insignificant. The problem with professionalism or institutional practice is that there is often such a stress on getting to the point (sometimes for understandable but nevertheless unwelcome reasons), that the point, expressed as it sometimes is in small details, gets missed altogether. Transcripts can be good as quick references, but one always has to think about what gets left out of them. As James Edward Young argues in his book, *Writing and Rewriting the Holocaust*,[13] what gets suppressed or deleted altogether from narratives is just as important as that which gets narrated, for the meanings of narratives lie in the articulation of both the foregrounded and the suppressed.

I think that the politicisation of oral poetry and history by our respondent is crucial for literary historians. Often the tendency in literary history is to provide the general socio-cultural and political contexts of a work of art, but to leave out the strongly personal motives that influence the choice of what is or is not narrated. As I have mentioned, our respondent showed himself to have the shrewd business skills one associates with a good publisher. However, an act of politicisation is also important in another way. A different respondent, for example, could not offer us enough of what he knew because, he explained, he did not have time to organise himself for the occasion. On close questioning, it turned out that organising himself meant that he needed to retrieve the sheets of paper where he had his poems written down. He indicated that he composed the poems himself, on paper, and then memorised them. However, these sheets of paper always helped him to remember as he recited. Without them, he explained, he was rather lost. That was why he preferred to recite for Radio Bantu (he was referring to the then Radio Lebowa) and to recite on important occasions at the chief's kraal, simply because they told him in advance that they needed his oral services and in this way accorded him an opportunity to get self-organised. Thus his oral artis-

13 James E. Young, *Writing and Rewriting the Holocaust* (Bloomington: Indiana University Press, 1988).

tic skills were inextricably linked to his writing skills. Nevertheless, he praised us for recording his contributions on video as he felt that oral poetry and history were vulnerable things these days, being gradually decimated by many forces. He saw the value of electronic media like the video camera and radio. But then an archivist interested in collecting poems could easily miss the complex relationship that the poet recognises between the oral, the scribal and the electronic, a relationship that again renders ungainly the discourse of authenticity.

However, with regard to radio and literature, both oral and written, one has to express a word or two of reservation. I speak in particular of Thobela FM and other radio stations like it. In the 1970s and 80s Radio Lebowa used to have a programme on Sunday afternoons called *Mmino wa Setšo* (Traditional Music).[14] The programme offered a wide range of this music. But often the musicians were not interviewed on the programme for the general public to know what motivated them, who had influenced them and similar questions that needed to be asked if their music was to be fully appreciated. Indeed, I remember learning more about Ernest Rammutla, one of my favourites at that time, just after his death. I suspect that it was exactly his death that led to the station telling us more about him. In other words, he could not speak for himself when the time allowed for it because the radio, as an archive, was more interested in his music than it was in him. The severing of the relationship between music and its producer is quite problematic, and an archivist wishing to record data on music might like to think carefully about how to keep the link as intact as possible. Similarly, an archivist interested in books might like to be sensitive to the link between books and their producers. I find it rather worrying when on Thobela FM, David Lebepe, a broadcaster who is accomplishing a great work in interviewing Sepedi writers on his programme *Di Tla Le Meso* (Things That Come with Dawn),[15] asks them about their life experiences and often fails to discuss in any significant detail the contents of their books. It is not clear to me whether it is because he has not read the books himself, but the audience comes away from the interview knowing more about the writer than it does about his or her works, a knowledge that cannot in itself hope to promote the buying and reading of these books or the possible subsequent appreciation of their value. Indeed, one could rephrase the point and suggest, rather, that the audience ends up knowing nothing about the writer as a writer. Radio, then, while it can be an invaluable source of information, also has a tendency to decontextualise the materials with which it deals. The product (like

14 Mosibihla I. Ramakgolo, *Mmino wa Setšo* (Radio Lebowa).

15 David Lebepe, Di Tla Le Meso (Thobela FM, 1998).

music) can become all-important, as in *Mmino wa Setšo*, at the expense of its producer, or the producer (like a writer) can become all-important at the expense of her or his product, as in *Di Tla Le Meso*. As with the news emanating from the Truth and Reconciliation Commission, the highlights can become all-important and the finer details remembered by the people offering these testimonies, the little things aiding their memories and the processes of narrating their testimonies, are shoved to the locus of insignificance.

In short, oral historians and professional archivists (whether they are interested in political history, literary history or other forms of history) should be wary of the discourse of authenticity and instead engage other issues such as what they are told, why it is told and how it is told. Researchers must also try to understand their relationship with their respondents. A respondent tells the story because she or he is interviewed, and this is obvious enough. But we must remember that the respondent is also trying to satisfy her or his motives for agreeing to be interviewed in the first place. For example, the KwaNdebele-Moutse interviews had enthusiastic respondents who thought that if Derrick Nielsen's Ph.D. research got completed, with their help, then the history of Moutse might well find its way into books and in that way become part of the larger history of political struggle in South Africa. For one respondent, whether published as a book or not, the research was going to be a long-lasting corrective to the Radio Lebowa news report that had failed to indicate to the general public that the people of Moutse rejected the idea of incorporation of their land into KwaNdebele. In the case of oral poetry and history, one of the respondents offered small reserves of what he had because he wanted us to come back. One might rightly ask: was this respondent committed to telling the truth? Maybe. Maybe not. But the point is that he knew what he was talking about, and this became part of his motive for selecting and articulating what he told us. And, of course, other sources of information through which oral history and literature are mediated are crucial. Radio, television and video are just some of the mediators. Print media are another, as is gossip.

Although the scope of this essay does not allow for a discussion of all the relevant issues, I want to dwell briefly on the question of translation. What are its processes, politics and their implications? For a researcher or an interpreter/translator, awareness of the complexities involved in translation can ease the movement between source and target languages. Yet, even with such an awareness and sensitivity, new meanings are sometimes created when moving from language to language. As Duncan Brown reminds us, a word in the source language may not have an equivalent in the target language, so that a phrase or an explanatory sentence or sentences have to be used to make up for the linguistic shortfall. This shortfall may be complicated further when the grammatical or poetic structures of the two languages are different. For these reasons, Brown argues, a translation, in many cases, cannot be said to be the same as the original – that is, to translate is to invent.[16]

As I illustrate elsewhere,[17] Sol Plaatje also was sensitive to these processes and politics of translation. Hence his translation of Setswana oral praise poems into English yielded poetic structures that are not found in the originals he provides. In the process of transcription these in turn might have been changed somehow, so that even they are not really originals. In some poems, for example, the translations have more lines than the originals. Also, he adds words like 'O', often accompanied by exclamation marks, and other punctuation marks that might help with pronunciation of Setswana words or names. In all these cases, Plaatje seems to have been in search of appropriate poetic registers in the target language, English, which do not appear in what he refers to as 'free verse' in Setswana. Sometimes his usage suggests that he was seeking equivalence by drawing on archaic registers of English. Comparison of meanings also shows some changes in meaning from the Setswana poems to their supposed English equivalents. But the point, too, is that this quest for English registers shows Plaatje's sensitivity to the new readership addressed by the translations.

Another fascinating example of what can happen in translation is contained in Maje Serudu's translation of Chinua Achebe's novel *Things Fall Apart*, into Sepedi. I must hasten here to add that the translation is generally good. However, there are instances where what appear to be minor linguistic shifts create new meanings. In Chapter Sixteen of the original, we learn of whites introducing Christianity for the first time to the Ibo people of what is now called Nigeria. The white person speaks through an interpreter who, although an Ibo man, speaks a different dialect from the audience. As a result, 'Many people laughed at his dialect and the way he used words strangely': 'Instead of saying "myself" he always said "my buttocks."'[18] Serudu's translation uses two words interchangeably, namely *marago* and *difularo*, to refer to buttocks.[19] *Difularo* is a euphemism and lacks the directness of the word 'buttocks' as used in *Things Fall Apart*. Indeed, *go furalela* is to turn one's back on a person or object, and *difularo* (either Serudu's

16 Duncan Brown, 'Oral poetry and literary history in South Africa', *Current Writing: Text and Reception in Southern Africa* 6, 2 (1994).

17 Phaswane Mpe, 'Sol Plaatje, orality and the politics of cultural representation' *Current Writing: Text and Reception in Southern Africa* 11, 2 (1999).

18 Chinua Achebe, *Things Fall Apart* (Oxford: Heinemann, 1986 [1958]).

19 Chinua Achebe, *Di Wele Makgolela* (*Things Fall Apart*), translated by Maje S. Serudu, (Johannesburg: Heinemann, 1993 [1958]), pp. 102ff.

coinage or a dialect, to the best of my awareness) can easily be taken to refer to one's whole back rather than just buttocks. It must also be noted here that *Things Fall Apart* does not use an alternative, euphemistic word for buttocks in this particular context.

Yet *marago*, another equivalent of 'buttocks', is sometimes used euphemistically or vulgarly (depending on the context and tone adopted by its user) to refer to female sexual organs. Hence, when people, often with disrespect, talk about *go ja marago* (to eat buttocks), the reference is to a male having sex with a female, obviously with the sexist overtone that the male is unquestionably in charge of the process. This sexual connotation, while perhaps unintended by Serudu, and arguably inevitable, is interesting, since the first African converts in *Things Fall Apart* are women and either male outcasts or untitled men, who are, at any rate, regarded as 'women'. Thus the sexual connotation of *marago* in *Di Wele Makgolela* (as the translation is entitled) further suggests and reinforces the lowly social stature of the converts, including males, in a way that the original does not. Thus, whether Serudu goes for directness or euphemism in this context, new meanings are created.

In our dealing with the Sepedi poems in our research at Acornhoek, we did not transcribe them. Thus one could have them on tapes, as intact as a tape-recorder and a cassette could leave them. However, Motopi Ramperi and I had the task of explaining (not reciting!) what some of the poems were about. In cases where the poems or folk tales were performed or narrated in Xitsonga, we had informants to explain them to us. The same applied to the historical narratives that some performers offered, either in Sepedi or Xitsonga. Given these layers of explanations and translations, much must have been lost in the processes. Similarly, much might have been gained, as the explanations and translations added something unknown to us, to be used as a point of reference should the performer or narrator not have provided such a clue for our benefit. Clearly, these layers of mediation, while diminishing the much-sought-after authenticity, have many benefits as well as disadvantages. How much the researcher gains and loses depends on many factors, and here the translator (who may or may not also be the person who transcribes) becomes a major factor.

Where the case of the land dispute in Moutse was concerned, I occasionally had to deal with the old man who referred to Sepedi idiomatic expressions and proverbs in order to draw me to his side. One fascinating example was when he asked me if anyone would keep quiet should another person persistently prick his/her buttocks with a stick. This idiomatic expression in Sepedi suggests one of the worst forms of disrespect, and indeed utter contempt. To keep quiet in such a case equally suggests either the worst kind of foolishness or cowardice. So I had to agree with him that, indeed, nobody could afford such a luxury. His point, of course, was that the Sepedi-speaking people of Moutse could not accept that their land be incorporated into KwaNdebele without putting up a physical fight, if necessary. They were therefore justified in fighting the Ndebele-speaking people favoured by the central government, to prove both to them and to the central government that the people of Moutse did not approve of this 'stick' being used to prick their buttocks so persistently.

My agreement with him was based on two things. One, there was clearly no way I could challenge the idiomatic expression, knowing what it meant. Two, had I decided to philosophise and question whether the people of Moutse were indeed right to use physical violence in the way they did – in the face of what they regarded as an obvious assault on them by both central government and the people of KwaNdebele, while the central government saw the matter differently, in administrative and economic terms – the old man might have reasoned that either I was naive or I sided with Moutse's enemies. Either way, he might then have decided I was not a worthy audience. Since my interest, and obviously Derrick Nielsen's as well, was to hear his narrative in its comprehensiveness and with as many nuances as it might finally contain, I also had to think quickly and facilitate the narrative by demonstrating to him that I was a sympathetic and intelligent listener. I assume, too, that the person who interpreted and translated the Ndebele interviews for Derrick Nielsen would have been sensitive to such politics and processes, and that, to get comprehensive and nuanced narratives from the Ndebele side, he or she would have obliged by demonstrating his or her sympathy and intelligence.

Now, who is the translator employed in your own oral history or literature research project, or the transcription of your research material? In all the case studies that I have looked at closely so far, the respondents were Sepedi-speaking. They often drew on cultural templates like proverbs, oral narratives or idiomatic expressions to clarify or reinforce their points, or, indeed, to win the audience over to their side. Does your translator understand these templates and what could go wrong should there be a misunderstanding? Is the translator sensitive to how much gets lost and gained in the whole process of translation and transcription? It is certainly not sufficient to know the

Sepedi language only in this case, and I think it is a pity that sometimes translators have taken no time in their studies (that is, those who went through formal tertiary education) to engage in in-depth learning about culture, language and/or media. Research skills in a social science are insufficient, just as a knowledge of culture and language without research skills is insufficient.[20] That is why it is disconcerting when student numbers in African language departments drop, for clearly then people are failing to appreciate the significance of African languages for good research and archiving. It is equally disconcerting when people talk disparagingly about African-language radio stations: a good understanding of their work is crucial as they influence popular memory, whether this memory be in the area of history or culture.[21] As long as these mediators of popular social memory are ignored,[22] the commitment of oral historians and archivists will remain a commitment to irony: a commitment to tell the true, authentic story or to keep the authentic document, yet brushing aside awareness of the mediators that make the story or document (both of them of doubtful authenticity) possible.

20 It is desirable, I think, for the researcher to research her or his prospective translator in order to ensure, to the extent that it is possible, that the translator is knowledgeable about the cultural, religious, political, etc., values of the prospective and/or actual respondents. Whether the focus falls on researching the cultural, religious or political knowledge of the translator will depend on the agenda of the research. Admittedly, this task is really demanding and in some cases might prove to be almost impossible.

21 Among the Sepedi-speaking people, I am convinced that Thobela FM, previously Radio Lebowa, has popularised the notion of the *setori* (story) more and better than any educator or cultural worker relying largely on books could have hoped to. 'Story' in English often means a fictional narrative, and occasionally a historical narrative as well. As *setori* is generally used in Sepedi, it can refer to fictional narratives as written in books (in both short story and novel forms) or narrated orally. In addition, it refers to radio and television drama, so that the terms tend to blur the distinction often made between these genres. A literary historian interested in the literatures of African languages will do well to find out what can be gleaned from listening to radio and watching television, because schools and tertiary institutions teaching these literatures tend to overlook these popular media and their significant role in the construction, development and distribution of popular cultural and historical memory.

22 The stories of Herman Charles Bosman sometimes reflect critically on the importance of books (and the classroom), radio and newspapers to a community and the way in which these mediators of historical knowledge are often erroneously assumed to be more important than oral history, especially in the form of gossip. I find them absolutely worth reading in this regard. See for example, 'The Music Maker', 'A Bekkersdal Marathon', 'Birth Certificate' and 'Day of Wrath', in *Herman Charles Bosman at His Best* culled by Lionel Abrahams (Cape Town and Pretoria: Human and Rousseau, 1965).

ada - shit (synonyms – guntsa, dantso)

ce - a soccer player who usually operates like an engine in the pitch

aiki - dagga rolled up with a paper to make a candle size

ayas - cap, usually with an average peak, in a plain or check

bhathula - hijack

bhari - young man who does not seem to understand anythi in the townships

Bhizzah - Boy, any young man who is feared and usually troublesome in any given area

bhobhlash - expensive dark sunglasses

chama - bribe

chamela - defeat in a soccer game

com tsotsie - persons who robs the people pretending t fighting for their basic rights

dima - keep a low profile

dladla - home; house

dlala - put on; wear; dance

four room - big police truck that usually roams the streets (synonym - gumbhagumbha)

goga - eye someone or something with suspicion

grizngirl - mother

jackroll - hijacking of lady or ladies

Jomo - soccer player with a big skull and an ext forehead

m - million

maphela - brown uniformed policemen who r townships

mratata - machine gun

nkomo - one who cannot play soccer

Memorials without facts: men loving: Clive van den Berg, Video still

Holdings: Refiguring the Archive

Jane Taylor

'The child knows no money apart from what is given him.'
(Sigmund Freud)

*'. . . we call those objects valuable that resist our desire to possess
them.'* (Georg Simmel)

*archive, ark iv, n. (in pl) a repository of public records or of records
and monuments generally: public records.* (Chambers Dictionary)

The exhibition *Holdings: Refiguring the Archive* celebrates the launch of
the University of the Witwatersrand's graduate seminar series
Refiguring the Archive. Arising out of the seminar series, the exhibition engages with issues that these seminars probe: questions of authority, the storing and transmission of knowledge, intellectual control. At
the same time, the exhibition, even in its naming (*Holdings* . . .), also
seeks to raise questions around value, desire, possession. What and why
do we hoard, catalogue, covet, exclude and authenticate? The exhibition aims, then, to foreground the psychological dimensions of the
ostensibly intellectual projects associated with archival procedures.

The *Holdings* exhibition consists of a range of works by contemporary South African artists who explore processes of documentation, and
how these are inevitably also processes of interpretation. Every act of
codification is also an act of selection. Every act of memory is also an
act of forgetting. In this show there are works of retrieval which draw
on historically ignored materials; there are works that imagine the private domestic archives of subjective life; there are linguistic archives
that compete with one another; other pieces suggest the relationship
between the religious relic and museum artefact. The works on show
use a variety of media and engage with the ear as well as the eye.

In the late 1990s South Africans have been confronted directly,
through the workings of the Truth and Reconciliation Commission,
with questions of who owns information, representation and memory.

The assumptions about what was relevant and what was irrelevant detail have been seriously challenged through the rewriting of history; reinvigorating while undermining the very project of history itself. In the recent past the hearings of the Commission have been documented, solidified, archived. At the same time, the findings of the Commission have been published and discussed, as well as interrogated. *Holdings: Refiguring the Archive* explores the larger question of who we are in relation to the retrieval and storage of information. At the same time the show is a more general inquiry into questions of value. The will-to-possess infiltrates our beings, marking not only our patterns of consumption, but also our erotic engagements. What we hold and what we surrender provide allegories of love and loss – stories of ourselves as a species.

Is the archive in the first instance a place for storing a body of materials: as the dictionary definition at the start of this essay suggests, 'a repository of public records'? Or is it in the first instance an idea, a conception of what is valuable and of how such value should be transmitted across time?

The writer Jorge Luis Borges, an Argentinian (the records tell us), spent much of his writing life exploring the vexing relationship between the material world and the ideal, and he persistently returned to the archive as his primary metaphor. His short story 'Tlön, Uqbar, Orbis Tertius' gives account of various experiments that test the relationship between representations and 'the actual'. He describes how in March 1941,

> a letter written by Gunnar Erfjord was discovered in a book by
> Hinton which had belonged to Herbert Ashe. The envelope bore
> a cancellation from Ouro Preto; the letter completely elucidated
> the mystery of Tlön. Its text corroborated the hypotheses of
> Martinez Estrada. One night in Lucerne or in London, in the
> early seventeenth century, the splendid history has its beginning.
> A secret and benevolent society (amongst whose members were
> Dalgarno and later George Berkeley) arose to invent a country.
> Its vague initial program included 'hermetic studies', philan-
> thropy and the cabbala. From this first period dates the curious
> book by Andrea. After a few years of secret conclaves and prema-
> ture syntheses it was understood that one generation was not suf-
> ficient to give articulate form to a country. They resolved that
> each of the masters should elect a disciple who would continue
> his work. This hereditary arrangement prevailed . . .[1]

1   Jorge Luis Borges, *Labyrinths* (New York: New Directions Books, 1964).

JANE TAYLOR

The imaginary landscape is recorded in a series of encyclopaedic volumes, and has its reality wholly within the realm of documentation. However, we are told, in 1942 'events became more intense' because it was in this year that the Princess Faucigny Lucinge received in the mail a small artefact, a compass around the circumference of which was lettering in one of the strange and unfamiliar alphabets from Tlön. Borges comments: 'Such was the first intrusion of this fantastic world into the world of reality.'

What should we make of Borges' strange fable about a virtual country, a place that was constructed through the infinite internal cross-references of an encyclopaedia in which each new term would be indexed within a circular system of meaning?[2] In some ways, his story is amusing but not disconcerting until this ideal world begins to take hold in another, apparently material world, although of course we have no way of knowing who Princess Faucigny Lucinge is or whether her existence is any more 'real' than that of the fictive country from which she receives the strange object. Borges baits us, his readers, by creating layers of text that make claims to their own authenticity. He thus establishes a kind of hierarchy of texts, teasing us into trusting some while rejecting others as frauds.

Archives similarly reinforce a philosophical hierarchy, in which the truth claims of various interpretations can be tested through reference to the real. Documents and objects are preserved, in part, in order to challenge interpretation. It is thus in the nature of the archive that it conceals its own role as a place of evaluation, selection and exclusion. Archives in this sense must trust material traces while remaining sceptical about interpretation.

This is perhaps one reason why institutions of public record and display generally suggest that what they possess and what they exhibit are the effects of the inevitable. Processes of selection are veiled, their mysteries shared between communities of initiates. However, in some exceptional and particular contexts such processes are privileged and valued. In recent decades, for example, the place of the curator in art installations has become increasingly significant; but the curator of the natural history display is still largely invisible.

This is not to say that material artefacts and documents do not make claims of a particular kind. In the *Holdings* exhibition there are objects and words that take part of their meaning from their assertions of authenticity. Until recently, the Enlightenment and its operations have been either celebrated or damned for inventing distinctive disciplinary procedures to verify such assertions. Increasingly, however,

2   We are ourselves living in what is now known internationally as 'the new South Africa', a country which came into existence as an idea and which the material world sometimes confirms, often undermines. The era of the virtual reality is of course also a material reality; changes in media technologies, global economies and information systems are in part productive of, in part produced by, new conceptions of the consumer subject and the objectified worker.

there are experiments in which different interpretative systems are confronting Western philosophy, contesting their own claims in their own terms. Perhaps every system presents, as part of its body of knowledge, an archive that forms an element of its argument?

I

Contemporary theory suggests that questions of 'being', for the human subject, cannot be separated from questions of 'having'.[3] The symbolic representation of who we are is manifest through what (or whom) we possess. At some level, it seems, we are at the mercy of the symbolic capacity of the things we own. As Baudrillard has commented, 'the system of needs has become less integrated than the system of objects; the latter imposes its own coherence and thus acquires the capacity to fashion an entire society'.[4] Marx's anxieties about the enigmatic processes of commodity fetishism are well known, in which he explored how agency and subjectivity seem to leach out of the producer and enter the product. Such diverse fields as exchange theory (from anthropology and economics); object-relations theory in psychoanalysis; philosophy; as well as experiments in performance and visual arts that reach toward the collapse of the horizon between the artist and the work of art have all in recent years explored the relationship between what we are and what we own. In such terms, then, what is the archive, that thing that is at once a system of objects, a system of knowledge and a system of exclusion? Do we possess the archive or does it possess us? These questions are becoming increasingly prescient with the blurring of boundaries due to the internet as web-sites become environments in which vast databases can be accessed, or sexual aids ordered, where virtual coffee-houses facilitate the transaction of desires.

A particularly compelling artistic meditation on human subjects and their objects that I recently saw is a work by the French-based artist Christian Boltanski. Titled *Verloren in München* (*Lost in Munich*), the artwork has various actual and virtual components. Boltanski appropriated one issue of the Sunday magazine *Süddeutsche Zeitung*, and used its pages to display small photographs of artefacts currently housed by the city of Munich's Lost and Found. The objects include teddy-bears, wristwatches, cassette-recorders, a guitar, a typewriter, false teeth, underwear, a camera, and several bars of Swiss chocolate. Through the assembled goods the viewer is led to wonder at who the Municher is, as manifest not only through what objects

3   See, for example, Mikkel Borch-Jacobsen, *Lacan: The Absolute Master*, translated by Douglas Brick (Stanford: Stanford University Press, 1991).

4   Jean Baudrillard, *Selected Writings*, edited by Mark Poster (Stanford: Stanford University Press, 1988), p. 15.

JANE TAYLOR

s/he owns or mislays, but also through what s/he returns, restores to an imagined original owner in a gesture of civility and 'publicness' that seems so distinctive. Given the contemporary socio-economic context of South Africa, a place in which the theft of telephone cables has jeopardised even the public telecommunications system, the Municher's engagement with civil society seems unimaginable. Particularly, Boltanski's exhibition stages a sense of community through which there is an abstraction of a public made up of *others with property rights*.

The objects in the *Lost in Munich* installation construct allegories of the city at several levels. On one hand, we are led to meditate on the character of the collective Municher identity as an ensemble. We ask, because of the curious diversity of objects, who or what is Munich? At the same time, the particularity of each thing asserts its singularity and calls upon us to recreate, to narrate, the 'ding-ness' of the object, as well as history: the circumstances whereby it had migrated into the city's Lost and Found. Who lost the toy hand-grenade; how did striped underpants enter the public sphere; who discovered, perhaps an hour too late, that their watch was missing?

And beneath it all, the wonder: these were all objects that had been returned. I could not wholly divorce my perception of the meaning of this public consciousness from my recollections of standing the day before, in another Munich art context, that of Hitler's showcase Gallery at the Haus der Kunst.

As an archive then, Boltanski's *Verloren in München* is in one sense an archive of the city, of the ordinary passage of being that marks itself through having. The objects manifest no obvious unifying characteristics: they are not of a particular size, or value, or function, or age. They are brought together simply as *those things in the Munich Lost and Found*. In this sense they set up a most extraordinary taxonomy.

Foucault, who has written so brilliantly on systematic models of mind, reminds us at the beginning of *The Order of Things* of a Borges story that records a 'certain Chinese encyclopaedia', in which animals are classified as:

'(a) belonging to the Emperor, (b) embalmed, (c) tame, (d) sucking pigs, (e) sirens, (f) fabulous, (g) stray dogs, (h) included in the present classification, (i) frenzied, (j) innumerable, (k) drawn with a very fine camelhair brush, (l) et cetera, (m) having just broken the water pitcher, (n) that from a long way off look like flies.[5]

5   Michel Foucault, *The Order of Things* (New York: Vintage, 1973).

What Foucault goes on to explain is how this incomprehensible ordering suggests a system of thought wholly exotic to our own, because we cannot fathom the classificatory hierarchy that establishes these categories in any kind of relationship with one another.

The implication is that any classificatory system looked at from an outsider's point of view will impose an incomprehensible order on apparent randomness. Penny Siopis's work in the *Holdings* exhibition (see Fig. 1) brings together objects of astonishing variety, and through the ordering principle of colour it contrives to craft a homogeneity out of the differences. So a pair of ice skates, a doll's head, a child's dress, a book cover, a menu, might all end up as elements of a single panel, unified only through a shared colour palate. And this sleight of hand is undertaken three times so that the three great window caverns of the exhibition space are stuffed, separately, with artefacts in red, white and beige, painting a great tricolour flag across one wall. By raising the coloured panels up against the surface of the window, the constructions took on a particularly iconic meaning, as if they were large stained-glass windows, radiating colour and mystical meaning. On the one hand, the work becomes a meditation on the contrivances of sameness enacted through the ideologies of nation-formation, whereby difference is effaced in the interest of mobilising sameness. On the other hand, the installation simultaneously invokes such taxonomic processes as are integral to language itself and which impose a unifying order over infinite chaos in order to make communication itself possible. So the class 'tree' replaces the single oak, with its unique pattern of branching arms, its community of squirrels and birds, its 15 wet winters and the two seasons of drought. But it is via an act of culture that we select, as the definitive feature of this vast growing thing, its 'treeness' as more distinctive than its other aspects: its greenness, or its age, or its height, or its number of branches. Siopis' mad assemblage of red objects brings together these things, subordinates their differences to their shared 'redness'. Archives invisibly impose similar logics. Recently in the Mütter Museum in Philadelphia, I and my companion came across a set of small drawers, which contained, on beds of cotton wool, the following assortment of things: safety-pins; buttons; badges for the American ornithological society; a small silver rattle; bottletops; nail scissors. We could not fathom the unifying logic that brought together these artefacts until we read the explanatory note: these objects were all from the collection of a laryngologist who had, over his career, removed each of them surgically from the throats of his patients.

Figure 1: Sacrifices. Penny Siopis
Installation: personal objects /
'found objects'
1998
Photo: Natasha Christopher

This might seem a perverse example but it reveals a practice of selection that is usually masked. This principle is clear when one considers the logic of the library, that archive probably most familiar to even nonspecialists. Every book that is filed in a catalogue is ordered in similarly contrived ways: the variety and differences of emphasis in each book will at some point be subordinated into sameness in order to conform to the classificatory logic of the librarian or, more recently, to global unifying practices such as those governing the subject catalogues of the Library of Congress, or the Dewey Decimal System. At what point does a book on Italian architecture become a history book, at what point does a herbal become a cookery book? With computer catalogues the serendipity of chance associations is increasingly diminished, producing an increasingly unified matrix of meanings for the researcher. It is now a rare institution that hangs on to its older cataloguing systems where archaic logics are still evident. The Newberry Library in Chicago, for example, contains a treasure trove for the period scholar. This is not only because of its wealth of specialist holdings but in part because it has retained, alongside the 'new', its old chronological catalogue. Here you can find, for example, the texts for works published between, say, 1680 and 1690, grouped together. Here the researcher might explore the unlikely conjunction of an ancient herbal, a tract about witch burning, a medical treatise, a map of North America, a new edition of Machiavelli, and a play by John Dryden, all of which suggest a textured web of intellectual and political life that more linear cataloguing systems, such as the computer catalogue, conceal.

II

> 'There, near that high building which is Mzimhlope station, is
> where I stay. This is Phomolong, beyond is Killarney. Further up is
> the hostel – the one that engaged in the faction of Seventy Six.
> The horizon is Meadowlands. The school with a green roof to the
> right of that ridge, is Orlando West High where the first bullet of
> Seventy Six snuffed out thirteen-year-old Hector Peterson's life . . .'
> My friend looked attentively at the living map I pointed at, like
> a determined school child in a geography class. (Mtutuzeli
> Matshoba, *Call Me Not a Man*)[6]

Over the past decade the artist Titus Matiyane has constructed panoramas representing different environments. An early work

6   Mtutuzeli Matshoba, *Call Me Not a Man* (Johannesburg: Ravan Press, 1979).

explored his own locality, Atteridgeville. More recently, he has produced a vast twenty-metre map of Gauteng, as well as a view of Lesotho; and his map of London is part of a new body of work that figures international cities (see Fig. 2). In his works we see an artist exploring the subjective orientation of the body in space. At the same time his drawings comment on the bureaucratic mapping of urban environments.

Formally, Matiyane's maps are a combination of visual elements. They invoke medieval maps that have a narrative trace in that they suggest the charting of a voyage. Such maps tell of a journey. Modern commercially produced maps, for all their increased particularity, are, in this sense, abstractions, because they do not point to a preferred route or a desired end. Rather, they make available (ostensibly) all possibilities. Matiyane's selection of boundaries, his use of scale, and his selection of colour all contribute to the texture of his map as a complex code of desires. At the same time, his use of three-dimensional projection drawings reminds viewers, on the one hand, of eighteenth-century urban panoramas or, on the other hand, of the 'SIM CITIES' of contemporary computer design.

Apartheid planners actively sought to separate various elements, various functions from one another, rupturing relationships, constructing boundaries, and concealing geographic links. In these terms it is particularly striking that several South African artists have, in the past decade or so, used maps, roadways and traffic signs as central elements in their visual world.

Apartheid law attempted to legislate identity and geography. It could not sustain this project because human subjects adapt, manipulate, refigure environments around their subjective needs. Matiyane's maps are graphs of human intervention. The early works show the inherited spaces of Group Areas as well as the arteries of movement between townships and urban-industrial centres. But, they are also highly personalised and subjective charts of Matiyane's own history of navigation in a country that attempted to tell the majority of its inhabitants that their real identity was always in an 'elsewhere'.

Information systems sustain our passage as we make our way in the world. We are largely unaware of the vast archives that make daily transactions possible. It is often only through the failure of such archives that we become aware of their existence. The neurologist Oliver Sacks, in his essay 'The Man Who Mistook His Wife for a Hat', tells of a patient who, because of a cerebral deterioration, could no longer distinguish the relationships between elements in

Figure 2: Panorama of London.
Titus Matiyane
Oil paint, ball pen, watercolours
and pastel pencils
10 m x 2 m
Photo: Natasha Christopher
Acknowledgement: Market
Theatre Gallery

his visual world:

> He saw all right, but what did he see? I opened out a copy of the *National Geographic*, and asked him to describe some pictures in it. His responses here were very curious. His eyes would dart from one thing to another, picking up tiny features, individual features, as they had done with my face. A striking brightness, a colour, a shape would arrest his attention and elicit comment – but in no case did he get the scene-as-a-whole. He failed to see the whole, seeing only details, which he spotted like blips on a radar screen. He never entered into relation with the picture as a whole . . .[7]

Sacks's patient (Dr P., as he calls him) is trapped in a universe that consists only of fragments. While he can see, in his wife's face, a pair of eyes, a nose, a mouth, he cannot bring the features together as a familiar face. He lost, as it were, his map of the world and could not tell how to connect point A to point B. To live in such a chaos is unimaginable. Much of our sense of well-being in the world is generated from the information systems that we use to give us accounts / evidence / myths of how various parts relate to one another.

III

Before 1683, the word 'museum' in English referred to a private study or place of learning. However, in that year the word and the place came together with new meaning. It was in 1683 that the first public exhibition space for the display of rarities was opened under the name of the 'Museum Ashmoleanum', now more simply the Ashmolean. Early visitors listed, among the wonders to be seen, the portrait of a 152-year-old man, the iron cradle of Henry VI, Anne Boleyn's straw hat, a bishop's crook belonging to Augustine, 'various very large goats' horns', a stuffed reindeer, a huge tortoise, a giant molar, and 'sundry strange creatures'.[8] This list is instructive because it brings together the secular and the sacred, thereby reminding us that the skeletonised index finger of St. John kept within a crystal casket on some church altar is not entirely distinct from the tray of humming birds secreted away in a drawer in the natural history museum. The relic is in some ways the original of the scientific specimen.

Peter Schutz's work on this exhibition explores some of the ambiguities and connections between belief and information systems by bringing spiritual and material iconographies together (see Fig. 3). Through the figures of the saint and the wooden carved figure famil-

7 Oliver Sacks, *The Man Who Mistook His Wife for a Hat* (London: Picador, 1986), p. 9.

8 Amy Boesky, '"Outlandish fruits": commissioning nature for the Museum of Man', *English Literary History* (1991), pp. 305–330.

Figure 3: Relic. Peter Schutz
Jetulong wood
850 mm height; 190 mm width;
180 mm depth
Photo: Natasha Christopher

iar as the 'dumb waiter' in Edwardian homes, he explores how objects become totemic and saturated with meaning or value. The saint and the waiter are in a way represented by what they bear: St. Sebastian has meaning because of his arrows; Catherine, because of her wheel. What is it that the waiter has on his tray?

Schutz's sculpted figures stand in attitudes of perpetual subordination, presenting icons – perhaps as some form of consolation. It is pleasing that the niches in which these figures are placed in the exhibition space are traversed by computer cables that serve the University of the Witwatersrand's own information systems. Schutz notes, further, that the images offered by the waiters are based on treasured objects stored within the collection of the Gertrude Posel Galleries at the University of the Witwatersrand.

IV

In recent years the artist known as ZEM has been producing a dictionary, a linguistic code-book for visitors to and inhabitants of Johannesburg, so that those unfamiliar with the language will understand what is being communicated by strangers around them (see Fig. 4). On the exhibition are several individual texts that are all part of ZEM's larger lexicographical project, a sense of which is communicated through the introduction to the dictionary. ZEM states:

> This mini-dictionary is a mixture of almost all languages that belong to original peoples of this country, but no nationality can claim Johannesburg as their own, it belongs to those people who have intermingled for years and therefore have their own *original* language which serves them in communication problems. Hence no one can boast his or her language as being superior to others. It is because of this reason that SCAMTHO was born by BLACK PARENTS for any one who might have interest in living in our townships. It began as a tsotsie taal (thugs language) [*sic*] simply because SOWETO was and still is regarded as a crime infested black residential area. But in a way SOWETO is very creative when coming to serve itself on whatever level of life. The parent is Soweto and the child was named Scamtho . . .

Figure 4: Scamtho dictionary. ZEM
Acknowledgements: Market
Theatre Gallery

What follows here is a selection of words and phrases from the dictionary. The selection is of course not random but has been assembled to demonstrate the characteristic concerns of the dictionary, its sense of language as a mechanism of both defence and offence, and a place for contesting value:

AADA – shit (synonyms – **GUNTSA, DANTSO**)

ACE – a soccer player who usually operates like an engine in the pitch

AIKI – dagga rolled up with a paper to make a candle size

AYAS – cap, usually with an average peak, in plain or check

BHATHULA – hijack

BHARI – young man who does not seem to understand anything about townships

BHIZZAH – boy, any young man who is feared and usually troublesome in any given area

BHOBLAS – expensive dark sunglasses

CHAMELA – defeat in a soccer game

COM TSOTSIE – person who robs the people pretending to be fighting for their basic rights

DIMA – keep a low profile

DLALA – home, house

FOUR ROOM – big police truck that usually roams the township streets (synonym – **GUMBHAGUMBHA**)

GOGA – eye someone or something with suspicion

GRIZNGIRL – mother

JACKROLL – hijacking of lady or ladies

JOMO – soccer player with a big skull and an exalted forehead

M – million

MAPHELA – brown uniformed policemen who roam the townships

MRATATA – machine gun

NKOMO – one who cannot play soccer

Language is also at the heart of the work by Willem Boshoff, whose artistic production over the past decade or more has engaged with the idea of the archive more directly than any of the artists involved in the *Holdings* exhibition. He has constructed dozens of projects of extraordinary obsessive clarity: false taxonomies, samplers of tree bark, specimens of sand, experiments in type fonts, alphabets for the blind: worlds within worlds within worlds. His work for *Holdings* reconstructs, in actual scale, the granite slab monument that rests within the Voortrekker Monument, the temple to the perpetuation of Afrikaner identity. The surface of the artful slab is covered in printed strips of language, which from a medium distance mimic the textures

Figure 5: Shredded evidence.
Willem Boshoff
Paper, ink, wood, glue
1997
Whole piece: 59 cm x 113 cm x
68 cm
Photo: Natasha Christopher
Acknowledgements: University
Art Gallery Collection: Gift of
Dean of Arts, 1998.

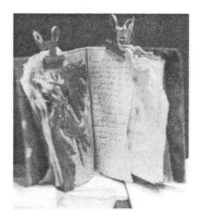

Figure 6: Diary. Maanda Daswa
Notes, journal, found materials
28 x 20 cm

of chromatic grain in a granite block. These ribbons of words are fragments of Afrikaner idiom associated with the languages of apartheid rule (see Fig. 5).

The languages of representation are explored in Maanda Daswa's journal (see Fig. 6). Daswa, who had recently been engaged on a research project around the work of Willem Boshoff, himself demonstrates an ironic sense of the relationship between the represented and the real. His literal incorporation of the little corpse of a bird into the pages of his diary suggests a commentary on the dilemma of the artist in South Africa, a context where the burden of documentation has at times all but overwhelmed the artistic project of interpretation.

The suspicion of metaphor and its capacity to 'betray' reality has had a long and honourable philosophical tradition. In recent history it is associated with the plain-style school coming out of the Puritan movement in the early eighteenth century. Thomas Sprat, the official historian of the Royal Society, decries: 'who can behold, without indignation, how many mists and uncertainties, these specious Tropes and Figures have brought on our Knowledg [sic] . . . this vicious abundance of Phrase, this trick of Metaphors, this volubility of Tongue'.[9] Hobbes similarly attacks metaphor in his *Leviathan*,[10] and by the time Daniel Defoe writes his *Complete English Tradesmen* he is advocating a new style of language that is adapted to its instrumental functions, particularly to the task of trade:

> All exotic sayings, dark and ambiguous speakings, affected
> words, and as I said in my last, abridgement, or words cut off, as
> they are foolish and improper in business, so indeed are they in
> other things; hard words and affectation of stile in business, is
> like bombast in poetry, a kind of rumbling nonsense, and nothing of the kind can be more ridiculous.[11]

In South Africa the suspicion of metaphor arises out of the unlikely conjunction of a Puritan and a Marxist tradition: both of which philosophies, in their instrumentalist versions, are suspicious of the idealist tendencies of the imagination. Artists of political conscience have had a difficult time of it feeling constrained by the obligation to produce engaged work.

A 'last word' on language in the exhibition is an installation based upon research generated by Professor Trail and the Department of Linguistics at the University of the Witwatersrand. There are three artefacts in this installation: one a sound text, the recording made in 1936 when a group of San women was brought to Johannesburg for the Empire Exhibition. While in the city, the university's Department of Linguistics made recordings of various speech acts, musical performances, and vocal imitations of animal calls. One of these recordings is a song, a lullaby sung by a Ku |khaasi woman, Kabara. She sings to her infant, whose vocalised responses can be heard as faint gurgles at certain points in the brief recording. This act of transmission of the language from mother to infant is the last known aural trace of Ku |khaasi. Apparently even in 1936, when the recordings were made, the only documented speakers of the language were several women who had married into other communities. This seemingly simple piece of information is enormously suggestive about questions of power and the transmission of culture. There is no indication that the relations between the Ku |khaasi women and the communities into which they married were hostile, or that the assimilation took place for any reasons other than mutual self-interest and regard. Nonetheless, one might ask, 'In what language(s) did these mothers sing their babies to sleep?'

There is a visual image of Kabara, with her infant strapped onto her back; there is also included in the installation a recording machine used by the Baptist missionary turned linguist, Clement Doke. Doke became a lecturer in the new Department of Bantu Studies at the University of the Witwatersrand in 1923 and his models of linguistic description in southern and central Africa dominated the field of study for decades. The recording machine documents vibrations in the head during the production of speech acts: three tubes are each held against different points of the head: one inside the nose, one against the throat, and one over the mouth. The instrument records, on a graphic roll, which portions of the head are resonating with the production of each sound in order to record how various clicks, diphthongs and vowels are being produced physiologically.

V

Another sound archive is activated through the composition and installation 'his reaction was instantaneous' by Philip Miller (see Fig. 7). Miller has used samples of sound recordings made in 1936 (the year of the Empire Exhibition, see above) by the ethno-musicologist Percival Kirby. From Miller's own notes:[12]

> In September 1936, over seventy Bushmen from the Kalahari were transported to Johannesburg by a big-game hunter, Mr

9   Thomas Sprat, *History of the Royal Society*, ed. I. Cope Jackson and H.W. Jones (St Luis: Washington University Studies, 1959), p. 113.

10 Thomas Hobbes, *Leviathan* (Harmondsworth: Penguin, 1985 [first published 1651]).

11   J. T. Boulton, ed., *Daniel Defoe* (New York: Schocken, 1965), p. 227.

12 Personal communication with Philip Miller.

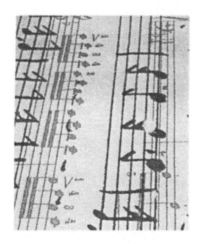

Figure 7: 'His reaction to the music was instantaneous'. Philip Miller Photos, photocopies, soundbooth

Donald Bain, to be put on show as an 'exhibit' for the Empire Exhibition.

Kirby, Professor of Music, visited the group at the Linguistics Department, where they were engaged in the process of making the recordings described above. In the spirit of cross-cultural experiment, Kirby invited a friend of his, Harold Samuel, to play a piece of music on the piano for the group, J. S. Bach's two-part invention in F major. Kirby describes the response in telling terms: This movement was in triple time and Mr Samuel had scarcely got into his stride when old Abrahams rose from his place and began to dance . . . his reaction to the music was instantaneous.' (Composer's notes)

Miller then notes how, when he was a child studying pianoforte in 1972, his teacher began to introduce him to the two-part inventions of Bach:

I have a strong memory of hearing my teacher play these inventions to me for the very first time. Although not old enough to understand the complexity of Bach's brilliantly constructed harmony and contrapuntal melodies, I remember that my reaction to the music was instantaneous . . . When I return to the music and sounds of my childhood, I realise that I was aware that there existed a music of 'the other' – whether it was at school seeing for the first time a grainy documentary film about 'the Bushmen people' and being mesmerised . . . or travelling with my parents on holiday to Johannesburg and hearing the rattles and stamping of feet by the Zulu mine dancers at an outdoor stadium for white tourists.

As a South African composer, today, I have begun to recognise how, as a young boy learning the piano, the music and sounds I heard and did not hear as a result of living in the white suburbs of Apartheid, has [*sic*] both informed and deformed the music which I write.

So, just as Kirby posed the question of what it would mean for a group of people from another culture with little access and experience of western music to hear the Bach inventions, I too ask myself, what it meant to me to hear the music of the Bushmen for the first time.

Originally, Miller intended to sample fragments of the Kirby recordings, and to structure these into a musical composition that would engage with the Bach invention. In fact, however, it proved impossi-

PLATE 1

PLATE 2

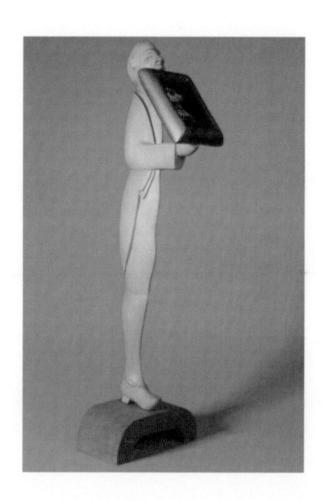

PLATE 3

PLATE 4

PLATE 5

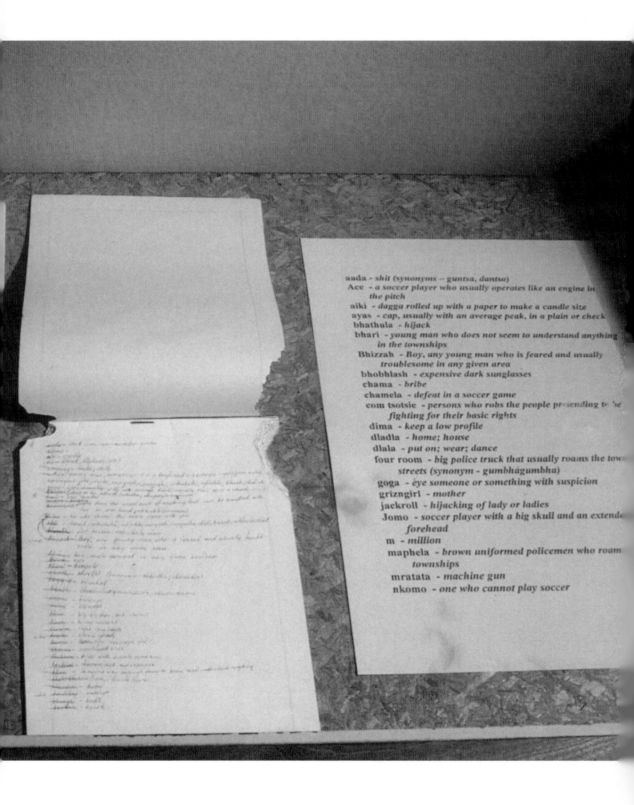

aada - *shit (synonyms – guntsa, dantso)*
Ace - *a soccer player who usually operates like an engine in
the pitch*
aiki - *dagga rolled up with a paper to make a candle size*
ayas - *cap, usually with an average peak, in a plain or check*
bhathula - *hijack*
bhari - *young man who does not seem to understand anything
in the townships*
Bhizzah - *Boy, any young man who is feared and usually
troublesome in any given area*
bhobhlash - *expensive dark sunglasses*
chama - *bribe*
chamela - *defeat in a soccer game*
com tsotsie - *persons who robs the people pretending to be
fighting for their basic rights*
dima - *keep a low profile*
dladla - *home; house*
dlala - *put on; wear; dance*
four room - *big police truck that usually roams the town
streets (synonym - gumbhagumbha)*
goga - *eye someone or something with suspicion*
grizngirl - *mother*
jackroll - *hijacking of lady or ladies*
Jomo - *soccer player with a big skull and an extended
forehead*
m - *million*
maphela - *brown uniformed policemen who roam
townships*
mratata - *machine gun*
nkomo - *one who cannot play soccer*

PLATE 6

PRINCE

HYDE PARK

GREEN PARK

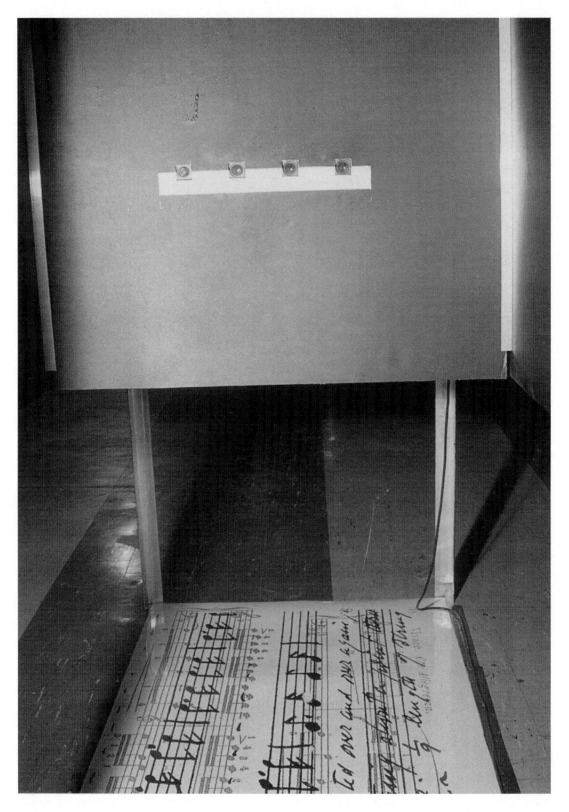

PLATE 9

ANALYSIS
OF THE
LANGUAGE OF THE BECHUANAS.

BY DAVID LIVINGSTONE.

A348   - - Papers, 1845-1871.   10 Items
The charred remains of 8 ALS and an
autographed copy of Livingstone's Analysis of
the language of the Bechuanas, (London, Clowes,
1858) rescued from the library fire in 1931.
Names of correspondents include W. Elwin, E.
Grimstone, W. von Haidinger, R. Moffat, B. Pyne
and J. R. Stebbing. Subjects include tribal rivalry
between Griquas and Barolong, the Boer
destruction of his books and medicines, the
Portuguese and slavery, description of his
explorations of Lower Zambesi and Shire Rivers
and English settlement in Africa.

PLATE 10

PLATE 11

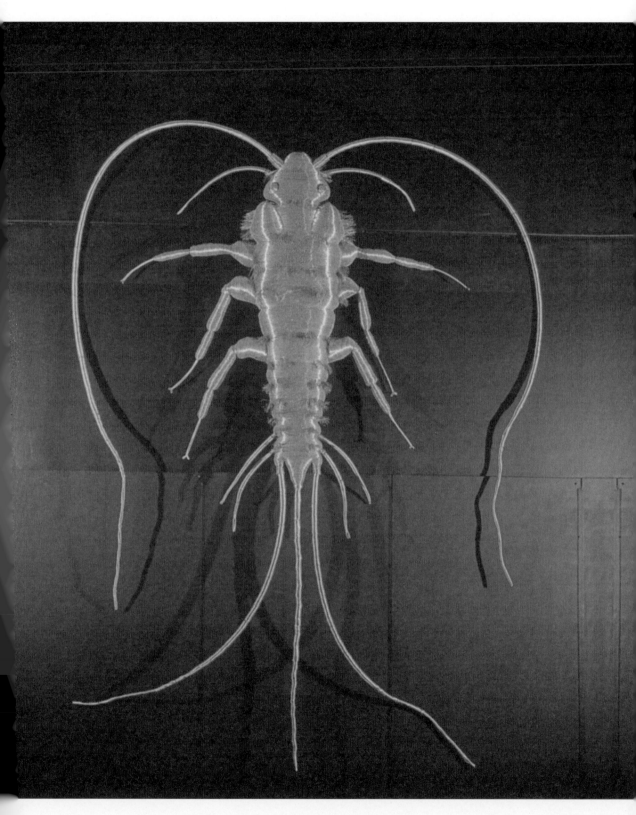

PLATE 12

PLATE 13

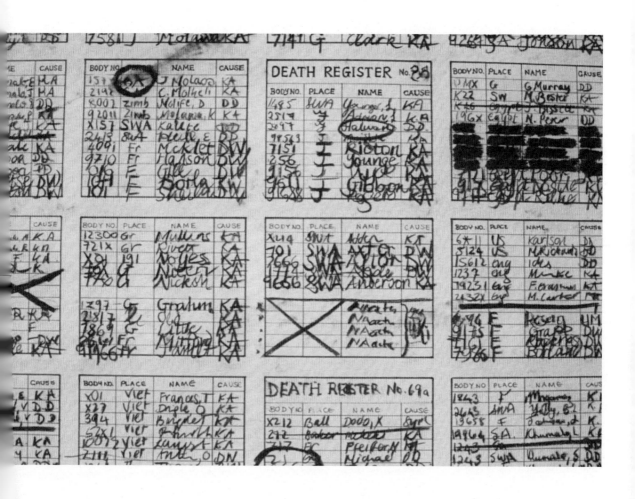

PLATE 14

PLATE 15

LIST OF PLATES

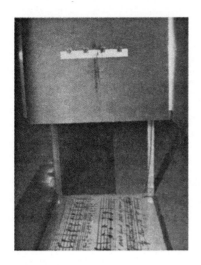

Figure 8: Miller's sound booth.

ble to trace the original wax recording drums, which have disappeared somewhere within the archive: it is unclear whether they have been misplaced or damaged beyond use (they are fragile objects and, being made of wax, particularly vulnerable to temperature changes).[13] In some ways the processes of working on this installation exemplified one of the characteristics of the archive: the archive is suspicious of the researcher. This is because the archive's *imperatives to conserve* are in some ways at odds with its *imperatives to inform*, so that at times it seemed as if the archive closed ranks against us, resisting our intrusions. The archivist feels a loyalty, an obligation of service toward the contents of the archive, a fidelity to keep the body intact which can override any sense of obligation to the individual researchers whose desire to 'use' can seem predatory and unnecessary.

Ultimately, Miller worked with Kirby's field notes from his research trips in the Kalahari, and used these documents to compile a musical language recreating some of the melodic and rhythmical patterns of Kirby's archive, working with a string ensemble and the high fragile sound of a countertenor voice to suggest something of the quality of song described. Having written the composition Miller then added, as a sound dimension to the work, the aural qualities of an old scratched record to evoke, if not recreate, the illusion of an archaic sound archive. The sound booth for the installation was constructed around a large-scale copy of a musical score of the Bach invention (see Fig. 8).

VI

Fire and the fishmoth: two of the terrors that stalk the soul of the curator and museologist. The one sings out its destruction, the other is an invisible menace that acts in secret silence. Within the *Holdings* exhibition there are safe and contained spaces for these enemies of conservation, as if by invoking the worst we safeguard ourselves through a totemic pact with our own fear.

Tongues of flame. But fire is silence. Or rather, it roars to consume competing voices. In Sarajevo, the city library became a pyre upon which diverse and contested cultural histories were devoured when, on 25 August 1992, the library was shelled from the surrounding mountains. It started to burn shortly before midnight. The fire could not be contained and it destroyed the building and most of the books. Sarajevans remember the ashes of books flying above the city.

Was it fire that destroyed, without trace, the fabulous library of Alexandria that had been built up under Ptolemy I and Ptolemy II

13 The last recorded institution where the wax drums were lodged was UCT Music School.

until it contained some 400 000 scrolls? Did the library succumb, as has been suggested, when Julius Caesar besieged the city?

Umberto Eco's *The Name of the Rose* considers the uses of fire in the management of information. Works too incendiary themselves are kept from the uninitiated through restricted access. When this control no longer suffices the works are committed to the flames. Eco's novel concludes with a conflagration that consumes a great monastic library and with it Aristotle's writings on comedy. The scholarly Franciscan, Brother William of Baskerville, attempts to quell the fire:

> Meanwhile, some sparks had flown toward the walls, and already the volumes of another bookcase were crumpling in the fury of the fire. By now, not one but two fires were burning in the room. William, realising we would not be able to put them out with our hands, decided to use books to save books. He seized a volume that seemed to him more stoutly bound than the others, more compact, and he tried to use it as a weapon to stifle the hostile element. But, slamming the studded binding on the pyre of glowing books, he merely stirred more sparks. Though he tried to scatter them with his feet, he achieved the opposite effect: fluttering scraps of parchment, half burned, rose and hovered like bats, while the air, allied with its airy fellow element, sent them to kindle the terrestrial matter of further pages.[14]

For the performance artist Laurie Anderson, the relationship between the fire and the library has become tropological. That is, it functions as a figure of speech, a metaphor:

Figure 9: Burn. Colin Richards
Mixed media: archival material, pen and ink, notebook
Photo: Natasha Christopher

> When my father died we put him in the ground
> When my father died it was like a whole library
> Had burned down.
> World without end remember me.
> — from Laurie Anderson, *World Without End*

Some time during the night of Wednesday 23 December 1931, a fire broke out on the campus of the University of the Witwatersrand. Many archival materials, largely irreplaceable, were destroyed. According to contemporary reports a fierce wind carried sparks and the charred pages of library books hundreds of yards to the west. Some 35 000 books were lost as were substantial ethnographic collections. Among the items saved were a number of documents relating to David Livingstone's tenure in southern Africa. These are now housed in the Cullen library at the University of the Witwatersrand. The frag-

14 Umberto Eco, *The Name of the Rose* (New York: Warner Books, 1984), p. 589.

ile fragments, carefully stored between tissue papers that function as a kind of protective epidermis, raise questions of value: what was lost, what retrieved? How are such accidents of preservation determined? Why did someone beat back the searing heat to retrieve, among other things, an autographed note from Livingstone, which bears the simple message, 'Thank you for the seeds.' Clearly this document was part of a bundle, a collection of texts of inherent significance because of their author, rather than any significance internal to the note itself.

Colin Richards, who has over the years worked in various ways with images and meanings around flame, assembled several of these as part of a small installation on fire and the vulnerability of the archive (see Fig. 9). Invoking figures of sacrifice, his works suggest that symbolic value accrues through a complex managing of both destruction and preservation, that these are part of one purpose rather than contradictory.

Clive van den Berg built a pillar of fire within a tin chimney which had a tracery of pinhole drawings about its surface and which was ignited at the opening of the exhibition in the spirit of perilous endangerment that is at the heart of many powerful works of art. All sat watching, enrapt, as the great chimney slowly subsided after half an hour of flickering visual magic, as the structure gave way under the pressure of heat, and gently threatened to set off another great fire at the University of the Witwatersrand (see Fig. 10).

Figure 10: Tower.
Clive van den Berg
Metal
Height: 4 m

Walter Oltmann's vast wire construction, *Silverfish*, hangs over the *Holdings* exhibition space like a great lunar capsule, all legs, tentacles and data-gathering apparatuses (see Fig. 11). The creature, so familiar in the diminutive scale of the everyday, becomes quite transcendent when massively enlarged. It also becomes something of a wonder of design as we become conscious of its myriad feelers and tiny hairs, all sensory receptors. The curious intimate repugnance we feel toward the little beast is perhaps best described in the artist's own terms:

> In recent works I have been making (amongst other things) large insects of the varieties that we commonly find in our homes but which are generally very unwelcome and despised, e.g. cockroaches, crickets, earwigs and other bugs. These creatures have a particular resonance for me in that they arouse in us such a strong sense of revulsion and yet they cohabit and share our everyday living spaces. They are as such the 'unfamiliar' (excluded) within the familiar. Monumentalised and displayed on a wall like samples or specimens to be examined, these insects allude to

Figure 11: Silverfish.
Walter Oltmann
Aluminium wire
3 m x 3 m x 0.25 mm
Photo: Natasha Christopher

scientific practices of scrutiny and categorisation while the magnified wall display also recalls trophies that makes them both comic and disquieting. They are both subordinated and somewhat frightening.

For this exhibition it seemed appropriate to make a large silverfish (order: Thysanura of the Arthropoda) as this insect is very much at home in the archive where it feeds on moulds and starchy materials, including book-bindings and the glue of cartons, and can cause serious damage to books and other papers. It is a fast-running, wingless insect, covered with silvery scales, that prefers dark and undisturbed spaces such as cupboards and bookshelves. Ideally adapted to these conditions it has very long antennae and numerous hairy feelers along its body. Enlarged to human scale the viewer confronts this creature on a bodily one to one and becomes aware of its features such as the antennae and feelers that underscore the tactile, information-seeking adaptation of this animal. The shiny aluminium wire lends itself to recreating the silky surface of the silverfish and there is some irony in the fact that a creature associated with destroying human fabrication is itself fabricated by hand using methods usually associated with domestic handicrafts (weaving, coiling, tufting). I find it interesting to play with these ambiguities.

VII

Figure 12: The Black Photo Album / Look at Me: 1890–1950.
Santu Mofokeng
Photographer: Unknown, ca 1900s
Unidentified albumen print
This photograph was found in a wooden box labelled (in Afrikaans) 'Aan M.V. Jooste van die personeel van Die Vaderland'. In the box there were 68 images including one of 'Their most Gracious Majesties: Edward VII and Queen Alexandra – in their robes of State'. This box belongs to Moeketsi Msomi whose grandfather, John Rees Phakane, was a bishop in the AME Church.

The photographic tradition in South Africa has, over the years, been dominated by the documentary imperative, that is, the obligation to record the conditions of being that were produced by apartheid legislation. Santu Mofokeng's *The Black Photo Album / Look at Me: 1890-1950* has another purpose. Through an act of retrieval Mofokeng has set about recovering photographic documents of black African families:

> These are images that urban black working and middle class families had commissioned, requested or tacitly sanctioned. They have been left behind by dead relatives, where they sometimes hang on obscure parlour walls in the townships. In some families they are coveted as treasures, displacing totems in discursive narratives about identity, lineage and personality. And because, to some people, photographs contain the 'shadow' of the subject, they are carefully guarded from the ill-will of witches and enemies. In other families they are being destroyed as rubbish during spring-cleans because of interruptions in continuity or disaf-

fection with the encapsulated meanings and the history of the images. Most often they lie hidden to rot through neglect in kists, cupboards, cardboard boxes and plastic bags.

If the images are not unique, the individuals in them are. Painterly in style, they are evocative (most of them) of artifices of Victorian photography. Some of them may be fiction, a creation of the artist insofar as the setting, the props, the clothing or pose are concerned. Nonetheless there is no evidence of coercion. When we look at them we believe them, for they tell us a little about how these people imagined themselves. We see these images in the terms determined by the subjects themselves for the subjects have made the images their own.

For Mofokeng the images represent acts of self-representation of Africans that he designates as 'integrationist', in other words, those who engaged in performances of bourgeois identity that would facilitate their integration into the hegemonic world of white affluent power. Mofokeng is keenly aware of the ideological meanings implicit in his archival project, funded as it is by De Beers Chairman's Fund and the Ernest Oppenheimer Memorial Trust:

> The project seeks to create an archive of images that Black working and middle-class families commissioned in the period 1890–1950 and the stories about the subjects of the photographs. Those of you with even a cursory knowledge of history will realise the significance of this period. While the world went to war twice, South Africa was busy articulating, entrenching and legitimating a racist political system that the United Nations proclaimed 'a crime against humanity!' A lot of research is still being done to place these images in a more comprehensive context. They belong and circulate in the private domain. That is the position they occupied in the realm of the visual, in the nineteenth century. It was never their intention to be hung in galleries as works of art. Their significance lies outside the framed image. They were made in a period when the South African state was being entrenched and policies toward people the government designated 'Natives' were being articulated.

What Mofokeng reminds us of is the way in which even the photograph intended for private circulation undertakes considerable work: it is a place for the performance and contest of identity. The retrieval of such hitherto unpublished and undocumented images is itself an act of historical redress and ideological conflict insisting on the insertion into an archive of new documents that have previously been excluded. The purposes of such inclusive acts can at times mask the purposes of the sitters and photographers, who become passive in relation to a contemporary gesture of historical inclusion. What did the photographs mean once? A recent exhibition of photograph albums from District Six (South African National Gallery, 1999) motivates itself in similar ways as the retrieval of a photographic archive, but it begs the questions about the conditions under which the original images were shot, and for what ends.

The family photograph is a highly charged canvas, in which the hierarchies of kinship structure are displayed and contested. The photograph album or, more simply, the shoe-box under the bed, constructs a dominant family narrative providing a mode of inclusion and exclusion. Bad elements are effaced, divorces staged, dominant lineages established. Given that this powerful business of managing the photographs is generally undertaken by women, family and clan members who often have few other forums for acts of cultural construction, the 'mistress narratives' of the photographs call for some interpretation.

IX

Clive van den Berg's video *Memorial Without Facts: Men Loving* both celebrates and mourns the invisible archive that documents the history of homosexual love. Cutting together sequences of himself chanting in melancholy loneness with archival images of Edwardian men and his own flame drawings, the whole assemblage creates a world of deep elegy, a longing that cannot even speak its name.

Jean Brundrit's pinhole photograph *Valued Families* patterns lines of affiliation and kinship upon two naked female bodies. It suggests a virtual network of relations that in form evoke the visual appearance of a family tree, but here the links are based upon affection and sympathy rather than the more conventional matrix that marks genetic lineages. This image is part of an evolving language of images for Brundrit through which she explores the idea of the lesbian family. Both artists confront the reality that the racial formations of violence and domination that characterised modernist South Africa have until recently made it all but impossible for other histories of oppression to be represented.

X

Bertrand Tavernier, the cinematic maestro, has explored memory in many tantalising ways, perhaps never more economically and ingeniously than in his *Life and Nothing But* (1989), a film set during the First World War. In the film there are two protagonists with apparently antithetical purposes: on the one hand, there is the French medical officer who has been detailed to identify the corpses of the French dead; on the other hand, there is another officer commissioned to choose the body that will be memorialised as the unknown soldier in the new monument. In the ironic encounter between the two men, the medical officer (Philippe Noiret) points out that it is his task precisely to confound the ends of the other: that as soon as the unknown soldier is selected, Noiret will work to identify him.

This conflict of ends provides something of an allegory of the dual purposes of memory and forgetting. While there is an imperative to document, to record, to memorialise, as part of the process of psychological health, there is also that aspect of memory that is a work of forgetting, through which an event is acted upon, transformed, metaphorised, repressed and managed in order to make psychic evolution possible.

Figure *13: Death register.*
William Kentridge
Charcoal on paper
129 x 160 cm
Part of the animation for the theatre production of *Faustus in Africa*, 1994.
Photo: Natasha Christopher

In the *Holdings* exhibition there are two works expressly engaging with such processes. William Kentridge's large charcoal drawing *Death Register* (1996, for the production *Faustus in Africa*), uses the inscription of the names of the dead as a visual field (see Fig. 13). The work is crossed by erasures and emphatic circles designating points of interest. The graphic quality of the text is uneven, at times mimicking a careful and precise bureaucratic hand, at times careless, hurried, overburdened and only just adequate to the task of documentation. The apparently simple transcriptions provide rich allegories of the work of writing and the project of memory as linked technologies, at times intense and exact, at times gestural and fluid. Kentridge points out the more literal purposes in the process. The precise area of the drawing is the central sphere within the image upon which the camera focused when the drawing was filmed for the stage production of *Faustus in Africa*. Consequently, this section had to be more precisely rendered than the surrounding section, which would only ever appear as a blurred border.

The source for *Death Register* is the catalogue, housed in the War Museum, of Africans killed in the First World War and the names are compiled into ordered lists that serve official memory, not personal longing: 'Name of Person'; KIA (Killed in Action); DD (Died of Disease); and DW (Died of Wounds).

Figure 14: GALA Scrapbook.

Also in the exhibition are two documents housed in the University of the Witwatersrand's Gay and Lesbian Archives (GALA). The one is a personally constructed list of names produced by a South African who worked with the Gay and Lesbian Association of South Africa, and it serves to document the deaths from AIDS of people who had received counselling from the Association. The second of these texts is a personal scrapbook of news documents, media reports, information pamphlets and cartoons about HIV and AIDS. The scrapbook suggests an attempt by one individual to accumulate and store information in the face of rumour, dread, fear and suspicion. The front cover of the volume carries the note: 'SCRAP BOOK KEPT BY L . . . E . . . WHO DIED IN AUGUST 1986. HE WAS THE 5TH CAPETONIAN TO DIE FROM AIDS.' L . . . E . . .'s name is in fact the fifth name on the list exhibited alongside the book. The two documents refer back to each other and suggest the intensity of the circulation of information between the members of a community perceived to be at such imminent risk. The names have, at the request of the Triangle Project, been masked for purposes of confidentiality for the public forum of the exhibition, although the documents themselves constitute part of a public archive held by the University of the Witwatersrand.

My comments on the *Holdings* exhibition gesture toward completeness through my attempt to provide a summary description of the installations. Fortunately the works with which a curator is involved generally escape and exceed those meanings that had precipitated the curator into selecting those same works. In other words, the whole is always more than the sum of its parts.

"I A M . . . . .N O T H I N G ."

——————————

THE SHEER AGONY OF BEING BLACK ......

The indignities and frustrations the
Africans suffer in their daily lives.

The exploitation due to the Hire Purchase
system.

The LAWS ..... and their repercussions

(Pass raids, influx control, mass
removals and resettlements, the
so-called separate facilities,
migratory labour and illegitimacy,
hostels system, immorality act,
low wages, job reservation, etc, etc.)

In fact, the whole of the South African
way of life ......

These are some of the subjects you read
about in this book - the first of its
kind - written by an African woman, relating
her experiences while working in
Metropolitan Radio, a store dealing in radios
and household electrical appliances, in the
city of Johannesburg.

——————————

OTHER TENTATIVE TITLES:

(1) "THEM AND US"

(2) "BETWEEN THE TWO WORLDS".

[For obvious reasons, names of persons
and places have been changed.]

Miriam Tlali's opening remarks in her draft novel 'I Am Nothing'.

Literature and the Archive: The Biography of Texts

Sarah Nuttall

In this chapter I track the story of a literary text, the first novel written by a black woman in South Africa. This novel by Miriam Tlali was published in 1975 under the title *Muriel at Metropolitan*.[1] Written by Tlali on a typewriter and now lodged in the archive of the National English Literary Museum (NELM) collection in Grahamstown, South Africa, the manuscript gives the original title of the book: *I Am Nothing*. The difference between the two titles is immediately striking: the new title does not reflect the spirit of the original title in any way. It is the sense of *extremity* that is lost, the notion of not being worth anything that is absent in the much more placid *Muriel at Metropolitan*.[2] This difference, reflected in the two titles, marks the two texts throughout. How did *I Am Nothing* come to be *Muriel at Metropolitan*? In the first part of this essay I discuss the two texts, one unpublished and yellowing in a makeshift folder and the other a now out-of-print but well-known novel, looking at what was left out and what was put in, and why that might have been. I focus on excision – the multiple excisions that mark the biography of *Muriel at Metropolitan*. I then move to a discussion of the questions for literature and for the archive that these and other texts raise. I argue that South African literature and the literary archive have been badly served by the mixture of belles-lettristic and New Critical formative pedagogical influences that paid little attention to the materiality and context of texts. In the third section, I move from the notion of excision to the notion of excess. I argue that the archive constantly moves between these two orders – excision and excess: between that which limits and that which is limitless. Finally, I consider how we can use the fecundity, the instability, of literary texts to rethink our notion of the archive itself: how we can project the dynamism of the literary project back onto the archive so that the border between the literary text and the archive begins to shift and refigure.

1 Miriam Tlali, *Muriel at Metropolitan* (Johannesburg: Ravan Press, 1975).

2 Tlali also provided two alternative titles on the first page of the manuscript: *Them and Us* and *Between Two Worlds* (see Fig. 1). M. Tlali, *I Am Nothing*, manuscript lodged with the archive of the National English Literary Museum collection in Grahamstown, South Africa.

I had thought I had seen everything there is to see, heard
everything there is to hear in my experiences with people black,
white and brown in this Republic of South Africa. But I was
sooner or later to realise that I had so far seen and heard
very little of this beloved land of ours; especially as far as
inter-relationships between the different races are concerned.

I am not an authority in the study of human behaviour. I
do not profess great knowledge. I am not a writer. But do not
have to be any of these in order to know about the Africans,
their feelings, hopes, desires and aspirations. I have read a
lot of trash by the so-called 'authorities' on the subject of
the urban Africans (that is, those who spend most of their
lives with the whites in their business places and their homes;
those who travel with them day and night from place to place
all over Southern Africa - in short, those who toil side by
side with all the other races in all walks of life to make
this country the paradise it is said to be.

The Republic of South Africa is a country divided mainly
into two worlds. The one, a white world - rich, comfortable,
for all practical purposes organised - a world in fear, armed
to the teeth. The other, a black world; poor, pathetically
neglected and disorganised - voiceless, oppressed, restless,
confused and unarmed - a world in transition, irrevocably
weaned from all tribal ties.

In the white world there are two main groups with two
distinct cultures - the English-speaking and the Afrikaans-
speaking groups. The former are aloof, almost indifferent.
They favour white domination. The Afrikaans-speaking group, are
composed of a bulk of the poorer whites of Dutch origin, who
prefer to be called Afrikaners. These, boasting of political
power earned through numerical superiority - are anti-African,
anti-Semitic, and to a lesser degree, anti-English. They are
dispised by the English-speaking groups as well as the other
non-whites and Africans. Infact, all the non-white groups
look upon them as proud, arrogant, aggressive, ethnocentric
and hypocritical.

The whites, with ofcourse very few exceptions, are quite
ignorant of the conditions of living of the Africans (their
black neighbours). This is partially due to their indifference
and partly to their misconceptions. The Africans on the other
hand, know more about the whites because they have to know them
in order to survive. With even fewer exceptions, (in fact a
very negligible proportion) their daily bread depends entirely
on their going into the white homes, factories, garages,
offices etc, etc. or standing at their doorsteps looking for
work, pleading or even begging. With the Africans it is a
matter of life and death.

...   .

A deleted section of 'I Am Nothing'.

SARAH NUTTALL

EXCISIONS

When one lays Tlali's manuscript next to her published novel, the most immediately striking dimension is indeed the difference between the two titles. Increasingly evident, however, becomes a desire throughout the published book to play down the feelings of worthlessness and also the anger that Tlali often expresses in *I Am Nothing*. The choice of quote on the back cover of the published book makes this vivid. This reprinted section of Sheila Roberts's foreword states:

> Muriel's story is *never strident in hatred or resentment* against those who have turned her, in Fanon's words, into an 'object in the midst of other objects'. There is even at times a *latent warmth in her attitude towards those 'on the other side'*, a warmth which she knows they will never allow to develop . . . this story should *enlighten, surprise and even delight* readers, both black and white. (emphases added)

These remarks, maybe somewhat true of the published version, emphasise a desire on the part of the publishers not to alienate white readers and to sell the book as a 'warm' or generous rather than angry or 'resentful' response. This is undoubtedly also the reason for the removal of Tlali's opening remarks about her novel, which refer, *inter alia*, to 'the sheer agony of being black' (see Fig. 1).

Large sections of the text have been left out of the published version of *I Am Nothing*. I am grateful to my research assistant, Angela Bull, for her work in tracking these unused parts of the text. The deleted paragraphs tend to be those where the narrative voice moves beyond the events of the story to issue broader, more critical and more omniscient social comment. One of these sections is to be found in Fig. 2. In it, Tlali explains the chasm she sees between black and white South Africa. Careful not to assume too much authority,[3] she nevertheless discredits those 'authorities' who have previously written 'trash' about the life of urban black South Africans. She offers subjective and harsh criticism of Afrikaners in particular, highlighting their ignorance of the living conditions of blacks. Other significant sections left out are Tlali's full explanation of why her previous employer did not write her a complete testimonial ('As a matter of fact, officially there is no such thing as a skilled African')[4]; her opinion that Mr Bloch had to be like he was because his aim was to extract as much labour and money as possible from blacks;[5] and that Mrs Stein's effi-

3   Muriel says: 'I am not an authority in the study of human behaviour. I do not profess great knowledge. I am not a writer. But I do not have to be any of these in order to know about the Africans, their feelings, hopes, desires and aspirations.' M. Tlali, *I Am Nothing*, p. 4.

4   Please note that I have used my own numbering of the manuscript pages here since the page numbers given on the original are faulty, erratic and not always legible. In this instance the text reference can be found on page 7.

5   Tlali, *I Am Nothing* , p. 14.

ciency was motivated by her 'unmistakable burning desire' to 'sit on the necks of black people'.[6]

Other significant passages include a conversation between Muriel and William no. 2 that contains derogatory and significant racial commentary.[7] This is one of the few occasions in the text where reference is made to both the intellectual inferiority and capacity for violence of some of the whites in charge. Many other passages omitted are concerned with everyday living conditions and difficulties of black people: pages 42 to 45 have been entirely scrapped and these deal with the description of how difficult it is for a black migrant worker (who calls himself a 'police-boy') to buy a radio for his girlfriend. Tlali has included the elaborate application form for doing so in the text, effectively highlighting inhumanities and difficulties (such as splitting up families, obtaining permission to travel and low wages) experienced by migrant workers.[8] Often Tlali has included in the text the 'actual' letters or forms that people had sent/filled in. Five out of seven of these have been cut out. Muriel's letter to Mr Bloch about why she has been absent from work has also been left out of the text.[9]

Occasionally the final sentence of a paragraph has been left out, changing Tlali's view on a particular situation. When Muriel is commenting on why she does not send Johannes out to buy her things from the shop, her thoughts end with 'We reserve a place, an elevated place, for our men'[10] – a sentence much quoted by critics of her work.[11] In the original manuscript, the paragraph ends with 'We do all the work and they sit', lending a far more dissatisfied and less admiring tone to the observation. Similarly, when Mrs Kuhn remarks on how blacks would rather buy a radio than food or clothing,[12] the paragraph ends with her looking at Miriam and saying 'Shame'. In the original manuscript, the conversation ends with her saying 'Isn't that so, Muriel?' and Muriel replying, 'Yes, Mrs Kuhn.' The latter stages Muriel's virtually obligatory submission to her white superior.

In the final chapter of the novel there is significant commentary on the discrepancies in salary between black and white employees and on the financial plight of most black people in South Africa. Furthermore, when Muriel cannot take up her new job because of the inadequate toilet facilities for black people, she comments angrily on 'the preposterous laws' of separate facilities and the 'abominable nauseating business' of separate toilets. She adds that she feels 'stifled', 'suffocated', 'in a dungeon without means of escape' and can understand why 'people resorted to suicide'.[13] These remarks (made just before the final paragraph of the novel) are crucial to assessing

6   Ibid., p. 29.

7   William says: 'They [the white employers] think I'm stupid. I may not be as educated as they are but I know how far to go. How can they ask for more when they themselves are not honest? . . . The white man is the boss in this land; he is the one holding the gun. You must just listen to him.' In reaction, Muriel thinks: 'They are crude; their grammar is bad; their spelling is even worse. But what does it matter? They have the say anyway – "They are holding the gun."' (p. 36) Reinforcing this is the omission of part of Muriel's speech about the matter of losing one of the customer's cards (p. 88), a sentence which reads: 'It will be that I failed because I am black – and "black" is synonymous with stupid.'

8   The form, in its sheer and intrusive request for detail, reveals the multiple levels of bureaucracy that governed a black person's every move during this period. Not only does the man, Cerjeva Pindela, have to fulfil all the requirements, but he has to provide his personal details to Muriel, who fills them in for him. Interestingly, from a narrative point of view, the questions on the form are interspersed in the text with the exchanges which take place between Muriel and the man, thus signalling to the reader the exhausting quality of the process. Seeing the form and the details of Pindela's life upon which it insists on the printed page makes his plight as a migrant worker more vivid than a summary recounting would: thus we see details like the following: 'Address: Room 87, "C" Compound, No.5 Shaft, Crown Mines' (p. 42). The anonymity of this address is confirmed by the man's incapacity to supply referees in Johannesburg – since his girlfriend is the only person he appears to know in the city.

SARAH NUTTALL

the tone and intention of this novel accurately yet they have been deliberately omitted.

Tlali's original chapter divisions and chapter headings have been changed and omitted respectively. This may indicate a desire on the part of the publishers to 'upgrade' the novel to one with longer, more conventional chapters without the kinds of headings Tlali uses. The headings indicate much of the general content and spirit of the novel and include sentiments such as 'Separated . . . and . . . United'; 'A Slap in the Face'; 'The Boss', 'The Final Kick', and 'I Quit'. The same reasoning may have motivated the removal from the published version of the List of Characters[14] and quotations from Patience Strong. It would seem that the publishers were intent on eliminating anything that could class this novel as popular[15] or as genre-bending. The removal of some of the letters and application forms may have been undertaken for the same reason. An interesting *insertion* into the text is made in the last chapter. Above, I mentioned that the Patience Strong quotes had been removed. The published version has Muriel describe a Patience Strong quotation that she receives on a card as 'trite' and by implication unrealistic – something that does not figure in the original manuscript at all. In the manuscript Tlali uses the quotation as the frontispiece for her chapter from which she launches into her opening paragraph, picking up on its significances for Muriel. Interestingly, phrases indicating Tlali's education or broader reading have also been omitted, such as her use of the phrases 'far from the madding crowd'[16] and 'tête-à-tête'.[17] The idea of what an African woman's novel should be – neither too popular nor too cosmopolitan – is somewhat clearly set.

Changes in diction have been made throughout the manuscript. Whereas in most instances Tlali has written about Mr Bloch as 'the Boss', all such references have been changed to 'the boss'. Other changes include the omission of phrases such as 'boss-boy',[18] 'so-called boy' following the description of an African[19] and 'township' to define Soweto.[20] The phrase 'non-whites', often used by Tlali, was replaced by 'blacks'. The alteration of these politically loaded phrases has an important impact on the tone and intention of the novel. '[W]hite women' is substituted for Tlali's use of 'white ladies'. This anxiety for Muriel not to seem too subservient is reinforced by various other deletions such as 'poor me, only a native'.[21] However, most of the sections where she asserts herself as independent and intelligent have also been omitted: 'it was another challenge to my intelligence I thought',[22] 'This was an insult I would not tolerate',[23] and 'I'm old enough to look

9 The letter explains her child's sudden illness, the fact that the child has to be taken to the local clinic for daily injections and has to be kept under quarantine at home for two weeks. The letter reveals Muriel's acute sense of responsibility and etiquette. (Tlali, *I Am Nothing*, p. 72.)

10 Tlali, *I Am Nothing*, p. 21.

11 See, for instance, Dorothy Driver, 'M'a-Ngoana o tsoare thipa ka bohaleng – The child's mother grabs the sharp end of the knife: Women as mothers, women as writers' in Martin Trump, ed., *Rendering Things Visible: Essays on South African Literary Culture* (Johannesburg: Ravan Press, 1990), p. 236.

12 Tlali, *I Am Nothing*, p. 24.

13 Ibid., p. 209.

14 The order and wording of this list of characters would be very significant in an analysis of the text. The characters are divided into racial categories, for example, 'European radio mechanics' and 'Non-European radio mechanic', and Mr Bloch is referred to as 'The Boss', without inverted commas.

15 Perhaps this is also why the word 'toilet' has sometimes been changed to 'lavatory' in the published version and sentiments such as 'in my heart I prayed to God to help me' have been excised.

16 Tlali, *I Am Nothing*, p. 11.

17 Ibid., p.16.

18 Ibid., p. 38.

19 Ibid., p. 33.

20 Ibid., p. 37.

21 Ibid., p. 50.

22 Ibid., p. 49.

23 Ibid.

after myself'[24] are cut out of Muriel's dialogue.

The case of *Muriel at Metropolitan* is a study in excisions. First, Tlali was writing into a context of excision. A wider culture of secrecy, of silencing and exclusions, a culture and politics of dismemberment meant that the lives and histories of entire black communities were actively dis-remembered during the apartheid period. Then, even among liberal or sympathetic leftist publishers, it was difficult for a black woman to get her manuscript published. Moreover, when such a manuscript did appear, it did so as an 'expurgated' text. In an interview, Tlali said the following:

> I finished writing the first novel, *Muriel*, in 1969, but it was only published in 1975, and even then, too, very much expurgated. A lot of material was removed from it to make it acceptable to the white reader. . . . Very little editing was done. It was presented the way I had written it, but the thing is, they just expurgated a lot of material from it, which they thought would not be acceptable. So the first version – the South African version – does not have all the right terms, the originality, that I had in my manuscript. Only later on did Longman come forward to ask for the manuscript to publish it abroad – with a lot of errors in it, I'm afraid.[25]

The Longman edition that Tlali refers to above appeared in 1979.[26] In this version, the title remains as '*Muriel at Metropolitan*' but the chapter headings are retained and a number of passages removed in the Ravan version are kept in. The List of Characters and the Patience Strong quotes, for instance, are left out. Whereas the Ravan edition has on its cover an indistinct outline of a woman's head, the Longman publication is much more assertive and oppositional: two black hands type on a typewriter and across the sheet of paper in the machine is written 'Final Demand'.[27] In this essay I have chosen to focus only on the Ravan version published in South Africa.

What is interesting and significant about the changes to the text I have discussed above is the many registers in which they can be read. First, we need to note the widespread repression by the apartheid state at the time of the book's publication of any activity, including publishing, that was regarded as inimical to its interests. Fears that the book would have been banned would have contributed to the excision of some of the references. Peter Randall, the director of Ravan Press at the time, has observed that 'it was inevitable that some self-censorship had to be practised for sheer survival'. By 'self-censorship' Randall

24 Ibid., p. 54.

25 Miriam Tlali, interviewed by Cecily Lockett in C. MacKenzie and C. Clayton, eds., *Between the Lines: Interviews with Bessie Head, Sheila Roberts, Ellen Kuzwayo, Miriam Tlali* (Grahamstown: NELM [National English Literary Museum], 1989), p. 71.

26 Miriam Tlali, *Muriel at Metropolitan* (London: Longman Drumbeat, 1979).

27 There is an interesting ambiguity to this image: in the text, letters to this effect are sent to customers as a final warning to extract payments from them. It is Muriel's dislike at having to dispatch these that contributes to her resignation. In the cover picture it is Muriel who is shown, also, to be making a 'final demand' for her own and other's humanity in the face of relentless racial prejudice – and by extension, Tlali herself, in writing her book.

SARAH NUTTALL

appears, from what he goes on to say, to be referring to the decision not to publish certain texts at all. He offers less reflection on what it was necessary to excise from texts in order to get them published. Of Tlali's text specifically he says the following:

> Tladi's [*sic*] manuscript consisted of a large ring binder crammed with disjointed writings including verses and prayers. It was clear, however, that embedded in this mass of material was an interesting and original narrative . . . The book launched Tladi [*sic*] on a writing career: Ravan subsequently published her *Amandla*, and it was disappointing when she later attacked the press on racial grounds and accused it of manipulating her work.[28]

His comments lead us to the second register in which the texts can be read. At the time, Ravan Press, along with David Philip and Ad Donker, was one of the most progressive publishers in South Africa. However, what we see from the removed sections of the text above is the result not only of what must have been fears of state banning of the text but what we might perceive as the construction of a very particular voice for Tlali based on the liberal-leftist suppositions of the Press. These become particularly evident in relation to how registers of subservience and anger are dealt with – as well as the range and type of cultural references that are made by the author. Tlali has commented specifically on the question of anger in an interview:

> *Interviewer:* Let's talk about your work now. Many critics tend to find your work 'modest' and 'subdued' (to quote Richard Rive), yet I find an element of anger, especially in the protest of Muriel . . . Would you agree with this?
> *Tlali:* Yes. There is very great anger, and I'm happy that it does show. My own grandmother was a very angry woman, and my mother was. You can discover this in Muriel, for instance . . . There's anger in almost every one of us.[29]

Where Tlali refers to the 'originality' of her manuscript that was subsequently altered, in the first quotation above, she may be referring in part to the generic fluidity of her book. In a letter written to John Rees of the South African Council of Churches in 1973, asking for help in finding a publisher for her book, Tlali describes the book as being 'made up of essays which have continuity'. Tlali has also spoken of her affinity for play writing, and her sense of the accessibility of theatre, both as a written and performed product, to an audience of black

28 Peter Randall, 'The beginnings of Ravan Press: a memoir' in G. E. de Villiers, ed., *Ravan: Twenty Five Years 1972–1997* (Randburg: Ravan Press, 1997), p. 9.

29 Miriam Tlali, interviewed by Cecily Lockett in *Between the Lines*, p. 76.

South Africans, 'especially women', for whom she sees herself writing. It is this generic instability of the unpublished manuscript that does indeed form part of its most original contribution to the archive. In so far as it shows the novel as a fissile and fissioning form, releasing new energies as it takes on an abundance of shape, it both eludes and nevertheless works to shift the archive's disciplinary function in relation to such categories as the 'novel', the 'autobiographical fiction', 'drama', 'essays' and so on. However, the published version does not reveal the generic fluidities of the manuscript and especially Tlali's inclusion of popular cultural references and devices.

CONTEXTS

The case of *Muriel at Metropolitan* starkly reveals the importance of a culture of the preservable text in the writing of literary history. It is precisely such a culture that was lost during the apartheid period. Frequently there was a 'parting of the ways' between author and text. Often writers were not allowed to possess copies of their own books; and their writings were confiscated. 'A piece of writing which was once a writer's pride and joy almost becomes an object of resentment,' Andrew Martin, a researcher at NELM, says.[30] Enormous gaps in black literary history have been left, then, as material has been destroyed – and as writers have been forced into the margins, through land legislation, exile and censorship, they have taken their writing with them. As a consequence, cultures of retrieval have come to dominate the construction and reconstruction of the literary archive in South Africa in the 1990s.[31] Even so, the circuits of cultural power and knowledge that shape the South African archive – and specifically the archive's capacity to render up details of everyday life, which has made it such an important form of cultural memory for writers – reveal particular strains and ambivalences. Wolfram Hartmann et al. have asked: 'What happens when the archive has not been organised on long-standing principles, but has been assembled unevenly, haphazardly, anonymously – not even called an archive but a "collection" or a "library" – and not easily rendered up for scrutiny?'[32] In black families archives were often eroded due to the problem of space and the pressures of moving a lot. In the twentieth century in particular there was also frequently an imperative to destroy things, especially papers: in the context of an increasingly repressive internal colonialism, black people would often not have been sure what could be considered as

30 E-mail interview with Andrew Martin, researcher based at the National English Literary Museum, Grahamstown, 3 November 1998. Martin observes further:

'Not being able to see one's book in print or even to see one's book on the library shelves because one was not allowed in the library likewise diminishes the value of the writing to the author. Where authors did get published, these publications only had limited runs, like the numerous "little magazines" which appeared during the 1970s and 80s, had little marketing potential. Authors who had their work published overseas often only received a number of complimentary copies of the work. These were often given away, lent out, or lost. Authors who have moved, either forcibly or by choice, will often have to discard material or give it away. Authors also lost ownership of the works. Plagiarism of poems and short stories by black authors was rampant during the apartheid era. In many cases works were published without any acknowledgement to the author.'

31 NELM is currently working on retrieving material written by black South Africans in foreign publications that are not available in South Africa. Martin also speaks of having 'reunited' a number of authors with their works, pieces which they had published and lost access to and in some cases subsequently forgotten about.

32 See W. Hartmann, J. Silvester and P. Hayes, *The Colonising Camera: Photographs in the Making of Namibian History* (Cape Town, Windhoek and Athens OH: University of Cape Town Press, Out of Africa and Ohio University Press, 1998), p. 6.

SARAH NUTTALL

'evidence' to be used against them. Internalised self-perceptions of not counting in the world may also have contributed to the often 'damaged' family and individual archives in the black community. Photographs were more often kept: they could be stored more easily than manuscripts or piles of papers – slipped into a Bible, for instance.[33] Writers like Elinor Sisulu, current biographer of the Sisulu family, have lamented the lost sources of the black family archive. However, there have been a myriad ways that black families do keep archival records albeit not in textual forms. A range of cases show that pieces of paper pertinent to claims and status are jealously preserved, even when the custodian is unable to read them, precisely because of the defence such papers offered against the implementation of certain policies.

Part of the task of reconstructing the archive, then, is first locating it since it may not exist in current institutional spaces.[34] Scholars like Sifiso Ndlovu are also beginning to study ways in which black intellectuals of the 1930s and 40s chose to write historical fictions in the vernacular rather than histories in English, partly to avoid censorship, but also to escape the constraints of Western history-writing conventions and epistemology.[35] Ian Glenn has argued that by uncovering literary writing about South Africa in the first half of the nineteenth century we find a body of work that investigated the political motivations and grievances of black South Africans more intensely than Schreiner or Pringle, hailed as the most 'progressive' writers before the twentieth century, was ever able to do. For Glenn, such archival work 'restores dimensions to the study of South African literature that a new South African literary culture will need'.[36]

At least some of this work, as I said at the beginning of this essay, has been held up by how the archive has been read. In particular New Critical literary influences have focused on content-based textual analysis at the expense of the material histories of texts. Psychoanalytic approaches, too, have frequently underestimated the contexts of textual production. In order to illustrate this further, I want to return here specifically to the treatment of the archives of fiction writers: not only to the manuscripts, documents and letters that they leave behind but to the ways in which this material has been theorised. I take the example of Bessie Head, a writer who spent her early years in South Africa and went into exile in Botswana in 1964. Head left a large range of autobiographical writings including a vast collection of letters. I look at a set of disputes that have emerged around her

33 Interview on 27 October 1998 with Karel Schoeman, novelist, archivist at the South African Library, Cape Town, and author of The Face of the Country: A South African Family Album 1860–1910 (Cape Town: Human and Rousseau, 1996). See also Hartmann et al. in The Colonising Camera, who show how infrequently photography has been taken seriously as archival material. Most researchers of Africa's social history have had limited interaction with photographs since ' . . . visuality is subordinated to textuality which itself is grounded and empirically validated by reference to documents and sources from the privileged site of the archive' (p. 2).

34 I am indebted here to a remark made by Bheki Peterson on the occasion of the launching of the Refiguring the Archive series at the Graduate School for the Humanities and Social Sciences, University of the Witwatersrand, August 1998.

35 See S. Ndlovu, '"He did what any other person in his position would have done to fight the forces of invasion and disruption": Africans, the land and contending images of King Dingane ("the Patriot") in the twentieth century, 1916–1950s', South African Historical Journal 38 (May 1998), pp. 99–143. Petros Lamula, for instance, decided to print, publish and market his 1922 history text uZulu kaMalandela on his own, to avoid such pitfalls. The only copy remaining within the country is held by the University of Natal, Pietermaritzburg. Ndlovu, citing other examples, suspects that there are many texts like Lamula's that it will be difficult to trace, catalogue and archive because writers kept the original manuscripts, which have often not been found. Ndlovu is beginning to reflect in his current work on how the state, language boards, school inspectors and publishers influenced and affected the quality of literature published by African authors – and how this in turn influenced literary criticism on African literature in South Africa. (E-mail correspondence with S. Ndlovu, researcher in Zulu history, 30 September 1999.) See also Chapter 2 of Ndlovu's forthcoming Ph.D. thesis, 'The image of King Dingane and Zulu nationalist politics'.

36 Ian Glenn, 'The future of the past in English South African literary history', Quarterly Bulletin of the South African Library 51, 1 (1996).

literary estate, disputes which are instructive, I think, about Head's life and writing, about the South African literary critical establishment and about notions of the archive itself.

Head is a writer who has been seen to possess a 'biographical legend', whereby the author becomes obliged to live a legendary life, or to make one up.[37] Head's by now famous account of her origins is as follows:

> I was born on the sixth of July, 1937, in the Pietermaritzburg Mental Hospital . . . The reason for my peculiar birthplace was that my mother was white, and she had acquired me from a black man. She was judged insane and committed to the mental hospital while pregnant. Her name was Bessie Emery and I consider it the only honour South Africa ever did me – naming me after this unknown, lovely, and unpredictable woman.[38]

In 1986 the South African critic Susan Gardner published an article called '"Don't ask for the true story": a memoir of Bessie Head'[39] in which she set out to contest Head's account. I want to examine briefly the set of readings and counter-readings that the article set in motion. Gardner writes that she 'started to think that [Head's story] seemed almost too "good" in its horrible way, to be true',[40] for what Head possessed was the 'ideal biographical legend'. Setting out to find the facts, she says that she 'discovered that, if Bessie was telling the truth about herself as she knew it, never in her lifetime did she really know who she was'.[41] She continues: 'such knowledge is an almost intolerable burden, and the only way I can handle it now is, in its essentials, to put it under embargo until after my own death'.[42] Gardner's revelation is that Bessie Head was not born in the Fort Napier mental hospital in Pietermaritzburg nor had her mother been a patient there. Her mother was committed to the Pretoria Memorial hospital before her birth, however. Her mother's family name was not Emery, since her mother had married an Australian railway worker, but that of a prominent white South African family, the name of which Gardner withholds. The 'truth' of Gardner's biography, then, is that Head's autobiography is false.

Three years later, in 1989, Teresa Dovey published a powerful riposte to Gardner's article.[43] Dovey focuses on Head's remark that 'I have always just been me, with no frame of reference to anything beyond myself'.[44] She interprets it as the expression of an 'impossible but liberatory desire to simply be identical to herself, to avoid the passage of the self through the Symbolic system, in which the

37 As such, she has much in common with another southern African writer, Dambudzo Marechera. Marechera constantly reinvented his own biography: revising, adding, deleting and magnifying scenes and sections according to his projected role. He, too, died young, leaving behind a tantalisingly large and scattered volume of unpublished writings.

38 Quoted in Susan Gardner, '"Don't ask for the true story": a memoir of Bessie Head', *Hecate* 12, 1-2 (1986), p. 114.

39 Gardner, '"Don't ask for the true story."'

40 Ibid., p. 115.

41 Ibid., p. 113.

42 Ibid., p. 125.

43 Teresa Dovey, 'A question of power: Susan Gardner's biography versus Bessie Head's autobiography', *English in Africa* 16, 1 (May 1989).

44 Bessie Head, 'Notes from a quiet backwater' in Craig MacKenzie, ed., *Bessie Head – A Woman Alone: Autobiographical Writings* (Oxford: Heinemann, 1990).

SARAH NUTTALL

individual subject receives a name and an identity'.[45] She goes on to say that Gardner's attempt to name Head is a violation of this desire and represents an attempt to locate her within a system that she herself preferred to negate. It also implies a refusal to recognise 'the potential for resistance in that which may be considered unnameable in terms of the system: Head is not white, not black, not feminist, not revolutionary. She wishes to be regarded as simply herself: like her mother, unknown and unpredictable.'[46] In her closing remarks Dovey writes the following:

> If Bessie Head's ability to survive, and to transcend in writing, the suffering she endured growing up in South Africa was in some sense made possible by the autobiography she constructed for herself, then surely this identity should not, and cannot, be taken from her.[47]

While Gardner chooses to focus on the 'terrible fact that [Bessie Head] did not know who she was, though she had pieced together a legend about herself which almost everyone still believes',[48] Dovey concentrates on writing, unnameability and the instability of subjectivity. Although Gardner's account is written as a 'memoir', it functions at least in part as a vindication of Gardner herself, whom Head had accused of 'professional misconduct' and with whom she had cut all ties.[49] The exchanges between Gardner and Dovey focus on a very particular set of questions for the literary archive – questions about the nature of subjectivity and language, which are also questions about literature, history and identity and their relationship to truth. Who owns the facts of our lives? And does 'own' here mean own as possession, or own as to acknowledge, admit to or confess – own to something? These questions relate to others, about the potential for misreading that lies between writing and its reception, and also resides internally to subjectivity itself. It is recent critical approaches to literature only that have criticised the celebration of a writer's unity, seeing it as a form of resistance to the complexities and difficulties of language and subjectivity that such unity resolves or denies.

In emphasising the relation of literary texts to truth these critics fail to consider adequately the relationship between texts and their contexts. For although their readings may tell us something about forms of denial, suppression and intertextuality, they tell us very little about what it is to write under conditions of censorship and about the question of address to which such a context would have made writers

45 Dovey, 'A question of power', p. 34.

46 Ibid., pp. 34–35.

47 Ibid., p. 37.

48 Ibid., p. 111.

49 See both Gardner and Dovey for more information on this.

in such contexts acutely attuned. Head's biographical texts have also to be read as strategic statements made to different audiences on different occasions. To whom she was speaking, and in what context, would have necessarily altered the content of what she was saying. Rather than a generalised sense of the 'instability of subjectivity' which may come from an unprocessed psychoanalytic model of reading, literary estates such as Head's might offer us novel ways of understanding the production of identity in this context.[50]

Such literary estates can be read as being not just about the meanings of texts but about the social production of value. The question for the archive becomes then not only 'How do you archive the instability of an author's sense of himself or herself?' but 'What role do archivists play where their attention is focused not so much on the truth of what the writer is trying to say as on the ascription of value to texts?'. Critics themselves have paid far too little attention to the latter not only in the examples above but more generally. If we remain with the Bessie Head archive we find this amply demonstrated.

The only collection of Bessie Head's letters to have been published so far is Randolph Vigne's *A Gesture of Belonging: Letters From Bessie Head 1965–1979*.[51] In his introduction, Vigne writes: 'The letters fall into sequences written from her various addresses. They call for little elucidation or comment from me . . . I have not attempted to draw from the letters any lessons about literature or life, but Bessie Head was a remarkably gifted writer caught in a painful dilemma from which there was to be no escape.' Clearly, Vigne is attempting to create an archive that can be used by others, but it is striking, nonetheless, how little analysis he offers of the act he is undertaking. 'Hurtful or libellous passages have been cut, as she would have wished,' he writes, somewhat cursorily. Little reading is undertaken, that is, of the editing itself, of the fact of the cutting, of the inevitable development of a teleology, according to which everything else is offered as waste.[52] Authors, too, work across genres in the literary archive, genres being conceptions that are not fixed but produced. What Head thought letters were, and how this differed from other conventions, poses a considerable interpretative challenge. She used them not only for establishing relationships and exploiting a range of strategies on which she drew in her fiction but for negotiating and experimenting with the relationship between reader and writer in an explicit sense.[53] How she saw, and used, the interview form, the foreword and the autobiographical sketch need

50 I am indebted here to Bheki Peterson who was the respondent to this paper in a presentation at the Refiguring the Archive seminar series, Graduate School for the Humanities and Social Science, University of the Witwatersrand, November 1998.

51 Randolph Vigne, ed., *A Gesture of Belonging: Letters from Bessie Head 1965–1979* (Portsmouth: Heinemann, 1991). Others are housed in the collection at Serowe; most remain in private collections, 'too contentious', it is said, to publish.

52 In another example from the South African academy, Richard Rive, when editing Olive Schreiner's letters, removed all the beginnings and endings of the letters, leaving only the body of the texts, and writing off the rest as superfluous. It was left to his assistant on the project to meticulously restore the deleted parts of the letters before the collection appeared in print.

53 I am grateful to Desiree Lewis for these observations.

SARAH NUTTALL

further research as part of the task of writing black South African literary history.

In the first part of this essay I focused on the question of excision – the excision of a particular text, and the excisions of a wider culture. The archive itself bears testimony to excisions and is itself marked by them. But what of the archive itself *as excision*? The archive exists as excision, as that which limits, since it is a composition. It has been composed, by someone, from certain objects and not others. If this 'composition' carries a certain inflection towards productivity, which I explore below, it is also always a process that will be based on a set of exclusions.[54] For Echevarria, the first law of the archive is a denial, 'a cut that organises and disperses'.[55] The archive is an institution, and in institutions there is always an element of embodiment or translation into people's interests. Is institutionalisation always a violence? If we mean by 'violence' here the production of particular notions of ownership, reception, classification and value that necessarily imply exclusion it would seem to be a violence we cannot get outside of.[56] By aiming at a reconstructed archive, then, we would be engaging (only?) as Peterson has put it, in new levels of contestation.[57] In these ways, the archive is *limited*.

But the archive also exists as excess, as *unlimited*, in the sense of the endless readings to which it gives rise. Above, I considered ways in which critics have read – and have not yet read – the archive of her origins created by Bessie Head. I showed how Gardner interrupted the 'truth' that Bessie Head had offered about herself; and how Dovey read differently, focusing on the conditions of Head's subjectivity, thus refiguring the material in the archive. A constitutive dimension of the archival object is that it lends itself to becoming the tool of the imagination. Thus it is capacious, inviting a promiscuity of meanings. Ultimately, the archive exists at the interface between both orders – excision and excess, the limited and unlimited – it plays itself out via both, as a product of and as a tension between both.

EXCESS

We have seen that the paradox of the archive is the movement between excision and excess. Even where there is excision this does not foreclose the possibility of excess, of imagination. What does this mean, then, for an understanding of the case of the Tlali manuscript, presented by me as 'a study in excisions'?

In the first part of this essay, excision was presented largely as an

54 Thomas Richards in *The Imperial Archive: Knowledge and the Fantasy of Empire* (London: Verso, 1993) writes about the imperial archive as a fantasy of knowledge, 'a myth of control', built on an allied belief in comprehensive knowledge. In fact, he shows it was a miscellany, fragmentary and full of gaps. 'The assumption of the whole', he writes, 'ended as a myth of imperial knowledge.'

55 Roberto Echevarria, *Myth and the Archive* (Cambridge: Cambridge University Press, 1990), p. 37.

56 This may invoke a more static notion of the archive than is necessary. What about archival projects such as the writing of biography – might these offer an alternative to institutionalisation as violence? What about family archives? Is 'protection' in this context necessarily always to be read as some kind of violence?

57 Bheki Peterson, commentary on a presentation of this paper at the Refiguring the Archive seminar series, University of the Witwatersrand.

intentional act. A series of excisions were shown to have been made according to what appeared to be a more or less consistent and coherent set of exclusions and it was suggested how these reflected what are likely to have been some of the dominant assumptions about writing, identity and politics at the time. But excision does not belong entirely to the order of intentionality; it is also an act of the imagination. If excision involves a cutting it also, in that very cutting, involves the creation of something *new*. In addition, I allowed the assumption to rest that the full version of Tlali's text, the version represented under the title *I Am Nothing*, represented an authenticity of voice, a healing, in a sense, of the mutilated text. But there never is, of course, any such authentic voice – a voice that represents in a pure and transparent way who or what a person or a text actually *is*. To speak, to write one's story, is always also to enter into the order of corruption – corruption in the sense of a destroyed purity and thus of an excess. If to speak and to write is, on the one hand, to enter into an altered and tainted relationship to an original state, then, on the other hand, out of this distortion, deformation or corruption comes also a superabundance of meaning. At all levels, then, there cannot be excision without excess. Nor, though, can there be excess without excision.

Why and on what terms does excision belong to the order of productivity? Excision is not only mutilation, although it is that because it involves a concept of 'waste'. 'Waste' is constituted by that which is left after excision has occurred, by that which is considered to be 'useless' and, in a context of censorship such as South Africa in the 1970s and 80s, as that which represents 'the dangerous'. Excision also implies a notion of 'remains', and the productivity of excision is that what remains comes to hold a powerful significance, which it may not have had before. Not only does it carry with it, in an overdetermined way, that which is regarded as useless in a certain project of the imagination, a specific notion, then, of utility, but what remains speaks with a voice which resonates in a way that is different from what it would have been if it had not been excised. From this concatenation of excision, excess emerges.

Thus we can return to a reading of Tlali's manuscript and of the book that was finally published as in themselves archives that move between excision and excess. We see that we cannot even have begun to exhaust our readings both of what was and was not there in each version, and why. Working on the Tlali manuscript makes it hard to exceed the pointed political readings that it so vividly suggests. There is a certain predictability to the way in which the text was treated at all levels. It struck me while working in the archive, for instance, that while the correspondence between the publishers and certain white writers was copious about what to cut and what not to cut and about how to avoid the censors and prevent the novel in question being banned without damaging the text too much, no correspondence of this nature was to be found in the case of Tlali. Yet without losing the power of these readings, it seems important, too, that the logic of the excisions be read in as many complex registers as possible: as we revisit the archive, we might see that it is a logic that also always belongs to an order of imagining.

In the final part of this section I turn to a text that presents the act of writing biography as explicitly archival. As such, it helps us to develop an increasingly clear sense of what the archive is or can be. Mike Nicol, in his 1998 text, *The Invisible Line: The Life and Photography of Ken Oosterbroek*,[58] attempts to tell the story of Oosterbroek's short life as a prominent press photographer before his death by 'friendly fire' just weeks before the democratic elections in April 1994. Nicol draws the attention of the reader to what is bric-à-brac, a heap of meaningless fragments of objects and documents which are incapable of substituting themselves either metonymically for what really happened or metaphorically for the narrative of what truly happened – but from which he will make a story. Besides the large body of photographs taken by Oosterbroek himself, the impact of which threatens to overwhelm the text, is a narrative, scattered through with excerpts from Oosterbroek's diaries, verses written by him and snippets of songs he wrote or liked, a tape recording, comments at a braai, a piece of dialogue between Oosterbroek and his wife from an unpublished film script by someone else. It is a repository of documents: this, Nicol shows, is first of all what the archive is – a repository of documents from which one is supposed to produce the story of what happened. The documents have to be written, both those that were not intended to be written (that were intended to remain private) as well as those that formed part of a conscious project of writing the story of the self. ('He must have known that his private life would be revealed,' writes Nicol of Oosterbroek's diaries.) The biographer must break up the surface of a life, which would make it a story with a beginning and an ending, and without abolishing these, he or she must decontextualise the fragments in order to recontextualise them. A construction must be made; and where there is construction another order also comes into

58 M. Nicol, *The Invisible Line: The Life and Photography of Ken Oosterbroek* (Cape Town: Kwela Books, in association with Random House, 1998).

play – that of the imagination.

Nicol's text is a biography written by a novelist – someone given to fictionalising, to the excess of fiction itself. It is a point to which he draws attention in his text: 'In the telling of a novel', he writes at one point, 'these are the sorts of statements I would scatter about. At this point, I would also interrupt the narrative to tighten the chronology. I would want to show my character under stress.' The novelist reveals himself as 'unreliable narrator', shaping his 'character' as a fiction, condemning him to a fictional world. Nicol, perhaps as a way out of this dilemma of finding a register and a voice, is at pains to show his text as a 'construct'. Moreover, he informs us that at the beginning he did not like his subject – because he perceived him as someone who manipulates images, who visibly *constructs* himself. Widespread public reaction to Nicol's book has focused, in turn, on the 'constructedness' of his subject – on a perceived failure on Nicol's part to render his subject 'into being'; in short, on a failure of the imagination.[59]

The chain of 'constructions' that surfaces in relation to this text allows us to think through precisely the tension between 'construction' and 'imagination'. If a construct involves first and foremost the erection of boundaries and the invention of forms, imagination, the capacity to imagine in all its dimensions, escapes these 'constructions'. Contemporary theorising, especially where it draws strongly on postmodernism, has tended to reduce the question of the imagination to the assertion of constructivism: to the idea that since there can be no truth everything is a construct. Where all we have are constructs – or images – imagination, according to this logic, must be reduced to an outdated mirage of modernity. Yet imagination exists in excess of 'construction'. 'Constructing' is imagining only in its positivist sense. Imagination carries with it that which escapes intentionality, the formalities of reasoning. It belongs to the order of excess. It is precisely this gap, this significant slippage between construction and imagination, to which the story of Nicol's book gives rise. Nicol himself introduces a tension between the fecundity of one kind of fictional imagination and a text that is a carefully honed construct; and his readers, too, pick up on the tension between the 'construct' with which they are presented and the sense, not only of someone who lived but of someone 'living', that they would want to inhabit their minds.[60] Nicol, it would seem, works too much with the order of excision and too little with that of excess.[61]

59 A number of the responses, too, including those by Oosterbroek's wife and friends, show a largely unthinking predilection for a misplaced 'authenticity': it is not that which I am invoking here, but rather those responses which suggest that a 'further act of the imagination' is required to conjure a vivid biographical persona into being.

60 See, for instance, Maureen Isaacson's review of the book, 'The tender vision and tragic death of Ken Oosterbroek', *Sunday Independent*, 27 September, 1998. Over and over again, interestingly, reader responses to, and reviews of, this text argue that it is in the photographs that they find the dramatic vitality and a fuller complexity of the biographical subject that the text can render (see, for instance, James Mitchell, 'Man and moment', *Star*, 12 October 1998 or Bronwyn Wilkinson, 'The invisible line and not returning', *Cape Times*, 25 September 1998).

61 To turn to the notion of excess, as a figuring of the imagination, is to turn to a sense of fecundity. I have argued above for the fecundity of the archive itself. But how, also, can we project the fecundity of a text onto the archive, to refigure it? To ask this question is to ask, 'In what sense are such books not archives: in what sense, that is, do they contain an excess of meaning which eludes the archive?' In her novel *Manly Pursuits*, South African writer Ann Harries uses the elusive concept of sound to disturb the rigid narratives of colonial history. She explores Rhodes' obsession with hearing British birdsong on the slopes of Table Mountain and reanimates the lives of Milner, Kipling, Wilde, Dodgson, Schreiner and others in a narrative that

SARAH NUTTALL

Both biography and archive exist via the orders of death (excision, limitation) and of life (fecundity, imagination). Both are part of a specific operation that consists in dealing with what life has left behind.[62] If both inhabit an intimacy with a world that is dead, both engage in a certain ritual of resurrection; at an articulation aimed at driving back the dead, at inserting them into time. Achille Mbembe has pushed this line of argument further to contend that what the historian, or biographer or archivist, does is not simply to bring back the dead to life: rather the 'ghost' is brought back to life 'precisely to kill it or to exorcise it by turning it into an object of knowledge'. Yet both – biography and archive – are open to the order of the imagination. They turn us towards life. Imagination can keep excising the archive, replenishing it with things that were not there at the beginning.

shuttles between England and South Africa. It is her work with the multiple ambiguous registers of sound which destabilises conventional readings of colonial history. Harries's work, a written, literary text, nevertheless lets us ask – what is sound? How could we archive sound? How may we consider, in the histories of time and place, the relationship between listening and the imagination, between sound and word? How does sound offer us new ways of reading cultures of the past, and of the present? Why is it that writing produces history – produces the archive? Harries takes us beyond the question only of the spoken, the verb, the word-of-mouth, orality, to the larger question of sound itself: what could sound be for an archive that is at once capacious and incomplete? A. Harries, *Manly Pursuits* (London: Bloomsbury, 1999).

62 As Echevarria puts it, 'The Archive [also] stands for loss, emptiness, frequently hypostatized as . . . death.' Roberto Echevarria, *Myth and the Archive* (Cambridge: Cambridge University Press, 1990), p. 177.

Nadine Gordimer was born in Springs, South Africa in 1923. At age 11 she began her writing career and was first published in the children's section of the Johannesburg *Sunday Express* in 1947. Since then she has written a number of novels. Excerpts of these, in addition to her countless short stories and articles have appeared in magazines and newspapers worldwide. Many of her works reflect the political and social dilemmas of living under apartheid in South Africa and consequently, several of her books were banned in that country until very recently.

Among her numerous awards are the Booker Prize for Fiction (1974), Modern Language Association of America award (1982), and the Premio Malaparte prize (1987). She was a four-time winner of the CNA Award sponsored by the Central News Agency, a book/stationery company in South Africa. In 1991 Gordimer's entire body of work was honored with the Nobel Prize in Literature. She has been decorated Commandeur de l'Ordre des Arts et des Lettres (France) and has received honorary degrees from such institutions as Harvard and Yale universities.

Apart from her many achievements in writing, Gordimer has been visiting professor and lecturer at several American universities. She is a founder and executive member of the Congress of South African Writers and has encouraged and supported new writers, especially young African authors and poets.

The Gordimer collection contains approximately 6,700 items covering the years 1934 to 1991 and consists of correspondence, short stories, novels, articles, lectures and speeches, a childhood diary, notebooks and research materials. Also included are scripts, many adapted from Gordimer's short stories and novels. There is extensive correspondence with her colleagues, literary agents and publishers, including magazines such as *The New Yorker* where many of her short stories and articles first appeared.

Extract from 'Guide to the Nadine Gordimer Papers', Lilly Library, Indiana University, 1994.

Keeping the Self: The Novelist as (Self-)Archivist

Ronald Suresh Roberts

INTRODUCTION

'Against the closed traditions of little despotic courts, he opposed an open tradition: he taught how to find originality within an established discipline; actually – how to live.'[1] What Sartre said of composer Johann Sebastian Bach also captures, I suspect, the quandary of art (anarchic, subversive) within the archive (disciplinary, hegemonic). The presence of art in the archive, the fact that art and archive (each somehow defined, on which more below) intersect, troubles the binary opposition between creativity and conservation.

The Conservationist (1974) is not only, in terms of form, Nadine Gordimer's most adventurous novel; it is also, despite its title, a place where things fall apart. The unruffled persona of a sophisticated industrialist disintegrates before our eyes; a flood destroys his farm even as the floodwaters bring intimations of new life, rebirth. The novel embodies a twinship of creativity and cataclysm, of cataclysm and (an enlivened form of) conservation.

For Sartre the pursuit of originality within discipline, freedom within constraint, is a lesson in how to live. But where part of what constrains us is a certain kind of cataclysm, the felt absence of disciplinary constraints – the lost prosthesis of objectivity – that lesson becomes doubly (or more) difficult to locate, to learn. In Sartre's picture originality is parasitic on constraint: so on what will originality feed if constraint has collapsed amidst relativism?

I will suggest in what follows that Nadine Gordimer's work can be read in ways that reunite us with our ability to walk, even without the lost prosthesis of objectivity. This question – how to act amidst absent origins – has remained a spectral presence throughout the seminar series at which this paper was first presented, and merits less oblique attention. Thus the first section of this essay ('Artist, archive, origin') directly addresses the recuperation of action in the absence of 'origins' – the question of how to act meaningfully (morally) in a climate of relativism.

Within these large questions of human agency and metaethics (comprising a vast literature) I find that Gordimer exemplifies a helpful Wittgensteinian tradition. I do not attempt a comprehensive defence of this tradition, which would be hubris in an essay of the present nature

1 Jean-Paul Sartre, 'The artist and his conscience' (1950), reprinted in *Situations* (London: Hamish Hamilton, 1965), p. 220.

301

and scale. And I do not suggest that Gordimer actively or consciously espouses this tradition or any other 'theory' in her work.[2] The tradition is immanent in the work. Its 'discovery' there is the work of reading, my reading, a supplement of interpretation. And yet I find the textual mandate for this reading strikingly explicit. (Much debate about Gordimer's work is more opinionated than informed; so this essay gives deliberate and extensive play to her own texts, a methodology that ideally should go without saying but, in her case, cannot.)

While the first section thus treats the ontological question ('How to archive amidst relativism?') as a branch of the question of human agency, the second section ('Enlivening the archive') asks how the liveliness of art – its human agency, now taken as read – can avoid extinction within the cemetery ethos of the archive. The second section argues that the presence of art in the archive itself alters the materiality of the archive, undoing its allegedly cemetery ethos and immersing it in communal forms of life, vividly. The archive begins to seem more womb (site of unborn art, unpublished manuscripts, nascent ways of being embodied in print) than tomb. But the author, too, inhabits and implements variants of discursive discipline. And she inhabits an uncertain space where dialogue (meaningful exchange) recurrently veers towards mere chatter (abdication of self, betrayal of the *being* that ought to reside in *writing*).

The third section ('Re-cognising the archive') first addresses the question of defining the archive, highlighting how public or communal norms *constitute* the archive. The section then explores the role of the artist in expanding the range and scope of this process of public recognition. Given the argument in the second section that archival and human materiality share a oneness, the artist's enhancement of society's archival recognition(s) is an enhancement of the range and scope of human *being* itself. The archive hosts the concepts that *move* a society, in the very particular sense that Rosa Burger experiences when she is moved by the sight of an owner brutalising his donkey, or a vagrant dead on a park bench:

> These are the things that move me now – when I say 'move' I don't mean tears or anger. I mean a sudden shift, a tumultuous upheaval, an uncontrollable displacement, concepts whose surface has been insignificant heaving over, up-ended, raised as huge boulders smelling of the earth that still clings to them. A shift that comes to me physically, as intestines violently stir and contract when some irritant throws a switch in the digestive tract. Earth, guts – *I don't know what metaphors to use to describe the process by which I'm making my own metaphors for suffering.*[3]

2   'A work in which there are theories is like an object upon which the price is marked' (Marcel Proust, quoted in Nadine Gordimer's unpublished Notebooks, on file with Ronald Suresh Roberts).

3   Nadine Gordimer, *Burger's Daughter* (London: Jonathan Cape, 1979; Penguin reprint, 1984), p. 196 (italics added).

RONALD SURESH ROBERTS

This passage summarises the tectonic quality of society's archival fabric (its collective mental space): it has the provisional stability of artefact or fossil, yet remains subject always to earthquakes of renewal. The passage also captures the artist's role in naming (which is a form of enabling) these earthquakes. And finally, in the questing and open-ended nature of its final sentence, in its *meta-metaphorical pondering*, we glimpse how the novelist's enabling (naming) function in relation to culture waits upon a chronically prior exercise of naming (and so enabling) her own activity, which means – because art is her essence – a naming of the self. In a sense, this passage from *Burger's Daughter* condenses and interlinks the questions of being, knowing, choosing (committing) and acting that I will attempt to unfurl, alas more discursively, in the three sections of this essay, below.

But before turning there I supply, in the following subsection of this introduction, a note on the title of this essay.

* 'Keeping the Self: The Novelist as (Self-)Archivist' is a title that might seem to bristle with narcissism, might seem to posture the novelist as navel-gazer. But this interpretation already assumes a particular concept of the self – a hermeticism of the self – which may be misleading. For another ethos of selfhood can be found among those 'people who, far from poring over the navel of a single identity . . . see the necessity of many'.[4] Among such folks, self-manufacture and societal remaking might well coincide. Gordimer explains in her 1994 Harvard Lectures:

> Where there is the necessity, through historical circumstance of time, place and birth, to 'make oneself' many processes take place at once. Because I had turned out to be a writer, because I was just that, because it was my fundament beneath all that has been done to condition my being, all my confusions, my false consciousness – because I was a writer, my principal means of 'making myself' was my writing.
>
> Only through the writer's explorations could I have begun to discover the human dynamism of the place I was born to and the time in which it was to be enacted. Only in the prescient dimension of the imagination could I bring together what had been deliberately broken and fragmented; fit together the shapes of living experience, my own and that of others, without which a whole consciousness is not attainable. I had to be part of the *transformation of my place* in order for it to know me.[5]

4   Ibid., p. 112.

5   Nadine Gordimer, *Writing and Being* (Cambridge: Harvard University Press, 1995), p. 130 (italics in original).

The writer is immersed in society and society is reciprocally drenched by the individual and collective consciousness of its writers, just as the fish is in the water and the water is in the fish. The self, others, and their collective inhabitance – compound of inheritance and habitat – these are reciprocally formative; they work upon each other: 'in the writing, I am acting upon my society, and in the manner of my apprehension, all the time history is acting upon me'.[6] It is this that enables the Gordimer corpus to be described, as it is by her most influential critic, as an embodiment of 'history from the inside', played out in an arena where 'human cannot be separated from historical experience'.[7]

Gordimer's own rejection of hermetic methodologies in art is wry and emphatic:

> Of course, there are distinguished examples of this [hermetic art] as a matter of *own choice*: the writers who are deliberately self-obsessed, genuinely finding revelation for us in the couplings of their own physical and thought processes as certain creatures are equipped with male genitalia at one end of their bodies and female genitalia at the other, so that they may perform a complete life cycle in themselves.[8]

While resisting hermeticism (the writer as self-sufficient universe unto herself), Gordimer also resists the opposite theorisation: the author as mere medium of language and history, wholly determined artefact of discourse. Gordimer locates this overdetermined concept of the author in Roland Barthes – she takes him to say that 'to interpret a text' is to 'appreciate what *plural* constitutes it' and that the author, the compiler, is not present in that plural.[9] In resisting this idea, in insisting on a notion of artistic *agency*, Gordimer in effect insists on the role of the artist as an origin(ator) of something called art.

In creating the self exactly through the transformation of place Gordimer thus confronts us with an idea of the novelist as a walking archive, possessing what she calls 'a facility that works upon while it stores fragments of perception' – an archive that is formative of the artefacts it possesses (produces) and, by extension, of the society that constitutes it. This facility intersects with the actual because it deals with imaginary lives that are nevertheless 'contained in time by aleatory real events of politics and history'.[10] Yet these elements of the actual are not stored static, are not merely conserved or preserved, in the novelist's archival facility. They are subject to transmutation.

6   Nadine Gordimer, 'Introduction' to *Selected Stories* (London: 1975; Penguin reprint, 1978).

7   Stephen Clingman, *The Novels of Nadine Gordimer: History from the Inside* (Johannesburg: Ravan Press, 1986).

8   Gordimer, *Writing and Being*, p. 14.

9   Ibid., p. 16.

10   Ibid., p. 8.

RONALD SURESH ROBERTS

We no longer (if we ever did) see the archive as a safe harbour from ontological flux, as a place of existential repose, where meaning drops anchor and stays, stilled. At once an instrument of historical study and a product of each history in which it claims instrumentality, the archive – its scope, identity, relevance, meaning – is as controversial now as are our practices of history, politics, law and literature themselves.[11] The disciplinary function of the archive – *its archival violence*[12] – is an expression of epistemic violence more generally: of the inherently coercive impact that socially hegemonic truths inflict upon insurgent or marginal communities of truth with whom they collide. The archive has lost its appellate function in the resolution of our disputes, has lost its judge's gavel of purportedly uncontroversial 'fact'.

But the artist need not make this claim of factuality, need never align herself with this alleged variety of usefulness: fact-finder for the archive. We expect from the artist, including the novelist, peculiarly creative contributions to the archive. (I mean now not only the walking archive of her body and imagination, but also society's archive, ostensibly external to her, into which her work is published.) If in her work she arrives with mere fact, she commits what V. S. Naipaul calls the 'documentary heresy',[13] a failure to complete the alchemy, to utilise the facility by which fact passes through artistic vision and arrives as something new, or at least different. Fiction 'enriches the corpus it claims to treat but which it enlarges and of which, in fact, it is henceforth a part'.[14] In this way, fiction secretes, it extrudes, fact that is not merely found but also at once made.

Beginning in imagination, in the intangible, fiction ends in *positivity*. Ilse Fischer is not Rosa Burger and yet she could say of Gordimer's novel: 'This was our life.'[15] *In some sense, perhaps, the artist is origin.*

This is certainly Gordimer's position (as mentioned above) when she demands that the artist be acknowledged as a causative force in the Barthesian plurality that constitutes the text. If the artist is denied human agency, then art collapses into anthropology: the 'author' is irrelevant; culture is the collective, impersonal creator. Gordimer has specifically objected that, within the Eurocentric curricula of the past, 'the arts of the African continent to which we belonged were relegated to the anthropology departments of universities. I remember, in the 1960s, being invited to give a talk on African literature – in the anthropology department of Witwatersrand University.'[16] In Africa, as in postcolonial places generally, insis-

11 Jacques Derrida, *Archive Fever: A Freudian Impression* (Chicago, University of Chicago Press, 1996), pp. 29, 90. ('Archive is only a notion, an impression associated with a word . . . nothing is less reliable, nothing is less clear today than the word archive'.)

12 Derrida, *Archive Fever*, p. 7 (italics in original).

13 V. S. Naipaul, 'The documentary heresy', *Twentieth Century* (Winter 1964), reprinted in Robert D. Hamner, ed., *Critical Perspectives on V. S. Naipaul* (Washington D. C.: Three Continents, 1977), p. 24.

14 Derrida, *Archive Fever*, p. 40.

15 Gordimer, *Writing and Being*, p. 12. (Ilse Fischer, daughter of anti-apartheid communist Bram Fischer for whom *Burger's Daughter* was begun as a form of homage, commenting on the completed manuscript.)

16 Nadine Gordimer, 'Gondwana 2000', unpublished paper delivered to the conference 'Writing the Deep South', held in Santiago, Chile, 2–7 November 1998.

tence on the identity of the author becomes a metonym for insistence on the dignity, the agency, of the individuals whom colonialism tellingly called 'subject peoples'.

The critic George Steiner – whose work Gordimer has long admired and which turns up frequently in her unpublished Notebooks – sees (following Ernst Bloch) 'the essence of man to be his "forward dreaming, his compulsive ability to construe 'that which is now' as being 'that which is not yet'."' This is what Gordimer, too, means when she speaks of the writer possessing 'the prescient dimension of the imagination' – why else that adjective ('prescient'), potentially odd in this context, to describe the imagination? Steiner continues:

> Human consciousness recognises in the existent a constant margin of incompletion, of arrested potentiality which challenges fulfil-ment. Man's awareness of 'becoming', his capacity to envisage a history of the future, distinguishes him from all other living species. *This Utopian instinct is the mainspring of politics. Great art contains the lineaments of unrealised actuality.* It is, in Malraux's for-mula, 'anti-destiny'. We hypothesize and project thought and imagination into the 'if-ness', into the free conditionalities of the unknown. Such projection is no logical muddle, no abuse of induction. It is far more than a probabilistic convention. *It is the master nerve of human action.*[17]

Whatever his other conservatisms, his perhaps rebarbative elitisms, Steiner here wonderfully captures the links between art, world and action. He captures the way in which art can be constitutive of human agency.

This possibility – art as origin – may assist those who are thrown into tremulous paralysis by the thought that facts have lost their bind-ingness, their quality of being facts, of settling debates. In this evi-dently fraught context the artist may help us find out how to act amidst existential discomfort, without the duvet of metanarratives, without some Archimedean point on which we might stand to gain ontological leverage upon the world, history, indeed the self. This very theme – discovering a basis for ethical action in a world bereft of epis-temological foundations – is an explicit, if insufficiently recognised, concern of much of Gordimer's fiction. In Gordimer's work art and the artist displace the 'relic present'[18] in favour of enlivened alternatives at once imaginary and actual.

'I find it very hard to tell the difference between the truth and the facts: to know what the facts are?'[19] says/asks Rosa Burger in an explic-

17 George Steiner, *After Babel: Aspects of Language and Translation* 3rd ed. (Oxford: Oxford University Press, 1998), p. 227 (italics added).

18 Gordimer, *Burger's Daughter*, p. 112. See also, Nadine Gordimer, *The Late Bourgeois World* (London: Jonathan Cape, 1966; Penguin reprint, 1982) ('The future was already there; it was a matter of having the courage to announce it'.)

19 Gordimer, *Burger's Daughter*, p. 142 (punctuation in original).

itly self-questioning utterance. She both says and asks at once. It is an utterance infused with relativism. Yet she says/asks in a moment not of paralysis but of its opposite – a moment of mission. Her mission is to deliver something to an anti-apartheid operative at a petrol station in a western Transvaal *dorp*: seemingly a stern anti-apartheid task.

But she is accompanied by a Swede who, ignorant of her secret mission, has his own in which she is assisting – the making of a documentary film. So is her presence *really* part of an archival foray: 'the material transcendence of a man's span by the recording, for posterity, on film, of landscapes and types of environment that formed his consciousness'?

Additionally, the Swede is her lover, so is the *real* meaning of the weekend instead the 'ecstatic energy consumed in the hotel bed between eleven o'clock in the morning when the Dutch Reformed church bells were tolling and midday when the xylophone notes of the lunch gong were sounded, an hour without any consequences whatever except a stain on the bottom sheet – stiff commemorative plaque that a Selena or Elsie would remark, without having her life altered in any manner, before it disappeared in the wash'?[20]

It is not enough to say that the western Transvaal weekend is all these things (mission, documentary foray, erotic outing) at once because these characterisations of the weekend carry mutually incompatible implications for the actualisation of Rosa's future self. Erotic outings of the giddy romantic sort are a way of being that is alien to Lionel Burger's emotionally austere communist ethos where, for instance, marriage to imprisoned comrades is arranged as a device for maintaining communication with them. To conflate giddy eroticism and the struggle is to jeopardise one's standing in the movement as Sonny learns in Gordimer's novel *My Son's Story* (1990), where his extra-marital relationship, taken too seriously, renders him 'unsound' and triggers something of a fall from grace.

Similarly, the documentary foray – with its explicit premise that human consciousness is formed by the physical or visual environment – contradicts the fact that it is the intensely *intangible* motions of Rosa's spirit (her secular–spiritual development) that push the novel forward. The weekend, viewed through the lens and language of the documentary project, borders on the 'documentary heresy' mentioned above: it suggests that the formative impacts on human spirit can be recorded, glibly, by a roving camera lens and it therefore places artistic vision into desuetude (if humankind can be understood in the straightforward documentary fashion, as an emanation of physical landscape, why bother with the elaborateness of art?). So I repeat:

20 Ibid.

these different glosses placed on the 'facts' of the western Transvaal weekend are inflected with fundamentally incompatible worldviews, ways of being.

Yet Rosa nevertheless can act amidst these proliferating documentary, erotic and political impulses which become severely and mutually incompatible as the novel develops. How? She *combines assertion with its own interrogation* (she both asks and says – questions and asserts – in the *self*-same utterance); and additionally she combines this utterance-question with action. In finding a path clear through to action amidst mutually incompatible selves, Rosa *embodies* ('I am the place in which something has occurred' is the novel's epigraph from Claude Lévi-Strauss) a process of moral and political self-construction that may be exemplary for us who fret in ontological despair.

Gordimer has said that while *Burger's Daughter* is superficially about white communists in South Africa it is actually, to her, something else. 'It's a book about commitment. *Commitment is not merely a political thing. It's part of the whole ontological problem in life.* It's part of my feeling that what a writer does is to try to make sense of life . . . It's seeking that thread of order and logic in the disorder, and the incredible waste and marvellous profligate character of life.'[21]

The interplay of commitment and ontology is evident as Rosa Burger ruminates on how her committed father must have viewed her self-absorbed bohemian friend, Conrad: 'Lionel Burger probably saw in you the closed circuit of self; for him, such a life must be in need of a conduit towards meaning, which is posited: outside self. That's where the tension that made it possible to live lay, for him, between self and others; between the present and the creation of something called the future.'[22]

By juxtaposing commitment and ontology; by immersing ontological concerns in the profligate character of life itself, rather than on a Platonic or Olympian mountaintop; by declining to corral ontology within sterile theoretical debate; by loosing it instead among our forms of life in all their fecundity – in all this Gordimer's metaethics are consonant with a powerful Wittgensteinian tradition best articulated by Stanley Cavell, whose *The Claim of Reason: Wittgenstein, Skepticism, Morality and Tragedy*[23] appeared in 1979, the same year as *Burger's Daughter.*

Briefly stated, Cavell says that when our moral disagreements are intractable it is often not because of the unavailability of rational reasoning to one or other party, but rather because of an incommensurability of selves that separates the disputants.[24] The solution – or, at

21 Nadine Gordimer, quoted in Nancy Topping Bazin and Marilyn Dallman Seymour, eds., *Conversations with Nadine Gordimer* (London: University Press of Mississippi, 1990), p. 140 (italics added).

22 Gordimer, *Burger's Daughter*, p. 86.

23 Stanley Cavell, *The Claim of Reason: Wittgenstein, Skepticism, Morality and Tragedy* (Oxford: Oxford University Press, 1979).

24 Cavell, *The Claim of Reason*, pp. 117–118 ('Who is crazy? I do not say no one is, but must somebody be, when people's reactions are at variance with ours? It seems safe to suppose that if you can describe any behaviour which I can recognise as that of a human being, I can give you an explanation which will make that behaviour coherent . . . And if I say "they are crazy" or "incomprehensible" then that is not a fact but my fate for them. I have gone as far as my imagination, magnanimity, or anxiety will allow; or as my honour, or my standing cares and commitments, can accommodate.')

RONALD SURESH ROBERTS

least, the work the disputants must do (with no guaranteed success) – involves the transformation of each self so that it becomes amenable, accessible, to the other. Where this accessibility exists from the outset dispute will be absent, or at least resolvable, and sensibilities will find themselves in mutual attunement based on shared 'criteria' (a term of art in Wittgenstein) of meaning. But where our attunements are dissonant, where we come up against limits of being (limits not only of knowledge but of experience), there is a moment of disappointment. 'The power I felt in my breath as my words flew to their effect now vanishes into thin air . . . I am thrown back upon myself; I as it were turn my palms outward, as if to exhibit the kind of creature I am, and declare my ground occupied, only mine, ceding yours.'[25]

For Cavell, the risk of failures of communication is a part of the human condition, the very fabric of tragedy itself, for which there is no merely intellectual or theoretical fix, unless we can envisage a human condition bereft of the capacity for sadness, for disappointment (and would it then be a *human* condition, or even a desirable one?).

Gordimer's work is rich in this sense of the fragility and ontological significance of (attempts at) human communication. She knows that words are never merely factual, that they entail judgements, inherently invoke *criteria*, which in turn mark the contours of being – and which therefore can bring us together or fling us apart:

> What I say will not be understood. Once it passes from me, it becomes apologia or accusation [i.e. it becomes *prescriptive*, cannot remain value-free fact]. I am talking about neither . . . but you will use my words to make your own meaning. As people pick up letters from a stack between them in word-games. You will say: she said *he* was this or that . . . I am considering only ways of trying to take hold; you will say: she is Manichaean.

The elements of self-questioning, of provisionality, that accompany Rosa's saying/asking get lost in the inevitable positivity of utterances, as they fly to their effects, between persons. The other person experiences (hears) in what Rosa says a categorical ingredient, inherent in language as a currency of communication, that can alienate, can enforce a separateness of selves, which contradicts Rosa's desire to reach that other. *At the outer edge or limits of communication language betrays being.*

A further example: Rosa ruminates on what she has learnt from her boyfriend Conrad. She sees what he means when he says that, in Lionel Burger's house, the people did not *know* each other in the important ways that reside outside of the public currency of political commit-

25 Ibid., p. 115.

ment. In this insight she and Conrad find affinity. But in this very act of acknowledging Conrad's insight Rosa has another of her own about the limits of Conrad's insightfulness, limits that mark, yet again, her separateness from him: 'But there are things you didn't know; or, to turn your criteria back on yourself, you knew only in the abstract, in the public and impersonal act of reading about them or seeking information, like a white journalist professionally objective and knowledgeable on the "subject" of a "black exploiting class."'[26] This turning away from Conrad can be read as an unconsciously explicit moment of Wittgensteinian dissonance, in which Rosa actively grasps, assesses, and turns away from Conrad's criteria of value, his ways of knowing the world. Rosa navigates relativism (her divergence from Conrad despite certain affinities with him) without paralysis.

Similarly, Rosa only rejects the tempting prospect of becoming mistress to a French professor after she rejects also his more basic assertion: that commitment to 'the blacks' back in South Africa is 'not open' to Rosa. As the professor attempts to insist upon her existential incompatibility with 'the blacks', Rosa discerns clearly her own existential incompatibility with *him*. When he says 'Ah, my reasons are not theirs'[27] he inadvertently sums up and acknowledges the notion that reasons are rooted in being, in forms of life, such as are now palpably looming up, incommensurably, to separate Rosa and himself as divergent beings, wrought of different reasonings.

For Wittgenstein–Cavell–Gordimer, we panic about lost origins, we succumb to the paralysis of scepticism, only because we repeatedly 'attempt to convert the human condition, the condition of humanity, into an intellectual difficulty, a riddle'; we constantly attempt to convert 'a metaphysical finitude into an intellectual lack'.[28] We succumb to the hubris of believing that we can solve problems of *being* by wordgames of *saying*.

There is no such solecism in Gordimer's work. Instead we find this paradox: intense writerly commitment, allegiance to words, alongside an awareness of the limits and hazards of runaway language, language unloosed from being, as when Rosa Burger talks to her father's biographer and finds him 'respectfully coaxing me onto the stepping stones of the official vocabulary – words, nothing but dead words, abstractions: that's not where reality is . . .'[29] To keep lit the spark of writing, firing the synapses of being – this is a job of work, a task of art, not an inevitability.

So there is a twofold challenge. *First*, the writer has (gives herself, is given by society) a mandate to invent, to extend the range and

26 Gordimer, *Burger's Daughter*, p. 171.

27 Ibid., p. 297.

28 Cavell, *The Claim of Reason*, p. 493.

29 Gordimer, *Burger's Daughter*, p. 142.

RONALD SURESH ROBERTS

scope of human being. But, *second*, by the cavalier discharge of this mandate the artist may career away from the essential gesture of being. Then writing becomes an *in*essential gesture, as it is for the decrepit white Russian writer, urbanely exiled in the south of France, whose manuscripts Rosa's stepmother types for four francs a page: sometimes the stepmother inserts her own sentences, for fun ('*Delphine sniffs cocaine from Marcel's manly armpit*') and the dissolute author does not even notice.[30] His seemingly 'private' authorial failing is part of the more general – call it 'public' – existential decay that slants across Rosa's sunny French self-exile and, eventually, propels her back to South Africa.

How does she *act* – what does she *do* – upon her return? 'Like anyone else, I do what I can. I am teaching them to walk again, at Baragwanath Hospital. They put one foot before the other.'[31]

If we wish to navigate the ontological flux of the external world (of archives, history, politics, law) perhaps we must take soundings that go to the very heart of inward being. This is the metaethical echo of Gordimer's theory of the novel (but 'theory' is too grand and sterile a word): her belief, with Georg Lukács, that in the writerly sensibility is fused 'the duality of inwardness and outside world'.[32] The private self-archiving of the writer and the lunge towards coherence (towards meaning) in the public sphere: these must together proceed, one foot before the other, as if in a three-legged race.

'To know and not to act is not to know' is the admonishing epigraph that launches Part Two of *Burger's Daughter*, in which Rosa attempts to 'defect' from her father's complex political legacy and to embrace the bonny climes of southern France, only to find that she is 'out of place: not I, myself . . . the manner of my coming – it doesn't fit necessity or reality here . . .' As Rosa here turns her palms outward, exhibiting the kind of creature she is, ceding French ground that is not hers, the entire novel can be read as a form of life that expresses the oneness of selfhood, knowledge, commitment and action.

To *be* and *know* and *choose* (*commit*) and *act* – these are perhaps the interlocking elements – each the other's catalyst and precondition – of a way forward, one foot before the other, through the blizzard of scepticism. During her existential sojourn in France, her 'out of place' exile from anti-apartheid action, Rosa's selfhood itself (her 'being') begins to fall away: 'Dissolving in the wine and pleasure of scents, sights and sounds existing only in themselves, associated with nothing and nobody, Rosa's sense of herself was lazily objective.'[33] To *be* without *choosing* (*committing*) is to forfeit humanhood, to swap strenuous human

30 Ibid., p. 236 (original emphasis).

31 Ibid., p. 332.

32 Nadine Gordimer, 'Living in the interregnum' in Stephen Clingman, ed., *The Essential Gesture: Writing, Politics and Places* (London: Jonathan Cape, 1988; Penguin reprint, 1989), p. 277. Lukács has a subtle but insistent determinism in his belief that historical materialism provides positivist knowledge about the real world. Georg Lukács, 'The changing function of historical materialism', in *History and Class Consciousness* (London: Merlin Press, 1968), pp. 223–225. This short-cut through the problem of scepticism loosens his interest in the present context. Additionally, Lukács did not directly address questions of ontology until very late in his career, and then not very satisfactorily. See Roy Pascal, 'Georg Lukács: the concept of totality' in G.H.R. Parkinson, ed., *Georg Lukács: The Man, his Work and his Ideas* (London: Weidenfeld and Nicolson, 1970), pp. 147 and 169.

33 Gordimer, *Burger's Daughter*, p. 115.

subjectivity for lazy objectivity: to inhabit objecthood rather than self-hood. It is to abandon the goal of 'living to be judged',[34] which is part-ly the core of moral motivation.

'Being' likewise requires *knowing* – call it memory. For Rosa the decay of the French way of life is epitomised in her encounter with an ageing beauty who, in her dotage, 'had slipped the moorings of nights and days . . . her fingers twitched like fleas'. When Rosa asks her what was wrong, the 'old girl' is bewildered: 'that was what was wrong – that she didn't know, couldn't remember what it was that was wrong'.[35]

Thus the absence of memory amounts, too, to the forfeit of self-hood. But memory alone is no panacea. Without commitment rudder-less memory seizes on misleading outer attributes of action, frustrating knowledge: Rosa imagines that the French community, amidst whom she is out of place, might remember her, were she to return another year, as 'the great love of the Parisian professor who was writing a book'.[36] This is an identity, a way of knowing Rosa, that Rosa herself cannot recognise, to which she is not *committed*. Within the limits of their commitments, the collective memory of their bonny French com-munity, they cannot know Rosa. Between her and them lies an iron curtain of being which mocks ostensible memory itself.

Knowledge in turn requires imagination (a variety of commitment) through which the artist secretes upon the external facts of the world the skeleton architecture of (new ways of) being. 'That utopia, it's inside . . . without it, how can you . . . act?'[37] In Rosa's mind – in a phenomenology of Rosa Burger – the link between knowledge and action is intimate, even as that knowledge insists on ingredients of the utopic. Utopia loses its ingredient of escapism. Rosa lives for (and through) the demolition of relic realities under the hammer blow of workaday – not grandiose – principles.

As evident in the phenomenology of Rosa Burger, Gordimer's idea of the novelist's vocation is ambitious to say the least, even romantic.[38] Fiction becomes the '*enactment of life*'[39] in a sense other than the mere duplication of existing realities: the point is to challenge them, as the protagonist says in Gordimer's 1970 novel: 'You can't be realistic with-out principles – that's just the convenient interpretation, that the real-ist accepts things as they are, even if those things express an unreal situation, a false one.' The 'practical application of principle' compris-es, says this protagonist, the ability to 'see over the head of that situa-tion, and instinctively reject it even as a temporary one . . .'[40]

Gordimer's deliberate use of the vocabulary of falsity to describe injustice, her undeferred, sometimes seemingly premature, rejection of

---

34 Ibid., p. 158.

35 Ibid., p. 300.

36 Ibid., p. 301.

37 Ibid., p. 296 (ellipses original).

38 Gordimer in Bazin and Seymour, eds., *Conversations*, p. 41. ('I am a romantic struggling with reality, for surely this very engagement implies innate romanticism'.)

39 Gordimer, *Writing and Being*, p. 18 (italics in original).

40 Nadine Gordimer, *A Guest of Honour* (London: Jonathan Cape, 1970), pp. 235–236.

RONALD SURESH ROBERTS

prevailing injustice as 'unreal' – combined with the fact that the deployment of tense and gyrations of time are never accidental in her work – all this adds up to an *assertion* of the artist's presence in the archive. The artist can be seen as the indispensable assurance against an unlively archive, against what Derrida calls '*an archivable concept of the archive*'. Because creativity – *origin*ation – is integral to the artist's presence in the archive, the artist keeps open the *question* of the archive: 'it is a question of the future, the question of the future itself, the question of a response, of a promise, and of a responsibility for tomorrow'.[41] For Derrida, the supposed savant of playfulness, the archive embodies a *responsibility*. Artistic and other creativity within the archive inoculates us against the naive idea of an archival *finality*.[42] The artist in the archive, additionally, assures us that we do not need, in order to act ethically, the hyperbolic (and unattainable) certainty that such finality would imply.

So perhaps philosophers may look to learn from literature, but whether they will must await resolution of Stanley Cavell's parting question: 'can philosophy become literature and still know itself?'[43] Meanwhile, both jostle together, in the archive.

Enlivening the Archive

In the Coolidge room of the United States Library of Congress hang the finest Stradivarius violins, violas, cellos on earth. They hang lustrous, each millimetre restored, analysed, recorded. They hang safe from the vandalism of the Red Brigades, from the avarice or cynical indifference of dying Cremona. Once a year, unless I am mistaken, they are taken from their cases and lent for performance to an eminent quartet. Haydn, Mozart, Beethoven, Bartok fill the room. Then back to their sanctuary of silent preservation. Americans come to gaze at them in pride; Europeans in awed envy or gratitude. The instruments are made immortal. And stone dead.[44]

What kind of dancer maims the dance? Archives can be the means by which culture becomes a variety of manufacture, intensely professionalised, domesticated, its should-be vibrancy dissipated. Culture becomes enervated so that 'its interactions with the community at large are those of ostensible presentment, of contractual occasion rather than of anarchic and subversive pervasiveness'.[45]

But archives – viewed for now as spaces cordoned off from 'real' life – are not alone in this ontological jeopardy. This jeopardy also inhab-

41 Derrida, *Archive Fever*, p. 36. Derrida locates a creative aspiration and achievement in Freud's *Civilisation and its Discontents*, indicating that an artist has no inherent monopoly on innovation. Foucault further suggests that authors like Freud and Marx are 'founders of discursivity' in that they author 'a theory, tradition or discipline in which other books and authors will in turn find a place', whereas the author of a novel 'is, in fact, no more than the author of his own text'. Michel Foucault, 'What is an author?' reprinted in *The Foucault Reader* (New York: Pantheon Books, 1984), pp. 113–114. The existence of novelistic theories, traditions or disciplines (geographic, generic, aesthetic, historical) renders Foucault's attempted distinction somewhat dogmatic.

42 See also Jean-Paul Sartre, 'The artist and his conscience' (1950), reprinted in *Situations* (London: Hamish Hamilton, 1965), p. 219: 'It is the artist who must break the already crystallized habits which make us see in the *present* tense those institutions and customs which are *already out of date*. To provide a true image of our time, he must consider it from the pinnacle of the future which it is creating, since it is tomorrow that will decide today's truth' (italics in original); Gordimer, *Writing and Being*, p. 21: 'the order of experience that anticipates and is carried over to form the future is the definitive one'.

43 Cavell, *The Claim of Reason*, p. 496.

44 George Steiner, 'The archives of Eden' (1981), reprinted in *No Passion Spent: Essays 1978–1996* (London: Faber and Faber, 1996), p. 283. Steiner's essay is controversial for its potentially jingoistic differentiation of 'European' and 'American' cultures, to the detriment of the latter. Those unattractive aspects of Steiner's argument are no part of my own. See generally, James Wood, 'George Steiner's unreal presence' in *The Broken Estate* (London: Pimlico, 1999), pp. 155–173.

45 Ibid., p. 286.

its 'real' life itself. In Nadine Gordimer's world – where 'to risk, I think, is to live'[46] – we meet people who, through their misguided existential risk aversion ('priggish absurdity . . . the virginal drawing away of skirts from the dirt'), become walking anachronisms: 'we are museum pieces, better put away in a cupboard somewhere'.[47] They are mummified, wrapped inside 'the bourgeois fate . . . to eat without hunger, mate without desire'.[48]

And while life can have about it a whiff of the mausoleum, art can so enliven itself and others as to enter fully into the realm of the corporeal. This was the experience of Marcel Proust (whom Gordimer describes as 'my great mentor')[49]: 'No days, perhaps, of all our childhood are ever so fully lived as those we had regarded as not being lived at all: the days spent wholly with a favourite book.'[50] This was likewise the experience of Proust's own mentor, John Ruskin: 'the real force of genius is to make us love a thought which we feel to be more real than we are ourselves'.[51] And of Gordimer herself: 'to be literate is to be someone whose crucially formative experience may come just as well from certain books as from events. I know that until I was at least twenty nothing and no one influenced me as much as certain poets and writers.'[52]

From this angle it seems an impertinence to question the 'materiality' of 'texts' as though they suffer a prima facie disability from which 'life' is inherently exempt. 'Life' (of the risk-averse variety) can be immaterial while texts, works of imagination, can have a jarring materiality. '[Outer] space is not of this world, either, and yet you can walk about alive in it, up there.'[53] We can live in books, inhabit them (and they us), in a sense as strictly literal as that which we mean when we acknowledge that astronauts can live in space.

The existential unity of life and art, a sense of their criss-crossing singularity, is the powerful impulse behind the title ('Writing and Being') of Gordimer's 1994 Norton Lectures, the same title that she gave the completely different text of her 1991 Nobel Prize lecture. 'Writing and Being' carries the force of a personal and aesthetic mantra. Her insistence that writing is a full-blown iteration of being (not an anaemic poor relation) is manifold and emphatic and it takes powerful forms in the fiction itself. If drama has its plays-within-plays, Gordimer has her books-within-books which enter fully into the materiality of her characters' emotions.

For instance: as the protagonist in *The Late Bourgeois World* (1966) awaits a dinner guest, the imminent arrival of this real person constipates her facility with texts (she cannot begin a letter), while the depar-

46 Gordimer in Bazin and Seymour, eds., *Conversations*, p. 70.

47 Gordimer, *A Guest of Honour*, pp. 213–214.

48 Gordimer, *Burger's Daughter*, p. 117.

49 Bazin and Seymour, *Conversations*, p. 224.

50 Marcel Proust, quoted by André Maurois. *The Quest for Proust* (London: Jonathan Cape, 1950), p. 26.

51 John Ruskin, quoted by Maurois, *The Quest for Proust*, p. 111.

52 Nadine Gordimer, 'Notes of an expropriator', *Times Literary Supplement*, 4 June 1964.

53 Nadine Gordimer, *The Late Bourgeois World* (London: Jonathan Cape, 1966; Penguin reprint, 1982), p. 92.

ture (by death) of another real person (her ex-husband, Max) alters the materiality of a book that she has half-finished reading. And, finally, the half-finished book itself seems to give a charged materiality to the deceased Max (whose death notice has 'already been dropped' from the late final edition of the daily newspaper, ostensible journal of 'fact'), which subsides only when she stops reading:

> There are so many things that ought to be done when I have the time, but an awkward little wedge of time like this is not much use. Whatever I began, I should not finish. I can never go back to a half-written letter; the tone, when you take it up again, doesn't match.
>
> And yet to put on a record and pour myself another glass of wine and sit – something that sounds delightful – made me feel as if I were on stage before an empty auditorium. I fetched the book I was reading in bed in the morning. *Since I stopped halfway down the page at which a dry cleaner's slip marked my place*, there was Max's death; it seemed to me a different book, I can't explain – it sounded quite different there in that inner chamber where one hears a writer's voice behind the common currency of words. The voice went on and on but ran into itself as an echo throws one wave of sound back and forth on top of another. I read the words and sentences, but my mind twitched to the single electrical impulse – the death of Max. *As soon as I gave up the attempt to read, it was all right again. I wasn't even thinking about him.* Through the walls there was the muffled clatter of dinner-time in the flats on either side of mine, and the bark of someone's radio at full volume. Car doors slammed and the clear winter air juggled voices.[54]

Her immersion in the book, *her place* marked by the workaday dry cleaner's slip, supplied her with a finely calibrated existential scale of reference against which to inhabit the lack of Max. This is a place – a strenuous and disturbing solace – that the ephemeral press report of Max's death could not provide. The objective furniture of the world that she re-inhabits after setting aside the book (slamming doors, muffled dinner-time clatter) is like the newspaper: indistinct, *immaterial*, by comparison to the book. The air juggles voices: the human (in its risk-averse suburban iteration) becomes the plaything of the inanimate and intangible wind.

Like the protagonist in *The Late Bourgeois World*, Gordimer herself, in her own real life, can inhabit a textualised reality, find solace there. For instance: although initially anxious about what Ilse Fischer's

54 Ibid., p. 73 (italics added).

response to the novel *Burger's Daughter* would be, she ultimately finds herself 'tranquil' as she awaits Ms Fischer's response: 'it was as if the three of us, the schoolgirl [Ms Fischer] waiting to visit her father in prison, my fictional character and I, together had a dimension of immaterial existence to be privately occupied for a while'.[55] Here the novel is itself doubly immaterial (fictional and, furthermore, not yet published: Ms Fischer was given it as a pre-publication manuscript). Yet it manifestly possesses materiality, providing the artist a source of actual emotional solace (tranquillity) and a dwelling space for the three of them, one of whom (Bram Fischer) was deceased. (That the 'real' Ms Fischer – not only the potentially self-congratulatory artist on her behalf – inhabits/inhabited this dwelling space is confirmed when Ms Fischer responds to the manuscript, saying simply: 'This was our life'.

So it looks as though the novelist can criss-cross with impunity the boundaries of the banal and sublime, material and immaterial, constructing and deconstructing at will: we glimpse the novelist as uber-archivist, as wayward and sovereign sensibility. By comparison, the traditional or stereotypical archivist (think dusty shelves, labelled boxes, reading rooms and regulations), a hyper-professionalised drone, can seem antithetical to the novelist, an apparent disjuncture that novelists themselves encourage:

> I think of professional life as something one enters by way of an examination, not as an obsessional occupation like writing for which you provide your own, often extraordinary or eccentric, qualifications as you go along. And I'm not flattered by the idea of being presented with a 'profession', *honoris causa*; every honest writer or painter wants to achieve the impossible and needs no minimum standard laid down by an establishment such as a profession.[56]

The novelist appears (constructs herself) as free-range forager, ostensibly unconstrained by any such professional or discursive disciplines as bind the conventional archivist.

But now the philosopher arrives to rival the novelist. He challenges 'the traditional idea of the author' as 'the genial creator of a work in which he deposits, within infinite wealth and generosity, an inexhaustible world of significations'. The philosopher doubts that 'as soon as [the author] speaks, meaning begins to proliferate, to proliferate indefinitely'. For this philosopher, 'the author is the principle of thrift in the proliferation of meaning . . . he is a certain functional principle by which, in our culture, one limits, excludes, and chooses; in short, by

55 Gordimer, *Writing and Being*, p. 11.

56 Nadine Gordimer, 'A bolter and the invisible summer' (1963), in Stephen Clingman, ed., *The Essential Gesture: Writing, Politics and Places* (London: Penguin 1989), p. 19.

RONALD SURESH ROBERTS

which one impedes the free circulation, the free manipulation, the free composition, decomposition, and recomposition of fiction'.[57]

Here the author is seen as one who exerts her identity, her selfhood, at the expense of the nascent proliferation of meanings immanent in her 'own' work. The death of the author, as of God, ought to be liberating for those readers who heed the philosopher's counsel. We ought to feel ourselves out from under the jackboot of the artist's existential self-governance. And yet we look to the footnotes to put a name, perhaps a face, to that anonymous philosopher.

For better or worse (or both), and perhaps paradoxically, we readers sometimes find writerly identity *empowering*. I feel that this is because having a notion of writerly identity allows us readers to shift from textual congress with the isolated page, to multitextual *conversation* with another person, the authorial being (not necessarily the same as the author 'herself'). We seek originality (inherently an attribute of personality?) within the disciplines of conversation. *Gordimer herself has said, quoting Nietzsche in an utterance of ontological significance, that 'truth begins in dialogue'*.[58] Dialogue (re)creates the constraints that the relativist cataclysm had washed away. But these constraints can only operate within a pre-existing mutual attunement, as the earlier discussion of Cavell will have clarified. Dialogue will not conjure constraints between divergent beings; word games will not resolve metaphysical dissonance.

There is an internal dialogue among the artist's plural selves as well as a dialogue among the artist, the reader and her characters. It can fail; it is plagued by the spectre of disappointment; we may find that we must cede the other's ground; disconnect. Such a moment is remarkably explicit in Gordimer's text where Rosa meets Brandt Vermeulen, a sophisticated New Afrikaner, determined to preserve the core of apartheid by reconfiguring it as a savvy, reasonable doctrine, beyond barbarism. Returning to South Africa equipped with his fancy foreign education (Leiden, Princeton, Paris, New York), he came back not to destroy the apartheid legacy, his precious inheritance, but 'with a vocabulary and sophistry to transform it' into a defensible late twentieth-century idiom.[59]

With the understated irony that is a kind of trademark in her work Gordimer places the most explicit rumination on dialogic ethics in the mouth of pro-apartheid Vermeulen, underlining the point that her commitment to dialogue is not a commitment to a romance of universal agreement. Truth may indeed begin in dialogue, but the link between truth and dialogue is not inexorable – there remains the

57 Michel Foucault, 'What Is an author' (1979) in Paul Rabinow, ed., *The Foucault Reader* (New York: Pantheon, 1984), pp. 118–119.

58 Nadine Gordimer, 'The novel and the nation in South Africa', *Times Literary Supplement*, 11 August 1961 (italics added).

59 Gordimer, *Burger's Daughter*, p. 175.

problem of Wittgensteinian jeopardy, the separateness of selves, divergences of being. Thus the rhetorical framework of Vermeulen's worldview is strikingly similar to Rosa's – there is an affinity of existential vocabulary – but the being immanent in his words could hardly be more dissonant:

> He had told me how much importance he placed on the human scale of policy action (the succinct phrases are his); that meant that when one has found the Kierkegaardian idea for which one must live or die, one must support its policy passionately in theory and at the same time take on the job of personal, practical, daily responsibility for its interpretation and furtherance. He gave me an informal luncheon-type address on the honourable evolution of Dialogue, beginning with Plato, the Dialogue with self, and culminating in 'the Vorster initiative', the dialogue of peoples and nations. With me he was self-engaged in that responsibility on the human scale; for him, his afternoons with Rosa were 'Dialogue' in practice.[60]

As Brandt Vermeulen finds his own way through the blizzard of relativism, placing one foot in front of the other, guided by a pro-apartheid ethic, the constraints of being that might *enable* his Dialogue with Rosa, that might facilitate a communion of selves, which is what genuine conversation amounts to – these constraints are absent. His 'succinct phrases' lack traction within Rosa's moral universe. Vorster's outward policy, which pre-dated the novel's 1979 publication date; Reagan's constructive engagement initiative, which followed – these are invocations of the trope of conversation, of Dialogue, in a denuded form. They were attempts to fill with words what is a void of being; to fix a problem of metaphysical finitude (the ontological divide between the respective vocabularies of apartheid and anti-apartheid) with the trappings of dialogue.

Dialogue, in its richly communicative Wittgensteinian sense, requires a strenuous coupling between language and desire. To respond to another speaker is to respond to her desire; art becomes the insistence on an authentic relation between language (vocabulary) and desire[61] and 'a strictness and scrupulousness of artistic desire thus comes to seem a moral and intellectual imperative'.[62] To conduct dialogue without this scrupulousness; to permit a wedge of détente to intercede between the self and its vocabulary, its desire; to permit this form of existential give-and-take is, in Cavell's vocabulary, to stupefy the self and ultimately the society.

60 Ibid., p. 194.

61 '. . . the degree to which you talk of things, and talk in ways, that hold no interest for you, or listen to what you cannot imagine the talker's caring about, in the way he carries the care, is the degree to which you consign yourself to nonsensicality, stupefy yourself . . . I think of this consignment as a form not so much of dementia as of what amentia ought to mean, a form of mindlessness.' (Cavell, *The Claim of Reason*, p. 95)

62 Ibid.

Rosa's dialogue with Brandt Vermeulen is just such a form of inauthentic conversation. She is calculating, hoping, that he will help her get a passport from the apartheid government, thus enabling her to travel to bonny southern France. Rosa's eventual stupefaction there, her flight from that 'out of place' French setting, is prefigured in the debased currency of her 'Dialogue' with Vermeulen. She is not her*self* in this exchange (in both the dialogue itself and the broader exchange of obtaining an apartheid passport, which she knows Vermeulen will parade as evidence that an enlightened apartheid is arrived). She explicitly enters a form of existential détente in which she, also explicitly, abdicates human agency: 'I hoped to be stopped. "Detente" (mispronounced and misappropriated) made my passport possible.'[63]

Thus, in Gordimer's work, dialogue is not inexorably a transparent window into the speaking self. When a self speaks it (she, he) raises a *question*: is it the true self that speaks? The conventional use of quotation marks ('like this'), which Gordimer eschews, invites the idea that speech and self are inherently parallel; that some part of the self is caught between those marks. *But, in fact, keeping the self is more complex than that.* It is a strictness and scrupulousness of artistic desire, a moral and political imperative, an existential agenda for interplay with others and with the world:

> A good deal of what is representative in modern literature, from Kafka to Pinter, seems to work deliberately at the edge of quietness. It puts forward tentative or failed speech – moves expressive of the intimation that the larger, more worthwhile statements cannot, ought not, be made (Hofmannsthal came to speak of the 'indecency of eloquence' after the lies and massacres of world war).[64]

At the beginning of her interaction with Brandt Vermeulen, Rosa Burger remains 'mistress of her own silences; as if he were the one waiting for her to speak instead of she herself looking for an *opportunity*'.[65] It is as she must speak, must embrace opportunism, that he draws her into the self-maiming dialogue (the abdication of self) that enables her departure for bonny France. In thus portraying Rosa, Gordimer enters into what is perhaps the writer's distinctive contribution to an enlivened archive: she helps us tell chat (where the self is absent and or jeopardised)[66] from Dialogue (which is self-formative and self-expressive).

63 Gordimer, *Burger's Daughter*, p. 193. The ethical significance of this lapse from human agency is enormous. Fifteen pages later, Rosa herself is horrified when she sees a black man abusing a donkey, seeming to act within a discourse of cruelty, signifying a self-perpetuating violent dynamo, seemingly unhinged from human will: 'I didn't see the whip. I saw the agony . . . I saw the infliction of pain broken away from the will that creates it; broken loose, a force existing of itself, ravishment without ravisher, torture without torturer, rampage, pure cruelty gone beyond control of the humans who have spent thousands of years devising it' (*Burger's Daughter*, p. 208). Juxtaposed with her own ethico-moral détente, this incident exposes Rosa as participating in exactly what appals her: a self-abdication (forgoing human agency) that facilitates an inertia of cruelty.

64 Steiner, *After Babel*, p. 194.

65 Gordimer, *Burger's Daughter*, p. 183 (italics added).

66 ' . . . when we chat, it is no longer we who speak.' Marcel Proust, *In Search of Lost Time*, vol. 2 (London: Chatto & Windus, 1992) (translated by Scott Moncrieff and Kilmartin), p. 263. Note, however, that in this passage, Proust also writes that the development of the artist is 'purely internal'. He portrays all conversation, all friendship, as a departure from artistic growth which, for him, is like the trees 'which draw from their own sap the next knot that will appear on their trunks, the spreading roof of their foliage' (p. 263). Enough will have been said in the introduction about Gordimer's rejection of artistic self-sufficiency – incestuous self-reproduction – to clarify that on this point she differs from Proust's protagonist. For Proust's protagonist, all talk is chat (worthless). For Gordimer, some talk is mere chat, but some rises to Dialogue.

If the archive is to be more than a mausoleum – the archivist more than an embalmer — what will the archive and archivist look like? What work may the archivist do? How to reconcile the archivist's *disciplinary* function with the indispensable fecundity of life left (somehow) alone? If the archive is a collective, communal or institutional record, can we *comprehend* an archiving methodology – one of 'anarchic and subversive pervasiveness', Steiner might say – that is so audacious as to renounce civic (perhaps also existential self-) governance itself?

A dictionary – that unruffled archive of meaning – says that to comprehend is to '1. Grasp mentally, understand 2. include.'[67] So even were one somehow to comprehend an anarchist methodology of the archive, this would merely defer the disciplinary moment (to the operations of the comprehending mind) rather than abolish it (by implementing somehow anarchist or non-disciplinary archiving principles). Thus the phenomenology of the archive – what the archive can *be* – is bounded (indeterminately, contestably) by the community of onlookers who are always more than merely passive observers, who must for instance accord the archive its recognition as such, must determine the real meaning of what the archive includes. *The expansiveness of the archive therefore hinges on the collective farsightedness of these onlookers, on their ability to re-cognise – to rethink – what counts as part of the archive, what the contents of the archive are and ought to be, mean and ought to mean.*

These onlookers (participants, really) are essential because the unacknowledged archive, the archive with no participants, like the imagined empty auditorium of *The Late Bourgeois World*, is both abject and comedic (think how royal-mindedly Imelda Marcos filled her closet with all those shoes, a podiatric archive that could amuse, versus appal, only after her fall from power and towards harmlessness, only after the eventual seizure of her overseas assets, which the excessive footwear aptly symbolised).

Imelda's path from the awe-inspiring dictatortress to the ludic unshod suggests that the rules of recognition,[68] by which societies acknowledge archives, have some relation to state power, legitimate or otherwise. The sanction of state or political power can enhance, its absence deflate, the archival status of a given entity.[69] Thus South Africa's own state-sponsored archive (or archival process), the Truth and Reconciliation Commission, commands a spectrum from enthusiastic allegiance to surly acquiescence, and even those who question its legitimacy cannot deny its materiality.

Nevertheless, others than the state also influence the recognition and

67 *Oxford Paperback Dictionary* (Oxford: Oxford University Press, 1994), p. 163.

68 The allusion here is to jurisprudential debates about how societies organise themselves to recognise what counts as a law. See for example H. L. A. Hart, *The Concept of Law* (Oxford: Clarendon Press, 1961) outlining how systems of 'secondary' rules, such as constitutional ones, assist in determining the bindingness or otherwise of ostensible 'primary' rules, such as that you must stop your car at red lights. See also Derrida, *Archive Fever*, pp. 2, 4. ('A science of the archive must include the theory of [its] institutionalization, that is to say, the theory both of the law which begins by inscribing itself there and of the right which authorizes it.')

69 The inverse also holds: not only is the archive parasitic on power; power is conversely parasitic on the archive: 'there is no political power without control of the archive, if not of memory'. (Derrida, *Archive Fever*, p. 4, footnote 1)

vitality of a society's archive, or of what we should perhaps call its archival milieu, the patterns of habit, intuition, doubt, solidarity, resistance, rebellion, affinity and aversion that contribute to collective self-knowledge as well as to the individual self-knowledge of citizens.

Only outright dogma (an archive just is much narrower than that) or a perhaps laudable concern for efficient administration (the professional archivist cannot arrive Monday mornings at a 'milieu', can draw no paycheck from that) can deem inadmissible these broader social processes in the construction of the archive. As Derrida puts it, 'effective democratization can always be measured by this essential criterion: the participation in and access to the archive, its constitution, and its interpretation'.[70] And once these social processes are admitted as constitutive of the archive, we will probably seek tools of increasing subtlety in order to comprehend the rules of recognition, defining the archive and supplying its contents, at work among us. Through law, history, sociology, media studies, the gamut of positivist inquiry, we will learn certain things (apartheid hit squads did *this*, not *that*) about which only the reckless will be dismissive. But for the more subtle outer banks of sensibility we may seek, beyond positivisms, the artefacts of imagination.

Thus Nadine Gordimer suggests that the novelist extends the vision of those archival onlookers (the citizens) whose vision constrains what the archive can be: 'What is a novel', writes Gordimer quoting Joseph Conrad, 'if not a conviction of our fellow men's existence strong enough to take upon itself a form of imagined life clearer than reality.' The novelist has a searchlight and can 'rescue work carried out in darkness'.[71] Gordimer even uses the language of geographic exploration (and, unintentionally, of conquest?) in describing the 'true purpose' of fiction as 'the discovery and registration of the human world'.[72] In 1979, she praised V. S. Naipaul because, in his best work, he 'expresses a whole consciousness that has not been expressed before'.[73] So the novelist becomes explorer of previously unknown reaches of an existential archive, opening up new vistas of farsightedness, expanding society's sense of what its archive, the components of its collective selfhood, can be. She expands our facility, in the vocabulary of Cavell and Wittgenstein, for human attunement.

In a paper entitled 'Writing the Nation', delivered in Santiago, Chile on 3 November 1998, Gordimer summed up the mix of conservation, creativity and subversion that the novelist brings to her role as archivist of self and society: 'The writer is both repository of the people's ethos, and the revelation to them of themselves. This revelation is what regimes fear, in their writers.'

70 Derrida, *Archive Fever*, p. 4, footnote 1.

71 Gordimer, *Writing and Being*, pp. 6–7 (quoting Joseph Conrad).

72 Ibid., p. 19 (quoting Frank Kermode).

73 Gordimer in Bazin and Seymour, eds., *Conversations*, p. 106.

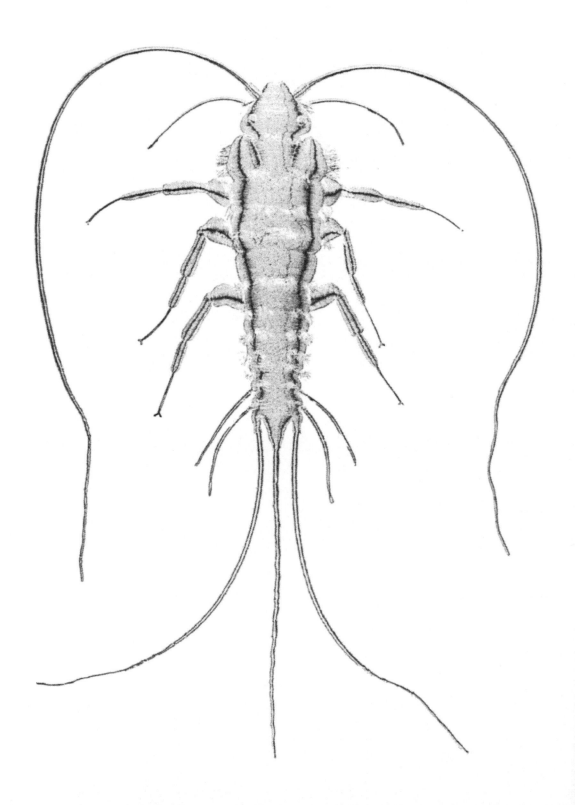

Electronic Record-keeping, Social Memory and Democracy*

David Bearman

Introduction

In his invitation to me to speak in the Refiguring the Archive seminar series, Verne Harris wrote that my contribution was to be 'part of a series exploring the role of archives in memory and knowledge construction. The key objective is to marry this exploration to South Africa's transition to democracy and reintegration in the global economy.' He asked me, 'In this context, then, what are the implications of electronic record-keeping? How can we ensure that electronic records contribute creatively to social memory and support democratic processes?'

In addressing his questions I am not exploring the symbolic or abstract archive but concrete records as kept or destroyed by organisations, in particular by government. And I am not examining the personal meanings of such archives[1] or their cultural uses and misuses after they have been collected[2] but rather the risks to legitimacy posed by the normally undocumented practices by which records are initially selected for archival retention. Despite the somewhat philosophical sounding title, the solutions advanced here are entirely pragmatic and addressed to policy makers weighing concrete options for programme structuring rather than to theoretical debate.

While I am advancing recommendations for South Africa's electronic records I do not know when South Africa will create significant electronic records. In ignorance of the South African technical landscape, I must focus exclusively on how to establish the policy frameworks, professional mindset and technical infrastructure for when this occurs. Additionally, I must stress that this essay is not about paper records at all. Although the theoretical possibility of transforming paper to electronic storage formats exists, it does not carry with it the different cost-benefit ratios that make electronic record-keeping desirable. I am sure that much scanning of traditional records will take place to promote access or preservation, but I am explicitly eschewing the offer of any suggestions here as to the implications or desirability of retrospective conversion to electronic formats.[3]

What I am contending is that the role of the archivist in modern society is untenable unless the archivist can engineer a means of serving two masters with conflicting expectations and authority. The archivist

* This chapter was prepared and presented in 1998. Recent reflections by the author on these themes are cited at http://www.archimuse.com/consulting/bearman

1 As explored by Jacques Derrida in *Archive Fever* and his contribution to this seminar series.

2 As brilliantly discussed by Martin Hall in 'Blackbirds and black butterflies' in this volume. Hall asserts the power of the material evidence, which pre-electronic records certainly possess, while I am examining only the post-physical electronically created evidence. At the heart of both our treatments, however, is the importance of authentic records. Protecting the authentic record from physical destruction is easy with electronic records, which can be rapidly and cheaply copied and thus protected by distribution; but ensuring authentic records can be more difficult with electronic records because only quite sophisticated systems and users can distinguish real from fabricated evidence.

3 My view is that copying records to promote access or preservation, whether into electronic formats or onto microfilm, is not fundamentally an archival policy decision but rather a social policy decision. Depending on the way it is done, who is involved and how it contributes to other social purposes, it may be beneficial, but that is beside the point of this article.

must find grounds on which these conflicting authorities can agree about archival decisions or the legitimacy of the enterprise will be threatened. Archives of disputed legitimacy are a source of social conflict rather than a means to resolve social conflict. In a new and fragile democracy archives must be carefully constructed on grounds of agreed legitimacy in order to contribute to building a shared social memory on which stable democracy rests.

SERVING TWO MASTERS

Society expects the archivist to create a bias-free record (imagining that archivists play little or no role in shaping the record in any case) and to protect it against political and other pressures. The archivists' employer, the state or an organisation, expects the archivist to create the record it needs, can afford and is able to live with. The state is largely indifferent to any greater social or moral imperative than itself.

This conflict in the loyalties of the archivist is relatively severe in any society in which there is tension between citizens and the state. In the United States, it erupts in periodic legal battles in which the archivist is sued in the public interest.[4] In Australia it seems to take the form of the archivist being fired by the administration s/he serves for putting public interests above its own.[5] The tension faced by a newly democratising country is especially great since new political and social institutions seem fragile and in need of protection (including protection from too thorough exposure) while the demands of the general society for legitimising documentation are strident, if inchoate.

Even though sophisticated academics and cynical politicians have abandoned it, the naive citizen still believes in 'Truth' with a capital T and assumes the possibility, and indeed the imperative, of bias-free records. The citizenry is almost unaware that the archivist has, historically, shaped the record dramatically by selecting what to keep.[6] The nature of the shaping depends on many factors including 'objective' criteria that seem 'obvious', like the destruction of copies of records in offices other than the office of their origin. But no matter how 'objective' or well justified, trimming the records changes the story. We know from experience that different decisions will be taken depending on how long after the event the records disposition takes place.[7]

The society, meanwhile, shapes social memory for different reasons but with equally distorting effects. What we remember is that which we choose not to forget. Just as individuals choose to forget, or to remember only what they need to get by, a society as a whole chooses

4   The National Archivist in every US Presidential administration for the past twenty years has been named in major lawsuits. State archives are not immune.

5   Western Australia, Victoria and Queensland have had the most notorious incidents at the state level in the past twenty years, but they are not alone.

6   Eric Ketelaar has noted the cultural context of this act, extending the personal aspect noted by Derrida in his essay 'Archivalisation and archiving', published in *Archives and Manuscripts* 27 (1999), pp. 54–61.

7   This is a strand in a broader discussion of just why it is that archivists perversely insist on making such decisions once and for all rather than over time. Elsewhere, recently, I have argued that the archivist would be better served deciding to keep records another x years, than deciding to keep them forever, and that disposal decisions could be simplified by incremental appraisal. See David Bearman, *Archival Methods* (Pittsburgh: Archives & Museum Informatics, 1989) and 'Archival strategies', *American Archivist* 58 (1995), pp. 380–413.

the past that it needs and on which it can construct a future.[8] This is, of course, not bad, but necessary. However, it means that whatever record the archivist selects to keep, it will be confronted in time by a social memory that contradicts it. Connections made after events will not be substantiated by the record and many factors that weighed during the process will no longer seem significant.

If the archivist's decision process was understood and accepted, this contradiction would be seen for what it is and accepted. But if the selection process (and hence decisions made by the archivist) have not received social sanction in advance, the society will judge that archivists have distorted the past unacceptably. It will be easy to find evidence that this is true because archivists are as much members of society as their fellow citizens. Like their contemporaries, they will not have seen the importance of certain facts and will have overestimated the importance of others. Even the best and most professional archivists, keenly aware of the importance of their jobs, and anxious to create an accurate record, will tend to think of the routine acts of their society as without interest and view the received explanations of how policy was arrived at without suspicion. Both of these they must do to survive as members of that society, but fifty years later their bias will have shaped a record that many will come to suspect is untrue.

Can archivists articulate an explicit basis for appraisal that is accepted by their professional colleagues and society? What would such a framework look like? In a manual for archival appraisal published by the UNESCO Records and Archives Management Program (RAMP) in 1991, Terry Cook, the leading Canadian theorist of appraisal, advanced the extraordinarily radical thesis that the published record of government will adequately portray the missions of government agencies and their programmatic intentions – archivists need not concern themselves with adding yet more to that story.[9] Instead, he suggested, only in the record of the transaction between the citizen and the state will the actual texture and import of that interaction be documented. The archivists' duty, he suggested, was to document the discrepancies between the official policies and documented practices of the agencies of government and the experience of citizens interacting with the state.

We could hardly ask for stronger evidence of the near impossibility of serving these two masters. Terry's suggestion, made to help archivists reduce the bulk of gigantic series of routine files of personal interactions with government, places archivists in direct opposition to the interests of the state that employs them. Whether we accept Terry's conclusions or not, the logic of his position leads to the same conclusion: some deci-

8   Major undertakings, such as Germany's 'recovery' of its memory of the Holocaust and Israel's recent reinterpretation of Palestinian history in its school texts, are examples of societies facing a need for a different future, reconstructing a different past on which to build it.

9   Terry Cook, UNESCO Records and Archives Management Program (RAMP) (1991).

sion must be made that will result in retaining, or disposing, of those files which document the individual experience in interaction with the state. If the archivist, and the record, are to be legitimised, the state and the citizen must be brought to place the same value on these files.

However much archivists wish to have their retention decisions understood and the process made transparent and accountable, decisions about keeping paper records must be carried out by individuals and their execution will vary. Methods of managing electronic records, on the other hand, virtually require that such decisions be executed algorithmically following explicit rules. As a consequence, these rules can be subject to debate and to agreement between parties. Rule-based retention decisions can build trust in records and in the government whose records are being retained.

ARCHIVIST AS RISK MANAGER

Archivists have been generally unwilling to cede that their role as absolute arbiter of truth is unacceptable. Protesting their professionalism, they have urged the society to accept their judgements. The prospect of systems that automatically execute records retention determinations is not one that appeals to most archivists. But their protestation of innocence when there is suspicion that they are manipulating the record is futile so long as the rules by which they make determinations cannot be examined openly. Ultimately, the archivist needs to have the state and the citizens understand and accept the basis for selection of the record and to acknowledge the trade-offs being made.

To obtain such a sanction, archivists would be best served by adopting the role of the manager of a process that sets known benefits and current costs against future, long-term and unknown risks. I recognise that this has been unattractive to the types of individuals drawn to archives who are humanists with largely non-technical training. Not only do these people find the many layers of reality an attraction and the reduction of their judgement to formulae offensive, but they are ill-equipped by training to take a more engineered approach. Nevertheless, I believe that this is in fact the correct way for archivists to make decisions and, ultimately, to gain the respect of their dual masters. It may be the only way forward in nations in which the legitimacy of the archive has the potential to be a major political liability.

Let us first acknowledge that any society has a certain quantity of its resources to expend on the preservation of its record. This quantity is not only finite but relatively small. Historically the equation has been different for different civilisations and times, with ancient China and the Jewish diaspora perhaps making the greatest investments. But societies do not need to believe that they are the only civilisation, or the true civilisation, to make comparatively large investments in archives – the modern Dutch state makes a relatively large investment because this is an important element in its civil ideology.

Regardless of the sums (and these can be increased or decreased with the political skills of the archivist), the finite amount that can be expended should be openly allocated with conscious risk assessment. A society that openly decides to take certain risks with its records will be in a better position to demand that appropriate actions be taken to ensure the preservation of those records that it has determined should be retained. Besides, identifying the nature of the risks allows the society to take measures against them, some of which go beyond the sphere of archives policy: legal actions and redefinitions, taxation incentives, adoption of technical standards and the like.

Serious risk analysis is a technical process leading to a political decision. Each supports the other. In so far as archival activity will distort the record (and any disposal of records will) it is preferable to undertake it consciously, systematically, and as a result of political decisions based on expert assessments of risks rather than as a consequence of unweighed judgements, however well-meaning. Not only do such decisions then themselves remain a matter of record, explaining the subsequent loss of accountability at whatever level of granularity they were applied, but they can also be applied rigorously, provably, auditably and systematically.

RETHINKING THE APPRAISAL

Archivists call the method by which they cull the historical record, choosing what to keep and what to discard, 'appraisal' or 'scheduling' since the action is often applied at a later date. Archivists assume that appraisal, and subsequent disposition according to the appraisal authority, improve the record. Despite the demonstrated difficulty of actually getting around to appraising most records, and the often less-than-impressive implementation of such findings, archivists have made appraisal the core of their professional contribution to record-keeping.[10] Appraisal costs a lot of money, even when it works, but the case made for it by archivists is based less on study than on 'common sense'. After all, the archivist will assure you, the goal of having fewer records is achieved first by reducing redundancy, then by disposing of

10 In *Archival Methods* and elsewhere I have argued that appraisal as currently practised does not work, gets the wrong records, costs so much that it cannot be applied to all records, and focuses on the wrong thing – records instead of the transactions that generate them. Leonard Rapport documented the failure of appraisal to actually retain useful content in his classic article 'No grandfather clause: reappraising accessioned records', *American Archivist* 44 (1981), pp. 143–150, which has been studiously ignored in the archival literature since.

routine, uninteresting records and 'housekeeping' records, and ulti-mately by disposing of records relating to internal decision processes while saving the decisions themselves. The trimmed result is, they say, easier to document, less costly to manage, quicker to search, and faster to retrieve from.

Archivists acknowledge that the incompleteness is, of course, a trade-off, but suggest that their methods are safe and effective. Yes, the reduced record can never be as complete. Yes, it is by definition biased in some way. Yes, significant effort is expended in the appraisal process. But archivists have not seen an alternative. In the world of paper records, despite evidence to the contrary that showed they were not working, these rationales held firm and seemed like facts of life.

Each of these commonsense rationales for appraisal, however, breaks down in the face of the realities of electronic records management, whose cost factors are fundamentally different. I explored this in a minor way in a critique several years ago of the National Archives of Canada report on their appraisal of the Free Trade Negotiation files. These files, from numerous different offices of the Canadian govern-ment, were all sent to the National Archives after the conclusion of the NFTA treaty. In total they amounted to 100 MB of wordprocessing files from a variety of then current wordprocessing systems. Two pro-fessional archivists worked for six months to assess these files and decide what to keep – reducing the volume to 10 MB. Given that storage costs for this final volume of data were less than $20 at today's back-up stor-age prices, it should be obvious that investing in value-added retrieval or ignoring this fonds altogether would have made more economic sense *and* avoided the possibility of bad decision-making that could come to light ten or twenty years from now.[11] What exactly was the hurry? In this case there was an element of experimentalism involved combined with a sense, of the software dependency of so much mid-1990s data. Fair enough, but not the basis for a regular policy.

After disposing of duplicate records it is now more cost-effective and will in the long term be more beneficial for retrieval, simply to retain all electronically created records digitally. If electronic records are truly redundant (and identity can be established quickly by an automated process), 'keeping' two copies requires no more than an additional index entry. If we discover that they are slightly different we can avoid the drawback of traditional appraisal, which might have disposed of potentially important information, and keep both copies electronically at very little extra cost. If documentation of records as evidence occurs as an automated process at the time of record creation

11 There are obvious parallels between this situation and that of the Truth and Reconciliation Commission, which I hope to have the opportunity to explore with South African National Archives staff.

DAVID BEARMAN

and is, indeed, the basis on which disposal decisions would be made anyway, then documenting records that are retained is no easier if some or even a large quantity are disposed of. As against the costs of the appraisal process itself (involving labour), the costs of storage (mainly hardware) are trivial and easily recovered by the reduced costs of implementing appraisals. It costs essentially the same to manage the full record as it does to manage the appraised and reduced version. Finally, the increase in speed of discovery made possible by reducing the volume of records is trivial, while the loss of precision and recall could be very great indeed.

What then is holding back the formulation of government policies to retain the electronic record in its entirety subject only to automatic disposal processes? Fear. There is the fear of politicians of too complete a record. There is the fear by bureaucrats (including archivists) of loss of control. And, of course, there is the lack of popular awareness of the problem or demand for a more effective solution. In countries where the risks of disposal are very high, due to tension or lack of social cohesion or distrust of government, the case for these policies is greater. South Africa may be the perfect place to break through the barrier created by fears since the prospect of loss of legitimacy is a far greater risk. Will South Africa be the first to make it?

BASIS OF ELECTRONIC RECORDKEEPING

Before answering such a question, we need to take a detour to explore just what it is that needs to be done.

It was fashionable a few years ago, for largely ideological reasons, to stress that electronic records did not change anything basic about archival practices. However, while they do not change deep-level principles, electronic records do change the economic, political, social and technological context of record creation, maintenance and use. As such, we need to look carefully at whether, and if so how, they might alter the conundrum we have just described of archivists serving masters with different agendas in an environment where every decision they make results in a differently biased record.

I believe that, in principle, electronic record-keeping could help for the simplest of all reasons – it is possible to design, and probably implement,[12] a cost-effective electronic record-keeping system in which archivists select what to keep with explicitly stated abstract rules that can be reviewed by outside authorities and will operate exactly as anticipated without room for human judgement.

12 My caution here is that implementation is always specific to the setting, and I frankly know much too little about South Africa to know what the hurdles would be or whether they can be overcome.

In this system the definition of what constitutes a record would be grounded in social consensus and expressed in data specifications. The record would be captured at the moment of its creation in its digital I/O format with appropriate metadata and a copy only would be passed to the recipient. The archival copy would resist all tampering and automatically destruct at the time it was scheduled to be destroyed. Until then it would be available only to those with proper authority and its uses could be logged. I have described such a system in a Reference Model for Business Acceptable Communication and in detailed work over the past four years.[13] It has been tested in city governments, universities and states in the United States and, despite problems in understanding my sometimes poor documentation, it has been found to work.

Such a system could be used to protect against purposive (interventionist) distortions of the record and to ensure that only articulated strategies govern retention. It could be used to ensure that records of higher-level decision-making were available to the archive. It does not change whom the archivist works for. It is likely to decrease overall costs (though we do not know this for sure) while making available many records that have not been included before.

Over time the approach is likely to cost less annually with each year. Not only is it able to take advantage of an independent trend in electronic storage, whose costs are halving every 18 months, but its costs will not increase with implementation of new hardware and software by the agencies, as do other approaches to electronic record-keeping

It is even imaginable to reach a social consensus to keep all electronic records of government; the costs of initially keeping all the records traditionally created by government are well within the same order of magnitude of expense as the cost of appraising them, and total retention reduces costs sufficiently in the future to make it plausibly less expensive to retain all records rather than expending human energies to decide which to keep (and risking human biases in the selection).

OPTIONS FOR CUSTODY IN RECORD-KEEPING

For political and pragmatic reasons there are many pressures to distribute the archives. The provinces want to have their record close at hand, the agencies are reluctant to part physically with records they use in their day-to-day business even if remote access is assured, and people like to have local repositories with records relating to their lives nearby.

13 David Bearman, 'Item level control and electronic recordkeeping', *Archives and Museum Informatics* 10, ch. 3, pp. 195–245. http://www.lis.pitt.edu/~nhprc/item-lvl.html. Extensions of this work are provided by National Archives of Australia, Recordkeeping Metadata Standard for Commonwealth Agencies, June 1999, see www.naa.gov.au, and Jusine Heazlewood et al., 'Electronic records: problem solved?', *Archives and Manuscripts* 27 (1999), pp. 96–113.

The advantages of distributing electronic archives are many, and there are few, if any, negative consequences, so it may be that the electronic record provides a way to satisfy the demand for distribution of the record and for improving public access. In the context of United States archival policy and for Australia I have argued that distributed custody is more likely to support the aims of the archives than is the effort to gather electronic records under a single physical control. This position assumes that the distributed or central electronic data support services are equally able, or the distributed services better able than the National Archives, to support the functional requirements of record-keeping. In South Africa, where telecommunications are still less reliable, even more reasons for distributing multiple copies of the archives can be imagined – it also provides a framework for easily implementing redundancy as the basic long-term protection strategy.

Tactically, the direction for government might be to outsource the effort, as private or academic operators would not be seen as having a political bias. Policies could be drafted that enabled universities or agencies to bid on managing parts of the archives, although whether the attitudes of individuals and organisations will support entrepreneurial government remains to be seen.

Conclusions

In short, I believe that the position of the archivist cannot simply be asserted in society: it must be negotiated and accepted. Particularly with respect to decisions about disposition of records, fragile cohesion can best be strengthened by open agreement on articulated outcomes. Electronic records require a more explicit, rule-based formulation of retention policies, and, because of their different economic factors, provide a locus for radical departure from prior practice. In particular, the range of options for South Africa in managing its electronic records includes the retention of the broadest possible electronic record at very close to the lowest cost. Because this is possible, and could forge a stronger bond among South Africans and between citizens and the state, it seems only reasonable to begin immediately to construct an infrastructure and policy framework for the systematic retention and control of electronic records of the South African government. Your social memory and democratic society may depend on it. There is no reason why South Africa cannot, in this respect, lead the world.

Blackbirds and Black Butterflies

Martin Hall

Mauritsstad, Brazil, 1636: 'since the local moradores knew his taste and inclination, each one brought him whatever rare bird or beast he could find in the back-lands. There he brought parrots, macaws, jacifs, canindes, wading-birds, pheasants, guinea-fowl, ducks, swans, peacocks, turkeys, a great quantity of barnyard-fowls, and so many doves that they could not be counted . . . in short there was not a curious thing in Brazil which he did not have . . .' (Father Manuel Calado)[1]

Sarajevo, Bosnia, 1992: 'black, sooty, still hot, butterflies . . . books and papers aflame, the library's treasure . . . flying around and falling over distant parts of the city'. (Ivan Lovrenović)[2]

I

In 1636, Prince Johan Maurits van Nassau-Siegen sailed from Amsterdam to take up his position as governor of the Dutch West India Company colony in Brazil; a charge that included South America, the Caribbean and the West African coast. Maurits' entourage included botanists, astronomers and artists and the governor established a botanical garden into which he attempted to gather every species of plant and animal: 'every kind of bird and animal that he could find . . . parrots, macaws, jacifs, canindes, wading-birds, pheasants, guinea-fowl, ducks, swans, peacocks, turkeys, a great quantity of barnyard-fowls . . . tigers, ounces, cissuarana, ant-bears, apes, quati, squirrel-monkeys, Indian boars, goats from Cape Verde, sheep from Angola, cutia, pagua, tapirs, wild boars, a great multitude of rabbits . . .'[3] When Maurits returned to the Netherlands he turned his palace at The Hague into a private museum of his Brazilian collections and, years later, sent a 'curiosity cabinet' to Louis XIV in the hope that its contents would be used as models in the Gobelin tapestry factory and woven into a perpetual representation of his achievements.[4]

Among Maurits' entourage was a young illustrator, Zacharias Wagenaer. In his subsequent career, first with the Dutch West India Company and then with the Dutch East India Company, Wagenaer

1 Fr Manuel Calado, in C. R. Boxer, *The Dutch in Brazil, 1624–1654* (Oxford: Clarendon Press, 1957).

2 I. Lovrenović, *The Hatred of Memory: In Sarajevo, Burned Books and Murdered Pictures* (New York: New York Times, 1994).

3 Calado, in Boxer, p. 116.

4 R. Smith, 'The Brazilian landscapes of Frans Post', *Arts Quarterly* 1, 4 (1938), pp. 238–267; M. Benisovich, 'The history of the Tenture des Indes', *Burlington Magazine* 83, 486 (1943), pp. 216–225.

5   O. H. Spohr, *Zacharias Wagenaer. Second Commander of the Cape* (Cape Town: A. A. Balkema, 1967).

6   S. Gray, *Southern African Literature: An Introduction* (Cape Town: David Philip, 1979).

7   The Mauritshuis can be accessed through http://www.nbt.nl. An example of a digital Gobelin tapestry (the original is available for $17 000) can be found at http://www.rodingallery.com.

8   M. Poster, *The Mode of Information: Poststructuralism and Social Context* (Cambridge: Polity Press, 1990); M. Poster, *The Second Media Age* (Cambridge: Polity Press, 1995).

9   This is a problem of the last decade of the millennium. A survey of national libraries in various countries carried out in 1989 showed that few were actively involved in issues raised by electronic material, although it was recognised that a great deal of information was being lost (P. McCormick and M. Williamson, 'Legal deposit and electronic publishing. Results of a survey', *Alexandria* 2, 3 (1990), pp. 51–63). Ten years on, the situation is very different with a widespread recognition that archiving dispersed digital information poses many problems. For example, the issue of 'non-tangible' forms of information was raised in the United Kingdom in a 1997 Department of Heritage consultation paper (D. Stoker, 'Tangible deposits', *Journal of Librarianship and Information Science* 29, 2 [1997], pp. 65–68; J. Lyon, 'The nation's virtual memory', *Information World Review* 124 ([997], p. 9.); has led to the establishment of the Nordic Digital Library Centre (S. Hedberg, 'Authorities and electronic publishing: an overview of the efforts to apply library legislation and established organizational patterns to electronic publications', *Alexandria* 8, 2 [1996], pp. 135–142.); and has prompted legal revisions of legal deposit legislation in France (O. de Solan, 'Les documents informatiques et l'avenir du dépôt légal', *Bulletin des Bibliothèques de France* 40,4 [1995], pp. 28-32; C. Vayssade, 'Le dépôt légal des documents informatiques', *Bulletin des Bibliothèques de France* 40, 3 [1995], pp. 34–38).

moved around the outer reaches of Europe's colonial world, seeing service in Japan and then as the Company's commander at the Cape of Good Hope.[5] Here, his major task was the construction of the new Castle. The foundation stone was laid in 1666 and the Company's chronicler embellished the archive with a poem:

> Thus more and more the kingdoms are extended,
> Thus more and more are black and yellow spread.
> Thus from the ground a wall of stone is raised,
> On which the thundering brass can no impression make.
> For Hottentots the walls are always earthen,
> But now we come with stone to boast before all men,
> And terrify not only Europeans, but also
> Asians, Americans and savage Africans.
> Thus holy Christendom is glorified,
> Establishing its seat amidst the savage heathens,
> We praise the great director and say with one another,
> Augustus' dominion nor conquering Alexander,
> Nor Caesar's mighty genius has ever had the glory
> To lay a cornerstone at earth's extremest end![6]

Today, the discovery of new things and the curation and distribution of knowledge of the world seem very different. Time and space – 'earth's extremest end' – have been conquered and digital images are dispersed across continents and oceans without the need for zoological collections, intermediaries such as artists, or the travails of tapestry-makers. Maurits' house in The Hague can be visited from anywhere through the World Wide Web, and the Gobelin works can be rendered digitally on any computer screen.[7] It has been suggested that this new 'media age' – the constant mêlée of communication and response across vast but inconsequential distances – is creating multiple, disseminated and decentred human subjects, a different sort of consciousness that has no need of 'walls of stone'.[8]

What are the implications of this digital world for the concept of the archive? Presumably, Maurits had no doubt that he was collecting rare and valuable things that would be preserved and displayed as part of a record and history of endeavour and discovery, and *generations of curators and archivists have been dedicated to this idea. The archive has been, above all else, a place of containment and safety, a mausoleum for the original, the rare and the exotic, a temple to erudition where civility and silence are expected. But now, at the turn of the millennium, things seem different. Archivists can be less certain that there is such a thing as an 'original'.[9] The British Library – as always a suitable monument to the times – has established a 'digital library', 'the use of digital technologies to acquire, store, conserve, and provide access to information and material in whatever form it was originally published'. Digital documents are available on demand, anywhere at anytime, and are held in more than one place, with a provenance in more than one institution; the antithesis of the conventional archive.[10] David Bearman (this volume) sees the distributed, electronic archive as the inevitable way of the future.

The concept of the digital world is firmly rooted in contemporary fantasy, whether this be the utopian vision of a new frontier, a post-bureaucratic civil society,[11] or the dystopian futures of cyberpunk – Neal Stephenson's[12] Hiro Protagonist racing through a virtual world to prevent the infocalypse. Such fantasies assume an 'information society' in which the traditional archive and the tangible assemblages of treasures that it contains are an anachronism. Cyberspace is seen as a 'virtual habitat' in which creative potential is realised and extended globally.[13] This is best represented in the work of one of the cyber-world's patriarchs. Howard Rheingold's *Virtual Reality*[14] and *The Virtual Community: Homesteading on the Electronic Frontier*[15] have been extraordinarily influential in mapping a new paradise. For Rheingold, Virtual Reality is transformative, 'a kind of new contract between humans and computers, an arrangement that could grant us great power, and perhaps change us irrevocably in the process',[16] while Virtual Communities are 'social aggregations that emerge from the Net when enough people carry on those public discussions long enough, with sufficient human feeling, to form webs of personal relationships in cyberspace'.[17]

This vision is exemplified in the Whole Earth Lectronic Link (the WELL), which grew from the Whole Earth Catalog in the 1980s. In its own words, the WELL is 'an online gathering place like no other – remarkably uninhibited, intelligent, and iconoclastic . . . a cluster of electronic villages that live on the Internet, with denizens from all over the globe . . . More than just another "site" or "home page," The WELL has a sense of place that is palpable.'[18] Visions such as these imply that such forms of computer-mediated communication make the old distinction between individual and community redundant because of the capacity of meeting individual and the community needs simultaneously. All will have access to this nirvana, which will be the 'spirit of community' – 'the subjective criterion of togetherness, a feeling of connectedness that confers a sense of belonging'.[19]

10 British Library Research and Innovation Centre; http://portico.bl.uk/services/ric/legal/.

11 B. Loader, 'The governance of cyberspace: politics, technology and global restructuring' in B. Loader, ed., *The Governance of Cyberspace: Politics, Technology and Global Restructuring* (London: Routledge, 1997), pp. 1–19.

12 N. Stephenson, *Snow Crash* (New York: Bantam Books, 1992).

13 D. Carter, '"Digital democracy" or "information aristocracy"? Economic regeneration and the information economy' in Loader, ed., *The Governance of Cyberspace*, pp. 136–152.

14 H. Rheingold, *Virtual Reality* (New York: Simon and Schuster, 1991).

15 H. Rheingold, *The Virtual Community: Homesteading on the Electronic Frontier* (Reading: Addison-Wesley, 1993).

16 Rheingold, *Virtual Reality*, pp. 386–387.

17 Rheingold, *The Virtual Community*, p. 5.

18 www.well.com.

19 D. Foster, 'Community and identity in the electronic village' in D. Porter, ed., *Internet Culture* (London: Routledge, 1997), p. 29.

In this essay I take a different view. Starting with recent work that links the global flow of information and the construction of local identity as an inseparable connection, I argue that the material evidence of the past is central to the ways in which identities are understood and maintained in today's global world. I want to show that the ethnic nationalisms that are increasingly a feature of the post-1989 world *inevitably* use and manipulate manuscripts, records, artefacts and architecture – either through conscious manipulation, or else because the varied records of the past trap us in identities that we cannot escape. The form of this refiguring of the archive tends towards a distinctive combination of local agency and global flows of information.

Unlike Bearman (this volume), who sees the distributed electronic archive as a means towards participatory democracy, I argue that the distinctive combination of local agency and digital media results in new sites of violence. Seventeenth-century conquests and nineteenth-century imperial possessions were a long way, in space and time, from Europe's metropolitan heartlands. Consequently, the accessions of the great archives of empire were sanitised of the blood and violence that was often inseparable from their acquisitions. The galleries of the British Museum, for example, display treasures from Africa, South America and the East in reconstituted ethnographies; the mundane brutalities of conquest and dispossession are rarely represented. In the British Museum's collections are parts of bodies collected from around the world – including shrunken heads stored in brown cardboard boxes and available for study by *bona fide* researchers.[20] But this separation from the viscera of conquest depends on distance in time and space, allowing the illusion of a detached and objective 'science of mankind'. Now the world economies of the past four centuries are being superseded by a global system, 'an economy with the capacity to work as a unit in real time on a planetary scale'. As a consequence of the quantum increase in computer performance and the capacity and speed of telecommunications, space now organises time.[21] Distance is dead, and death seems to be returning to the centre, taking the form of ethnic violence, racism and hate politics across Europe and North America; what Arjun Appadurai[22] has called the 'heart of whiteness'.

II

Maurits' archive of conquest was one of many that followed from Europe's colonial expansion and from the transport of the exotic and

20 P. Skotnes, ed., *Miscast: Negotiating the Presence of the Bushmen* (Cape Town: UCT Press, 1996).

21 M. Castells, *The Information Age: Economy, Society and Culture*, vol. 1: *The Rise of the Network Society* (Oxford: Blackwell, 1996), pp. 92, 376.

22 A. Appadurai, *Modernity at Large: Cultural Dimensions of Globalization* (Minneapolis: University of Minnesota Press, 1996).

rare from the perimeter of the known world to its core. Such zoological, botanical and ethnographic collections form one category in a typology that includes national archives, museums and libraries, local records and myriad special collections. Very often, such collections are stored and displayed in monumental buildings that themselves make references to earlier traditions of architecture and culture. In the 'high nationalisms' of modernity, autonomous countries had national archives, libraries and museums in their capitals. Together, such treasure houses of the past formed a vital part of national patrimonies, focal points for learning and discovery, and part of the way in which the 'imagined community' of the nation state was itself curated and sustained.[23] The emblem of knowledge about the past was the respected scholar closeted in a gilded reading room and shielded by a neo-classical portico.

Today, the nation-state is weakened by globalisation and myriad expressions of collective identity:

> caught between these opposing trends, the nation-state is called into question, drawing into its crisis the very notion of political democracy, predicated upon the historical construction of a sovereign, representative nation-state . . . subjects, if and when constructed, are not built any longer on the basis of civil societies, that are in the process of disintegration, but as prolongation of communal resistance.[24]

As a result, it seems simplistic or misleading to map 'national patrimonies'. Archives and artefacts are often dispersed, and circulate in global systems of loan, exchanges and markets. Then again, the archive's treasure is often a simulacrum, simultaneously everywhere in mass media and digital images. There is a parallel dispersal of information, opinion and interpretation. As Edward Said has observed, today everyone can be an organic intellectual.[25] Transnational media feed into the complex construction of local identities and are linked in turn with large-scale movements of people. Contemporary diasporas claim the archive of the homeland and adapt and modify it to local circumstances in faraway places, while local ethnographies gain authority from universal claims for recognition.[26] In turn – and this is the particular point of interest in this essay – this has implications for the concept of place and for the material authority of records of the past.

This can be illustrated by means of one striking example of the connection between global media flows, issues of local identity and competing, violent claims for possession of the material evidence of

23 B. Anderson, *Imagined Communities: Reflections on the Origin and Spread of Nationalism* (London: Verso, 1991).

24 M. Castells, *The Information Age: Economy, Society and Culture* vol. 2: *The Power of Identity* (Oxford: Blackwell, 1997), pp. 2, 11.

25 E. Said, *Culture and Imperialism* (New York: Vintage, 1994).

26 S. Hall, 'Cultural identity and diaspora' in J. Rutherford, ed., *Identity: Community, Culture, Difference* (London: Lawrence and Wishart, 1990), pp. 222–237; Appadurai, *Modernity at Large*.

history – the destruction of a mosque in the northern Indian town of Ayodhya, the consequential violence and worldwide attention. The rise to prominence of India's Bharatiya Janata Party (BJP) began with a sacred pilgrimage through the continent to Ayodhya, birthplace of the god-king Rama. This Rath Yatra was a media event in which aspirations for religious revival – Hindutva – were focused on the outrage that Rama's birthplace had, for the last four centuries, been the site of a mosque.[27] Appeals for the demolition of the Babri Masjid, and the construction of a temple for Lord Rama, were based on interpretations and counter-interpretations of archaeological evidence.[28] Two years later – on 6 December 1992 – the mosque was torn apart, stone by stone, by a crowd fired with religious fervour; an event that received huge media coverage. More than three thousand people died in the subsequent riots between Hindu and Muslim communities across India. Once in power in New Delhi the BJP was committed to Hindutva in the spirit of Lord Rama – asserting Indian sovereignty with a series of nuclear tests that caused a worldwide political crisis. Meanwhile, Hindu revivalism was promoted throughout the world, and particularly through the Web. An example is the electronic journal *Hinduism Today*, based at the Himalayan Academy on the Hawaiian island of Kauai.[29] 'As the new millennium approaches, the world's oldest religion is donning shining new clothes. The age-old Hindu philosophy passed from mouth to mouth in tiny villages across India is now going high-tech . . . bringing . . . every aspect of Sanatana Dharma to millions of Internet users across the world.'[30] In New Delhi, the Vishwa Hindu Parishad (World Hindu Council) challenged BJP political expediency by announcing that massive columns for a reconstructed temple – replicas claimed to be based on authoritative archaeological evidence – were being assembled in secret workshops in preparation for transport to Ayodhya; a campaign that rested on its appeal to a global media.[31]

The example of Ayodhya shows clearly how global media (broadcast coverage of the Rath Yatra and mosque destruction, and Internet sites), the political manipulation of the past (the Bharatiya Janata Party's use of Hindu tradition), the materiality of the archive (the vital importance of the Temple site, the visceral action of the mosque's destruction, and the appeal of the announcement of its secret reconstruction), and violence (the thousands of deaths that followed the assault on Babri Masjid) are all part of a common nexus. Both Arjun Appadurai and Manuel Castells have argued that it is the connection between global media, large-scale movements of people and the con-

27 K. R. Malkani, 'BJP history: its birth, growth and onward march', http://www.bjp.org/history.html (1998).

28 D. Mandal, *Ayodhya: Archaeology after Demolition* (Hyderabad: Orient Longman, 1993).

29 http://www.hinduismtoday.kauai.hi.us/ht_home.html. For a South African-based Hindu site, see http://www.hinduism.co.za.

30 L. Melwani, 'Hey, just who are you guys, anyway?' http://www.hinduismtoday.kauai.hi.us/Newspaper/History/LavinaStory.html, (1998).

31 S. Miglani, 'Hindu group plays archaeology card in temple row', Reuters (1998).

testation of interests and identities on a local scale that renders the late capitalist world so singularly unstable.[32] And, just as diasporic Hindus assert an ethnic identity through claims to Rama's birthplace, so other ethnic identities are asserted through recourse to the past: Croats who have long lived in South America or the United States; Algerian 'guest workers' in Germany; Chinese in Indonesia or Australia; white South Africans in Seattle, California or New Zealand.

Responses to Ayodhya and other flashpoints where ancient rights, traditions and monuments are the ammunition in contemporary political struggles inevitably lead to attributions of primordialism: the conclusion that such conflicts are the consequence of age-old rivalries inherited through the generations. Such assumptions are deeply rooted, and continually sustained in contemporary media: Shakespeare's Montagues and Capulets, revived in futuristic setting in Hollywood's *Romeo and Juliet*; the medieval horror of Africa, canonised by Joseph Conrad in *Heart of Darkness*[33] and sustaining the assumption of the inevitability of genocide in Rwanda. Indeed, the reach and authority of global media allow such assumptions to be rerouted as fact, sustaining the political agendas they are simultaneously reporting. News media present the politics of Ayodhya as an expression of an inevitable clash of ancient and essential titans – Hindu India versus Muslim India. The BJP and many Hindu Web-sites do the same, essentialising Hindutva as the expression of age-old ethnic identities that must always move towards a pure form of their expression. But historical analysis shows how Hindu and Muslim India were colonial constructs – the colonial bureaucratic simplification of thousands of local identities for the purposes of administration and control.[34] And more probing journalism has shown that before the arrival of the Rath Yatra in 1990 the town of Ayodhya accommodated many faiths, temples and mosques, and was relatively untroubled by the domes of the Babri Masjid over the place where Rama was rumoured to have been born.[35] Six years after the destruction of the Babri Masjid, local Hindus and Muslims were attending one another's weddings in Ayodhya, and blaming the riots on the political agitation of outsiders.[36] [37]

III

The Ayodhya story reveals the particular relationship between the mobilisation of identity in the context of global media flows and the materiality of the archive in localised claims to land and its history. The extent and impact of changes in the representation of heritage are

32 Appadurai, *Modernity at Large*; Castells, *The Rise of the Network Society*; Castells, *The Power of Identity*; M. Castells, *The Information Age: Economy, Society and Culture*, vol. 3: *End of Millennium* (Oxford: Blackwell, 1998).

33 J. Conrad, *Heart of Darkness* (New York: W. W. Norton, 1971).

34 Appadurai, *Modernity at Large*.

35 Nandini Rao, personal communication.

36 M. Iijima, Feature: 'Indian temple town just wants peace', Reuters (1998).

37 Asking questions about the manner in which the archive is appropriated in the contemporary world leads to a re-evaluation of the concept of culture. In rejecting the idea that 'culture' is a thing in itself, Appadurai suggests the concept of 'culturalism', 'the conscious mobilization of cultural differences in the service of a larger national or transnational politics . . . frequently associated with extraterritorial histories and memories, sometimes with refugee status and exile, and almost always with struggles for stronger recognition from existing nation states or from various transnational bodies' (Appadurai, *Modernity at Large*, p. 15). Culturalist movements are 'self-conscious about identity, culture and heritage, all of which tend to be part of the deliberate vocabulary of culturalist movements as they struggle with states and other culturalist forces and groups' – 'deliberate, strategic and populist mobilization of cultural material' (Appadurai, *Modernity at Large*, p. 15).

further illustrated in the contested history that prefigured the out-break of the war between Yugoslavia and NATO in Kosovo in early 1999.

The Balkans have long stood for the backward, primitive and bar-barian within Europe. Maria Todorova has argued that 'Balkanism' evolved independently from Said's Orientalism, with a Christianity opposed to Islam but also non-Western:

> geographically inextricable from Europe, yet culturally con-structed as 'the other', the Balkans became, in time, the object of a number of externalized political, ideological and cultural frus-trations and have served as a repository of negative characteristics against which a positive and self-congratulatory image of the 'European' and 'the west' has been constructed. Balkanism con-veniently exempted 'the west' from charges of racism, colonial-ism, Eurocentrism and Christian intolerance: the Balkans, after all, are in Europe, they are white and they are predominantly Christian.[38]

One of the more prominent revivals of Balkanism has been Robert Kaplan's *Balkan Ghosts*.[39] Described as 'a dreadful mix of unfounded generalizations, misinformation, outdated sources, personal prejudices and bad writing',[40] Kaplan's travelogue was, in its turn, a revisiting of Rebecca West's Balkan journey of 1937. Kaplan carried West's *Black Lamb and Grey Falcon*[41] with him and revelled in his perception of a centuries-old continuity of experience. Here, Kaplan describes the archive of thirteenth-century paintings and frescoes in the Church of the Apostles in Peć:

> The workings of my eyes taught me the first canon of national survival: that an entire world can be created out of very little light. It took only another minute or so for the faces to emerge out of the gloom – haunted and hunger-ravaged faces from a pre-conscious, Serb past, evincing a spirituality and primitivism that the West knows best through the characters of Dostoyevsky. I felt as though I were inside a skull into which the collective memories of a people had been burned. Dreams took shape, hal-lucinations: St. Nicholas, with his purple robe and black, reminding eyes at the back of my head; St. Sava, Serbia's patron saint and founder of this very church, who descended through the watery void to proffer gifts of mercy and inspiration; the Ascended Christ, a dehumanized peasant-god beyond the last

38 M. Todorova, 'The Balkans: from discovery to invention', *Slavic Review* 53, 2 (1994), p. 455.

39 R. D. Kaplan, *Balkan Ghosts: A Journey through History* (New York: Vintage, 1994).

40 H. Cooper, 'Review of Robert Kaplan, "Balkan Ghosts,"' *Slavic Review* 52 (1993), p. 592.

41 R. West, *Black Lamb and Grey Falcon* (New York: Viking Press, 1941).

stage of physical suffering, more fearful than any conqueror or earthly ideology. Apostles and saints intermingled with medieval Serbian kings and archbishops. They all appeared through a faith's distorting mirror: with elongated bodies and monstrous hands and heads. Many of the saints' eyes had been scratched out. According to a peasant belief, the plaster and dye used to depict a saint's eyes can cure blindness.[42]

Ten years later, these same medieval frescoes and icons could be visited through the Web. By 1998, every monastery in the Kosovo diocese of Raška and Prizren had its Web-site and gallery of images. Visoki Dečani Monastery, for example, described its history (beginning in 1327) and its incomparable art and architecture. The twenty black-robed members of its brotherhood were introduced and their daily routine described: prayer from 5 a.m., individual obediences, kitchen duties, breadmaking, iconography, farmwork. The monks' current project was publishing, using computers, scanners and the Internet: 'in this way the brotherhood is trying to revive the ancient tradition of the monastery scriptoria where hundreds of books were written and translated'.[43]

But can a manuscript collection be reduced to a virtual scriptorium? Do the digital obediences of Visoki Dečani's monks replace the experience of seeing the image of Christ ascended by the light of hundreds of candles in an atmosphere laden with beeswax? In Rheingold's world, the answer is emphatically 'yes' – there are potentially no limits to the sensory experiences of Virtual Reality. But Visoki Dečani's monks were protected by young Yugoslav army conscripts who guarded the monastery from the Kosovo Liberation Army and the surrounding Muslim communities under the pall of imminent conflict; there was no digital escape from an AK-47, as the months ahead would show.[44] As with Ayodhya, the treasures of the local site were of vital importance – and the violence was palpable.

Kosovo is at the heart of Serbian nationalism; mythologised as the place of defeat by the Ottoman Turks in 1389, the stain of Muslim occupation, and the core of the Serbian Orthodox Church.[45] Religious and historic places in Kosovo were the ground zero of Serbia's nationalist politics. At the same time, Serb nationalists were dispersed throughout the world maintaining a fierce loyalty to the idea of 'greater Serbia'. Local identities in faraway places were formed around the idea of Serbia – its history, memories of 'home' and imagination of the past and future. Such was the Serbian Unity Congress (SUC) of the

42 Kaplan, *Balkan Ghosts*, p. xx.

43
http://www.decani.yunet.com/edecani.html.

44 'Marooned Serb monk calls for Kosovo ceasefire', *The Times*, London, 29 April 1998.

45 J. V. A. Fine, *The Early Medieval Balkans* (Ann Arbor: University of Michigan Press, 1983); J. V. A. Fine, *The Late Medieval Balkans* (Ann Arbor: University of Michigan Press, 1987); N. Malcolm, *Kosovo: A Short History* (New York: New York University Press, 1998).

United States of America, an 'international organization representing Serbs and friends of Serbs in the diaspora, committed to ensuring the continuation of the Serbian heritage'.[46] In the run-up to the 1999 war the SUC was lobbying in Washington, organising fundraising events and conventions, and running a large Web-site. This featured 'electronic exhibitions' of Serbian culture, including coinage[47] and medieval material culture:

> This unique electronic exhibition organized by the Serbian Unity Congress presents, for the first time, the attire, jewelry and ornaments of the Serbian kings and czars in the 12th through 15th centuries. Symbolic significance, political influences and pure fashion can all be traced as they intermingle in this fascinating presentation featuring 24 pictures with careful reconstructions of masterpiece frescoes found in churches and monasteries throughout the Serbian lands.[48]

The SUC's electronic galleries led directly to Slobodan Milošević's Belgrade and attempts to whitewash atrocities in Bosnia-Herzegovina that were reminiscent of Nazi propaganda,[49] while the very tangible situation of Visoki Dečani's virtual scriptorium in Kosovo's impoverished and bitterly contested landscape pointed to the vital connection between the virtual and material worlds.

As with Ayodhya, this example illustrates the differing nuances that 'place' and its materiality can have. In the months before the war the Yugoslav army was defending sacred sites against the Kosovo Liberation Army – a form of action that invited a line of association through epic (or notorious) events back to the beginning of history. But claims to rights over places that may be thousands of kilometres distant (and perhaps never visited) were also central to the construction of networks of 'local subjects' in a world of global media flows and large-scale migrations.[50] The result – both within embattled Serb communities inside Yugoslavia and among those who saw themselves as ethnically Serb in New York, San Francisco and other cities around the world – was ethnographies of neighbourhoods in which the archive of documents, records and historic artefacts (and their simulacra) was deployed within landscapes, domestic architecture and urban structures. This interpretation insists on an ineluctable connection between the material world and the rich play of circulating media representations. It is the opposite of the transcendental fantasy of the digital subject, ever circulating and materialising at will in different parts of cyberspace.

46 http://www.suc.org. 'The SUC's "Blago Fund", based in San Francisco, has as its goal "to preserve and promote Serbian treasures in a way that ties together the past, present and future."'
http://www.suc.org/Blago/Blago_mission.html.

47 R. Bozinović, 'Serbian history through coinage', http://www.suc.org/exhibitions/coins/ (1998).

48 T. Vuleta, 'Medieval Serbian royal ornaments', http://www.suc.org/culture/history/Medieval_Orn aments/ (1998).

49 V. Dabić and K. Lukić, 'Atmosphere of fear and ethnic cleansing in Vukovar', http://www.suc.org/politics/war_crimes/vukovar/ vukovar7a.html (1997).

50 Appadurai, Modernity at Large.

Serbian and Croatian nationalisms stem from one major distinction – religion. This has led to a continual emphasis on the differing physical experiences of Catholicism and the Orthodox Church, expressed and constantly recreated through art, architecture, iconography, and the divergent experiences of daily belief and worship.[51] Bogdan Denitch, a Serbian political scientist who divides his time between Croatia and New York, makes the point that Serbo-Croatian (or Croato-Serbian) was standardised in the mid-nineteenth century and is spoken by Muslims, Catholic Croatians and Orthodox Serbians. Prior to the disintegration of 'old' Yugoslavia in 1990, 80 per cent of its population spoke the same language and, within local areas, shared the same dialects irrespective of religion.[52][53]

These perceptions of difference have been fervently held for many years. However, the generally held belief – fuelled by Kaplan and by the archive of Balkanist writing before him, and claimed as a matter of record by the *New York Times*[54] – that the war between Croatia and Serbia and the sequential Bosnian conflict were the consequence of an upwelling of ingrained ethnic character does not stand closer scrutiny.[55] In the last Yugoslav census more than 25 per cent of the population were in intermarried families while a significant proportion of urban communities declined to describe themselves with the ethnic identifiers of Muslim, Orthodox or Catholic.[56] In contrast to the concept of primordial inevitability there is clear evidence that ethnic affiliations and historical referents were overtly manipulated in struggles for power in the vacuum that had existed since Tito's death in 1980.

In her definitive account of the destruction of Yugoslavia, Susan Woodward[57] shows how economic reforms forced on Yugoslavia by the international community, and particularly by the International Monetary Fund, destabilised the movement towards multi-party elections. As Todorova[58] has shown, Balkanism had taken on a new tint after the end of the Second World War: 'a new facet of the image of the Balkans was added . . . when a new demon, a new other, communism, was grafted onto it'. Consequently, Yugoslav nationalists were championed by the West in their opposition to reformist Communists, strengthening the position of political figures such as Slobodan Milošević.[59] Milošević– Serbia's leader through the war with Croatia and the Bosnian conflict and subsequently president of the 'new' Yugoslavia – established his power base in 1986 as the leader of the Serbian League, manipulating Orthodox suspicion of Islam and Serbian historical pride to oppose Kosovar demands for greater autonomy. In Bogdan Denitch's view this ignited a chain reaction of nation-

51 N. Malcolm, *Bosnia: A Short History* (New York: New York University Press, 1996).

52 Denitch, *Ethnic Nationalism: The Tragic Death of Yugoslavia* (Minneapolis: University of Minnesota Press, 1994).

53 Kosovo was an autonomous province in 'old' Yugoslavia and is still at the time of writing a province in Serbia, albeit under NATO supervision following the 1999 war. Kosovars are overwhelmingly Muslim and speak Albanian. Separatist aspirations have focused on the rights of Kosovo's people to be educated in Albanian rather than Serbo-Croatian. Bogdan Denitch is a Serb who has long been resident in the United States as an academic at a university in New York. Denitch spends his summers in Croatia on the Island of Brač and was one of the founders of an anti-nationalist political party standing against Slobodan Milošević in Serbia and Franjo Tudjman in Croatia. He is both a perceptive analyst of ethnic politics, and an example of the way in which the international diaspora relates to local issues.

54 Appadurai, *Modernity at Large*.

55 Noel Malcolm, in his history of Bosnia: '[t]he biggest obstacle to all understanding of the conflict is the assumption that what has happened in that country is the product – natural, spontaneous and at the same time necessary – of forces lying within Bosnia's own internal history. That is the myth which was carefully propagated by those who caused the conflict, who wanted the world to believe that what they and their gunmen were doing was not done by them, but by impersonal and inevitable historical forces beyond anyone's control.' (Malcolm, *Bosnia* p. xix)

56 Denitch, *Ethnic Nationalism*; Malcolm, *Bosnia*.

57 S. Woodward, *Balkan Tragedy: Chaos and Dissolution after the Cold War* (Washington: The Brookings Institution, 1995).

58 Todorova, 'The Balkans', p. 478.

59 Woodward, *Balkan Tragedy*.

alist politics led from the 'top':

> Albanian self-assertion in the Province of Kosovo led to
> Milošević's awakening of the Serbian nationalist populist genie in
> the mid-1980s. The fear-ridden reaction of the leaders of the
> other republics to Serbian bullying tactics had encouraged the
> reactive growth of varying nationalisms in Slovenia, Croatia, and
> even among Bosnian Muslims and in Macedonia. This in turn
> provoked predictable fears of the minorities about the increasing
> nationalism of the major national groups in their own republics.
> There were no instruments at the federal center that could have
> effectively mediated between the republics. The fat was well and
> truly in the fire . . . Rather than being caused by a popular
> upsurge of national hate from below, the civil war was the result
> of policy decisions from the top combined with the all-too-
> effective use of the mass media, especially television. I claim this
> in the teeth of the journalistic insistence by many observers that
> there is something almost biologically imprinted that, for
> example, would make Serbs hate Croats and vice versa.[60]

The central importance of Kosovo to Serbian nationalism rests on
the myth of the 'Field of the Blackbirds'. Serbian epic poetry and folklore record that Prince Lazar, elected leader of the Serbian nobility, was
converted to piety by Elijah (in the form of a grey falcon) and built an
Orthodox church at Kosovo Polje on the eve of a battle that was lost
to the Ottoman Turks on 28 June 1389.[61] Hence the doubly inscribed
significance of Kosovo to Serbian nationalism: the site of the battlefield where humiliation at Muslim hands must be avenged and the
place where fourteenth-century monasteries preserve a direct line, in
their art and architecture, to a proud and independent medieval kingdom. The six-hundredth anniversary of the Battle of Kosovo Polje was
marked in 1989 by the culmination of a celebration that had started a
full year earlier. A funeral procession of Prince Lazar's disinterred coffin travelled through every town and village in Serbia drawing 'huge,
black-clad crowds of wailing mourners at every spot'.[62][63] This culminated in the battlefield ceremony:

> in the courtyard of the monastery at Gračanica (south of
> Priština), while people queued to pay their devotions to the
> Prince's bones inside, stalls sold icon-style posters of Jesus Christ,
> Prince Lazar and Slobodan Milošević side by side. At the cer-
> emony on the battlefield Milošević was accompanied by black-

60 Denitch, *Ethnic Nationalism*, pp. 61–62.

61 Malcolm, *Bosnia*.

62 Kaplan, *Balkan Ghosts*, p. 38; Malcolm,
Bosnia.

63 Noel Malcolm points out that the battle of
Kosovo Polje was less decisive than Serbian
epic poetry recalls: both sides suffered heavy
losses, and the battle itself left the conflict
unresolved. The eventual Serb defeat was due
to the Turks' ability to follow up with repeated
attacks on Serbia (Malcolm, *Bosnia* p. 20.)

robed metropolitans of the Orthodox Church, singers in traditional Serbian folk costumes, and members of the security police
in their traditional dress of dark suits and sunglasses . . .[64]

Similarly, contemporary Croatian nationalism is constructed from
a deep history given form by sites, monuments and the material
archive of the past. A palimpsest of a rich Adriatic archaeology and
architecture – Roman Dalmatia, overlain by early Christian sites and
medieval towns and villages – supports the remembrance of tenth-
century kingship. This is captured in the life and work of Nenad
Jeptanović, a Croatian born in Chile, educated at Princeton and now
returned to the Adriatic island of Brač (and living in the same village
where Bogdan Denitch spends his summer months). A paragon of
Said's contemporary organic intellectual, Jeptanović is curator of a
family mausoleum built in 1927 at the behest of Francisco Petrinović,
Jeptanović's uncle made rich by Chilean phosphates.[65] The
mausoleum's sculptures express the essence of Croatian historical identity: the unity of Greek and Roman influences, the principles of
Catholicism and the struggle between good and evil. Its dome is
capped by a bronze sculpture of the Archangel Michael and its vaults
house the coffins of Petrinović family members, including the mummified corpse of Francisco himself, returned to Brač in 1961, a decade
after his death. The mausoleum is set on an ocean promontory backed
by terraced vineyards that predate the Roman empire, a medieval village and church and the beach where four teenage patriots were executed by Italian soldiers half a century ago. Jeptanović uses this richly material setting as a stage – a living archive that expresses his sense
of place, history and identity. He is obsessed with the graves that surround the mausoleum and with graveyard maintenance; how, after the
passage of years, bones in a sarcophagus are swept aside to make way
for new corpses and how the bones leach into the limestone soil. As
such, he is the curator of his past written across the landscape and of
his own grave.[66]

Serb and Croat nationalisms came into direct conflict after elections in 1990, resulting in a war that was to last from 1991 to 1995.
Milošević's nationalist counterpart and bitter rival in Croatia, Franjo
Tudjman, won a substantial victory at the polls and promulgated a
constitutional change that declared Croatia a 'state of Croats', rather
than a 'state of Croatians'. This change of a single word signified the
final abandonment of 'old' Yugoslavia's multi-ethnic politics and
prompted a revolt by Croatian Serbs in the Krajina region that was

64 Malcolm, *Bosnia*, p. 213.

65 For the complex history of Croat
nationalism and the emergence of the concept
of Yugoslavia within the Austro-Hungarian
Empire, see Malcolm, *Bosnia*, Chapter 12.

66 Nenad Jeptanović, 'Mausoleum of the
Family Petrinović in Supertar, Island of Brač'
(photocopy), and personal communication,
May 1998. The mausoleum's sculptures were
by Thomas Rosandić, one of Croatia's foremost
sculptors, who carved his own face in the
figure of Christ crucified.

backed by Serbia (in the guise of the 'new' Yugoslavian army). The war that followed resulted in some three hundred thousand Catholic refugees who fled to other parts of Croatia and about the same number again of Orthodox Croatians who moved into exile in Serbia. The ceasefire agreement specified that only ethno-religious groups would be recognised in negotiations, contributing immensely to the political myth of primordialism that had been carefully nurtured by nationalist leaders on both sides.[67]

Later in 1992 the focus of conflict shifted to Bosnia. Bosnia had been conquered by the Turkish army in 1463 and subsequently many Bosnians had converted to Islam, often to improve their social, legal and economic status within the Ottoman Empire.[68] Islamic communities dominated major towns such as Sarajevo and Mostar, which thrived under Ottoman rule (although there were prosperous Catholic, Orthodox and Jewish minorities). Changes in the system of land tenure had a huge impact on the countryside. The earlier, military-feudal system, in which both Christians and Muslims could be landowners, was replaced by a system of hereditary estates, almost all owned by Muslims and on which the majority of peasants were Christian. Through the years the major causes of conflict in Bosnia had not been religious or the result of 'ancient ethnic hatreds' but economic; the resentment of a mainly Christian peasantry towards Muslim landlords and Muslim administrators and merchants in the principal cities.[69] Within Bosnia's cities – and in common with other parts of the former Yugoslavia – there had been increasing secularisation, and by the late 1980s 30 per cent of marriages in urban districts were 'mixed'. For many rural Muslims, and almost all urban ones, being Muslim consisted of a set of cultural traditions: 'Muslim names, circumcision, baklava and the celebration of Ramazan Bajram, getting a godparent to cut a one-year-old child's hair, a preference for tiny coffee cups without handles, a sympathy for spiders and various other traditional practices, the origins of which are frequently unknown to those who practice them.'[70]

Rather than being an ethnic inevitability, the destruction of Bosnia between 1992 and 1995 was a further consequence of Western support for nationalist leaders combined with political manipulation by the Serbian government. Following initial engagement by Serbian security forces and volunteers, serving to mobilise Bosnian Serbs, the Yugoslav army withdrew from Bosnia claiming that the conflict was an inevitable civil war based on ethnic rivalry, playing into Western belief in the theory of 'ancient hatreds'. The pattern of European inter-

67 Denitch, *Ethnic Nationalism*.

68 Malcolm, *Bosnia*.

69 Ibid.

70 C. Sorabji, *Bosnia's Muslims: Challenging Past and Present Misconceptions* (London, 1992), pp. 5–6, quoted by Malcolm, *Bosnia*, p. 222.

vention helped enormously. The Vance–Owen Plan of October 1992 envisaged ethnically defined 'autonomous provinces', essentially similar to South African bantustans, and insisted on an arms embargo that prevented the multicultural Bosnian government from resisting Serbian expansionism.[71]

The reinvention of Croatian, Serbian and Muslim ethnicity by rival power blocs in the wake of Tito's multi-ethnic Yugoslavia was facilitated by the manipulation of a wealth of material symbols, records and the tangible evidence of centuries of history. The use of mass media – newspapers and, particularly, state-controlled television services – depended critically on the sensory presence of history, the visual and tactile presence of the archive in the everyday experience of the people. This is not to suggest the action of some false consciousness – a media brainwashing at the hands of an evil genius. On the contrary, the particular power of the tangible archive is to make the claims of history seem everywhere in their evidence and incontrovertible in their logic. The political direction of 'invented tradition' may be given by a Tudjman or a Milošević, but its success depends on organic intellectuals such as Nenad Jeptanović who will recreate their sense of identity on a daily basis in the fabric of the landscape, urban architecture and sacred books and relics in the local museum and church, reinforced by shared experiences in cafés, political meetings and Sunday sacraments.

An inevitable corollary of celebrating an identity rooted in the archive of manuscripts, records and architecture is the belief that competing claims, passionately denied, can only be defeated if the archive is restored to purity. As Bearman (this volume) has noted, most people see the archive as the residence of 'truth', and so it follows that its contents will be the popular benchmark for claims of the veracity of identity. From the first weeks of the conflict between Croatia and Serbia, 'ethnic cleansing' was more than driving communities into exile. In the border town of Vukovar, rival ethnic nationalisms escalated as harassment, attacks on individuals and, particularly, damage to houses. In the summer of 1991 the town was besieged by the Serbian army. Some thirty thousand Croats fled into exile. The Eltz Manor House, which housed the Vukovar Municipal Museum, was destroyed and the art gallery and other museums in the town extensively damaged. Systematic shelling by Serbian artillery reduced most of the historical precinct to rubble. Many surviving art works, archaeological collections and archives were stolen and are believed to be in collections in Belgrade and other parts of Serbia; some have been offered for

71 Malcolm, *Bosnia*; Woodward, *Balkan Tragedy*.

72 Denitch, *Ethnic Nationalism*; V. Pavić, 'The register of war damage to museums and galleries in Croatia' in *War Damage to Museums and Galleries in Croatia* (Zagreb: Museum Documentation Centre, 1997), pp. 55-166.

73 Dabić and Lukić, 'Atmosphere of fear and ethnic cleansing in Vukovar'.

74 B. Sulc, 'Museums in war' in *War Damage to Museums and Galleries in Croatia* (Zagreb: Museum Documentation Centre, 1997), p. 14.

75 J. Vinterhalter, 'Protection in museums – the first wartime task. Six years later', *War Damage to Museums and Galleries in Croatia* (Zagreb: Museum Documentation Centre, 1997), pp. 19–38.

76 War damage in Croatia has yet to be fully assessed but has been claimed to include damage to more than sixty museums and galleries. Inventories of war damage are compiled by the Museum Documentation Centre (Pavić, 'The register of war damage to museums and galleries in Croatia'), but it is not clear to what extent these records are an accurate representation of what happened, and to what extent they are anti-Serbian propaganda. However, from an early stage in the conflict, it was argued that destruction of cultural property on this scale was not just the 'collateral damage of warfare', but rather the 'assassination of culture', following the 1948 Genocide Convention and other international protocols. It has been argued that such 'cultural genocide' should be formally recognised by the United Nations Criminal Tribunal for the Former Yugoslavia (H. F. Hodder, 'Bibliocide', *Harvard Magazine* http://www.harvard-magazine.com/nd96/right.biblio.html [1996]).

77 P. Maass, *Love Thy Neighbor: A Story of War* (New York: Vintage, 1996).

sale in Belgrade markets.[72] Despite counter-claims by organisations such as the Serbian Unity Congress attributing the beginning of ethnic cleansing to the Croatian Democratic Union,[73] it is clear that, in this first major exchange of the war, the Yugoslav army and the volunteer militia were intent on wiping away the historical traces of a Croat presence from the banks of the Danube.

Buildings and archives continued to be specific targets as the war continued. Branka Sulc, Director of Croatia's Museum Documentation Centre, claims this as a 'scorched earth' strategy, an attack on 'the Croatian National identity': ' . . . the systematic destruction and damage was inflicted not only on historical town units, but also on sacral buildings, traditional architecture – especially villages, archaeological sites, entire cultural landscapes, libraries and museums. The inventories of churches, museums and private collections – that for the most part form the reference points of collective memory – were destroyed and plundered . . . '.[74] In October 1991 the first Serbian air raids on Zagreb's upper town – the historical quarter of the city – resulted in damage to historic buildings and museums. In the same autumn, the Yugoslav navy moved along Croatia's Adriatic coast, first shelling Diocletian's Palace, a fourth-century World Heritage Site celebrated by Croatian nationalists for the association with the glories of Rome, and then moving south to the thirteenth-century city of Dubrovnik, which was to remain under siege for a year.[75][76]

Those who experienced this war at first hand, or who have written about it, describe a conflict far removed from the Hollywood stereotype of high-tech scientific attack on distant targets, although Hollywood has indeed been closely implicated. In the play between locality and global media, focused attacks on the archives of arcane histories have been mingled with the paraphernalia and memorabilia of transcontinental imagery. Robert Kaplan's description of Albania in 1990 well captures the mix. Oxcarts were driven by shaven-headed soldiers, women tended wheat and tobacco fields with shovels and scythes, the air was polluted with factory fumes – and a family watched *Dynasty* and CNN (through a Greek frequency) on an ancient black-and-white Russian television. Throughout the war both the Croatian and Serbian governments maintained a tight hold on all media, and particularly television.[77] The consequence has been a material expression that encapsulates the global and the local. Many of the direct attacks on civilians and their culture were carried out by volunteer paramilitary units under the protection of the professional army. These militias were often made up of unemployed youth and other marginalised groups – 'the same alienated groups from which xenophobic skinheads and soccer gangs have been recruited in Western Europe'.[78] Serbian Chetniks adopted long hair and beards, peasant caps and daggers in reference to past struggles.[79] Serbian Volunteers, organised by Belgrade gangsters, chose US-style camouflage costumes, were clean shaven with the exception of moustaches, and were strongly influenced by American Vietnam movies. Croat reservists adopted Cherokee roaches and shaved heads, with black headbands, Rambo-style. French and German skinhead mercenaries were formed as a black-shirt legion.[80] As the next Balkan conflict began to escalate, the Kosovo Liberation Army was reported as fashioning its identity on Stalinist Albania and Mussolini's fascist blackshirts.[81] Global images – a deadly cyberpunk fantasy – had been brought to bear on the specifics of local histories: Prince Lazar's tragic piety, the Emperor Diocletian's retirement to grow cabbages in Dalmatia, the Vukovar museum's assertion of Croat history on Serbia's doorstep.

In 1992, the epicentre of conflict shifted to Bosnia-Herzegovina. Again there were repeated attacks on cultural property:

> It is as if the protagonists, unable to strangle the last living representatives of what they see as an alien culture, seem to think that with the destruction of place, an architectural cleansing, as it were, they can eradicate the people who inhabit that place . . . Like the horrifying rapes of women . . . these are violent efforts to remake the world in another image. Like the women of Bosnia, for many of whom the preservation of their traditional culture and the creation of home is an essential role, so too architecture creates home, represents memory, and preserves culture. Without minimizing the scale of human suffering, this attempt to destroy architecture, to annihilate place, like the violence against the women, is criminal warfare and cultural genocide.[82]

A young Muslim man, after his five-hundred-year-old mosque had been destroyed, said: 'it's not that my family was burned down, but it's my foundation that burned. I was destroyed.'[83]

There were specific attacks on archives – libraries, manuscript holdings, museums and other cultural institutions. This applied as much in the cities – Sarajevo, Mostar – as in the towns and villages, and it has been estimated that the cadastral registers, waqf documents and parish records of more than eight hundred Muslim and Croat communities have been destroyed by Serbian nationalists,[84]

78 Denitch, *Ethnic Nationalism*, p. 10.

79 The Chetniks were formed by a Yugoslav army colonel, Draža Mihailović, as a Serbian royalist opposition to the German invasion of 1941; the name recalls bandit heroes of earlier Serbian history. Elements in the Chetnik movement argued for a 'Greater Serbia', including land all the way to the Adriatic, and that this territory should be 'cleansed' of Croats and Muslims, who should be expelled to Turkey or Albania. The Chetnik resistance was opposed by Tito's partisan resistance movement. After the formation of communist Yugoslavia, Chetniks were seen as fascist (Malcolm, *Bosnia*). Consequently, the Chetnik revival recalls epic Serbian nationalism, guerrilla resistance, fascism, and rejection of Yugoslav modernism – a potent and contradictory bundling together of diverse historical referents.

80 Denitch, *Ethnic Nationalism*.

81 K. Schork, 'Analysis – KLA shatters Europe's placid self-image', Reuters, CNN, (1998).

82 N. Adams, 'Architecture as the target', *Journal of the Society of Architectural Historians* 52 (1993), p. 389.

83 Hodder, *Bibliocide*.

84 A. Riedlmayer, 'Destruction of libraries in Bosnia-Herzegovina', *Middle East Studies Association Bulletin*, http://www.cua.edu/www/mesabul/bosnia.htm (1995).

and that more than twelve hundred religious and cultural sites have been destroyed or damaged, including mosques, the historic centres of many towns, Muslim graves and pilgrimage sites, Catholic churches, monasteries, cemeteries and Jewish religious buildings. More than twenty thousand civilian homes have been reduced to rubble.[85]

Attacks on cultural property were carried out by nationalists on all sides, reinforcing Manuel Castells's[86] argument that nationalism attempts to obviate the conditions of the present by means of constructing a shared interpretation of the past for use as a political instrument to mould the future. Mostar – Bosnia-Herzegovina's second city – had grown from a small village to a prosperous town under the Ottoman Empire. Its focal point – and the key to its economic prosperity – was the bridge over the gorge of the River Neretva: Stari Most ('old bridge'), built in 1566 and a UNESCO World Heritage Site. Through the 1980s the historic core of Mostar had been conserved and restored in a world-renowned project run by an inter-ethnic group of Croats, Serbs and Muslims, winning the Aga Khan Award for Architecture in 1986. Such a project was anathema to nationalists intent on eradicating all traces of other histories from Bosnia. Much of Mostar's historic precinct was destroyed by systematic shelling in November 1993.[87] Stari Most, widely recognised as a symbol of Bosnian unity and culture, was blown up by the Croatian army.[88] [89]

In Sarajevo itself, the pattern of Serbian shelling suggests that libraries and museums were specifically targeted for destruction; surrounding buildings were often left intact. In the summer of 1992 Serb forces bombarded the National Museum. Two hundred thousand volumes were rescued under sniper fire, including the fourteenth-century Sarajevo *Haggadah*, brought to Sarajevo in the fifteenth century by Jews fleeing the Spanish Inquisition and considered one of Bosnia's principal cultural treasures. The building was badly damaged by shells and the museum's director was killed while arranging for plastic sheeting to protect what was left of the collections.[90] In May 1992 the Serbs attacked Sarajevo's Oriental Institute with phosphorus grenades, weapons designed to maximise damage by fire. This time the entire holdings were destroyed, including 5 263 bound manuscripts in Arabic, Persian, Turkish, Hebrew and Serbo-Croatian-Bosnian in Arabic script, as well as tens of thousands of Ottoman-era documents.[91] Serbian forces also occupied the Franciscan Seminary in Nedzariči, a western suburb of Sarajevo, looting and destroying col-

85 'Republic of Bosnia-Herzegovina', Washington Embassy;
http://www.bosnianembassy.org.

86 Castells, *The Information Age*.

87 S. Ozkan, 'The destruction of Stari Most', *Development Network* 14 (1994), pp. 5–7.

88 Woodward, *Balkan Tragedy*.

89 'Damaged or destroyed Islamic objects in Mostar',
http://www.haverford.edu/relg/sells/mostar/mostar.html. During 1997, blocks from the destroyed Mostar Bridge were hoisted from the Neretva River by a Hungarian military unit, part of the international stabilisation force in Bosnia-Herzegovina. The last block was bedecked in flowers and raised in a public ceremony. An attempt will be made to rebuild the bridge; 'Efforts to reconstruct the Mostar Bridge', *MTI Hungarian News Agency*, 1 December 1997;
http://www.applicom.com/manu/mostar.htm.

90 Riedlmayer, 'Destruction of libraries in Bosnia-Herzegovina'.

91 A. Riedlmayer, 'Fighting the destruction of memory: a call for an ingathering of Bosnian manuscripts',
http://www.applicom.com/manu/ingather.htm (1998).

MARTIN HALL

lections of books, sculptures and paintings.[92]

The attack on the National Library of Bosnia and Herzegovina came later in the summer, on the night of 25 August. Like the Oriental Institute, the National Library was known for the richness and diversity of its archive, preserving the record of centuries of Serb, Croat and Muslim interaction. Known as the Vijecnica (the name of the elaborate nineteenth-century building in which it was housed), this was a legal deposit library for the 'old' Yugoslavia, Sarajevo University's library and the major archival depot for Bosnia-Herzegovina.[93] The bombardment was witnessed by Sarajevo writer Ivan Lovrenović, whose own library was destroyed the same summer by Serbian militia in an *ad hoc* street ritual. Hundreds of incendiary rockets were fired from Serbian artillery in the hills surrounding the city, followed by machine gun and mortar fire to deter people from rescuing the books and manuscripts: 'black, sooty, still hot butterflies – books and papers aflame, the library's treasure – were flying around and falling over distant parts of the city'.[94][95]

The ferocity of the attack on the archives of Croatia and Bosnia-Herzegovina in the wars of the 1990s, and the way in which the politics of mobilised ethnicity were translated into actions by individuals, are captured in this description of a Serb raid on a Croat artist's studio in the Sarajevo neighbourhood of Grbavica:

> Serbian soldiers broke into his studio looking to steal money and equipment. They were incensed to discover an Islamic levha – a calligraphic inscription from the Koran – which the painter had mounted as a wall hanging. They took it down and, cursing, butchered it. According to witnesses, they then took all the artist's paintings, drawings and sketches, lined them up against the front wall of the house and executed them with machine-gun fire until they were in shreds.[96][97]

IV

Four hundred years ago when Maurits' chroniclers documented his archive, the ethnographic subject – and the violence of its subjugation – was six months away by sea, given exotic value through distance. Today, ethnos is everywhere and so is the violence latent in claims for purity, difference and heritage. The 'Bosnia fallacy' – that 'land, language, religion, history, and blood are congruent'[98] – leads in turn to the USA and the 'heart of whiteness'. Here, the triumphalism of global dominance and a new economic order masks a counter-culture of

92 Lovrenović, *The Hatred of Memory*.

93 E. Kujundzić, 'From ashes: the fate of the National and University Library of Bosnia and Herzegovina', http://www.geocities.com/CapitolHill/6777/library.htm (1997).

94 Lovrenović, *The Hatred of Memory*.

95 'Many tried to rescue books as the Library burned for three days. Librarian Aida Buturovi, was killed by a Serb sniper while trying to rescue books from the flames' (Riedlmayer, 'Destruction of libraries in Bosnia-Herzegovina').

96 Lovrenović, *The Hatred of Memory*.

97 There is a direct connection between the destruction of Bosnia-Herzegovina's libraries and the creation of digital archives. The Bosnian Manuscript Ingathering Project aims to track photocopies and microfilms of the Oriental Institute's manuscripts held by other institutions around the world, in order to restore a 'copied archive' (Riedlmayer, 'Fighting the destruction of memory'). A parallel project to re-establish the Bosnian National and University Library centres on the reconstruction of its catalogue. This is being achieved through the use of on-line catalogues – Online Computer Library Center Inc.'s WorldCat – linking information from libraries around the world to establish 'Bosniaca' – 'all documents in any format written in any language on or about the territory of Bosnia and Herzegovina'. A search of 36 million records has resulted in more than one hundred thousand matches, and is being followed by the use of refined search criteria to search other library catalogues that are not incorporated in WorldCat (E. T. O'Neill, J. A. Young and Bremer, 'The Bosnian National Library: building a virtual collection', http://www.oclr.org/oclr/research/publications/review96/bosnia.htm [1996])

98 Appadurai, *Modernity at Large*, p. 21.

ethnic conflict and hatred that has all the characteristics of the tribalism that is assumed to be quintessentially un-American.

One consequence of essentialising ethnic conflicts in Croatia and Bosnia-Herzegovina – and in other parts of the world geographically distant from Western Europe and North America – is the pretence that such conflicts are organic and therefore organically impossible in the heartlands of late capitalism. But the particular play between the global and local – the 'death of distance' that is the characteristic of the 'media age' – makes old geographical distinctions redundant. As commentators such as Bogdan Denitch have pointed out, the revival of Serbian and Croatian nationalism has been reinforced by substantial financial support from the Balkan diaspora. Aggressive nationalism in Croatia and Bosnia-Herzegovina has been sustained as much by Serbs and Croats in North America as by Belgrade and Zagreb. Croatian ethnic fervour is felt as much in West Germany – or among Chilean exiles such as the Petrinović family – as in Croatia. Seen in this way, 'Bosnia' cannot be simply bracketed off as an obscure tribal war in a distant corner of the world.

The ways in which conflicts in areas such as Bosnia-Herzegovina are connected with the rest of the world can be seen in the use of the Web to mobilise and direct global media flows around the locally manifested 'places' of ethnic identity. In 1995 besieged Sarajevo was connected to the outside world via an e-mail satellite link. This led to the foundation of 'Domovina Net' (Homeland Net) in Amsterdam, providing video and audio streams on Bosnian issues, including (in 1998) real-time audio-feeds from the International War Crimes Tribunal in The Hague. Domovina Net was visited by an estimated twenty-five to fifty thousand people, from all parts of the world, each week.[99] 'New' Yugoslavia used its official Web-site – signified by the flag, coat of arms and a sound file of the National Anthem – to claim the Federal Republic's legality of existence and commitment to 'peace, security, stability, cooperation and prosperity in the region and in the World of Future'. But the main emphasis of the site was to claim a sustained and deliberate media conspiracy throughout the last decade of Balkan conflicts against the legitimate national aspirations of Serbs throughout the region and in exile throughout the world. This position was supported and extended by the US-based SUC. Through its Web-site, the SUC offered an extensive apology for Serb expansionism, denied claims of atrocities, and presented counter-claims for war crimes by Croats and Muslims. These positions were contested at other points of presence. The Croatian Institute for Culture and

99 www.domovina.net; 'Balkans turn to Web for news', www.computerworld.com, 6/26/98.

Information, for instance, published an on-line newspaper every week, addressing issues such as religion, cultural heritage, politics and Croatia's rights of self-determination, and repeating well-tried constructions of history: 'the Croats are among the oldest peoples in Europe. They have inhabited the territory between the Adriatic Sea and the Drava River for at least thirteen centuries. And yet it was only six years ago that they managed to establish their own independent and democratic state . . .' The government of Bosnia-Herzegovina presented its position – and the extent of criminal injustice against the rights of its citizens to self-determination – on a Web-site from Washington, D.C.[100]

Not surprisingly, because of technological advances in the intervening years, the Internet played a greater role during the 1999 Kosovo war. E-mail discussion lists were used extensively by both Serb and Kosovar nationalists, stretching the idealism of advocates of free opinion to the limit as strident claims and counter-claims were made. In the words of *The Economist*, reporting at the height of military action,

> now we have war on the net. As NATO planes bomb the former Yugoslavia, American government web-sites display what is destroyed. The Yugoslav government ripostes with numbers of planes shot down, targets missed and civilians killed. Albanian web-sites chronicle the flood of Kosovar refugees. Serb ones list atrocities by Kosovar terrorists. All of this against a backdrop of interactive maps, living histories, bile-filled bulletin boards and eye-witness e-mails. This is the first web war.[101]

There are, of course, important distinctions between broadcast media and more recent forms of digital communication. The ways in which Serb and Croat nationalisms were shaped by state-controlled television services in the late 1980s and the first half of the 1990s are different from the use of the Web in the second half of the 1990s. For example, Peter Maass[102] has argued that Milošević's control of Serbia's television service was the key to his ability to control the sway of public opinion by denying all reference to alternative points of view. In this respect Web-based information is the inverse of broadcast television. By the time war came to Kosovo, Milošević was not able to prevent at least some Serbians from seeing, and being influenced by, any Web-site that they could find (a quality explicitly exploited by Domovina Net). But the crucial issue, of course, was access. The majority of citizens of Bosnia-Herzegovina, Croatia and Yugoslavia, battling to survive the

100 The Federal Republic of Yugoslavia Official Web Site is at http://www.gov.yu, and the Serbian Unity Congress at http://www.suc.com. The Croatian Institute for Culture and Information's 'Croatia Online Weekly' is at http://www.croatia.hr; the quotation is from the edition of 15 January 1998. The government of Bosnia-Herzegovina is at http://www.bosnianembassy.org.

101 See, for example, the Nettime list, 'a moderated mailing list for net criticism, collaborative text filtering and cultural politics', archives at http:www.nettime.org. Vigorous exchanges between advocates of Serb and NATO positions brought into question the viability of list discussion within the context of war. *Economist*, 'War on the Web', 15 May 1999.

102 Maass, *Love Thy Neighbor*.

rigours of poverty and the effects of war, were hardly likely to become cyber-surfers. Thus the attention that is being given to the Web as a medium for claims and counter-claims of regional ethnic rights emphasises again the ineluctable connection between global media and local place in the cultural construction of identity. *The Economist's* 'war on the net' is the conflict of international opinion – the global distribution of snatches of information pioneered by CNN in the Gulf War at the beginning of the war. Local opinion within Yugoslavia was the domain of broadcast media, a point well understood by NATO strategists, who identified Serbian television stations and transmitters as prime targets for bombing.

The use of the Web in war was shown starkly in the escalation of conflict in Kosovo and Albania's borderlands in the months before the NATO airstrikes began. Albania is often presented as the savage heart of this part of Europe; ancient mountain chiefdoms; a place where Byron found primordial inspiration; the most repressive of Cold War regimes; a place of blood feuds where an AK-47 can be traded for a carton of cigarettes; and one of the poorest countries in the world.[103] But Albania was presented on the Web through a cheerful home page that was pitched at the diaspora: 'you may ask yourself, why is this the Albanian home page, rather than a Albania home page. Albanians cover a far larger territory than the country of Albania, and to speak of Albania only would mean excluding half of the ethnic Albanian population'.[104] This Albanian identity was marked by means of a classic suite of ethnic markers: a description and history of language, folk music and folk costume; a history that is traced back to 2000 BC and the Illyrians; and a 'virtual menu', including local delicacies ('take a wild duck, clean it well, and keep it in vinegar overnight . . .'). The claim to a 'greater Albania' (reflecting the same ideology as 'new' Yugoslavia's claim to a 'greater Serbia') was expressed in a map that embraced Albania, Kosovo and parts of Macedonia and Montenegro. But the most active link on the page was to the 'Kosovo Crisis Center,' with news updates on the breaking war and a gallery of images of destroyed buildings and victims of the fighting. To navigate the Web-site was to move through graphics of historic landscapes and buildings – a deep ethnic past – to folk culture (people in folk costume, dancing) and then to images of buildings destroyed by Serbian militia, twisted and mutilated bodies and close-ups of men, women and children with limbs and faces torn away. The sponsor of this Web-site was the Albanian-American Academy, based in the US, and selling 'all kinds of Albanian music and movies'. The Kosovo news page is linked

103 As with the wars in Croatia and Bosnia, economic factors played an important role in the Kosovo conflict. Kosovo has rich mineral resources and coal reserves essential to Serbia's economy. In the words of Novak Bjelić, director of the Stari Trg mine in Kosovo: 'the war in Kosovo is about the mines, nothing else. This is Serbia's Kuwait – the heart of Kosovo. We export to France, Switzerland, Greece, Sweden, the Czech Republic, Russia and Belgium. And in addition to all this, Kosovo has 17 billion tons of coal reserves, Naturally, the Albanians want all of this for themselves.' The Trepca mining complex is valued at US$5 billion and is of key strategic importance. In 1988 the mines were a focus of fierce opposition to Serbian expansionism, with strikes by the 75 per cent Albanian-speaking workforce against nationalist Serbs who were in positions of power at the mines. Subsequently, miners were replaced by Poles, Czechs and Muslim prisoners from Bosnia (C. Hedges, 'The spoils of a blood feud: rich veins buried deep beneath Kosovo', *International Herald Tribune* [1998]). In July 1998, major conflict between the Kosovo Liberation Army and Serbian forces centred on the huge open coal mine of Belačevać. The mobilisation of Serbian national pride around the memory of Turkish defeat five centuries ago has to be seen in the context of Kosovo's essential contribution to the Serbian economy, and the potential value of the region in a 'greater Albania'.

104 http://www.albanian.com.

to one of the world's largest Web-based bookstores, Amazon, for purchases of the latest books about the region.

This example of the use of the Web in a local war is a striking illustration of Appadurai's theory of culturalism at work. The political goal was a 'greater Albania' – the independence of Serbia's Kosovo province and its realignment with neighbouring Albania, and less specific claims to parts of Macedonia and Montenegro. To this end, long-standing images of regional ethnicity were appropriated and revitalised in history, language, costume, custom and food and were related to the qualities of a fiercely beautiful, primitive landscape. This construction of an integrated Albanian culture was projected at the world and was instantly available to anyone, anywhere, who had access to the Web. Particular targets were Albanians abroad – those with remembered identities living in Western Europe or the US who were also interested in purchasing books, CDs and videos. From this digital perspective it seemed only natural that Albanians should have the right to live within their landscape as they had for centuries and that Serb aggression was a travesty of this natural order. The images of twisted bodies of children, headless torsos and destroyed faces of pregnant women made the claim that the Serbian militia were monsters outside this natural order, completing the nexus of local claims to place and identity, the global circulation of the essence of imagination, and violence – the digitally enhanced, visceral detail of horror.

The further fallacy of primordialism – matching the view that distance still protects the West from tribal conflicts on its old peripheries – is the belief that such cultural conflicts are inherently alien to Western democracies and either are an inevitable burden of foreign policies or should be the focus of pressure for reform. Such arguments of exceptionalism are countered by returning to the very 'heart of whiteness' – the ways in which forms of culturalism are operating within North America and Western Europe – and mobilising combinations of global media, local identity and violence in ways that are comparable to the Balkans and other parts of the world.[105] Again, there are many ways in which this could be explored. I will use the incident that was the most prominent in the ebb and flow of the digital media at the time of writing the first version of this essay (June 1998), and show how a local act of brutality connects to claims of identity, global media and the refiguring of the archive.

On 6 June James Byrd, a black 49-year-old father of three, was walking home in Jasper, Texas. Three young white men in a pickup

105 Appadurai, *Modernity at Large*.

offered him a lift. Byrd was driven to a deserted area, beaten and chained by his ankles to the back of the truck. He was dragged behind the truck for two miles. Parts of his body, including his head, were dispersed along the dirt road.[106] The three men were easily found and arrested - the truck was splattered with blood. One, 23-year-old John William King, had tattoos associating him with the Confederate Knights of America, an organisation linked to the Ku Klux Klan, and 'Odinism', a neo-Nazi sect. Initial reports also suggested a link with Aryan Nations, a white supremacist group. The claim of such an association was immediately denounced by Klan affiliates asserting that they are law-abiding citizens exercising their democratic rights. The language of denial, however, was designed to escalate the issue well beyond the small town of Jasper, Texas. For instance, the Knights of the White Kamellia were quick to post a statement on their Web-site: 'the scumbag, child killing, church burning, jack booted Zionist Occupational Government is using this opportunity to further their course of genocide against the White Race by attempting to link White Christian Patriot organizations to a heinous crime that none of us in the movement would orchestrate, condone, or even permit within our ranks'. The Imperial Wizard of the Knights, speaking from his 'CyberKlaven' in the 'Invisible Empire' of the Kamellia Internet site, called a White Pride rally at the Jasper County Courthouse.[107] He was matched by the Houston-based Black Muslim Movement, whose leader, Quanell X, travelled to Jasper with guns for Jasper's black community. President Clinton was represented at the funeral service of James Byrd by the Revd Jesse Jackson. On 27 June, supporters of the New Black Panther Party walked though Jasper's streets chanting 'black power' while about 18 robed Klansmen stood with Confederate flags outside the courthouse, protected by the Texas Highway Patrol.[108]

It is to be expected that an ugly racial killing will achieve national symbolic importance in the US where the history of discrimination by race is recent and raw. What is of interest here, rather, is the extent to which groups such as the Knights of the White Kamellia are representative of claims to local cultural identity, mobilised through the use of widespread media and expressed as the violent rejection of difference. As is well known, one person can establish an Internet presence and claim to reflect mass support. Is the Imperial Wizard's CyberKlaven little more than a cyberpunk fantasy?

The formation of the 'second Klan' in the first quarter of the cen-

106 'Man decapitated in possible racial killing', CNN, 8 June 1998; 'Byrd's friends pay last respects to a murder victim', CNN, 13 June 1998. Both reports from http://cnn.com.

107 http://members.aol.com/realmoftex/index1.html; http://www.kamellia.com.

108 'KKK rallies in town of dragging death victim. New Black Panthers vow to protect Jasper's blacks', CNN, 27 June 1998.

tury was intricately bound up with mass media. Appealing to a populist hostility to established elites,[109] Klan organisers made skilful use
of a nostalgia best represented by the novels of Thomas Dixon, in
which the Klan was presented as the saviour of the South. Dixon's *The
Clansman, an Historic Romance of the Ku Klux Klan*, was first published
in 1905 and was made into the first full-length movie epic by David
Griffith as *The Birth of a Nation*. The film was released in 1915 and
was seen by an estimated fifty million people:

> The movie's climactic scene was unforgettable. Here is the beau-
> tiful heroine surrounded by violent blacks about to break into
> her cabin. A bugle sounds. The Klansmen mount and ride to the
> rescue. The orchestra matches thunderous strains from 'In the
> Hall of the Mountain King' to the rhythm of galloping hooves.
> The camera pans back and forth, switching from shots of the
> menaced heroine to clips of the onrushing, rescuing Klansmen.
> Will the heroine be raped? Will the Klansmen get there in time
> to save her? The tension became almost unbearable as audiences
> waited for those questions to be answered. In the cities of the
> Old South, men leaped to their feet. They yelled, whooped, and
> cheered. On one occasion, they became so carried away that they
> even shot up the screen to save the beautiful heroine from her
> assailants.[110]

Reaching a zenith between 1920 and 1925, with an estimated
two million members and $44 million in revenue, the Klan was a
slick marketing operation, offering regalia, books and magazines,
real estate and life insurance, and '100 percent Americanism': an
avenue of hatred for blacks, Jews, Catholics, immigrants and radi-
cals.[111] Subsequently, the fortunes of the Klan rose and fell, frag-
menting into splinter groups marked by internal dissent and alle-
gations of corruption, reviving with the civil rights conflicts of the
early 1960s and again with the backlash against affirmative action
in the late 1970s.[112] The Klan's continuing attraction has rested on
its versatility – its appeal to changing, diverse and often localised
threats to 'all-American' communities by outsiders: 'like the
proverbial phoenix, the Klan has died in one setting, only to be
reborn in another'.[113]

But in recent years, the Klan has been eclipsed by a diverse collection of far-right groups that regard the 'hooded order' as insufficiently aggressive.[114] Many of these organisations are committed to
the religious orientation of 'Christian Identity'. This loose assemblage

109 N. MacLean, *Behind the Mask of
Chivalry: The Making of the Second Ku Klux
Klan* (New York: Oxford University Press, 1994).

110 F. Cook, *The Ku Klux Klan: America's
Recurring Nightmare* (New York: Julian
Messner, 1980), p. 36.

111 Cook, *The Ku Klux Klan*; MacLean,
Behind the Mask of Chivalry.

112 Cook, *The Ku Klux Klan*; P. Sims, *The Klan*
(Lexington: University Press of Kentucky,
1996).

113 MacLean, *Behind the Mask of Chivalry*.

114 Sims, *The Klan*.

of churches, sects and militia units holds three key beliefs. First, that white 'Aryans' are the descendants of the biblical tribes of Israel and have a divine mission to save the world; secondly, that Jews are unconnected with the Israelites and are the literal children of the Devil; thirdly, that the world is on the verge of a final, apocalyptic struggle between Aryans and a Jewish conspiracy.[115]

How extensive are these groups? The Southern Poverty Law Center, widely acknowledged as a leading monitor of US hate groups, reported in the same month as the Jasper killing that while many such groups had disbanded, others were becoming more extreme in their politics and were going underground. They are no longer a feature of the South alone. Despite the reduction in monitored groups, the number of organisations and chapters known to be active through marches, rallies, publications or criminal prosecutions is substantial: 523 listed Patriot groups, many active in war games, and over 200 different Klan, neo-Nazi, Skinhead, Christian Identity and Black Separatist organisations. Many have more than one chapter and are active in several states: American Knights of the Ku Klux Klan (18 chapters, from New York to Texas), Knights of the White Kamellia (12 chapters in six states), Aryan Nations (13 chapters), National Alliance (22 chapters), National Socialist White Peoples Party (11 chapters), and the National Association for the Advancement of White People (with 79 branches).[116]

History, and historical destiny, are particularly important for many of these groups. Some rely heavily on material representations of the Nazi past. Aryan Nations, associated with one of James Byrd's killers, sets out its manifesto and policy on a Web-page titled 'the Aryan Warrior'. Pastor Richard G. Butler (a veteran of Christian Identity)[117] gives a Nazi salute beneath a swastika, and the site is illustrated from the archive of Nazi propaganda graphics. This material connection with the past is emphasised throughout the Internet site:

> Behold the sign! – Look at the proof! By this thundering call the Aryan Warrior awakens his racial kindred from his sleep of death. By this SIGN does he smash the lying, murdering jew! By this SIGN do Aryan sons of God arise; unite and live. By this SIGN does the Aryan show his love for his Father and God!

A hypertext link takes the visitor to the 'Aryan Nations Literature Archive'; books, pamphlets, posters and memorabilia for the Aryan Warrior; an Aryan Nations arm patch, bronze belt buckle, pendant, collar tabs or an Aryan Nations Youth Korps Dagger at $25.[118]

115 M. Barkun, *Religion and the Racist Right: The Origins of the Christian Identity Movement* (Chapel Hill: University of North Carolina Press, 1994).

116 'Southern Poverty Law Center say groups plan for race war', CNN, 17 June 1998; http://www.splcenter.org.

117 Barkun, *Religion and the Racist Right*.

118 Aryan Nations is at http://www.nidlink.com.

The National Alliance offers a more measured, intellectual version of prejudice. Contesting 'Semitic ideology', the site claims a 'natural order' that includes a 'law of inequality' counter to the Jeffersonian principles of the US constitution: 'those races which evolved in the more demanding environment of the North, where surviving a winter required planning and self-discipline, advanced more rapidly in the development of the higher mental faculties . . .' Consequently, it is the responsibility of 'Aryan men and women to strive for the advancement of our race in the service of Life . . .' This takes the National Alliance directly to archaeology's archive: 'a knowledge of and appreciation for the history of our Aryan ancestors are absolutely necessary for even the short-term survival of our people. We need to have a good acquaintance with our roots before we can know who we are and make sound plans for our future . . .' Books available through the National Alliance's Web-page cover such subjects as medieval Iceland, megaliths, the Celts, Anglo-Saxons, Stonehenge, Avebury and Colin Renfrew's *Archaeology and Language*: 'the scholar who has revolutionized our understanding of the chronology of civilization in northern Europe returns to prove, in highly readable prose, that the Indo-European-speaking peoples appeared earlier than we'd been led to believe by conventional-thinking anthropologists . . .'[119]

Although the context is clearly different, it is difficult to justify a categorical distinction between the Knights of the White Kamellia and Serb Chetniks, or between Pastor Richard Butler's Aryan Nations page and Slobodan Milošević's assertions of Serbian destiny and superiority. James Byrd's killing has all the face-to-face brutality of an ethnic execution in Bosnia-Herzegovina or an atrocity in Kosovo.

V

Prince Johan Maurits van Nassau-Siegen's Brazilian archive was rich in tangible textures, colours and shapes – a testimony of the exotic lands at Europe's colonial periphery and a collection that owed its value in The Hague to its rarity, to the distance it had travelled. The refigured archive of the digital age depends on the global circulation of images of material things that are located at specific places where they are valued, and often contested. Thus the difference between the archives of early and late modernity is not, as is often claimed, that the concept of the original has been superseded by infinitely reproducible sets of binary code. It is rather that information technology has completed a four-hundred-year development from a six-month voyage in

[119] http://www.natall.com. It is obvious that this claim of support for the philosophy of this neo-Nazi group would horrify Renfrew and many of the other authors whose work is cited.

a sailing ship to the instantaneous delivery of a packet of digital data.

Given that aspects of the early archive were shaped by the consciousness of distance – the exotic value given Maurits' collection by the very extent of the space between Brazil and The Hague – it follows that the demise of the authority that rests in distancing is affecting the archive today. Building on Arjun Appadurai's work, I have argued that the materiality of the archive remains of critical importance. However, rather than following the modal form of the nineteenth-century national archive, the refigured archive of the 'digital age' is increasingly local in its contestations of manuscripts, books, artefacts and architecture, and simultaneously global in the circulation of claims to identity and images of ethnic identity. In this, the contemporary archive is part of the politics of global capitalism.

The result of this 'culturalism' has been a refiguring of tribal ethnography. It is no accident that commentators on the Balkans such as Noel Malcolm – Bosnia's most recent historian – draw analogies between Serbia's nationalist politics and the Bosnian settlement, and South African bantustans. Appadurai's 'Bosnia fallacy' – the assumption that contemporary politics are driven by 'ancient hatreds' that are somehow inherited and can only be resolved by partition – is a rediscovery of the assumptions that characterised Imperial conquests of Africa and apologies for apartheid. Similarly, nostalgia for the Old South, appeals to 'one hundred percent Americanism', and the preservation of 'Aryan identity' in the face of blacks, immigrants and a Jewish conspiracy are the organising principles of local identities that have their own ethnographies. Rather than Wagenaer's 'stone wall' that kept 'Hottentots' and 'savage Africans' at bay as curiosities, today everyone is an ethnic subject.

A consequence of this simultaneous play between the local and the global has been a refiguring of violence. In Maurits' and Wagenaer's day violence was pushed out to the colonial periphery contrasting the core of 'holy Christendom' with the civilising mission at 'earth's extremest end'. An archive such as Maurits' was initially stained by the blood of those who had been dispossessed and subjugated but collections of the exotic had been wiped clean, ordered and neatly labelled by the time they were deposited in the collections of Europe's great libraries and museums. But an effect of the defeat of distance – the achievement of today's information technology – has been to cancel this displacement of violence. Ownership of the archive – possession of the documents, artefacts and architecture that are the entitlement to a place in the world – is now claimed and defended at home, whether in Sarajevo, Ayodhya, Waco or Oklahoma.

An appropriate avatar for this 'heart of whiteness' is David Duke, one-time National Information Director and founder of the National Association for the Advancement of White People. Hatewatch considers David Duke to be America's most influential and politically active white supremacist. Here is his vision of the role of the digital world – and the archive – in the coming millennial conflict:

> the alien, anti-White media has been my unrelenting enemy. It has been yours as well, because it supports every pernicious liberal program that you can imagine. Up until now, unless someone met me personally, or read my material, the only way they could judge me is by what the liberal-biased media says. Now, that situation has changed. Millions of people are going online in America. Now, if they want to find out about me and my ideas and issues all they have to do is go into one of the search engines and search for 'David Duke'. Hundreds of sources will show up. There they can access my site and read my writings and reference material, and even hear my radio program which is broadcast 24 hours-a-day to the four corners of the earth . . . When egalitarians say that no mainstream scientists believe in inherent differences, instantly they are refuted by lucid and fascinating articles on my page by the leading psychologists, biologists, geneticists, historians, archeologists, anthropologists, and educators of the world. Right now I have dozens of articles from our point of view on my Internet site.[120]

A hundred years ago Joseph Conrad wove together prejudices and assumptions about the colonial periphery in his novella *Heart of Darkness*, and Marlow's discovery of the horror at the end of the long journey into the bowels of Africa has provided lasting images and metaphors for the twentieth century. But the tale of Kurtz's destruction was told on a ship anchored in the Thames and at nightfall – expressing Conrad's sense of the corruption at the heart of the metropole.[121] At the turn of the millennium there is no longer the possibility of a long sea voyage to insulate the colonial core from its colonised peripheries. Conrad's prescience has been fulfilled.

120 D. Duke, 'The coming white revolution: born on the Internet', David Duke Online Report (1998), http://www.duke.org/data/internet.htm.

121 Said, *Culture and Imperialism*.

Biographical Notes

DAVID BEARMAN is President of Archives & Museum Informatics. He consults on issues relating to electronic records and archives, integrating multi-format cultural information and museum information systems and is Founding Editor of the quarterly journal *Archives and Museum Informatics*, published by Kluwer Academic Publishers, in The Netherlands. Since 1991, he has organised and chaired the biennial International Conferences on Hypermedia and Interactivity in Museums (ICHIM), and more recently the annual Museums and the Web Conferences, as well as directing numerous educational seminars and workshops on related topics. Bearman is the author of over 125 books and articles on museum and archives information management issues.

JACQUES DERRIDA has been variously labelled 'French philosopher', 'literary theorist', 'postmodernist', 'deconstructionist', 'structuralist' and 'post-structuralist'. Born in Algiers in 1930, he has spent most of his working life in France and

the United States. A prolific writer and speaker, his work cuts across disciplines and genres, resisting (although, ironically, attracting) easy categorisation. He is, without doubt, one of the most influential thinkers of the late twentieth century.

MARTIN HALL is Professor of Historical Archaeology and Dean of Higher Education Development at the University of Cape Town, and President of the World Archaeological Congress. He has written extensively on the origins of farming settlement in southern Africa, the archaeology of colonialism and theories of materiality. His latest book, *An Archaeology of the Modern World*, was published by Routledge in 2000.

Currently Director of the Graduate School for the Humanities and Social Sciences and Associate Professor in the Anthropology Department at the University of the Witwatersrand, **CAROLYN HAMILTON** has served on the board of the South African History Archive and on the pilot committee of the Gay and Lesbian Archives. She has been a longtime researcher in archives and her recent book, *Terrific Majesty: The Powers of Shaka Zulu and the Limits of Invention* (1998), explores the processes of the making and the limiting of the archive of knowledge about the early Zulu king, not just in written text, but in oral accounts, discourses of domination and colonial authority, in forms of material culture and in performance.

BRENT HARRIS is currently a doctoral candidate in History at the University of the Western Cape. He is conducting research on 'National Identity in the Transition to a Post-Apartheid South Africa'. His doctor's thesis is entitled 'Memory and Subjectivity in Transition: Vision, Experience and Identity in the Transition to a Post-Apartheid State'.

VERNE HARRIS is Director of the South African History Archive, an independent archive dedicated primarily to documenting the struggles against apartheid. He is also co-ordinator of the University of the Witwatersrand's postgraduate course in archive studies. Previously he was with South Africa's State Archives Service for thirteen years before becoming a deputy director in the National Archives when it was established in 1997. He holds an MA in history from the University of Natal, and has published widely in the fields of archives, records management, history, music and fiction. He participated in a number of key processes leading to the transformation of South Africa's apartheid public records system: from 1992 to 1993 he served on the African National Congress' Archives Sub-committee; in 1995 he chaired the working committee of the Consultative Forum, which drafted the National Archives of South Africa Act; and from 1997 to 1998 he was a member of the team established by the Truth and Reconciliation Commission to investigate the destruction of records by the apartheid state. Between 1988 and 1998 he was editor of the *South African Archives Journal*.

WOLFRAM HARTMANN holds degrees from the universities of Hamburg and London, teaches in the History Department of the University of Namibia and recently completed his doctorate at Columbia University in the City of New York. His research fields include queer studies and colonial and visual history. Together with Hayes and Silvester, he is co-author of *The Colonising Camera*, which represents the first serious historical engagement with archived photograph collections in Namibia, and begins to consider a 'visual turn' in relation to the discipline of History.

PATRICIA HAYES was born in Zambia, grew up and went to school in Zimbabwe, and did her university training in the UK. She now teaches in the History Department at the University of the Western Cape,

and continues to do most of her research on Namibia. She is co-author of *The Colonising Camera*.

TREFOR JENKINS was Professor and Head of Department of Human Genetics, School of Pathology, the South African Institute for Medical Research and University of the Witwatersrand, Johannesburg, from June 1975 until his retirement in September 1998. He is now Professor Emeritus and Honorary Professorial Research Fellow in the same Department. He received the centennial award for Science and Humanity at Case Western Reserve University, USA, in 1988, and was the Galton Lecturer of the Galton Institute, London, in 1989. He is an Honorary Fellow of the College of Medicine, University of Wales, Cardiff, and author or co-author of over 300 scientific publications including two books, *Health and the Hunter-Gatherer*, with G.T. Nurse (Kargen) and *The Peoples of Southern Africa and their Affinities*, with G. T. Nurse and J. S. Weiner (OUP).

ACHILLE MBEMBE holds a PhD in History from the University of Paris (Pantheon Sorbonne) and a DPhil in Political Science from the Institut d'Etudes Politiques of Paris. He is currently a Senior Researcher at the Institute for Social and Economic Research at the University of the Witwatersrand. His latest book is *On the Postcolony* (University of California Press, 2001).

MS BHARTI MORAR is a Research Assistant in the Department of Human Genetics, South African Institute for Medical Research and University of the Witwatersrand, Johannesburg. She obtained her PhD degree in 2000 from the University of the Witwatersrand. She is actively involved in research on the origins and diversity of human populations in sub-Saharan Africa and Madagascar.

PHASWANE MPE'S research interests lie in literary publishing and reception in Africa, and in media, oral literature and his-

toriography in South Africa. He is author of the short story collection *Brooding Clouds* (University of Natal Press, forthcoming), which he has adapted into Sepedi as *Maru a Maso* (Heinemann, forthcoming) and of the novel *Welcome to our Hillbrow* (University of Natal Press, 2001).

SARAH NUTTALL completed her DPhil at Oxford University, and she lectures in the Department of English at the University of Stellenbosch. She is editor of *Text, Theory, Space: Land, Literature and History in South Africa and Australia* (Routledge, 1996); *Negotiating the Past: The Making of Memory in South Africa* (Oxford University Press, 1998) and *Senses of Culture: South African Culture* (Oxford University Press, 2000). She has published widely on South African and postcolonial literature and culture.

BHEKIZIZWE PETERSON is Associate Professor in the Department of African Literature at the University of the Witwatersrand. His most

recent works include the screenplay for the feature film *Fools* (1997) and *Monarchs, Missionaries and African Intellectuals: African Theatre and the Unmaking of Colonial Marginality* (University of the Witwatersrand Press, 2000).

MICHÈLE PICKOVER is the Curator of Manuscripts, in the Department of Historical Papers at the University of the Witwatersrand. She is also an Executive Committee Member of the South African History Archive Board of Trustees, and a member of the Advisory Committee to the Gay and Lesbian Archives. Since 1998 she has been the national chairperson of the South African Society of Archivists. She has published various inventories of collections and several editions of the *Guide to the Archives and Papers* as well as a number of journal articles on archival topics. Apart from archives and access to information issues, Michèle's other passion is animal rights and she is the chairperson of South Africans for the Abolition of Vivisection.

GRAEME REID has an academic background in African Literature and Social Anthropology, both of which he has studied at postgraduate level at the University of the Witwatersrand. Formerly the co-ordinator of the Gay and Lesbian Archives, he is currently a researcher at the Institute for Social and Economic Research at the University of the Witwatersrand.

RONALD SURESH ROBERTS, a graduate of Balliol College, Oxford, and Harvard University, is writing a biography of Nadine Gordimer. He is the author of *Clarence Thomas and the Tough Love Crowd: Counterfeit Heroes and Unhappy Truths* (New York University Press, 1995) and co-author with Kader Asmal and Louise Asmal of *Reconciliation Through Truth: A Reckoning of Apartheid's Criminal Governance* (David Philip, 2nd ed., 1997).

RAZIA SALEH has worked at the SA History Archive (SAHA) from its founding in 1989 until the end of the 2000. She is currently Archives Coordinator for

ANC Archives. She is co-editor of *SASA News*, newsletter for members of the South African Society of Archivists (SASA), and serves on the national committee for SASA.

JEREMY SILVESTER lectures in Namibian history at the University of Namibia. He has previously taught in the United Kingdom at the universities of the West of England, Bristol and Keele. He is currently involved in a number of projects concerning public history in Namibia, and is a member of the Executive Committee for the Museums Association of Namibia. Since 2 February 1997 he has written or edited the fortnightly 'Picturing the Past' column in *The Namibian* newspaper. He can be contacted on jsilvester@unam.na.

DR HIMLA SOODYALL is a Medical Scientist and Senior Lecturer in the Department of Human Genetics, South African Institute for Medical Research and the University of the Witwatersrand. She obtained her PhD in Human Genetics in 1993 working with Professor

Trefor Jenkins and then conducted postdoctoral research with Professor Mark Stoneking at Penn State University under the auspices of a Fogarty International fellowship from the NIH. She is currently the Director of the Human Genomic Diversity and Disease Research Unit of the Medical Research Council, the South African Institute for Medical Research and the University of the Witwatersrand. She is the recipient of the Vice-Chancellor's Award for Research (1999) from the University of the Witwatersrand and the President's Award from the National Research Foundation.

ANN LAURA STOLER is Professor of Anthropology, History and Women's Studies at the University of Michigan, Ann Arbor. In more than twenty-five years of ethnographic and archival research, she has worked on questions related to gender, racial taxonomies and political economy in colonial and contemporary Indonesia, colonial Vietnam, and in The Netherlands and France. Her recent books include *Race and the Education of Desire: Foucault's History of Sexuality and the Colonial Order of Things* (Duke University Press, 1995) and *Tensions of Empire: Colonial Cultures in a Bourgeois World* (University of California Press, 1997, co-edited with Frederick Cooper). Forthcoming books are *Along the Archival Grain: Colonial Cultures and their Affective States* (Princeton University Press) and *Carnal Knowledge and Imperial Power* (University of California Press).

JANE TAYLOR holds the Skye Chair of Drama at the University of the Witwatersrand. She has a background in theatre studies, and a PhD in English from Northwestern University, Chicago. In 1996 she curated *Fault Lines*, an exhibition about issues of truth and reconciliation, at the Cape Town Castle. In 1998, she curated *Holdings: Rethinking the Archive* for the launch of the University of the Witwatersrand's new Graduate School. In 1996, she wrote the play *Ubu and the Truth Commission* for the Handspring Puppet Company. She is currently working with the Handspring Puppet Company on a new work of theatre for the Kennedy Center. She has written reviews and catalogues on contemporary South African culture, and in 1987 she co-edited an anthology on South African resistance culture, *From*

South Africa, with David Bunn (University of Chicago Press).

CLIVE VAN DEN BERG lives and works in Johannesburg. He works in and outside of gallery spaces in a variety of media ranging from video to fire. Much of his recent work is part of a series titled *Memorials without Facts*. In this series he explores some aspects of the nation's memory that are left out of official accounts, both new and old. He exhibits widely in South Africa and abroad, and has won numerous awards for his work.

SUSAN VAN ZYL (PhD, University of the Witwatersrand) lectures in Applied English and Psychology at the University of the Witwatersrand, where she has been teaching in a variety of departments for over twenty-five years. Her interests include literary theory, cultural studies and, especially, Freudian psychoanalysis. She has published a number of scholarly articles in these areas.

Index

access 11, 17, 20-1, 30, 32-4, 85, 139, 145, 321, 331, 335; restrictions on 29, 98-9, 137-8, 140, 148, 193-4

Acts. Archives Act of 1962 138; Cultural Institutions Act of 1998 224; Legal Deposit Act 144; National Archives of South Africa Act of 1996 143-8, 224; National Heritage Resources Act of 1999 224-5; Promotion of Access to Information Act 144-5; Promotion of National Unity and Reconciliation Act 163-4, 168

anti-apartheid organisations 138, 141-2

apartheid 11, 31, 60, 62, 67, 137, 140, 250; and the TRC 164, 168-9, 174-5; archives system 138-41, 229, 277; control over social memory 137, 140-1, 144; destruction of records 135, 138, 140, 290; influence on publishers 143, 288-9, 297

archives 16-17, 19-20, 22, 69, 81, 116, 136, 151, 161, 177, 206, 244, 246, 250, 297, 299, 305, 320-1, 334, 337, 347, 360-1; and epistemology 15, 17, 51, 83, 144, 149-50, 161-2; appraisal of material 146-7, 150, 325, 327-30; as monuments to power 9, 15, 29, 40-1, 53, 139-40, 144, 229; conflict of loyalties 324, 326, 329; limits of records 135-6, 295; power of 20-3, 44, 79, 89, 200; relationship with the state 23-4, 89-90, 139-40, 320; status of 20-2; transformation of 149-50

archives, kinds of: African 30-3; anti-apartheid organisations 138, 141-3; colonial 83-6, 88-91, 93-4, 98-9, 114-15, 121; community 11-12, 201, 203; cultural 182, 185, 247, 302, 313; digital 360-1; electronic 336; genetic 182-4, 188-91; imperial 89, 115; literary 283, 290-4; oral 10, 12, 209, 213, 215, 219, 225, 227; sound 254-6, 274; visual 103-5, 107-9, 114-17, 119, 277-9

Arendt, Hannah 80

artefacts 24-5, 119, 206, 245, 254, 304, 337

authenticity 236, 240, 245, 296

authority 20, 22, 24, 41, 43, 45, 84-5, 88, 91-2, 97-8, 337, 360; of TRC 162-3, 165-8

(auto)biography 128-9, 131-3, 283-90, 291-4, 297-9

Barthes, Roland 126, 176-7

Cohen, David William 87, 209-12, 216-17, 219, 226-7

colonialism 11, 29, 83-5, 89, 90-2, 95-8, 105-8, 119, 217, 306

construction of knowledge 12, 16, 30, 151, 232-3, 297-8, 316, 321, 339, 355

DNA 179-82, 184, 188-91; as an archive 180-2

De Certeau, Michel 84, 100

death drive 42, 44, 51, 59, 66, 67, 68, 72

deconstruction 10-11, 16, 39, 45, 56, 58, 60, 64, 65, 72, 81, 316

democracy 150, 207, 229, 321, 324, 331, 336

Derrida, Jacques 10, 13, 15-17, 38, 40, 42-80, 81, 86, 88, 136, 161-5, 313, 321

destruction of records 23-4, 26, 42, 44, 50, 135, 138, 140, 145-6, 193-4, 274-7, 290-1, 297, 324, 327-9, 347-1

discourse 10-12, 15, 30, 136, 148, 164, 166-7, 173-4; on authenticity 236, 240; on homosexuality 202, 206; on transformation 142-6, 148-9

evidence 9, 43, 45, 57, 90, 94, 135, 165, 290-1, 328-9; at TRC hearings 163, 172-4; in historiography 212, 226, 347; in photographs 111, 113, 118, 121, 126-9; oral 135, 229-30

exclusion of material 9-12, 16, 20, 30, 81, 177, 230, 234, 295-6

fiction(alisation) 43, 65, 89, 98-9, 149, 151, 278, 291, 298, 305, 317, 321

forgetting 14, 24, 35, 143, 151; and forgiving 78, 80; and remembering 68, 75, 137, 243, 280, 324-5; in discussion of Archive Fever, 41, 49, 50, 51, 54, 57, 66, 67, 68, 72, 75, 76, 78, 79; in oral history 211, 220-3; see also memory

Foucault, Michel 9, 87, 89, 94, 118, 202, 247-8

Freud, Sigmund 41, 42, 43, 45, 47, 49, 51, 52, 53, 55, 57, 59, 67, 70, 72, 123-4

Gay and Lesbian Archives (GALA) 11, 194, 200-1, 204-5, 281

Habermas, Jürgen 173

historiography 25-6, 47, 84, 86, 88-9, 92, 129, 141, 143, 150, 184, 209-11, 215, 227, 291

history 21, 83, 85-6, 92, 96, 176-7, 215-16, 244, 347, 358-9; African 29, 209-10, 212; link between oral and visual 121-2, 220-3, 227; literary 233-4; public 172-4, 177; and literature 293; role of archive in production of 161-2, 165, 177, 305

identity 294, 317, 337, 339, 354, 360; local 336-9, 345, 347, 354-5, 360

ideology 126, 176, 278, 327, 341

imagination 20-3, 26, 75, 79, 87, 89-90, 149, 206, 244-5,

Editorial Collective: Carolyn Hamilton, Verne Harris, Jane Taylor,

Michèle Pickover, Graeme Reid, Razia Saleh

Project Manager: Libby Lamour

Design Team: Jane Taylor, Clive van den Berg

Book Design: Jenny Sandler and Joss Thorne

ACKNOWLEDGEMENTS

We acknowledge the financial assistance of the Department of Arts, Culture, Science and Technology, Codesria, Interfund, the Mellon Foundation, and the Faculty of Arts, University of the Witwatersrand. We are indebted to the Gay and Lesbian Archives, South African History Archive, National Archives of South Africa, Department of Historical Papers and the Graduate School for the Humanities and Social Sciences, University of the Witwatersrand, for contributing their staff, facilities and expertise to this project.

We gratefully acknowledge permission to reproduce materials in this volume from the Chamber of Mines of South Africa, Algemeen Rijksarchief, *The Namibian*, the South African Government Printer, Chris Roper, Truth and Reconciliation Documentation Centre, Rabson Wuriga, Gay and Lesbian Archives, Church of the Province of South Africa Archives, Swaziland Oral History Project, Willem Boshoff, Penny Siopis, Walter Oltmann, Colin Richards, ZEM, Maanda Daswa, William Kentridge, Natasha Christopher, Peter Schutz, Clive van den Berg, Titus Matiyane, Santu Mofokeng, Philip Miller, Miriam Tlali and the National English Literary Museum.

Achille Mbembe's essay was translated from French by Judith Inggs.

Our thanks to Jacques Derrida for giving us permission to publish the transcript of his 1998 seminar at the University of the Witwatersrand, and to Johann Rossouw for liaising with Derrida on our behalf.

Endpapers: from 'Sacrifices' by Penny Siopis